T0307826

Blacks in the New World

Edited by August Meier and John H. Bracey

A list of books in the series appears at the end of this book.

Freedom's Port

Fitzhugh Lane's 1846 oil painting *View of Baltimore from Federal Hill.*
Courtesy of the Shelburne Museum, Shelburne, Vermont.

Freedom's Port

The African American Community
of Baltimore, 1790–1860

Christopher Phillips

University of Illinois Press
Urbana and Chicago

© 1997 by the Board of Trustees of the University of Illinois
Manufactured in the United States of America
1   2   3   4   5   C   P   6   5   4   3   2

This book is printed on acid-free paper.

Library of Congress Cataloging-in-Publication Data
Phillips, Christopher, 1959–
Freedom's port : the African American community of Baltimore,
1790–1860 / Christopher Phillips.
p.   cm. — (Blacks in the New World)
Includes bibliographical references and index.
ISBN 0-252-02315-3 (alk. paper). —
ISBN 0-252-06618-9 (pbk. : alk. paper)
ISBN 978-0-252-02315-6 (alk. paper). —
ISBN 978-0-252-06618-4 (pbk. : alk. paper)
1. Afro-Americans—Maryland—Baltimore—History—19th century.
2. Free Afro-Americans—Maryland—Baltimore—History—19th
century. 3. Baltimore (Md.)—Race relations. I. Title. II. Series.
F189.B19N47   1997
975.2'600496073—dc21
96-45818
CIP

For my parents and for Bill

Contents

Acknowledgments

In preparing this book, I have asked far more than I have given to many different institutions and individuals. None could I hope to repay at all, much less adequately. A summer stipend from the National Endowment for the Humanities, a research fellowship from the Andrew W. Mellon Foundation at the Library Company of Philadelphia, and a summer research grant from the Faculty Research and Creativity Committee at Emporia State University allowed me to complete the research necessary to transform a dissertation into a book. The interlibrary loan staffs of the libraries at the University of Georgia and Emporia State University assisted me in locating obscure sources and provided direction in my search for others. The staff at the Maryland State Archives proved remarkably efficient and helpful, setting an example of institutional excellence. Becky Gundy and Tom Cotter of the Baltimore City Archives were unbelievably patient and helpful and provided friendship during the long periods of research in Baltimore. I also wish to thank the staff at the Maryland Historical Society for assisting me in the earliest phases of research for the project. The Reverend Edwin Schell of the Lovely Lane United Methodist Church in Baltimore provided special help on the black Methodists of early Baltimore. Phil Lapsansky and the rest of the staff at the Library Company of Philadelphia were most helpful in completing research on the book.

Friends and scholars sustained me through various and often difficult stages of research and writing. I offer special thanks to Phoebe Jacobson, who shared her wealth of knowledge on African Americans in early Maryland, and to her and Bryce Jacobson, who opened their home to me in Annapolis, Maryland, for several weeks. In Pennsylvania Emma Lapsansky and Aaron and Dottie Whitman generously offered me their homes so that I could complete research for the book. The DeFreezers offered me a second home in Georgia and became two of my best friends, blood ties notwithstanding. Bennie Heard and Paul Heard offered their home and hearts to their adopted southerner. At Emporia State Phil Kelly, chair of the Division of Social Sciences, and Lendley Black, dean of Liberal Arts and Sciences, provided complete support for my work and on more than one occasion secured financial support for travel and illustrations. Clay Arnold, Kim Arnold, Charles Brown, Pat O'Brien, and Yvonne O'Brien, good friends all, have sustained me through trying times. At the University of Georgia Kirk Willis offered an always-open door, as well as empathy, encouragement, and collegiality at a time when I needed all of them. Andy Chancey and Fitz Brundage provided amity on a journey that is not known for inspiring either. Dr. Joe Coté and Danny Bridges gave me five years of camaraderie, both on and off the baseball diamond and basketball court, on which I could not hope to place a value. Brian Wills, Jon Bryant, Randy Patton, Glenn Eskew, Carolyn Bashaw, Jennifer Lund-Smith, Sharon Flanagan, Mark Clark, Lesley Gordon, and Glenna Schroeder-Lien each lent collegial support that was equally immeasurable. As always, Russ Duncan provided friendship that most closely resembles brotherhood.

Many scholars have guided this project to its completion. Lois Green Carr and Lorena Walsh each read the first chapter and offered trenchant criticisms on my interpretation of the agricultural transformation in early Maryland. Emory Thomas (who has continued to provide friendship, encouragement, and assistance), Jean Friedman, Eugene D. Genovese, Robert Pratt, and Bennett Wall provided early yet essential criticism. I extend special thanks to Numan V. Bartley, whose rigorous and perceptive mind shaped graduate students' historical perspective at the University of Georgia. James M. McPherson has continued to offer his time and encouragement despite no institutional mandate to do so. To Steve Whitman, I owe a particularly deep intellectual debt, for his keen insight into slavery and labor in early Baltimore allowed me to make the connection necessary to form the book's primary thesis. He is also a consummate host and friend. At the University of Illinois Press, Richard L. Wentworth and especially my copyeditor, Jane Mohraz, have expertly guided the book to its completion. John Bracey read the entire final draft of the manuscript and helped me prune my prose and sharpen my thoughts at a particularly important point. Conference commentators at the Mid-America Conference on History, the Southern Historical Association, and the Organization of American Historians made criticisms of preliminary presentations of my work that helped shape the final draft, and the editors at *Southern Studies* and *Maryland Historical Magazine* graciously allowed me to use material published in their journals in article form.

I owe my deepest debts, whether professional or personal, to several individuals. August Meier saw the potential worth of this project and consistently encouraged and challenged me to expand my thinking and explain my ideas. William McFeely deftly guided the dissertation to its completion, and his constant entreaties to write the story continue to shape my approach to history. His brilliance is matched only by his humanity. For Dulcie, there are just enough words in the language: thank you. Though available, they still are woefully inadequate. And for Jill, words, no matter the number or availability, will never be enough. Finally, for my family, I offer thanks again for their unflagging love and confidence. I could not have completed this without them. Any errors, whether factual or interpretive, are purely my own.

Freedom's Port

Introduction

The current of African American studies in American history has shifted its course appreciably during the past two and a half decades. The successes of the civil rights movements, the active participation of black troops in the Vietnam War, and the contemporary struggles of minority groups for social rather than just legal equality have all affected modern scholars' portrayals of black Americans in studies of not only more recent U.S. history but also early America. A spate of works on the subject of the slave experience in the American South has offered the foundation for much of the modern canon of African American historical literature. Although such revisionist historians as Kenneth Stampp and Stanley Elkins portrayed black people prior to the Civil War as a victimized and largely silent minority, shackled within a repressive society in which they were unable to exert significant influence,[1] postrevisionists have depicted African Americans as active and often conscious agents of change in the shifting social landscape. Such scholars as John Blassingame, Herbert Gutman, Eugene Genovese, Peter Wood, Leon Litwack, Albert Raboteau, and Eric Foner have effectively challenged the notions of slave victimization and have each offered compelling portraits of individual and institutional strength and autonomy among African Americans in the South before and after emancipation.[2] Moreover, such historians as Richard Wade, Claudia Dale Goldin, and Robert Starobin have each addressed the nature of slavery in the southern urban setting, interweaving its complexities and seeming incongruence with plantation slavery to offer even greater breadth to the already sweeping panorama of the U.S. system of chattel bondage.[3]

Although most work on antebellum African Americans has centered on plantation slavery, several significant books have focused on the free black experience in early America. The most important of these studies are Leon Litwack's *North of Slavery*, Jane H. Pease and William H. Pease's *They Who*

Would Be Free, and Ira Berlin's landmark *Slaves without Masters*. These works have provided broad overviews of the experiences of free Negroes, North and South, but they offer less specificity on regional or even state characteristics.[4] A number of dated works (several unpublished, written as dissertations) have treated free Negroes in individual southern states, but many of these early regional studies portrayed free Negroes as inferior people incapable of affecting their own histories and focused on laws, court decisions, and the views of contemporary whites, which invariably reduced these people to the status of objects.[5] In two later seminal articles Ira Berlin offered future scholars sage caveats on the subject of regional variation, warning that African American social development "must be viewed within the specific social circumstances and cultural traditions of black people. These varied from time to time and from place to place."[6]

Prior to the 1970s perhaps most noticeably absent in the works on antebellum African Americans was literature on antebellum urban free black communities. While a significant number of published works have provided valuable analyses of postbellum black urban communities,[7] especially in the North, few have offered such comprehensive treatment of antebellum communities. This is surprising, for, as Ira Berlin has written, "free Negroes were the most urban caste in the South." Of the nearly 500,000 "free persons of color" in the United States in 1860, just under half of them lived in the slave states, and of those better than a third dwelled in cities or towns; by comparison barely 15 percent of southern whites and about 5 percent of slaves lived in urban areas. Free Negroes were more than twice as likely to live in cities as whites were and seven times as likely to be urban dwellers as slaves were. Several important studies of black urban communities have been published in recent years by such scholars as Gary Nash, Michael Johnson and James Roark, and Shane White, but nearly all concentrate on communities in the North or Deep South.[8] That no such community study has yet been published on a city in the Upper South is most surprising, given that on the eve of the Civil War the region boasted not only the South's but also the nation's largest urban black community, Baltimore.

This book recounts the multifaceted growth and development of Baltimore's black community, which both reflected and contributed to its unique social structure and ideological stance in the Upper South. Yet the book serves a larger purpose and weaves a broader story. The study traces the societal transformation of the city's black population, from a transient aggregate of migrant freedpeople, most of whom were fresh from slavery, to a strong overwhelmingly free community, less racked by class and intraracial divisions than in other comparable cities, such as Philadelphia, Charleston, and New Orleans, and inclusive of free Negroes as well as slaves. The demographic makeup, family structures, gender roles, occupations, and social construct each contributed to the fabric of the city's "internal" community, and all evolved collectively according to regional conditions and then particularized according to local conditions. Independent of wealth or any distant, wealthy leadership for community strength, Baltimore's black community derived its vitality from a relatively concordant populace that was overwhelmingly poor. This economic deprivation allowed Baltimore's African American residents to forge a community within which they not only avoided the deep fissures common to other black urban communities but also weathered the racial tempests of the antebellum years. Far from a monolith, however, the community found in its maturation both social differentiations based on structural forces and a group identification that sustained the development of a people who proudly considered themselves Baltimoreans. The coexistence of unity and divergence within the growing internal community distinguished the foundation on which "external" community development (characterized by group organization and identification) later occurred.

Communal organization and group solidarity allowed Baltimore's black people to create a mature community, one that looked within for identification yet also demonstrated a centrifugal solidarity that reached black residents throughout Maryland and even the Upper South. Through its benevolent associations, fraternal organizations, churches, schools, and other social institutions, the black community actively participated in defining its race relations with whites of the same economic stature. Yet the crosscurrents created within its class relations reflected the community's coexistence with urban workers and artisans in a slave society. While this mature community was internally complex, its organizational development—which was largely a response to external pressures threatening to dismantle the multilayered social structure and to abrogate those hard-won societal privileges that black Baltimoreans had long considered rights—not only offered agency but also served to unify the community in times of crisis.[9]

Baltimore's city of transients slowly gave way to, in the words of one historian who has written of northern black communities, a "community of commitment."[10] So I have divided this book. Baltimore's African American community exemplifies, perhaps more than any other such population in the North or South, the multipartite nature of a community—internally divided yet capable of coalescing in the face of external challenges. This study uncovers the lives of the community's individual members and their efforts to carve out and maintain their place in the rapidly changing economic and social structure of Baltimore, a city in the Upper South that reflected both southern and northern urban black experiences. In this anomalous confluence Baltimore's African American experience was unique. A city through which North and South reached each other, a notorious entrepôt for fugitives between the slave states and the free states, and a safe harbor for the development of autonomy as well as community, Baltimore proved itself to be the true "freedom's port" of antebellum America.

Part 1

A City of Transients, ca. 1790–ca. 1820

1

Slavery and the Growth of Baltimore

In the spring of 1825, after serving as a cabin boy aboard his master's sloop, the *Sally Lloyd*, the adolescent slave Tom Bailey returned to Wye House, the grand Eastern Shore plantation of the Lloyd family, one of the richest and most powerful families in Maryland. Tom had just come from Baltimore, the great city across the wide Chesapeake, an occasion that never failed to gain him celebrity status among the slaves of the Lloyd plantation—especially his nine-year-old cousin, Frederick. "When he came from Baltimore," a mature Frederick Bailey, now known as Frederick Douglass, recalled, "he was always a sort of hero amongst us, at least till his Baltimore trip was forgotten." The older boy's "eloquent description of the place" inspired in his precocious young relative "the strongest desire to see Baltimore." As Douglass recalled of his cousin's epic accounts that so piqued the interest of the plantation's slave community:

> I could never tell him of anything, or point out anything that struck me as beautiful or powerful, but that he had seen something in Baltimore far surpassing it. Even the great house itself, with all its pictures within, and pillars without, he had the hardihood to say "was nothing to Baltimore." He . . . told what he had seen in the windows of stores; that he had heard shooting crackers, and seen soldiers; that he had seen a steamboat; that there were ships in Baltimore that could carry four such sloops as the "Sally Lloyd." He said a great deal about the market-house; he spoke of bells ringing; and of many other things which roused my curiosity very much. . . .[1]

Similarly, Levi J. Coppin, a post–Civil War Methodist minister in Philadelphia and a former Eastern Shore slave, wrote of his first trip to Baltimore as a seven-year-old boy: "Three score years have not been sufficient to obliterate the scenes of the Patapsico harbor, nor to wipe out the impression made, upon my first visit there."[2]

Douglass's descriptions of the powerful response Baltimore evoked among slaves on Edward Lloyd's plantation, as well as Coppin's recollection, provide insight into the reasons why the city on the Patapsco attracted so many black migrants in the decades following the Revolution. Unlike Tom Bailey or Frederick Bailey (who himself would soon move to the city across the bay), however, most African Americans who traveled to Baltimore in the early decades of the nineteenth century were not plantation slaves on an infrequent sojourn in the city. The overwhelming majority were free Negroes moving to the city in pursuit of liberties to which they may have been legally entitled but which were in reality unavailable to them in the countryside. Baltimore's sights and sounds inspired among such migrants far more than simple awe; to both slaves and the newly freed, the city's name rightly had become synonymous with freedom.

A century earlier Baltimore had been little more than an inconsequential hamlet. In 1729 an intrepid group of Baltimore County planters, seeking to facilitate tobacco marketing and boost cultivation in and around the basin of the Patapsco River, petitioned the Maryland General Assembly to authorize a charter "for erecting a town on the north side of the Patapsco, in Baltimore County, and for the laying out into lots sixty acres of land. . . ." Once granted, the small village—with no more than three dwellings, a mill, a few tobacco houses, and an orchard—appeared to hold great potential for growth. Charles Carroll, an Annapolis lawyer looking for speculative investment and believing that the Patapsco village site would offer a quick return, eagerly bought twenty-six lots in Baltimore Town in 1736. Carroll proved no more prescient than the town's founders; for eight years he was unable to sell even one lot.[3]

Baltimore Town owed its initial lack of growth largely to the Chesapeake's seventeenth-century cash cow, tobacco. Residents of southern Maryland—on both shores of the bay—had quickly grown dependent on the cultivation of tobacco, which thrived in the sultry summer heat and "lusty soyle" of the tidewater and required far more effort than capital to produce. For nearly a century immigrants to Maryland sought patents in those tidewater areas, which best supported "the stinking weede" and where broad rivers and innumerable creeks carved up the low, level landscape to allow quick access to the bay from the many small plantations that had been established alongside them for miles upstream.[4] Because tobacco shipping was best carried on directly from the planters' homes, only a few inconsequential villages dotted the rivers of southern Maryland. These were invariably around ship landings and warehouses associated with the tobacco trade. Until the mid-eighteenth century the entire Chesapeake tidewater was one expansive port.[5]

Yet tobacco simply would not sustain Baltimore Town's future. Although its production played a role in the early development of Baltimore County, tobacco culture never dominated the local society as it did in Maryland's tobacco coast. By the 1660s a number of ambitious individuals, such as Robert Gorsuch and Charles Gorsuch, had claimed patents at the Patapsco basin, but only a handful of men actually settled in the frontier wilderness of the colony's two northernmost counties, Charles and Baltimore. Planters of southern and Eastern Shore Maryland held many of these patents as future investments, either for themselves or for their children and grandchildren, confident that the tobacco coast would ultimately extend to the bay's distant upper waters.[6]

Though they could and did grow tobacco, farmers in northern Maryland found the crop difficult to market without easy water access to the bay. The hilly terrain of the upper reaches of the Chesapeake proved decidedly less conducive to tobacco production than that of southern Maryland. Unlike the low-lying tidewater counties, Baltimore County had few waterways, much less of sufficient depth to transport tobacco. Steep hills and deep valleys, gouged by fast-moving creeks as they spilled toward the bay, afforded settlers poor opportunity to market their leaves. To market them, planters were forced to have their bulky, heavy hogsheads rolled over the area's few wretched roads, hacked from the mixed hardwood forests, to the Patapsco's mouth. It was not until 1750, two decades after Baltimore Town was chartered, that the first cargo of tobacco—just a single hogshead—left by water.[7]

Moreover, shortly after the town's incorporation, tobacco's fortunes took a decided downturn. In the decade prior to the 1755 census Maryland tobacco prices suffered the century's most severe downturn, fetching well under a penny a pound—half of what it had been two decades earlier. In 1747 the passage of the Tobacco Inspection Act posed an additional hardship, requiring planters to destroy rather than sell poor quality crops. One historian has argued that as a result almost half of the tobacco grown on the Western Shore of Maryland could not pass inspection, including most of that grown in the upper reaches of the Chesapeake, though the amount of tobacco actually destroyed because of this act appears to have been small. Such economic adversity visited on fledgling Baltimore County farmers encouraged many residents and prospective settlers not to stake their future on the enormously fickle plant, at least not in Baltimore County.[8]

Consequently, Baltimore County planters were, in reality, merchant-planters. The term must be used liberally when regarding early Maryland, for the scale of tobacco farms in much of the colony was quite small. Most

tobacco planters possessed estates worth less than £100 sterling.[9] As one
historian has reminded us, the term "planter . . . simply describes an occupation without indicating the economic status of the individual." Such diversification proved necessary, because the changing fortunes of the southern Atlantic tobacco market had so depressed the price of the weed that few
could succeed solely on tobacco profits. A number of planters did manage
to establish themselves in the northern section of the colony, but few attained
the power and prestige of the great planters of the lower Western Shore,
and those who did seem to have engaged in business endeavors beyond mere
tobacco planting, especially land speculation and tenancy, to a far greater
extent than their elite rivals to the south. After 1700 the commercial trading activities of the merchant-planters largely accommodated the needs of
Baltimore County residents until the arrival of large-scale, specialized mer-
chant-factors from England (individuals who handled large-scale mercantile operations and acted as agents for tobacco houses in England) a generation or more later. The entwining of the crafts and agriculture characterized
the Baltimore County economy during the eighteenth century, as well as the
development of Baltimore Town itself.[10]

As late as 1752 Baltimore Town was still, in the words of one resident,
just "a struggling village of about 25 houses," inhabited by a mere hundred
people, two inns, and a church, all of which were clustered irregularly on
the low hills and along the marshy shoreline of the Patapsco. That year a
local enumeration listed only thirty families, including the two innkeepers,
a cooper, a tailor, a drayman, a carpenter, a barber, and a midwife. The small
town stood little chance for sustained growth. It did not serve the colony's
tobacco economy, it had only a limited iron industry, and it was not particularly important to the backcountry trade.[11]

Economic changes both in and outside Maryland soon altered the future
of the hamlet at the Patapsco basin, however. During the mid-eighteenth
century people of southern Pennsylvania spread westward and southward.
Many of them were German and Scots-Irish immigrants who landed in Philadelphia and followed the fertile valleys in search of cheap land. As a result,
the character of northern Maryland became distinctly different from that of
the tidewater. Following the tradition of their homelands, these newcomers
had little interest in tobacco cultivation. Instead, they planted cereal grains,
especially wheat, which were far more familiar and proved better suited to the
rolling hills of western Maryland. This practice was encouraged by the start
of a half-century of price increases for cereal grains as a result of increased
world demand, especially in Europe and in the West Indies, where full conversion to sugar production had produced the need for foodstuffs.[12]

The character of Baltimore County's farms changed with this shift in production. Following the lead of larger planters on the Eastern Shore, many of Baltimore County's middling and larger planters often diversified their acreage by adopting slave-based wheat production, a transition to plow agriculture made possible by capital and the presence of 4,140 Baltimore County slaves in 1755. Only three of the fourteen Maryland counties had more slaves.[13] While small tobacco farmers on both sides of the Chesapeake (particularly those in Baltimore County) often lacked the labor necessary to grow both tobacco and grain commercially, the merchant-planters in Baltimore County appear to have adjusted to their production with relative ease. Upper and Eastern Shore Maryland's conversion to grain was so dramatic that from 1747 to 1791 nontobacco exports increased from 10 percent to 54 percent of Maryland's whole. By contrast, between 1747 and the outbreak of the Civil War just over a century later, production of tobacco fell from 90 percent to just 14 percent of Maryland's agricultural whole.[14]

Unlike tobacco production in the tidewater and on the Eastern Shore, upcountry grain production could not depend on direct exchange. Trade in grains required a centralized source for export, where farmers could mill and market their grain to merchants, who in turn could find buyers and store it until ready for shipment. Many farmers who had settled recently in such western locales as Frederick County found it impossible to lumber their ox-carts over nearly impassible country roads to distant Philadelphia, the nearest market for their grains. Consequently, manufacturers in the outlying areas of the county clustered at mill seats from the Patapsco to the Gunpowder. With a number of such mills located on Jones' and Gwynns' Falls, Baltimore Town grew quickly as a place of export for this grain trade. As early as 1752 local residents owned two ocean-going vessels that made regular voyages from Fells Point to the West Indies, carrying not only tobacco but also barrels of flour and corn, bread, beans, and hams.[15]

Because of Baltimore's proximity to the wheat-producing areas of northern and western Maryland and its access through the Patapsco to the bay, it continued to grow in commercial importance as well as in population. Already in 1756, just four years after its first enumeration, the town boasted three hundred residents. By 1770 eight main roads crossed the recently surveyed Mason-Dixon line southwest of the river, in addition to those connecting Baltimore with the western counties, attracting farmers even from the counties of southern Pennsylvania, west of the Susquehanna, who brought "a considerable quantity of grain . . . from hence, by land carriage, to Baltimore, for exportation to the European markets." By 1804 fifty flour mills were in operation within a radius of eighteen miles of Baltimore Town.

By that time Baltimore had long supplanted Annapolis as the hub of Maryland's trade.[16]

With the grain industry in place, Baltimore Town grew with such staggering speed that astonished observers chronicled its growth for European readers. William Eddis, who served as the Crown's surveyor of customs at Annapolis, recalled in 1771 that "within these few years some scattered cottages were only to be found on this spot, occupied by obscure storekeepers, merely for the supply of the adjacent plantations." Now, Eddis proclaimed with noticeable enthusiasm,

> persons of a commercial and enterprising spirit emigrated from all quarters to this new and promising scene of industry. Wharfs were constructed, elegant and convenient habitations rapidly erected; marshes were drained; spacious fields were occupied; . . . and within forty years, from its first commencement, Baltimore became not only the most wealthy and populous town in the province, but inferior to few on this continent, either in size, number of inhabitants, or the advantages arising from a well-conducted and universal commercial connexion.[17]

The writer had grounds for such fervor; in 1774, just a quarter of a century after being described as a hamlet of "nine miserable log houses," Baltimore—designated the county seat in 1768—had 564 houses and nearly 6,000 residents. The grain trade, which had made the city the region's leading center of export, had spawned a number of directly and indirectly related light industries, especially flour mills, bakeries, distilleries, leather tanneries, wagonsmitheries, and blacksmitheries.[18]

A thriving shipbuilding trade at Fells Point, a mile and a half east of the city, was equally important to Baltimore's rapid growth. The Point was the nearest place where the river's channel ran deep enough for deep-draft ships to land or launch, and it soon boasted many satellite services connected with the shipbuilding industry: block and tackle making, pump making, rope making, and sail making. A diverse yet interrelated community of tradespeople and laborers operated such industries, including craftworkers who produced goods, both on site and in small shops, and semiskilled and unskilled workers.[19] On the eve of the Revolution these industries had attracted to Baltimore many immigrants—English, German, Scots-Irish, and even French Acadian (who settled on the heights overlooking the basin south of town, which the locals called Frenchtown)—lending texture to the social fabric of the city that seemingly overnight had become the ninth largest in British North America. As John Harriott, an English visitor, observed, "Baltimore has had the most rapid growth of any town in America."[20]

As spectacular as Baltimore's growth had already been, the American

Revolution only accelerated it. Maryland's central location and relative absence of enemy incursions allowed Baltimore to become a major supply center to both military and civilian populations. By commissioning, building, and outfitting at least 248 privateers, the city gained a reputation as a source of patriotism, employment, and profit amid the general deprivations of wartime. Moreover, the acceleration of grain production to capitalize on the inflated wartime prices hastened the decline of tobacco in upper Maryland and solidified Baltimore's stature as a center of export and trade. Merchants rather than planters thus came to dominate Baltimore's economic and social structure.[21]

When Robert Gilmor recalled in 1844 the Baltimore of his youth, he remembered that in 1778 it had been a growing town of mostly wooden houses and buildings and unpaved streets, rivaled only mildly by its neighbor, Fells Point, and surrounded by cornfields and woods, with a large marsh at the foot of Jones' Falls, where townspeople crabbed with forked sticks. The city of the postwar years appears to have resembled Gilmor's reminiscences only slightly. Such a large number of merchants and traders had moved to Baltimore from Philadelphia that as early as the mid-1780s the town contained an estimated 1,100 shops and 1,900 houses. Commerce had become so important to the town's growth that in 1783 Johann David Schoepf, a surgeon with a Hessian regiment who remained after the war, observed that "Philadelphia excepted, there are nowhere in that country [the mid-Atlantic states] so many merchants. . . . In several places next [to] the harbor, each square foot of ground yields a guinea a year in rent. . . ."[22]

By 1790 Baltimore had become, in the words of the historian Lawrence Larsen, "North America's first boom town." The onetime village at the mouth of Jones' Falls had spread crescentlike around the basin from the upper Patapsco to Fells Point. Many of the town's houses, shops, and mills were being constructed of red brick. Though improvements lagged behind construction, many of Baltimore's tangled streets—most notably the wide principal thoroughfare, Market Street—boasted wide sidewalks, were lit with oil lamps, and were paved with cobblestones. Finally, plans were afoot to capitalize on the city's rapid growth by dredging the basin to allow larger ships to land at Baltimore rather than at Fells Point.[23]

During the colonial period Annapolis had been the dominant urban center in Maryland. By the end of the Revolution Baltimore not only had far eclipsed Annapolis as Maryland's largest city but also stood as the fifth largest in the new nation, behind Philadelphia, New York, Boston, and Charleston. As European demand for American foodstuffs increased during the postwar decades, encouraging even more flour millers to locate in and around Baltimore, the city became the export center of the entire region below Philadelphia. Between 1790 and 1795 two-thirds of Maryland's exports left through the port at Baltimore.[24]

By 1790 the city had a population of 13,503, the fourth largest in the nation, and was impressive enough to be considered as the site of the federal capital. A decade later its population had again doubled. By 1800 at least 150 warehouses lined the docks and wharves along the basin, or inner harbor, servicing some fifty mills within eighteen miles of the flour merchants who operated nearby. Baltimore merchants handled such a volume of incoming goods that many flew private flags from the masts of incoming ships to announce the arrival of cargoes of merchandise and signal the need to prepare room in their warehouses. The city soon had more than a hundred inns, taverns, and coffeehouses for patrons of this dizzying trade. Baltimore's transformation into a center of commercial import was so rapid that in 1812 the *Niles' Weekly Register* boasted that within the "short period" of three decades the city had been "raised from absolute insignificance, to a degree of commercial importance, which has brought down upon it, the envy and the jealousy of all the great cities of the union."[25] In a remarkably brief span of time Baltimore had become the Upper South's Queen City.

In all of this remarkable growth little record remains of black people in colonial Baltimore Town. Though no exact figures are available, few of Baltimore Town's two hundred residents in 1750 were African Americans, and those few were most likely slaves. By contrast, in 1748 the slave population of Maryland already numbered 36,000, and seven years later Baltimore County had 4,143 black or mulatto slaves, constituting nearly 25 percent of the county's population. One merchant recorded the earliest evidence of slaves living in Baltimore's population in a journal citation that traced the births of all "Negroes in Balto. Town" back to one slave woman, Dina, who bore a total of four children between 1751 and 1763.[26]

As it had done for the Baltimore economy, the Revolution spurred the growth of slavery. No figures are available for Baltimore's bondpeople at the outbreak of the war, but Fells Point's slave population grew fourfold during the war, from 65 to 276. By the end of war Baltimore's slave population stood at an estimated 1,000, which increased again by nearly 25 percent in less than a decade. By 1810 Baltimore's slave population was 4,672, another fourfold increase in just two decades, and now constituted nearly 13 percent of the city's overall population.[27]

Moreover, during the two decades following the Constitution's ratification, the growth of the city's slave population had outpaced that of Maryland as a whole. Between 1790 and 1810 the number of slaves in the state rose by just over 8 percent, while Baltimore County, not including the city of Baltimore, witnessed a 12 percent increase in slaves during the same period. Baltimore City's slave population, however, nearly tripled to 4,672 in 1810, which accounted for three-quarters of the county's overall increase. The number of slaves in the city grew faster than that of any county in the state. From 1790 to 1810 the city's numbers nearly quadrupled, from 1,255 to 4,672 (see table 1), while Baltimore County's slave population increased less than 15 percent. In 1790 the slave population of Baltimore County was 7,132, of which only approximately 18 percent lived in Baltimore City, but by 1800 over 29 percent of the county's slaves lived in the city. In 1810, 4,672 of 11,329 (42 percent) of the county's slave population resided in Baltimore.[28]

Baltimore appeared to be developing a dependence on slave labor that certainly matched cities farther south. At least for these early decades slave-owning in Baltimore was not yet confined to the realm of status display

Table 1. White, Slave, and Free Black Populations of Maryland and Baltimore City, 1790–1860

Year	Total Population	White Population	Slave Population	Free Black Population
MARYLAND				
1790	319,728	208,649	103,036	8,043
1800	349,692	222,402	107,703	19,587
1810	380,546	235,575	111,502	33,469
1820	407,350	261,305	107,306	38,739
1830	447,040	291,224	102,878	52,938
1840	469,232	317,575	89,619	61,938
1850	583,034	417,943	90,368	74,723
1860	688,029	516,918	87,189	83,922
BALTIMORE CITY				
1790	13,503	11,925	1,255	323
1800	26,514	20,900	2,843	2,771
1810	46,555	36,212	4,672	5,671
1820	62,738	48,055	4,357	10,326
1830	80,620	61,710	4,120	14,790
1840	102,513	81,147	3,212	17,980
1850	169,054	140,666	2,946	25,442
1860	212,418	184,520	2,218	25,680

Sources: Wright, *Free Negro in Maryland*, 86–88; Fairbanks, *Statistical Analysis of the Population of Maryland*, 105; McSherry, *History of Maryland*, 403–4; Fields, *Slavery and Freedom on the Middle Ground*, 70.

(i.e., domestics and menials) for wealthy merchants and professionals, as numerous studies of slavery in southern urban settings have suggested about the later antebellum years.[29] In increasing numbers and proportions, the city's tradespeople and manufacturers, large and small, employed slave labor in their shops. In 1790 craftspeople made up nearly one-fourth of the city's slaveholders and held a like proportion of the city's slaves; by 1810 artisans and manufacturers constituted 35 percent of the slaveowners and held a third of Baltimore's slaves. Slave labor thus appeared to be indispensable to many entrepreneurs seeking profit during Baltimore's meteoric years of expansion.[30]

Many of those slaves became available because of the economic changes sweeping upper Maryland during the eighteenth century. Planters saddled with field hands without steady work during two seasons of the year often sought additional income from their bondpeople by hiring them out either to other farmers or to craftspeople and manufacturers in small towns and occasionally in cities near their farms. Before the economic disruptions of the Revolution forced many planters to abandon the production of tobacco in favor of foodstuffs, Maryland plantation owners, in their drive for self-sufficiency, generally trained their slaves in skills necessary for the daily maintenance of the farms. Consequently, rural areas generally boasted an ample pool of trained slaves and whites to perform such skills for the local residents. After the move to the production of grain, slaves' work routines changed even more. Planters often diversified their farms, thus allowing their slaves, particularly males, to acquire such skills as carting, mowing, lumbering, and milling. One historian has found that in rural St. Mary's County, one-fifth of male slaves over the age of sixteen worked outside farming. The skills most prevalent among those slaves were carpentry, blacksmithing, and sailoring.[31]

As the number of slaves in Baltimore swelled, keeping pace proportionally with the white population's growth, the number of free blacks increased at approximately the same rate during this period. By attracting slaves as well as freepeople, Baltimore as late as 1810 had nearly the same number of slaves and free blacks. That the slave population of the city grew more quickly than that of the outlying county suggests that forces beyond the general migration of Maryland's population—both white and black—to its northern and western sections fueled the slave population growth in Baltimore. Obviously, slaveholders in Baltimore City were buying and hiring slaves from outside the city.[32]

Rural slaveowners recognized that in Baltimore they had a market for unneeded or unemployable slaves, and they often solicited urban buyers in city newspapers. One advertised in the *Baltimore American and Commercial Daily Advertiser* in 1804: "For Sale, A likely Negro Man, of good character—sold for want of employment." Another wrote similarly in the *Federal Intelligencer, and Baltimore Daily Gazette:* "To be Sold for a term of years, AN ACTIVE NEGRO BOY, about thirteen years of age. Sold for no fault but want of employment." Struggling to profit from their slaves, Maryland owners viewed slave pregnancies as unwanted hindrances to maximum labor—as well as additional and unaffordable maintenance costs. One disgusted owner advertised his "young NEGRO WENCH, with a Male Child two years old. She can wash and iron, and is sold for no fault but for being pregnant." Other masters peddled their slaves in Baltimore as punishment to them for bad behavior. Nicholas Worthington of Anne Arundel County advertised his mulatto slave man, Wat, as having been "used as a waiting man till about two years ago, when, for his misdeeds in rifling when abroad, I was obliged to turn him to labour." With no need for their slaves' labor, rural Marylanders looked to Baltimore to relieve themselves of their burden.[33]

Rural owners found a ready market for male slaves in the shipyards of Fells Point. Many of the owners of the largest shipyards used slave labor in the shipbuilding trade, which became one of Baltimore's largest industries. In 1800 nearly half of the thirty-five shipbuilders owned slaves, the largest proportion of whom were working-age males employed in the yards.[34] Large shipbuilders generally owned more than one slave. In 1798 John Steel owned eight males between the ages of twenty-four and thirty-five; David Burke and William Price owned six males each. In 1800 the average shipbuilder owned between five and six slaves, the highest average among tradespeople in the city, and that number appears to have grown as the years progressed. By 1820 Price had twenty-four slaves, while four others possessed seven or more. Some of those in trades peripheral to the shipbuilding industry acquired male slaves as well, such as David Stoddard, a shipwright who in 1798 owned sixteen slaves, thirteen of them working-age males, and William Jackson, a block and pump maker, who owned five.[35]

Because Baltimore had few tobacco manufactories and iron foundries, which traditionally purchased slaves to meet their needs, the number of slaves in the city working in industry appears to have been low when compared with those later working in such southern cities as Richmond, Virginia. Even so, small tradespeople and industrialists sought to purchase slaves for use in their shops throughout the city. In addition to enhancing status, male slaves could provide valuable labor to small shopkeepers who strived to improve their businesses and their financial standing. In 1798 Christopher Raborg, a Fells Point copper and tinsmith, owned a male slave, Frank, aged twenty-five, who was assessed at £45 sterling. This assessment, higher than for most males that age, suggests that Raborg probably employed Frank in his shop, where he was still learning the trade. John Welsh, a Baltimore cordwainer who operated a small boot and shoe factory, owned five slaves, three of them male. The oldest, twenty-three-year-old Joe, was listed in the tax assessment as a "tradesman" and received the highest assessment, £60, which likely indicates he was more highly skilled than John, an eighteen-year-old, who was valued at £45 and was probably still learning the shoemaking trade.[36]

The records of the Baltimore County Court provide evidence of the transfer of slaves into Baltimore from a variety of places. Between 1792 and 1830 Maryland slaveowners filed declarations for the entrance of 598 slaves into Baltimore County from outside the state; more than 350 of these slaves came into Baltimore County during the 1790s alone.[37] Of the total brought into the county through 1830, more than 60 percent came from Virginia, with another 31 percent arriving from such Caribbean islands as Guadeloupe, Martinique, and especially Saint-Domingue (present-day Haiti).[38] The remainder came from such places as the District of Columbia, Delaware, Kentucky, Louisiana, South Carolina, New York, Pennsylvania, Tennessee, Massachusetts, and North Carolina. Of those slaveholders who petitioned to transport slaves into Baltimore County, eight out of ten lived in Baltimore City.[39]

Hired slaves also appear in the early Baltimore economy, particularly in the city's shipyards or one of the shipbuilding industry's various satellite industries. Benjamin Denys, a local grocer, hired out his slave Caesar to work at the city's wharves. Sixteen of the twenty-eight slaves owned by James Price, a merchant and the city's largest slaveowner in 1798, were males; of them eleven were between the ages of fifteen and forty-five. Price likely had little need for so many male slaves in his trading business and might well have hired out some or all of them. In a market in which unskilled laborers received wages of between fifty cents and a dollar per day—as opposed to just forty cents per day for agricultural workers—many owners hoped they could hire out their slaves in the city for six-month or, more desirable, twelve-month contracts. This enabled them to reduce the cost of caring for their slaves while guaranteeing themselves a steady income for the coming year.[40]

Rural and urban owners seeking to hire out their slaves in Baltimore appear to have found ready takers. The 1798 tax records for the city list 1,539 slaves owned by city residents; however, this figure falls short of the 2,843 slaves that federal census takers enumerated in the city only two years later. Moreover, Baltimoreans appear to have not yet hired out slaves within the city; the 1798 tax assessment includes only fifteen slaves owned by city residents yet not living with their owners. Most likely, the 1,304 slaves not accounted for in the tax assessment list were the property of absentee owners living outside Baltimore and had been either hired out or sent to live with city residents.[41]

It would appear that if the opportunity were presented to them, rural slaves rarely declined the chance to make Baltimore their new home. While fewer slaves than freedpeople had the freedom of choosing their occupation and living arrangements that brought most free blacks to the city, the chance to escape the oppressive ennui of the countryside for the breathless excitement of Tom Bailey's Baltimore lured many to the city. Others had deeper motivations. In 1809 William Winchester appeased his slaves' requests by sending them to Baltimore to labor "in the neighbourhood of thier wives & children." Indeed, a perceptive J. D. B. DeBow noted that slaves preferred the urban setting. "The negroes are the most social of all human beings," asserted DeBow in 1860, "and after having [been] hired in town, refuse to live again in the country."[42]

Slave numbers grew in Baltimore prior to 1810 as craftspeople and early industrialists transferred the prevailing source of labor to the urban venue. Indeed, judging by the high percentage of Baltimore craftspeople who were slaveholders, the market for slaves in the various industries appears to have been fairly substantial. As one historian has determined, between 1790 and 1810 craftspeople made up from one-fourth to perhaps more than one-third of the city's slaveholders and held a like proportion of the city's slaves. Such a high level of slave ownership suggests that slavery was briefly used profitably in the urban industrial setting.[43]

Despite the relative availability of industrial employment opportunities for male slaves in Baltimore, the ages and sex ratio of the city's slaves hint that a significant number of those slaves, both male and female, were employed as house servants. The 1804 tax assessment reveals that nearly a third of the slave population was composed of females between the ages of fourteen and thirty-six, the most desirable ages for domestic service. Similarly, slave bills of sale and declarations registered for Baltimore between 1787 and 1830, which specify slaves' sex and age though not the work they would perform, suggest that many slaves labored as domestics and menials. Of the 1,984 slave sales registered in Baltimore during the period for which sex was indicated, 1,031 (52 percent) were for women, while 953 (48 percent) were for men.[44]

Similarly, the 191 declarations of slaves brought into Baltimore from outside the state between 1792 and 1830 indicate an almost equal number of females and males.[45] The fact that relatively equal proportions of black men and women were being bought, sold, and transported into the state casts doubt on contentions that urban slavery was from the start primarily a female institution. Moreover, this parity suggests that slavery in Baltimore was never predominantly industrial in character and that the institution was never crucial to the city's economic growth.

Though owners manumitted Baltimore County male and female slaves at about the same rate until 1830, in subsequent decades the growing demand for female domestics meant the city's slave population was increasingly composed of women. The size and gender patterns of slaveholdings in Baltimore suggest that most homeowners acquired slaves for household chores. As in most antebellum southern cities, the demand for domestics in Baltimore outstripped that for industrial slaves. Not only was a merchant rather than an industrialist the city's largest slaveowner in 1798, but also over 70 percent of the city's wholesale merchants and professionals and nearly 50 percent of its retail merchants owned slaves in 1800. Together, merchants, traders, and professionals owned 61 percent of the city's slaves.[46] Of the 1,529 slave adults owned by residents in 1798, 833 (54.5 percent) were females. The 1820 federal census revealed that 55.0 percent of the city's 4,357 slaves were females, 5 percent higher than the percentage of women making up Baltimore's white population. By 1860 nearly two-thirds of Baltimore's slaves were female, unusual for such an important port and center of industry. While some male slaves were employed as domestics, the great majority of domestics were female.[47]

Slavery's initial expansion in Baltimore was linked to the increase of affluent urbanites who sought black servants for personal comfort as well as for status. The surest sign of gentility in the urban milieu was the presence of domestic servants, and in Maryland black servants were the most desirable. Many Baltimoreans preferred slaves to hired labor or even an indentured servant, who was worth much less in price. In 1794, for example, the saddler David Armour advertised the "Time of an Irish indented Servant Woman, . . . who has upwards of two years and a half to serve. . . . The cause of my parting with her is, because I have got a slave that I mean to put in her place."[48]

The Baltimore newspapers published daily advertisements for domestic slaves for sale, and sellers were quick to list the skills that suited their slaves to the needs of prospective urban masters. One such owner advertised "A STRONG Negro Woman, with 2 Children—She is capable of doing a great deal of family work, such as scrubbing, washing, plain cooking, &c." In March of 1800 Thomas Smyth advertised that he intended to sell a male and female slave, the man "a good house servant and understands that business well, being brought up in the house from a small boy," the woman "bred chiefly to plantation business, but is a good spinner, and is handy at kitchen work. The above negroes will be in Baltimore in a few days, where they can be delivered to the purchaser, and are sold for want of employment." Such rural owners took their chattel to the city, confident of the rapidly growing market for slaves there.[49]

Yet urban slaveholders, like their rural counterparts, often found themselves in possession of a surplus of domestic slaves. To exhibit their class stature, merchants, traders, and professionals attempted to hire out their domestic slaves to other fashionable urban households. Domestic slaves provided the household labor that freed mistresses from such unrefined tasks as cleaning, cooking, mending, and even nursing. "To Hire," read one 1804 newspaper advertisement, "A Negro Boy, accustomed to house-work." Another owner was somewhat more flexible: "FOR SALE, Or, will be hired by the month," his solicitation read, "*A valuable dark Mulatto Man*. He is well acquainted with driving a carriage, and taking care of horses—he is sober and careful, and is parted with for no cause but want of employment." Another advertised his "YOUNG MULATTO WOMAN of good character, with a good breast of milk," knowing that he likely could "engage [her] as Wet Nurse in a genteel family."[50]

Genteel families seeking to hire slave labor for their homes often placed their own advertisements in the city's newspapers. "CASH Will be given to a likely NEGRO or MULATTO WENCH, aged from 14 to 18 Years, who can work at her Needle, and bears a good Character," read one such message. Another wrote, "Wanted to Hire, A BLACK or MULATTO MAN, To drive a Carriage and wait in the House occasionally: Good Wages will be given to one of approved Character."[51] As their personal wealth grew, so did many Baltimoreans' desire to display their hard-won gentility.

In this bourgeois urban setting, a market existed for domestic slaves even among those who were less wealthy but wished to emulate their social superiors. Some Baltimoreans, in their quest for social and economic status, hired slaves despite not having the wherewithal or personal possessions in their households to justify the expense. In 1798 Charles Vallet, a confectioner, hired a female domestic slave from one Mr. Bogue to tend his rented home.[52] The pressure to keep up pretenses for their neighbors might well have led some to have black domestic servants in their modest homes, even if they could barely afford the expense involved in owning and maintaining them.

Slaves other than those hired as servants labored in the homes of Baltimoreans who could little afford to maintain them. Many Baltimore slaveholders inherited slaves from family members in Maryland and other slave states. In 1794 Lucy Stilk and Jannet Stilk of Baltimore Town brought to the city four slaves of different ages and sexes, inherited from their father's Virginia estate. Similarly, in 1820 Richard Janson inherited a male and two female slaves from his uncle's estate in Virginia and petitioned to move them to Baltimore.[53] Such acts were not isolated; in their quantitative study of slavery, Robert Fogel and Stanley Engerman found that in Maryland nearly half of all slave sales resulted from the breakup of the estates of deceased planters whose heirs were unable or unwilling to assume the obligations of the plantation or the maintenance of the bondpeople who had labored on it. The remainder of estate slaves were distributed throughout the family, to members who were willing to assume responsibility for slaves willed directly or granted to them for use in the property settlement. Thus, John Lee, a Fells Point ship carpenter, owned no real property but held two slaves, Jim and Dinah, while the schoolmaster Burch Demmett, similarly without real estate and with just £37 sterling worth of personal property, owned a young slave woman. More notable, Hugh Auld, a struggling shipbuilder who never owned more than $50 worth of private property, twice took in the young slave Frederick Bailey. Auld did this once while Bailey was owned by his brother's father-in-law and again after his brother had inherited the young man. This was done even though Auld had no real need for a slave and would incur additional expenses by providing Bailey a home.[54]

The ability to hire out slaves provided the incentive for many masters to keep them, even if they could not afford to maintain them and pay taxes on them while serving in their own households. Daniel Bowley, a laborer, hired out his working-age bondwoman, assessed at £30 sterling in 1798, to the attorney Richard Moale. Masters preferred to sign yearly contracts for their slaves, guaranteeing a wage that was steadier than that commanded by those doing day labor.[55] James Long, the clerk of the central market, advertised his thirteen-year-old slave girl—"active and smart in taking care of children, and according to her strength, can do house work tolerably well"—for hire by the month or year, "or I will let her go to any person in Baltimore for a longer term, if required." While lengthy contracts were desirable, the rapidly glutted market for slaves forced owners to accept shorter terms. In 1810 the sugar importer Ambrose Clarke hired a Negro named Fanny from Elizabeth Lawson for two months for the sum of eight dollars. Another such master advertised, "To be Hired by the Day, a black woman. She is a good Washer, and her Honesty and Sobriety may be relied on." For employers, the situation was a boon, allowing them great flexibility in the length of the contracts.[56]

The ability of slaveholders in Baltimore to find steady work for their slaves appears to have played a significant part in their decision to keep, sell, or free them. The records of the Orphans' Court of Baltimore County are replete with petitions that reveal just how often the city's residents could not afford to keep their slaves without hiring out their labor. In 1798 the court allowed William Mathews to sell his "Negro Slaves, consisting of a Man, his Wife and Six Children," which he inherited as part of an estate settlement, as "the said Slaves haveing constantly been, and Continue to be an expence beyond the Amount of their earnings." Similarly, in 1803 Thomas Derochbrune, the administrator of his father's estate, petitioned that though his father's will had stipulated "that Sundry Negroes . . . are entitled to Freedom at certain periods, Your petitioner finds that at this dull time when there is no certain employment to be got that they are more expence to keep, than they Earne." Convinced that "the said part of the deceased's Estate is wasting fast," the court granted Derochbrune's request to sell off some of the slaves.[57]

The increase in slave ownership in Baltimore's early years proved short-lived. Moreover, it belies its relative insignificance when compared with slavery in other cities in the Upper South. According to the city's tax records, of the 2,100 assessed property owners in Baltimore City in 1798, 563 (26.8 percent) owned slaves. Collectively, those owners possessed a total of 1,539 slaves. The average Baltimore slaveowner thus owned less than three slaves. By contrast, in the rural areas of Maryland, such as the Eastern Shore, slaveowners held on average eleven slaves, while in southern Maryland the average slaveholder owned as many as fifteen.

For most Baltimoreans of the first decades of the nineteenth century, regardless of their occupation, slaveowning was an unaffordable luxury. Simple economics alone ensured that this would remain the case; slaves, no matter what their initial cost, were expensive to maintain. As that initial cost climbed with the nation's economic growth (as well as the cost of living in the city), fewer individuals could manage the purchase price, much less the cost of maintenance. Even among small businesspeople, who wanted cheap labor for their shops and manufactories, slave ownership peaked early in Baltimore and then declined precipitously. For these struggling businesspeople, paying wages for labor proved far more appealing than purchasing a slave, primarily because of the great flexibility of wages in a rapidly changing market and the minimal or nonexistent investment that one stood to lose.

Slaveowning in Baltimore diminished steadily as the century progressed. In 1800 nearly a third of the city's households included at least one slave, but there was a gradual decline between 1810 and 1830 and a marked decline thereafter. By 1850 slaveowners represented just over 1 percent of the city's white population, and by 1860 slaves constituted only 1 percent of the city's total population and less than 8 percent of the city's black residents. Baltimore served as the model for Frederick Douglass's later observation that "slavery dislikes a dense population."[58]

Because the number of slaves available far exceeded the demand, masters who had no need for their services and yet needed to hire them out in Baltimore occasionally were forced to allow their slaves considerable liberty to solicit prospective employers who would not mistreat their valuable chattel. Some masters granted their slaves permission to hire their own time, by the day or the week, even going so far as to allow them to "live out," away from the master's home. Self-hiring slaves leased out for various periods, either annually or semiannually, would negotiate their own employers, wages, hours, and type of labor, as well as certain privileges, such as time off and the ability to retain wages earned for extra work. Slaves given the privilege of living out would do the same, but they carried the extra burden and risk of paying their own expenses from the weekly earnings left after giving their owners a minimum weekly wage. In allowing slaves to self-hire, masters avoided the problem of finding work for them or paying the 5 to 8 percent fee charged by hiring brokers.

Largely unknown in states in the Deep South, the practices of self-hire and living out, though barred by state law since 1787, did exist in Baltimore.[59] Alfred Pairpont, an English visitor to the city, noted that Baltimore had a noticeable preponderance of self-hired slaves, who "let themselves out for every kind of work, paying their masters a given sum for the loss of their services, and keeping a trifle for themselves."[60] Frederick Bailey's agreement with Hugh Auld stipulated that from his earnings as a ship caulker, the young slave would provide his own board, clothes, and caulking tools and would still bring home $3 each week. From 1801 to 1803 Ambrose Clarke, a sugar importer, allowed "his Negro man Slave Named Cesar To go at Large for Hire," for which Clarke paid a bond of $30 to city officials to guarantee his chattel's good behavior.[61]

Slaves appear to have welcomed the opportunity for self-hire and especially living out, which likely contributed to the decline of slavery as an institution. In the words of one historian of the Upper South, such practices were "a step towards freedom" and were psychologically important to the slave's pursuit of liberty. Such practices also allowed considerable latitude for slaves to improve the negotiating skills that no doubt enabled them to have been allowed to hire themselves out in the first place. Indeed, in Baltimore it would appear that some masters granted this privilege as a means by which their slaves could purchase their way out of slavery. In 1815 the merchant Alexander Robinson contracted with his slave, Jeffery McHerd, that once the slave had paid $400.00 to him, he would be free. When Jeffery began hiring his own time in July, Robinson charged him interest for needed clothing, which was added to the purchase price. By November of the next year, Jeffrey had paid off $153.10 of his debt, at which time Robinson transferred his account to a Mr. Timington, who was to give Jeffrey his freedom when he had paid off the remainder of the debt. In at least this instance, hiring one's own time appears to have been part of the process of self-emancipation.[62]

While a slave living away from the master's home—and paying his or her own expenses—might well have held some financial appeal, owners appear to have been more willing to grant gradual manumission as incentive to good service than to relinquish authority over them. By allowing their slaves to live out, masters lost virtually all direct control over them. By all indications, prior to 1830 few slaves in Baltimore received permission from their masters and mistresses to live out. The 1790 census lists only one household composed entirely of slaves, headed by "Negro Peter, the property of Charles Wells." No such households appear in the federal census for 1800, and only five such entries appear in the 1820 census, including John Benson's household of five slaves in Ward 1 and George Hammond and his wife, a free woman of color, living at Fells Point. Although the 1830 census lists forty-four households headed by slaves, these constitute a minute one-third of a percent of the city's households.[63]

Despite its attractiveness to slaveowners, slave hiring for industrial and craft usage appears not to have flourished in Baltimore as it did in other southern cities. One historian has found that among all of the cities in the slave states, Baltimore had by far the least slave-hiring activity.[64] Hard-pressed craftworkers (who made up the bulk of the city's white petite bourgeoisie) found little extra capital with which to take on the expenses of clothing and feeding a hired slave, in addition to paying the master for his or her services.[65] In 1850, well after slavery's peak in Baltimore, once the difficulty of finding employment for them would have only been heightened because of free labor competition, only a hundred people reported employing slaves. A decade later over half of the hired slaves in the city were employed by people who engaged only one such slave. In both of those years the average number of slaves individuals in Baltimore employed was less than two, compared with six in Richmond and Charleston.[66]

Financial considerations notwithstanding, factors peculiar to Baltimore—other than the law—may have played an equally important role in both the weakness of slave hiring and the relative lack of success of industrial slavery in Baltimore. Historians have shown that while the South ultimately failed to integrate slaves fully in the industrial setting, slavery was profitable and relatively successful in that venue.[67] Baltimore was no exception. Such industries as the Maryland Chemical Works did employ slaves and free workers profitably throughout the early decades of the nineteenth century. As one historian has shown, the owner David McKim quickly realized that the differing legal statuses of slaves in Baltimore fostered diverse and often inscrutable motivations and behavior among slave employees, forcing him to adapt his management techniques to suit the complexities of his labor force. McKim provided cost and wage incentives to his slave laborers, whether hired or owned for life or a set term, and selectively retained only those who provided security for his investment in them by laboring diligently and especially by not running away. Most telling, hired slaves—the most likely to run off—consistently cost the Chemical Works more than either term or life slaves, and in 1829 a hired slave actually cost only pennies less per week than did a free laborer.[68]

Free white workers in Baltimore openly resented the use of hired out slaves, especially self-hired ones. In 1808 the House of Delegates heard a petition from "the owners of hack-stages, draymen, carters and laborers" of Baltimore, who complained that they were "deprived of employment by the interference of slaves who engross the same."[69] Autonomous slave behavior influenced Baltimore employers profoundly, not only by forcing them to adapt their hiring practices and management techniques to maximize and enforce productivity but also by increasing labor costs significantly when slaves freed themselves by running away.

A limited market for slave hiring and the prevalence of such flexible forms of control as self-hire and living out suggest that Baltimore's economic rise never rested on the institution of chattel slavery, as it did in other southern cities. Indeed, the proportion of slaves in Baltimore City's population peaked at just over 10 percent in 1800, a figure that paled in comparison with that of Maryland as a whole, where slaves constituted more than 30 percent of the population (see table 2). Though Baltimore rivaled and even surpassed several other southern cities in its absolute number of slaves during this period, it had the lowest percentage of slaves. By 1820 slaves made up less than 7 percent of Baltimore's population, which was far less than in Charleston, where half of the population was in slavery. Even in Richmond and Norfolk in the Upper South, slaves constituted over a third of the population. Baltimore's slaves continued to decline in both real and relative numbers during the rest of the antebellum period. In only one other city in the

Table 2. White, Slave, and Free Black Populations as Percentage of Total, Maryland and Baltimore City, 1790–1860

Year	Total Population	White Population	Slave Population	Free Black Population
MARYLAND				
1790	319,728	65.2%	32.2%	2.5%
1800	349,692	63.6	30.8	5.6
1810	380,546	61.9	29.3	8.8
1820	407,350	64.1	26.3	9.5
1830	447,040	65.1	23.0	11.8
1840	469,232	67.7	19.1	13.2
1850	583,034	71.7	15.5	12.8
1860	688,029	75.1	12.7	12.2
BALTIMORE CITY				
1790	13,503	88.3	9.3	2.4
1800	26,514	78.8	10.7	10.5
1810	46,555	77.8	10.0	12.2
1820	62,738	76.6	6.9	16.5
1830	80,620	76.5	5.1	18.3
1840	102,513	79.2	3.1	17.5
1850	169,054	83.2	1.7	15.0
1860	212,418	86.9	1.0	12.1

Sources: Fairbanks, Statistical Analysis of the Population of Maryland, 105; McSherry, History of Maryland, 403–4; Fields, Slavery and Freedom on the Middle Ground, 70.

slave states—St. Louis—was the incidence of slaveowning ever as low as in Baltimore, but that was not until 1860.[70]

Why slavery never took root in Baltimore as it did in other southern cities is a subject of some debate among historians. Robert Starobin, among others, has demonstrated that numerous industries throughout the South utilized slave labor both efficiently and profitably.[71] Certainly, Baltimore boasted ample large industries as well as middle-sized and small manufactories that could well have made use of slave labor, as many industries did elsewhere in the Upper South, such as in Richmond, Virginia. Yet Baltimore failed to attract the slave factory hands so prevalent in Richmond. In Fells Point, soon to be annexed, where the shipbuilding industry would ultimately provide Baltimore's greatest demand for industrial slave labor, less than half of the 276 slaves residing there at the end of the Revolution were working-aged males, those most likely employed in the shipyards.[72] While some industries near Baltimore City, most notably the Principio and Baltimore Iron

Works companies, employed slave labor in their operations, for the most part free rather than unfree laborers served the needs of Baltimore's booming economy.[73]

A clue might lie in the diversification that had long typified the Upper South economy. As alternative means of accumulating capital came to the Chesapeake, planters appear to have turned away from slaveholding as a means of building capital. Inheritance patterns in probate records during the late eighteenth and early nineteenth centuries suggest that planters consciously stopped bequeathing slaves to their surviving loved ones; instead, they often left instructions to the executors of their estates to sell them and invest the proceeds in enterprises offering more secure returns. Maryland's proximity to the now-free states and the increased threat of slaves' escaping no doubt influenced many slaveholders' thinking.

Baltimore amplified industrializing practices already well established in the Chesapeake. Between 1800 and 1820 the number of charters granted by the state of Maryland to various businesses and industries (especially commercial banking, turnpikes, insurance companies, and manufactories) increased nearly sevenfold over the previous sixteen-year span, from a mere 17 to 118. Such an expansion of investment opportunities was not lost on Maryland residents, especially those in Baltimore, where most of these industries were locating. The plethora of capital-building ventures beckoned residents of the city to invest in enterprises apart from slaveholding. Such factors hint at the ultimate demise of slavery in the city.[74]

The very need for rural slaveowners to send their slaves to the city for employment attests to, as one historian of slavery in Maryland has found, an institution in decline. The slave population of Maryland reached its zenith in 1810 and declined steadily thereafter, more than 21 percent over the next half-century. In Baltimore the flexible terms and diverse arrangements owners were forced to accept in order to hire out their slaves only validate the contention that the system was eroding. Stated simply, slavery as a widespread economic institution was largely impractical in the integrated and volatile urban industrial setting of Baltimore. While it could and did work for some industries, such as the Maryland Chemical Works, the large complement of free laborers—white and black—who required neither high purchase price nor even servitude contracts rendered slavery in the city simply too inflexible to justify its high cost, especially given the trend of rapidly increasing slave prices during the later antebellum period. Only in such southern cities as Richmond, where heavy industry and tobacco production dominated and where slave labor remained a bulwark of the region's economy, did industrial slave hiring proliferate. With so much at stake, Baltimore industrialists turned increasingly to its ample supply of workers who were free rather than slave.[75]

❖   ❖   ❖

At the dawn of the nineteenth century, as the young nation struggled to define itself politically, socially, and economically, Baltimore was poised to become one of its most important urban centers. In only half a century it had grown from a rude hamlet to one of the republic's largest cities; by 1850 it would boast nearly 170,000 inhabitants, trailing only New York and Philadelphia in size.[76] While Baltimore was still largely preindustrial in 1800, its prowess as a shipping locus, primarily to and from the West Indies and continental Europe, each year brought hundreds of fast-sailing sloops and schooners, as well as the larger ships and brigs, and thousands of smaller bay crafts to its harbor in pursuit of trade. The development of the Baltimore clipper, the fastest cargo vessel yet introduced, only augmented the shipbuilding industry already crucial to the city's economy and hastened the industrial process by complementing the grain trade. As this trade began to blossom in the final decade of the eighteenth century, a result of the increased demand for grain impelled by the beginning of a series of European conflicts, Baltimore witnessed an explosion of satellite services and industries of the grain trade that would soon attract ever larger numbers of immigrants to the city, both white and black.

Yet unlike cities in the Deep South, Baltimore achieved this remarkable growth with only marginal dependence on the institution of slavery. Obviously, the growth of the city did not occur completely devoid of chattel bondage; indeed, until 1810 slavery grew in Baltimore at a rate that paralleled the blossoming of the city itself. Yet such growth was to prove ephemeral. Slavery lived and died quickly in the city. Far more important to the future of the city, Baltimore would soon create its own liberating momentum that carved deep fissures into the edifice of slavery. With the epicenter in Baltimore, the shock waves were felt throughout the Upper South seaboard. The wellspring of this impetus, which would ultimately crumble the institution in the South, emanated from several sources, not the least of which were the people of color, slave and free, of Maryland and Baltimore themselves.[77]

2

The Roots of Quasi-Freedom

In 1827 Nicholas Brice, chief judge of the Criminal Court of Baltimore County, issued a public letter to Joseph Kent, then governor of Maryland, in which he commented on a social phenomenon he believed had become an ominous threat to the state's social order. Reacting to the frequent cases he heard involving bondpeople for a term of years ("very rarely indeed are any of them slaves for life," he wrote), Brice argued that slaves freed in such a manner menaced the institutional stability of slavery in Maryland. "The manumission of slaves on contingencies, or at a certain age, or after a term of years," in the judge's estimation, "appears to be peculiarly injurious in its effects on the negroes themselves, and often renders them wholly unfit to enjoy the benefit designed them." As such, term slaves had come to believe they were "possessed of some rights in common with free men, which encourage them in acts of insubordination."[1]

Judge Brice called not for the statutory death of gradual emancipation but for the imposition of more stringent institutional controls over manumission. "If I might venture an opinion on this subject," the judge wrote, "the State should take this matter under its own management, and either make a law for the gradual emancipation of these people at proper ages, or establish some tribunal to decide on the proper objects for manumission, when desired by their owners, who are inclined to bestow that favour on any of their slaves, and not leave a matter of such importance to the community, to the caprice . . . of individuals, who in general consult only their own interest."[2]

Brice's objections lay bare a fundamental dilemma of gradual manumission. Considering the granting of such freedom in essence a "favour," Brice the idealist saw that the bestowal of freedom at a future date could be and was used by slaveholders as a form of paternalistic incentive to good behavior on the part of their slaves. Yet Brice the realist, a judge charged with overseeing the maintenance of Maryland's public good by enforcing its legal statutes, recognized that the availability of such terms set a precedent that could and did undermine masters' authority by creating "a sort of middle class, neither slave nor free; exempted from many of the motives for obedience which influence slaves" for life.[3]

In effect, Brice, in daily witnessing the clash of human wills in disputes over property, recognized a fundamental incongruity in the legal conflict over freedom and slavery. In granting freedom sometime in the future in hopes of encouraging slaves' good behavior or productive work habits, masters actually risked the far greater possibility of precisely the opposite. Judge Brice saw rightly that Baltimore slaves, bolstered by rising expectations, badgered, demanded, and even threatened their masters for varying degrees of freedom. His plan to emplace a "tribunal" to decide on future manumissions was both an attempt to establish a new balance between positive and negative mechanisms of controlling term slaves and a protection for masters against the pleas, cajolery (often in the form of offers of self-purchase), threats, and even violence by their far-from-placated slaves. By offering the legal power to deny or rescind the manumissions of those slaves who shirked or absconded, Brice believed that the state could reinstitute masters' waning control of their slaves, for term and for life.[4]

Ironically, the racial attitudes of white Baltimoreans (as much as the autonomous efforts of slaves to attain freedom) contributed to the problems of black autonomy against which Judge Brice protested so strongly. Like the evolution of African American culture itself, the racial perceptions of whites in the city directly reflected time and space. Nowhere was this more evident than in Baltimore City. As Baltimore became the principal port for exports from most of the upper Chesapeake and the fertile western Maryland countryside, migrants—both black and white—poured into the city to take advantage of the expanded economic opportunities. Baltimore raced to maturity during a period that witnessed a complex transition of such attitudes in postrevolutionary America. Just as the war itself had prompted many to view slavery as incompatible with the philosophy of American freedom, so had it spawned a proslavery ideology that many social conservatives employed to challenge liberal theories of natural rights. Even before the war ended, proponents had lent such theories to a growing class and race consciousness, which not only defended slavery as the natural status of those of inferior development but also branded black-skinned people as the most suitable for a permanent laboring class. Ironically, as the ideas of the Enlightenment acted as midwife to the birth of an era of liberty, slavery in America began its harshest period.[5]

Yet crucial ideological shifts and changes do not emerge as monoliths, and they progress anything but linearly. The hardening of racial philosophy during the late eighteenth and early nineteenth centuries ebbed and flowed with economic, political, and social circumstance, tossed about even further by regional and rural and urban distinctions. Early national Baltimore embodied such a transformation; amid the swirl of its breakneck growth social boundaries became imprecise, which invariably made for equally inexact ideological parameters. As more people crowded into the city, physical proximity alone daily forced all of its inhabitants to confront people from many different backgrounds. Baltimore's residents were consequently forced to assess each situation—and each person—differently, if not more adaptively, than did those in the cloistered countryside. The sheer size of the city's populace made blanket generalizations about others difficult, even when dealing with former and present slaves, especially term slaves. As a result, Baltimoreans defined and redefined their race relations according to need. In this context economic status had everything to do with racial distinctions.[6]

Obsessed with economic expansion, white residents of Baltimore appear to have grown marginally color-blind. The decades-long transition from slavery to free labor had already forced many white residents of upper Maryland to assume an ideological middle ground on matters of slavery and freedom, and this ambiguousness manifested itself in a subdued ambivalence on the concept of race—nowhere more evident than in Baltimore. The inherent ambiguities of Baltimore's racial lines allowed whites ample room to redefine continually the code of racial etiquette to suit local circumstances. The seeming insignificance of freedom papers, the nonexistence of slave-labor badges, the city government's failure to enforce the state's 1794 prohibition of self-hire in Baltimore, and the fact that city directories did not separate black from white householders until 1819 and that tax directories did not do so until much later all attest to a relatively liberal racial atmosphere in the city. So much so that a black man from the city could announce himself a candidate for the House of Delegates in a slaveholding state, while another could openly criticize white domination in that state. Between 1788 and 1792 at least five slave couples secured marriage licenses from the county clerk to legalize unions the state would not have recognized.[7] In an extraordinary example of the city's racially tolerant atmosphere, Peter Douat, a white French émigré from Cap-François, Saint-Domingue, was married to Mary Frances, a free black émigré, in the city's St. Peter's Catholic Church in January of 1794. This despite a 1715 enactment that imposed a fine of five thousand pounds of tobacco for ministers and magistrates performing such ceremonies. Whether such penalty applied to French Caribbean émigrés—probably not yet citizens of Maryland—is unclear, but such actions only enhanced the atmosphere of ambivalence already present in the city.[8]

Ambivalence about racial boundaries in early Baltimore grew in part from the general climate of colonial Maryland, where, according to one historian, "differences between the status of free whites and free blacks were small and often ill-defined." Not until after 1785, three decades following Virginia's lead, did Maryland bother to fashion a legal definition of the term *Negro*, deciding somewhat liberally (compared with neighboring Virginia and North Carolina) that one was considered black if he or she could claim an African ancestor in either of the previous two generations.[9] Tempered by the prevailing notion of black inferiority, white people's relations with black residents in early Baltimore were sufficiently relaxed that in 1785 (not ironically the same year that Maryland codified its parameters of blackness) at least one resident actually wanted to extend to them certain social privileges customarily reserved for whites. This sentiment is captured in a newspaper advertisement: "A person of a liberal Profession is desirous of trying a benevolent Experiment, by instructing an ingenious Negro Lad in a Business that will give him if ingenious and docile, an accurate knowledge of the English language, and besides rendering him really a rational Creature, will enable him in due time, to earn handsome Wages."[10]

Such a climate prompted a northern visitor to Baltimore, Ethan Allen Andrews, to note as late as 1835 that "it is said that the free blacks in Maryland are not by law excluded from any trade or employment which may be practised by the whites. . . . In New York, on the contrary, a colored man, it is said, cannot drive his own hack or cart."[11] Consistent with this observation, in late 1794 at least one of the city's newspapers carried advertisements for the newest regional almanac of Benjamin Banneker, a Baltimore County African American, which described its "ingenious and humorous anecdotes and jests," its "select maxims calculated to improve the mind and inform the judgment," and its "choice collection of the most useful receipts." Banneker's identity was hardly a secret; his almanac, a self-styled "first attempt of the kind that ever was made in America by a person of my complexion," was used widely, and he had achieved such fame as a scientist and mathematician that he was appointed to the three-man government commission to survey the proposed boundaries of the District of Columbia. Banneker's intellectual abilities reputedly caused some members of the British Parliament to reverse their beliefs about innate black intellectual inferiority, and in 1791 Thomas Jefferson, after reading Banneker's first almanac, was prompted to write the author that he would have to rethink his own notions of such inferiority.[12] In such a climate it is not surprising that Baltimore avoided for most of the early nineteenth century virulent, class-based racial tensions and legalized proscriptions against black workers that were becoming common in the northern port cities.

Yet no matter how casual its race relations might have been, Baltimore in the 1780s was not the seventeenth-century Eastern Shore of Virginia, where in its infancy, distinctions of color appear to have held even less importance.[13] Marylanders had a long history in which to acquire their racial baggage, and the late rise of Baltimore's star allowed plenty of room on which to build up the palisades of racial inferiority. At the beginning of the nation's second decade Baltimoreans could not completely evade the long-developed ideological construct of race. No matter how liberal Baltimore might be, its late emergence allowed white residents to have established a color line of sorts. Inherently imprecise, Baltimore's appears particularly blurred. However defined, such a barrier involved white Marylanders' making intellectual and even moral valuations of human nature and society that legitimized the obvious incongruity of racial discrimination in the midst of a virtuous republic. As white Baltimoreans entered the hectic era of the nascent market revolution, black Baltimoreans did not threaten their cultural hegemony, but white residents found ample reason to discriminate mildly, if not overtly, against them.[14]

Ironically, the city's racial tolerance was largely a result of the continued presence of slavery in the state of Maryland. The maintenance of slavery provided white residents, both rural and urban, with a powerful legal and psychological edifice to deflect racial hostility born of economic insecurities. By maintaining slavery (unlike Pennsylvania, its neighbor to the north), Maryland held on to a racial trump card that assured white residents of social control over not only its slaves but also free Negroes. While northern states disfranchised, segregated, and economically oppressed black people because they were afraid extending legal freedom to them might beget social equality, residents of such southern states as Maryland feared no such loss of racial dominance so long as their laws maintained that all Negroes could be held in—or returned to—bondage. In reality, remanding free black people to slavery occurred only occasionally, usually illegally. Yet by maintaining the power to make such a portentous decision if provoked, white people imposed a tacit control over black Marylanders, which both recognized and which unavoidably affected their relationship. In Baltimore this relationship manifested itself as one of ostensible racial harmony, a veneer, perhaps, but one reflecting a distinct ideological climate during the first three decades of the nineteenth century that again set the city apart from other places, whether in the North, South, or even rural Maryland.

As witnessed in the debate over term slavery and the resultant slave behavior, in the four decades following the War of Independence the black
population of Baltimore was increasingly made up of those who were, in
more than one historian's words, "quasi-slave" and "quasi-free."[15] Baltimore's
black residents, who were mainly slaves but rapidly were becoming free,
experienced only limited constraint compared with those rigid distinctions
that continued to delineate the statuses of African Americans living in such
cities of the Lower South as Charleston. In large part this relative autonomy resulted from the methods used and precedents set by Maryland slaves
who gained their freedom and quickly went to Baltimore. In particular the
manumission process proved singularly important to the Upper South, especially Maryland.[16]

As in other states in the North and the Upper South, the Revolution
unleashed a host of storms in Maryland that buffeted the ideological stance
of many white Americans toward African Americans. The age's revolutionary egalitarianism, ensconced in the Jefferson-cum-Lockean words "We hold
these truths to be self-evident, that all men are created equal," had provided for many the salient reason for fighting a war with Britain. Yet such beliefs also prompted many Marylanders to reevaluate their position on slavery and forced some even to pronounce it contradictory to republican
ideology and dangerous to the future of the new Republic. The message of
the evangelical revivals of the mid-eighteenth century had encouraged many
to this profession of faith and in some ways presaged revolutionary ideological rhetoric by espousing the idea that all were equal in God's eyes. To fulfill
this covenant, many of these congregations accepted black and white communicants for full membership into their churches. This powerful combination of impulses compelled many in the young nation either to reconsid-
er their stance on slavery or to take action against a practice they might
already have deplored.[17]

With revolutionary principles persuading many Maryland leaders that
slavery was wrong, the resultant intellectual climate quickly yielded a liberalization of manumission laws. Following Virginia's lead, in 1790 Maryland
modified its 1752 enactment, which had allowed manumission by a deed,
by extending the additional right of manumission by a will. Moreover, the
assembly passed certain pieces of legislation during the postwar period that
appear to have been designed to ameliorate slaves' conditions. In 1786 courts
began allowing oral evidence of slave petitioners' white ancestry in "freedom suits," which greatly increased the chances of the case's success. Seven
years later lawmakers decreed that these freedom suits, normally heard before the general court, would be tried in the counties in which the slave

petitioners brought suit, allowing more facile assemblage of witnesses for the slave and compelling masters to be present in court to bear proof of ownership. In a law passed in 1796, which provided the clearest definition of the conditions for manumission by both will and deed yet legislated, Maryland legislators attempted to prevent owners from freeing their superannuated charges (apparently, a common occurrence by which masters unburdened themselves of slaves who had outlived their productiveness) by setting an age limit of forty-five on future manumissions. While the law no doubt prevented many slaves who both desired and were physically capable of enjoying their freedom from obtaining it legally, it did hinder masters who sought to evade responsibility for aged slaves who were no longer able to provide profitable labor.[18]

Because Maryland did not abolish slavery during the First, or Revolutionary, Emancipation (as its neighbors to the north did) or greatly restrict the practice of private manumission in the early years of the nineteenth century after the initial liberalization of those laws following the American Revolution (as its neighbor states to the south did), Maryland witnessed a continuously high rate of manumissions throughout the early national period. Marylanders manumitted thousands of slaves by individual acts recorded in deeds or wills, again diverging from both the North and the Lower South.[19]

Despite its strong allure, however, revolutionary idealism alone could not account for the wave of manumissions in the Upper South that began in the years immediately following the Revolution. Just as white moral and political values awakened, compelling economic changes rendered slavery less attractive and financially too risky for many upper Marylanders. In a small state with small western holdings, hemmed to the north by what was now a free state, Maryland planters found little room for the westward expansion of a slave-based agricultural economy. Moreover, many farmers who were clearing raw grain land in the western counties soon found their new crop somewhat less suited for slave labor than was tobacco. Requiring more seasonal labor than year-round tending (a maximum work force at harvest but work for only a marginal crew during other seasons), grain production encouraged marginal farmers to trim surplus labor costs whenever possible, especially for women and children. With such seasonal demands, hiring and firing wage laborers was more appealing than slave labor, especially since hired labor was fast becoming readily available among the state's growing white and, eventually, free black populations.[20]

Moreover, during the Revolution slave prices plummeted by nearly one-half, and although they rose again somewhat by 1790, in the ensuing decade they gradually slumped. The collapse of the European tobacco market because of the wars there and the abolition of the French tobacco monopoly resulted in the removal of an important buyer of Eastern Shore tobacco. Though large planters with productive lands in southern Maryland might have benefited from low slave prices and acquired more slaves, they were already well supplied through inheritance. Middling and small farmers in Baltimore County, whose peers in other counties largely sustained slave purchases in the state during this period, could hardly have been encouraged by this trend. When those same wars sparked soaring grain prices, the decline of tobacco culture, in combination with a postwar depression, prompted even large western farmers to begin growing corn and wheat as cash crops, while rotating pasture and cover crops to prevent depletion and erosion caused by plowing. They, too, soon found their need for slave labor limited.[21]

With slavery declining as a labor system, Maryland masters often freed their slaves. Yet the pattern of emancipations in the Upper South was wholly unlike that of the Lower South, where slavery remained an essential labor source. Lower South masters most often freed only a select few, mostly mulattoes, who were generally illicit slave offspring—either their own or of white servants—or personal favorites. By contrast, masters in Maryland liberated their slaves more widely and less discriminatingly, generally involving not just one or two but most or all of the master's chattel property. The powerful economic changes during the years following the Revolution created a huge surge of emancipations in Maryland, as hundreds of slaveowners chose either to liberate or sell off their slaves or to allow them to purchase their own freedom.[22]

Despite efforts to limit manumissions, the practice remained popular in much of Maryland. In the three Eastern Shore counties of Caroline, Dorchester, and Talbot, masters freed 1,833 slaves between 1783 and 1799, and more than 3,000 were freed during the ensuing three decades. Between 1789 and 1830 residents of Baltimore County freed at least 2,448 slaves by deeds of manumission. Even in sparsely populated Dorchester County, the land and chattel records for 1799 to 1830 contain more than 1,000 such manumissions. The Maryland State Colonization Society noted 2,342 manumissions statewide in 1831–41.[23] The large number of manumissions created in Maryland the largest free black population of any state in the nation, so large that on the eve of the Civil War the state possessed nearly equal numbers of free Negroes and slaves—an anomaly among slave states.

In attempting to explain the wholesale manumissions in the Upper South, such writers as Gary Nash, Jean Soderlund, and Ira Berlin have posited that a powerful combination of republican principles, religious persuasion, economic pressure, and antislavery activity during and immediately after the Revolution played equally important roles in fashioning a unique course for freedom and slavery in Maryland. These writers have noted the wording of wills, such as that of William Cox of rural Baltimore County, who in 1768 liberated his six bondpeople because he "Believ[ed] it inconsistant with the rules of Christianity to Continue them in Slavery during life." They gain similar impressions from deeds of manumission, such as those of one Harford County owner, who declared when emancipating his seven bondmen in 1782 that "the holding of negroes in perpetual bondage and slavery is repugnant to the law of God and inconsistent with the strict rules of equity and that freedom and liberty is the inalienable right of every person born into the world." Finally, as late as 1846 Ishmael Day of Baltimore County evinced a wide range of liberal sentiment when he freed his woman Eliza because he lived "under a *Republican Government* & *believing as I most sincerely do*, that all the *Human Race without respect to sex or Coulour should* & *ought to be free.*"[24]

Such evocative statements provide some insight into the complex philosophical conflicts many Maryland slaveowners faced in keeping their servants in bondage. Few of those who manumitted them, however, included such lofty inspirations in their documents. Even in the earliest surviving manumissions, such revelatory confessions are quite rare and by the turn of the nineteenth century had become virtually nonexistent. By that time, court clerks and local attorneys had developed a stylized code for manumissions that satisfied the legal requirements for such documents but revealed little of the manumitter's intent. Unfortunately for the historian, the statement most often indicated with formulaic reticence that the individual acted of "diverse good causes and considerations."[25]

To be sure, republican virtue as well as religious fervor played a role in the spread of manumissions in Maryland. Quakerism and Methodism had considerable influence in the state's northernmost counties, particularly on the Eastern Shore. One historian has found that in the Eastern Shore counties of Caroline, Dorchester, and Talbot by 1790 at least three hundred Quaker-owned slaves had gained their freedom by deeds of manumission, and "untold numbers of others" were set free by wills. Similarly, another has found that in Annapolis between 1825 and 1830, 42 percent of Methodist slaveowners took steps to manumit their slaves, resulting in 55 percent of Methodist-owned slaves receiving their freedom, either immediately or by term. During the same period only a quarter of non-Methodist slaveowners participated in such manumission activity.[26]

The egalitarianism of the American Revolution had a substantial impact on the course of manumissions in early national Maryland. As one noted historian has written, "the philosophy of natural rights" did assist in the destruction "of the intellectual foundations of slavery." The manumission deed of one Caroline County owner bears stark witness to its imprint by its statement that the manumission of his ten slaves was consistent with the inalienable rights of mankind "as well as every principles of the glorious Revolution that has lately taken place in America." Another stated laconically that "Black people are as much entitled to natural liberty as whites."[27]

Ironically, this revolutionary egalitarianism as applied to black Marylanders appears not to have been expressed in deed during the era itself. The Miscellaneous Papers of the Baltimore County Court include no deeds of manumission during the years of the Revolution, though manumission by deed was the only legal mechanism for freeing slaves during those years. Of 326 free blacks with known dates of manumission who applied for certificates of freedom in Baltimore County between 1806 and 1816, only 2 had received notice of their freedom during the war (both of them in its final year), while a mere 15 more had been manumitted during the ensuing decade. Still others failed completely to understand the notion of morality as it pertained to slave property, such as the Baltimore County owner who in his 1794 will chided his son for converting to "a religious profession (called Methodist) and it being common for their professors . . . to manumit their slaves." He consequently refused to leave any of his slaves to his wayward offspring.[28]

Like the War of Independence itself, the destruction of slavery occurred only after a lengthy conflict rather than any single pitched battle. While revolutionary fervor and Christian ethos may have hastened the process, neither can receive sole credit for the proliferation of manumissions in Maryland. When late eighteenth-century Americans set about building their nation on the foundation of revolutionary liberty, they deepened a war of conscience over the propriety of African American freedom that had begun even before any musket flashes erupted on the Lexington green. This struggle was nowhere more evident than in upper Maryland. As proponents of emancipation celebrated the triumph of liberty and equality by advocating the expunction of slavery, such talk also gave rise to a vigorous proslavery argument, which appears to have quickly tempered much of the era's idealism.[29]

Far more prospective manumitters than not found their resolve sorely tested when they contemplated setting free such a costly investment as their slave property without financial compensation. Creditors did not accept idealism as legal tender, and slaves cost money to maintain. As a result, economic reality generally tempered the probity of all but the most fervent of Christian or patriot masters. When contemplating the liberation of their slaves, monetary considerations appear to have weighed more heavily on owners' minds than did republican principles, religious persuasion, or anti-slavery activity. Thus James Rigbie of Baltimore County, who though manu-mitting his seventeen slaves as a result of his "having Undergone much Uneasyness and Trouble of Mind on account of the Bondage & Captivity of those poore distressed people," did so only after each had reached the age of twenty-four. Monetary considerations, however, could not completely overshadow moral and social concern. The wording of Rigbie's deed of manumission provides insight into the philosophical conflict faced by many Maryland slaveowners during the period, who "In Justice to them [their slaves] Engaged to sett them at Liberty" yet at the same time felt themselves "Under a Sense of Duty Conscienciously Scruple to keep them."[30]

Prior to 1790 manumission by deed was the most frequently used means of legally liberating slaves in Maryland. Not until 1796, however, did law-makers codify the process of manumission by this method. To grant free-dom, the manumitting document (written in the hand of the manumitter) required two witnesses and had to be acknowledged before a justice of the peace. The county clerk then was to record the deed in the county property deed book after endorsing the date of the transaction. Such time endorse-ments were essential, for the deed was to be recorded within six months of the manumission to be valid. Only then could the freedperson obtain a certificate of freedom, legal proof of his or her new status, required of all freed slaves in Maryland after 1752. Because such freedom papers were never standardized in Maryland, as they came to be in Virginia and even the nearby District of Columbia, forgery was a constant problem, enabling slaves to pass as free.[31]

In drawing up their deeds of manumission, such owners as James Rig-bie occasionally recorded the dilemma that plagued many upper Maryland slaveowners during the late eighteenth and early nineteenth centuries when providing for their chattels' freedom. Balancing economic necessity with religious and moral pressure, slaveowners who formally manumitted their slaves as often as not did so by term, meaning that they would be freed at a future date rather than immediately upon registering the document.[32] Masters held the legal option to write deeds that granted freedom "from this day forward," but instead they frequently established a future date on which the slave would be freed. One scholar has estimated that just over half of all manumissions registered in Maryland prior to 1832 were delayed, while nearly four out of ten were done as such thereafter. In Baltimore

County between 1789 and 1814, 506 of the 1,048 manumissions by deed (48.3 percent) were delayed, though in nine of the first fifteen years after 1800, a majority of those manumissions occurred on the condition of a further term of service.[33]

Prospective manumitters could also free their slaves by wills once the state lifted the legal prohibition of the practice in 1790. This method not only allowed masters the full services of their slaves during the masters' lifetime but also often provided a term of service for their beneficiaries. While some masters provided that the slave or slaves would be liberated immediately upon their death, many more willed their slaves—along with livestock and furniture—to children and grandchildren until the slave reached a certain age, so that the masters' descendants might have the benefits of inherited slave property before setting them free. Of the wills involving manumissions registered with the county clerk of Baltimore County in 1796 and 1797, half stipulated the "deferred manumission" of slaves. Similarly, in 1810 and 1811 eleven of thirteen manumissions by will provided for delayed emancipation. In 1797 Luke White of Baltimore County bequeathed to his granddaughter, Rachel White, "one Negro Girl named Priscilla till she is forty years old and then to go free and be given a good Suite of Close she being Eleven Years old. . . ."[34] Manumission by will was the most conservative—and convenient—method of freeing slaves, for it afforded the greatest amount of protection for the master's purse while still appeasing the troubled conscience. As the historians Michael Johnson and James Roark have written of delayed manumission in general, doing so by will was a "tidy solution to the conflict between the rights of property, which the master retained during his lifetime, and liberty, which the slave received thereafter."[35]

Baltimore manumitters appear to have believed themselves entitled to compensation for the loss of their human property, and whether freeing by deed or by will, they often manumitted their younger slaves only after they had labored years as adults. In 1793 Mary Wilmott manumitted Fanny, Lydia, and George, aged four, two, and one, respectively, all children of her slave woman Jenny, after terms ranging from twenty-two to twenty-seven years. Similarly, in 1801 Jesse Weatherby freed his six slaves, who ranged in age from sixteen to infancy, after terms of anywhere from ten to twenty-six years.[36] The deeds of manumission in the Miscellaneous Court Records of the Baltimore County Court are replete with such examples. While some masters might have felt some responsibility for holding their slaves until they deemed them mature enough for freedom, most likely considered such time to be ample compensation either for the purchase price or for the costs of rearing such slaves, often from childhood. In Baltimore nearly half of all freedmen were over the age of thirty when granted their freedom; three of four were over twenty-five. Black women tended to be freed at younger ages; about two-fifths had reached thirty when freed, and more than six out of ten were over twenty-five.[37]

Masters who manumitted their slaves immediately appear to have been no less interested in obtaining full return on their investment in human property than were those masters who liberated them gradually. Among those manumission deeds filed in the Baltimore County Court, men and women manumitted immediately were older than those freed by term. More than six of every ten men manumitted immediately were over the age of thirty, while more than half of women manumitted immediately were thirty or older on the date of their freedom.[38] Of those granted delayed manumissions during the same time period, only 50 percent of the men and 40 percent of the women were thirty or older. Adult slaves of both sexes manumitted immediately received their freedom on average at nearly forty years of age, suggesting that manumitters routinely demanded an extended period of labor from their slaves before releasing them. Indeed, in 1830 Hezekiah Niles lamented in his *Niles' Weekly Register* the "unpleasant and oppressive fact—that aged and infirmed and *worn-out* slaves from all parts of the state, are turned to Baltimore, to live if they can, or die if they must."[39]

In addition to those Maryland masters who provided gradual and immediate manumissions, whether by will or deed, some sought to free their slaves while recovering directly at least a portion of their value. Locked in an economic transformation that rendered more and more slaves superfluous as laborers, coupled with the growing antislavery movement and an especially strong patriot heritage, Maryland witnessed the proliferation of the unique practice of term slavery. All but unheard of in the Lower South, term slavery became common practice in Maryland and resembled a system practiced by Dutch slaveholders in seventeenth-century New Amsterdam known as "half-freedom," which grew out of the diverse needs of an expanding mercantile economy.[40] Term slavery provided a convenient vehicle for small slaveowners from northern Maryland who were plagued by conscience or could not afford to keep their slaves or liberate them. By providing at least partial remuneration for their lost property and delaying manumission, term sale—like manumission by will—solved the problem of the owners' pocketbook, as well as their consciences about burdening society with those they deemed not yet ready for freedom. George W. Brown, the mayor of Baltimore, later described them as a people "grown up in bondage" who "can hardly be made to assume the part, and practice the moderation of men educated in the habits of regulated freedom."[41]

Masters often sold their slaves with the stipulation in the bill of sale that the new owner would liberate them after a limited term of service, guaranteed either by a will or by the deed itself. The various county clerks recorded such transactions as they would all other transfers of property, such as land and livestock. In 1797 John Beale Howard of Baltimore County sold his twenty-five-year-old female slave Sarah to James Cox "for six years then manumitted."[42] Court records indicated that buyers and sellers appear to have been actively engaged in the market for such slaves, and many unrecorded term sales obviously occurred. In 1817 the state legislature passed a law requiring that sales for a term of years be registered, implying that buyers and sellers had failed to do so often enough to prompt such legislation. Of the nearly 450 term sales included in the Baltimore Court records between 1787 and 1830, just 182 were registered during the twenty-eight years prior to the passage of the 1817 law. Of the surviving court papers for Baltimore City and Baltimore County prior to 1831, slightly more than 20 percent of bills of sale for slaves are for a term of years.[43]

The combination of many gradual manumissions and long terms of service created a steady market for term slaves, whom prospective buyers could buy at prices well below those prevailing for slaves for life. In 1813 Devezeaux O'Rourke drew up both a term deed of manumission and a bill of sale, the latter stipulating that for "the sum of forty dollars value received I do hereby transfer my *right* to the time of said negro boy . . . Nicholas Tessouint Sheriff . . . to Leau Shorptile Hiloure who will make use of him as his slave till the sixth of September 1834 at which time said negro will be free." While Hiloure purchased the boy for a long term of labor, others looked for a shorter duration for their investment. In 1808 Joshua Shedden of Baltimore County purchased for a term of seventeen years Harry Gray, aged eleven, for $205 from William Meluy of Talbot County. In August of 1811 Shedden sold Harry for $250 to James F. Winchell, a Baltimore baker, who eight months later sold the slave to William Lovell and S. Sultzer, biscuit bakers in the city. Because Winchell sold Harry for his purchase price, the baker obtained eight months of labor without direct cost.[44]

The availability of term manumission by deed, will, and sale in combination often yielded a complex series of events before the actual granting of freedom. In 1802 Richard Berry registered a deed of manumission for his mulatto slave, Peggy Loveden, originally owned by Jonathan Hanson, who had willed her first to his granddaughter, Esther Spicer, who sold her to Caleb Cockey, who in turn sold her to John Stark, who then sold her to Berry. Berry then allowed Loveden to purchase her own freedom and manumitted her, wishing her "to have a Pass as a free person." Many of the surviving bills of sale provide evidence of such multiple transfers of an individual slave or slaves to various purchasers, registered as notes recorded on the backs of the bills themselves when the slaves were sold from master to master during their term of service. In 1807 Frederick Eislen, a Baltimore butcher, purchased a Negro named Jerry, then fifty years old, from Joseph Woodard of Prince George's County for $115. The bill of sale noted that Eislen then sold Jerry to a Baltimore victualler, John Kelso, in 1808, who two years later sold the slave to Stephen Hill, also of Baltimore City. Jerry had a total of four masters in three years.[45] Perhaps a third of the bills of sale in the Baltimore County Court records between 1789 and 1830 mention a previous owner for the slave, probably to provide more precise identification of the slave being sold.

Manumitters who granted their slaves freedom by term often appear to have been as concerned with obtaining the maximum amount of labor from their slaves as were masters who liberated them at death or never freed them. "Slaves for a term of years" typically faced a long wait between the registration of their manumission and the actual date on which they obtained their freedom. More than half of the delayed manumissions in Baltimore set a ten-year term, while one in three masters stipulated fifteen years or more.[46] This prevalence of long terms of servitude factored especially into the prospective emancipations of younger slaves. Between 1790 and 1830 Baltimore masters registered deeds of manumission for 534 slave children aged eighteen years or younger; of those, less than a third were manumitted immediately. The typical slave child or adolescent manumitted by deed waited for freedom more than sixteen years, though shorter and longer terms were not uncommon. While in 1804 Ellen Gist freed her fourteen-year-old girl Harriot, effective in less than a year (most likely on her fifteenth birthday), in 1805 Sarah Price stipulated her one-year-old slave John was to receive his freedom only after he turned forty-five, the maximum legal age masters could liberate their slaves.[47]

Such extended terms of bondage for young female slaves played a critical role in perpetuating slavery, despite the proliferation of manumissions in Maryland that had precipitated the institution's slow decline. Because the majority of slave girls freed by term attained sexual maturity and lived through most of their childbearing years while still legally slaves, the likelihood that they would give birth during their slave term encouraged the state of Maryland to enact legislation in 1809 to forestall any pregnancies that would reduce their female slaves' capacity to labor and to allow masters to gain from such unwanted behavior. That same year the state decreed that any children born to term slave women would be slaves for life, unless specified otherwise in their deed of manumission. If the deed made no mention of the female slave's offspring born during her term of slavery, the children were by law born as slaves for life.[48] A great many gradual manumissions of female slaves explicitly stated the status of unborn children of their term bondwomen. In her 1811 term manumission of the slave Jane Harris, Susanna Bowen actually went to the extent of crossing out the lines on her standardized manumission form that freed "the issue of the aforesaid female born after the date of these presents," thereby denying freedom to any children born to Harris prior to her manumission date, set in 1822. Rarely did masters permit such future children to be born free; far more often, children born to term slaves would serve a term of slavery generally lasting until age twenty-five if they were male and until age twenty-one if they were female. In other words, like their parents, unborn children of term slaves would labor long enough to pay for their own upbringing.[49]

Because of such legislation, masters had a simple vehicle for actually perpetuating their own slaveholdings. In 1802 Charles Weir arranged for his six-year-old slave girl Maria to be manumitted at age twenty-five; any children born during her nineteen-year term would be freed at twenty-one if male or at sixteen if female. The manumission provided Weir with reasonable security that he and his heirs would have slave labor available to them for as many as forty years. Such imaginative and manipulative use of term manumission by masters as both a path to a general emancipation and a perpetuator of the institution of slavery in their own lifetimes can be no better illustrated than by the 1804 manumission deeds registered by Sarah Turnbull of Baltimore County. Each of Turnbull's twenty slaves was to gain freedom on his or her forty-fifth birthday, but in the deeds Turnbull stipulated that any children born to her slave women or girls during their terms would serve as slaves until their forty-fifth birthdays. Turnbull and her children could expect some kind of slave labor throughout their lives.[50]

Obviously, Sarah Turnbull's intent was not to terminate slavery, either immediately or gradually; rather, she intended to extend it for herself and her own children, as well as to new generations of slaves. Such actions raise several questions. Given the dwindling need for superfluous slave labor and the availability of slave traders in the Upper South, including Maryland,[51] why during Baltimore's early years did more masters not opt to sell their slaves to the Deep South or the new Southwest rather than manumit them, whether immediately or gradually? Though the preponderance of interstate transfers of slaves occurred later, after the banning of international trade to the United States in 1808, a recent historian of the slave trade has estimated that nearly 200,000 interregional slave transfers took place between 1790 and 1819, accounting for more than a fifth of the total number of such displacements.[52]

Without question many postwar Maryland masters did resort to the market in human flesh, enough so that the *Federal Intelligencer, and Baltimore Daily Gazette* reported as early as 1819 that "the selling of slaves has become an almost universal resource to raise money."[53] Buyers and sellers were particularly active in the Eastern Shore towns of Cambridge and Easton during the 1820s, where Baltimore traders had opened branch offices. In Easton traders established an annual slave auction at a local tavern as early as 1818.[54] With a burgeoning demand for laborers elsewhere and with means so readily available to potential sellers of slaves, why did so many Marylanders free their slaves rather than market them? Or, just as perplexing, why did those owners who still needed or at least wanted to retain their slaves as laborers not simply keep them as slaves for life rather than go to the trouble and expense of freeing them after a long term of years?

The surviving records reveal evidence that might help explain these thorny questions. Masters obviously manipulated the system of slavery to maximize its benefits in an atmosphere of gradual decline and to maintain control over the terms of freedom. It is equally obvious that many individual slaves could, and did, escape its oppression. In pursuit of one crowning goal—unconditional and permanent freedom—slaves and free blacks together conspired to win greater autonomy for those still in bondage. Efforts to gain such liberty often involved a lengthy contest, pitting masters against slaves and free blacks in an endless series of negotiations that took the form of pleas, bargains, and even threats. Recent studies of slavery have revised its traditional portrayal as a one-sided relationship in which masters had almost complete control of their slaves to a more complex one in which slaves, at once autonomous agents and victims, exerted significant influence in forging slavery's social parameters. A close study of the Baltimore experience suggests that slaves on this middle ground might well have enjoyed an even greater degree of independence than historians have imagined. By various tactics slaves coerced their masters into limiting their terms of bondage, a decision that masters made often reluctantly to ensure the system would continue to operate while their slaves were still theirs. As the combatants on this sloping field maneuvered for advantage over the contours of freedom or quasi-freedom, shaping and reshaping the terms and conditions of gradual manumission, unwittingly they not only altered the very nature of slavery and freedom at the margin but also redefined their perceptions of themselves and their future.

Self-purchase was one of the most common methods slaves used to gain their freedom. Although most surviving deeds do not give individual motivations for manumission, they frequently mention monetary sums, which suggests strongly that slaves and their families—whether slave or free—played an instrumental role in bargaining with their masters. In addition to the large number of delayed manumissions, which ensured years of labor to the master as compensation for their loss, nearly one-fourth of the deeds included a stipulated payment of a specific sum of money, ranging from as little as $1 to as much as $450. In 1814 Joseph Hill registered a deed of manumission for his slave, Mich Whatt, then twenty-nine, conditional upon his paying $350 within three years, plus 6 percent interest annually. This example notwithstanding, only rarely do any of the hundreds of manumissions that specify payment identify its source. These manumissions probably involved slaves purchasing their own freedom or free black families or benefactors purchasing family members.[55]

Likely, self-purchase agreements proved so commonplace in early Baltimore because they were easy and advantageous to both masters and slaves. Such transactions provided funds to masters who wished to buy replacement slaves and offered some insurance against a slave's debilitation or death prior to their receiving full payment. Conversely, slaves who lacked capital initially gravitated to that person with whom they had the most contact and who, because of the stakes involved, would be most likely to work out some sort of financial agreement with them. Masters generally did not do so without exacting their own quid pro quo. Many used the agreement for self-purchase as leverage with which to ensure the good behavior of those slaves who now labored in earnest for their freedom. In 1811 Sarah Thomas of Anne Arundel County sold her slave Grace for $140 to John Sands, a Baltimore tailor. Thomas included Grace's manumission in the bill of sale, to take effect after ten years, specifying that "if the said negro shall abscond from the service of the said John Sands, . . . then and in such case the said negro, so absconding shall serve . . . such time over and above the said ten years as negro shall remain absent from [Sand's] service."[56] The prevailing logic that slaves facing a lifetime of bondage who were promised freedom would be less likely to run off—far more than a mere possibility, given Baltimore's close proximity to Pennsylvania—prompted many Baltimore masters to offer the opportunity for freedom as an incentive for slaves to work even harder in an effort to build for themselves the solid reputation so crucial for even a modicum of success once they were freed.

The manumission deeds and slave bills of sale recorded by the Baltimore County Court testify to the struggles and sacrifices slaves and free blacks faced as they labored to amass the purchase price for slave wives, sons, daughters, and other close relatives and friends. These documents also reveal the wide variety of conditions offered by term slavery and the manifold permutations of quasi-freedom under which slaves and free blacks existed during their struggles. In 1820 the Baltimorean James Carroll sold his slave Rebecca and her son Henry for $150 to William Watkins, Rebecca's husband and later a teacher and leader of the city's black community. Rebecca was to serve a five-year term, while Henry was to remain in bondage for twenty-six years. Three years later, once Watkins was "fully paid up," Carroll drew up a deed of manumission, noting carefully that the two slaves were "to serve the times above set forth." Though he had released them to their husband and father, Carroll made clear that they should not yet consider themselves free.[57]

Despite nearly herculean efforts, many slaves and free blacks might never have been able to overcome such obstacles had they not found assistance. Most often this relief came from the largess of the masters themselves, generally by the offer of a reasonably low, or even token, purchase price.[58] In 1807 Joseph Moffitt of Baltimore County manumitted his twenty-year-old slave, Anna, upon payment of $50, though, considering her age, she likely would have fetched a considerably higher sum if sold to another master. Similarly in 1824 Mary Hodges of Baltimore City manumitted Samuel Dixon, then thirty-six, for $75, though again he was probably worth considerably more at auction or sale. In both cases these self-purchases were registered as immediate manumissions, suggesting that the participants had made prior agreements that had determined the terms of freedom.[59]

Many of those Baltimore slaves and free blacks who managed to persuade their own or their loved ones' masters to allow them to purchase their liberty also appear to have convinced their owners to allow them to pay off their debt in installments. In 1819 Mary Norwood agreed to free Betsey Jones and her son John when the husband and father, David Jones, paid $300. Two hundred dollars of the purchase price was due in two years, and the final hundred dollars was to be paid by Jones's boarding Norwood's slave Charles Jones, most likely another son, for five years. In 1824 Catherine McMeal, administrator for the estate of her father, Daniel McMeal, petitioned the Baltimore County Orphans' Court to sell the slave Matthias because he was not only useless but burdensome to the estate. Matthias's mother made an offer to purchase him. The court allowed the sale at a price set by the estate's appraiser, with one-third of the purchase price paid immediately in cash and the balance due in one year, secured by a promissory note bearing interest.[60]

On occasion, assistance in obtaining capital for self-purchase came from white benefactors other than the slaves' masters, who put up the purchase money and then, presumably, required repayment. In 1807 Robert Guy freed his wife, Ruth, and son Moses, who were, as he put it, "bought of John Paul by William Tomkins for me and conveyed to me after I became a free man."[61] This often occurred when the original master refused to allow the slave to purchase his or her freedom by installment or when the time limit for such a purchase was nearing its end and the slave had not accumulated the purchase price. In 1793 Thomas Biddeson freed his slave Manesseh Medos when Isaac Darnell paid the £20 purchase price. Such assistance sometimes arrived under dramatic circumstances. In December 1812 Elisha Tyson, a wealthy Quaker flour miller and merchant from the county and a famed abolitionist who came to the aid of many black Baltimoreans during his twenty years in the city, purchased John Hamilton and Edward Williams at Caspar O. Muller's wharfside auction house within two days of each other, saving each from being sold out of state. Tyson manumitted each the same day he bought him, effective immediately.[62]

Possibly at the suggestion of the slave, benefactors often stipulated continued bondage as repayment of the debt of freedom. In 1791 Samuel Owings, a Baltimore Town merchant, manumitted a slave named Hagar, whom he "lately purchased . . . with intent to give her her Freedom & Liberty after she had, by her Service, made me my Heirs and Assigns a Reasonable compensation for the sum of Money paid for her." Owings provided for Hagar's freedom on Christmas Day 1795, but he retained the services of any potential children she might have during her term of servitude until the males reached the age of twenty-one and females the age of eighteen. Similarly in 1814, one year after purchasing forty-eight-year-old Betty Green from Sarah and Deborah O'Donnell, Robert Jones freed her, upon receiving payment of a hundred dollars.[63]

The negotiation process often involved slaves arranging their own sales, in hopes that new masters would free them in the future. In 1809 William Winchester petitioned the Baltimore County Orphans' Court to allow him to sell the estate's slaves because he found "it Very difficult to hire out the Slaves belonging to the Said estate, and that the negros are themselves, dissatisfied with the Uncertainty of their homes and which to be sold, representing that they can find masters in the neighbourhood of thier wives & children." The court granted Winchester's request. Similarly, in 1834 William E. Moale freed Curtis Frederick, who "was purchased by me some years ago, at his own request from a certain Thomas Dorsey attorney of Catherine Nabb of Harford County for the sum of three hundred dollars, which said Sum he has fait[h]fully repaid out of his own Earnings, and according to the original agreement, I now give him this Deed of Manumission, warranting him free."[64]

For many slaves and free Negroes, the decision to ask whites for assistance in obtaining freedom for themselves or loved ones was not made easily. Most likely, few black residents were personally acquainted with whites who possessed the wherewithal to afford such succor. Even fewer had relationships with whites intimate enough for either party to feel comfortable doing so. Black people probably sought out any and all avenues of relief before asking whites for aid. One example provides evidence of the length of such delays as well as the toll levied on black families by their long separation—if not always physically, certainly legally and emotionally. In 1808 Richard Mackall of Baltimore manumitted James Byas [likely Biays], then thirty, to take effect after a thirty-month term. The following year Mackall shortened Byas's term to twelve months, presumably as a result of his good service and likely arranged at the time of the original manumission.[65] A full thirteen years later, in 1822, Isaac Tyson, son of Elisha Tyson and heir to his milling industry, purchased Byas's wife and two children from Paul Bentalou of Baltimore for fifty dollars. Tyson acted as a broker for other free blacks in Baltimore, requiring them to repay him in full before he would release them, no doubt to ensure that those he assisted would demonstrate the industry and self-discipline necessary not only to pay back the purchase price but also to survive in a white-dominated society.[66]

That slaves and free Negroes only reluctantly turned to whites other than their masters for assistance in their quest for freedom may stem in large part from the unsavory terms potential benefactors often exacted. Freedpeople and others often dealt with demanding lenders, and without liquid security they were forced to offer their labor power, the only commodity they did possess. Ironically, the widespread practice of term slavery provoked some free blacks to broker the possession that many would spend their lives striving to attain: their own legal freedom. In 1819 Edward and Elizabeth Brown mortgaged "all the right, title, Interest and claim . . . to their freedom" to James Blair, to whom they owed four hundred dollars. The debt was due in full in one year, but if they could not pay it at that time, Blair stipulated in the mortgage that he would release them from their debt if "they serve faithfully for 5 years" and that they would then regain their freedom. In an ironic reversal of history, the Browns, former slaves, now entered into debt bondage, an arrangement that in many ways resembled indentured servitude, the contractual labor system that slavery largely replaced in British North America.[67]

Free blacks, such as the Browns, who leveraged their freedom likely did so to acquire capital for purchasing other family members held in bondage. In 1804 John Richardson, "a free Black Man," sold to Peregrine Browning "my Negro Girl Named Julyan, Six Years old," for twenty dollars. Julyan, most likely Richardson's daughter, was to serve a term of fifteen years and then would again be free. That same year Richardson purchased George, his son, from David Stewart, a Baltimore merchant, for twenty-five dollars. Such arrangements appear to have been very much like an apprenticeship, except they involved an up-front purchase price.[68] In all likelihood, because of the specter of reenslavement, few free blacks entered into such arrangements, although financial concerns might well have compelled some to sell themselves back into slavery, not just for term but for life. In 1819 Matilda Moore, a Baltimore City "free woman of color," sold herself and her nine-month-old infant son, George Moore, to James Blair of Baltimore County, for a dollar. Her child was to serve until the age of twenty-one, while she herself would serve for life. Moore stated clearly in the bill of sale that she did so "of my own free will and accord and not influenced by fear or reward or any unlawfull means." Such a low selling price suggests that Moore might well have been destitute and saw no other means to provide for herself and her child. That Blair entered into contractual agreements with two different free Negroes in the same year indicates that he either was acting as, in effect, a broker for "freedom loans," with the collateral being service, or was a shrewd, if callous, businessman who recognized (and doubtless reaped) the great labor value of such arrangements.[69]

More often slaves and free blacks seeking purchase money turned to free Negroes who were in a financial position to help them obtain their freedom. In 1797 Ebo Prince and Richard Russell, prominent free Negroes, purchased the slave Lant, then forty years of age, from Joshua Wood of Harford County "for the consideration of the sum of Eighty pounds paid on the 24th of January and the 24th of July last." In 1808 Jacob Gilliard, a respected free Negro blacksmith, purchased his two adult sons, Jacob Jr. and Nicholas, along with fourteen-year-old Henry Williams, from John Merryman, a gentleman from Baltimore. Gilliard freed his sons immediately but freed Williams after a four-year term, presumably to allow Williams to work off his purchase price in Gilliard's smithery.[70]

At first glance, such often desperate efforts on the part of slaves and free Negroes in Baltimore affirm the sovereignty of the slave system in Maryland as well as owners' near-complete power over their slaves. Yet evidence offers a significantly different picture that dramatically changes the image of slavery and freedom in Baltimore, and perhaps Maryland and even the Upper South. The willingness of free blacks in Baltimore to reenter slavery in pursuit of others' freedom suggests slaves and free blacks recognized that masters who granted delayed manumission actually conceded substantial autonomy to their slaves. In Maryland a recorded deed promising gradual manumission was a legal contract and thus irrevocable, which actually provided term slaves legal rights over their masters. The practice of term slavery, which so many Baltimoreans engaged in, created a legal and social contretemps by which term slaves were neither slave nor free, but both at the same time. Moreover, in 1817 the state legislature decreed that masters could not sell term slaves out of state, thus even further decreasing slaveholders' power by restricting their right to dispose of their property at their discretion while augmenting those few legal rights term slaves already enjoyed.[71] Consequently, free Negroes appear to have felt fairly confident that they could safely relinquish their free status, or that of family members, to return to slavery temporarily. The situation instilled in Maryland slaves a recognition that slavery and freedom were circumstances that could be bargained for like any other commodity and that they themselves were capable of far more than simply lessening the oppression of bondage through cunning manipulation of the existing circumstances.

Negotiations in Baltimore between slaves and free blacks on one side and masters on the other figured prominently in many manumissions, with slaves and free Negroes themselves initiating many of these actions. Yet masters, too, appear to have recognized that those slaves who were promised their freedom at a future date gained substantial legal protection by the act and that those who granted freedom by term yielded some of the slaveholders' prerogative during the time preceding the slave's final manumission.[72] Consequently, masters strove to maintain as much power as possible in the process of granting freedom. The frequency with which manumission deeds set conditions that slaves should not abscond during their term alone suggests the power that not only masters but also slaves wielded in the negotiation process. Even those masters who freed their slaves immediately rather than by term occasionally did so in response to pressure the slaves exerted. In his 1825 deed of manumission Frederick L. Shaffer provided immediate freedom to his slave Charlotte Matthews, "for the cause that she has repeatedly asked to be freed from my service, and is not satisfied to remain in slavery. . . ." Matthews's badgering caused a disgusted Shaffer to grant the manumission only on the condition that she "shall leave the City of Baltimore and State of Maryland within thirty days from the date hereof; and shall not again return to said State of Maryland, under the penalty of being sold out of said state a slave for life."[73]

Masters who granted their slaves freedom after a term of years appear to have done so largely as an incentive to good service. The length of terms varied widely, depending on the slave's age, service value, and temperament.

The initial term of service was occasionally long, but it was often shortened or removed altogether if the slave worked hard and exhibited good behavior. In 1794 Adam Barnes of Baltimore County registered a deed of manumission for Jenney, then ten years old, which was to free her after twenty years. A year later Barnes filed a second deed, which shortened Jenney's term to fourteen years, presumably as reward for her diligence. Lewis Atterbury of Baltimore County, acting as administrator of Barnes's estate, subsequently freed Jenny in 1807, two years before the end of her already reduced term. That Barnes offered no further term alteration during his lifetime suggests that the two might well have struck a mutual bargain and that each lived up to its terms.[74]

Obviously not all masters were receptive to their slaves' overtures at gaining freedom, however resourceful or insistent. In many cases frustrated or desperate slaves resorted to more forceful attempts to persuade their masters, often with dire consequences. One of the most common forms of resistance was poor behavior, such as work stoppages or malingering, which not only proved a burden to masters but also often cost them the chance to hire out such slaves. In 1822 Benedict Sanders complained to the court that an unnamed male slave he had inherited "is no use or benifit . . . having Hierd out Said Boy to Sundry persons and at different employments but being of an Indolent disposition all his Employers refuse to Keep him and have returned him as being a burthen to them." Similarly, in 1824 Basil Stevenson complained to the court about the seven term slaves left to him and others as executors of Joshua Stevenson's estate: "it is attended with great difficulty to get places for to hire them as there are but few persons that wish to hire such property that there is apart of them that are Passionate Lazy and ungovernable fillows." Mary Spence, who was left nearly forty slaves when her husband died, complained that her attempts to hire out her slaves met with a "precarious . . . receipt of the wages and generally [were] accompanied with mutual complaint. There is also great danger, if they are hired out and dislike their master, of their absconding from service altogether." At least one potential employer recognized the behavioral differences between term and life slaves when she advertised for servants to work in her home but added emphatically that "they must be SLAVES FOR LIFE."[75]

Slaves' verbal threats to run away, particularly to neighboring Pennsylvania, caused other masters to sell rather than free them. In 1817 Mary Arnold petitioned the court asking to sell "those negros [who] are ungovernable and your petitioners are fearfull they will abscond." Years later Samuel Hopkins petitioned the court that his term slave Lewis Hall "has repeatedly proved refractory and has threatened to run off from the custody of your petitioner, which threat has induced your petitioner to confine said slave in the jail of Balt Co for safe keeping. . . ."[76] In demanding their freedom, especially once term slavery had become so prevalent in Maryland, some slaves actually resorted to physical violence against owners who refused to grant them a manumission. In 1828 Job G. Stansbury asked the Orphans' Court to allow him to sell his man John, who was "in every manner obstrepulous, has been in the habit of running away, [and] Recently he has gone so far as to have stabbed your petitioner twise in the breast and once in each arm which now confines him to his bed." In each of these cases the court allowed the sale, but not the freedom, of the miscreant.[77] However unsuccessful, these incidents illustrate the lengths Baltimore slaves would go to pressure their masters for their freedom. Perhaps as illuminating to the autonomy slaves enjoyed in Baltimore is the fact that slaves believed they could go to such extremes to obtain freedom.

A noticeable trend emerges from the petitions to the Orphans' Court over the course of time. In the years before 1810 petitioners who asked to relinquish their ownership of slaves generally did so on the grounds that their financial privations and the lack of work for them prevented the owners from supporting them. After that date the petitions show a marked increase in claims of "refractory" and "ungovernable" behavior on the part of slaves. Many of these claims stemmed from the Maryland law of 1817 that prohibited selling term slaves out of the state. Although this law might account for much of the increase in immediate manumissions after its passage,[78] it was obvious that term slaves understood their rights under the law, which might well have played a large role in this increase, just as masters came to understand the rights they surrendered when manumitting their slaves by term and instead kept their promises unwritten until granting immediate liberty.

Such activity in gaining freedom was not reserved to male slaves only. While previous studies on urban slavery have portrayed it as a largely female institution,[79] manumission data from Baltimore do not lend much support to this, at least in the city's early years. By all appearances through the first three decades of the nineteenth century male and female slaves received manumissions in Baltimore in relatively equal proportions (see table 3). Between 1789 and 1830 male slave manumissions made up more than 47 percent of all manumissions; in fact, males made up only slightly less than half of slaves who received their freedom by manumission during the entire period prior to 1815 and actually constituted a majority from 1801 to 1815. Although previous studies have maintained that the slave trade from the Chesapeake to the Southwest was subscribed to largely by masters who

Table 3. Manumissions by Sex in Baltimore, 1789–1830

Years	Total	Males		Females	
		Number	Percentage	Number	Percentage
1789–1795	115	44	38	71	62
1796–1800	147	67	46	80	54
1801–1805	209	118	56	91	44
1806–1810	377	192	51	185	49
1811–1815	322	154	48	168	52
Subtotal	1,070	575	49	595	51
1816–1820	433	188	43	245	57
1821–1825	352	146	41	206	59
1829–1830	359	171	48	188	52
Total	2,314	1,080	47	1,234	53

Source: BCC (Miscellaneous Court Papers), MSA C1, MdHR.

sold valuable black men to traders while more frequently holding less valu-able women for domestic service or manumitting them, the data from Bal-timore suggest that this occurred for the most part only later, certainly af-ter 1815.[80]

Surprisingly, the change of agricultural base in and around Baltimore County appears actually to have contributed to the gender balance in Balti-more's early black population. As fixed labor forces gave way to more flexi-ble sources of labor, surplus unskilled field hands (most often young black males) became disposable, and masters hired out some but apprenticed, sold, or freed many others. Upper Maryland masters, however, often retained their skilled male slaves, who could be worked in the fields and whose trade skills could be hired out locally in slack time. Yet they also kept a significant por-tion of their bondwomen to serve as domestics and personal servants, pre-venting the immigrants who crowded into Baltimore from being exclusive-ly female. Only in the decades after 1815, once the increasingly lucrative slave trade to the Old Southwest began to deplete a large portion of the state's male slaves, did free black and slave women outnumber their male counter-parts in Baltimore. In 1820 free Negro women constituted over 57 percent of the free black population of Baltimore City; by 1860 just under 60 per-cent of free Negroes in the city were women.[81] At least initially, however, an equal number of black men and women newly freed and marginally skilled looked to Baltimore for a new life and a better future than they could find in the Maryland countryside.[82]

❖   ❖   ❖

In Baltimore term slavery and term slaves—like the "half-free" slaves in seventeenth-century New Amsterdam—had slowly reshaped the terms and conditions of gradual manumission, to win greater autonomy and to become in Judge Nicholas Brice's words "a sort of middle class," entitled to legal notice and protection, however precarious, before masters could change their status. The autonomy that slaves (for term and for life) and freed blacks demonstrated while held in the shackles of bondage allowed these former slaves and future freedpeople to make the abstract notion of liberty real. In effect Baltimore slaves themselves pulled a heavy oar in achieving their own freedom.[83]

Yet the concomitant growth and ultimate singularity of Baltimore's African American population entail far more than a social by-product of any inevitable decline of chattel bondage in Maryland; together, they signify the culmination of a decades-long process of self-empowerment in which slaves and free blacks themselves played a subtle yet vital part. The process of manumission in Maryland—immediate, gradual, by term, or by self-purchase—reveals more than fleeting glimpses of a developing autonomy already begun during enslavement. In this sea change term slaves maneuvered for and seized a unique yet chartable course to liberty, and in weathering its tempests, they demonstrated a resiliency and resourcefulness that would characterize their future free lives. Once free, black Baltimoreans not only undermined the legitimacy of slavery but also forged a genuinely autonomous and cohesive community that would, by the truest definition of the terms, actually reflect Judge Brice's unlikely portrayal.

The Town of Baltimore in 1801. From John Warner and William Hanna's *Plan of the City and Environs of Baltimore*. Courtesy of the Library of Congress.

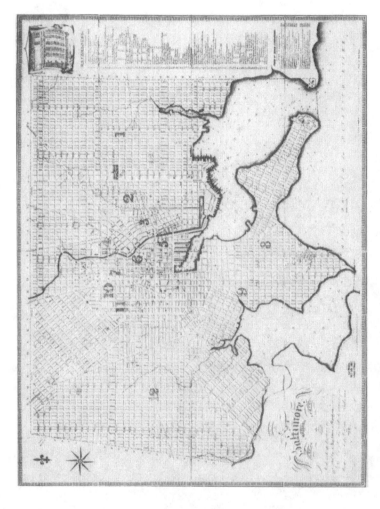

The growing city of Baltimore. From Fielding Lucas Jr.'s 1822 *Plan of the City of Baltimore*. Courtesy of the Library of Congress.

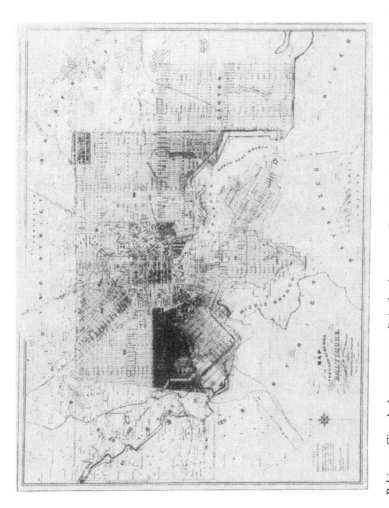

Baltimore City, the largest metropolis in the slave states. From Isaac Simmon's 1853 *Map of the City and Suburbs of Baltimore*. Courtesy of the Library of Congress.

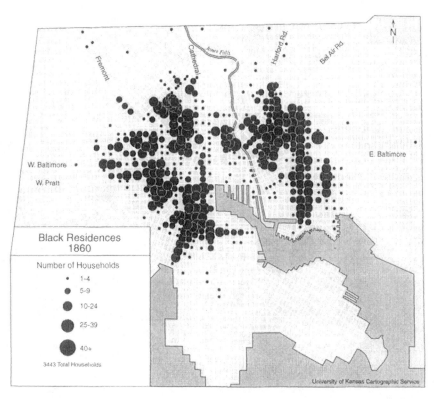

Map of black residences in 1860. From John W. Woods's *Woods' Baltimore City Directory* (Baltimore: John W. Woods, 1860).

3

The Urban Mélange

Frederick Douglass said of his days in Baltimore, comparing them to his boyhood days on the Eastern Shore, that "a city slave is almost a free citizen . . . [he] enjoys privileges altogether unknown to the whip-driven slave on the plantation."[1] True to Douglass's recollection, the early years of growth of Baltimore's black population witnessed a remarkable blurring of the city's people of color, both free and slave. Nearly all were either slaves or had been freed only recently. They were not former house slaves or sons and daughters of masters but field hands, craftspeople, cooks, and washers. Low in the hierarchy of the plantation, their backgrounds often were virtually identical. Most had come from the same regions and had worked the same crops in the fields; many had even known one another before they went to Baltimore. Once in the city, slaves and freedpeople competed for the same occupations, frequently took home the same wages, and lived on the same streets and alleys—often even in the same households.

The complex network of legal statuses and economic practices of black people in Baltimore—lifelong slaves, slaves for a term of years, slaves hired out or even living out, as well as free Negroes—increased the ambiguity of their situation during the city's early years. Adding to the confusion, prior to 1820 Baltimore's slave and free black populations increased rapidly—though free blacks did so at a far higher rate—primarily because of delayed manumissions, the migration of white slaveholders and their slaves to the city, and the growth of industries in the city based largely on free rather than slave labor. Consequently, the majority of Baltimore slaves lived their lives more like their free urban counterparts than their plantation brethren.[2]

In the years following the American Revolution, as the number of slaves in Baltimore grew, the city experienced an even more dramatic increase in the number of free Negroes. This growth mirrored that of Maryland itself, which, prior to the war, had few free black people living within its borders.

The colony's 1755 census (the only enumeration made in the Upper South during the colonial era that included black people) counted 1,817 free Negroes, who constituted only about 4 percent of its black population. Only 212 lived in Baltimore County at that time. By 1790 the state's black population had grown more than threefold, to just over 8,000. In the next decade alone, while the nation's free black population grew by over 82 percent (some of it the result of the prohibition of slavery in the northern states), the growth of Maryland's free black population was no less than staggering, increasing by nearly 150 percent, to 19,587, and outstripping that of all other states, even neighboring Virginia. In 1810 two Eastern Shore counties—Kent and Queen Anne's—had higher percentages of free blacks than did any other counties in the entire Chesapeake region. Between 1790 and 1800 nine of nineteen Maryland counties reported decreases in their slave populations. Many of those former bondpeople had left the countryside for Baltimore.[3]

The growth of Baltimore's free black population surpassed that of even Maryland (see table 4). In 1790 the city boasted nearly four times as many slaves as free blacks (see table 5); over the next decade (while the number of the city's slaves more than doubled, to 2,843), Baltimore's freedpeople increased by over 757 percent, from 323 to 2,771—until it was nearly equal to the city's slave population. By 1810 the number of free blacks had again more than doubled, and by this time free blacks outnumbered the city's slaves, 5,671 to 4,672. A decade later free blacks in Baltimore outnumbered slaves by more than two to one, and their increase of more than 3,000 percent during the three decades following the first federal census far eclipsed that of even the nation itself. Between 1790 and 1830, while the city's white population increased more than fourfold, from 11,925 to 61,710, Baltimore's black population swelled by nearly 1,100 percent, from 1,578 to 18,910, representing nearly one-fourth of the city's population (see table 6).[4]

As Baltimore's black population grew proportionately larger, so did a larger proportion of it become free. Clearly, the institution of slavery was in slow decline in Maryland, as well as in the border states in general. Widespread manumissions in the region resulted in Maryland's having nearly equal populations of slaves and free blacks by 1860, an anomaly for slave states. This decline was magnified in Baltimore, where by 1830 free people of color outnumbered slaves by well over ten thousand and constituted 78 percent of the city's black population. Within three decades slaves in Baltimore would represent just 8 percent of the city's black residents.

Surprisingly, this free black population explosion did not quickly set off Malthusian alarms among the white populace of early nineteenth-century Maryland. Eighteenth-century white Marylanders do not appear to have

Table 4. Free Black Population Increase, 1790–1810

	1790			1800			1810		
	Population	Percentage Increase	Free	Population	Percentage Increase	Free	Population	Percentage Increase	Free
United States	59,466	—	7.9	108,395	82.3	10.8	186,446	72.0	13.5
North	27,109	—	40.2	47,154	73.9	56.7	78,181	65.8	74.0
South	32,357	—	4.7	61,241	89.3	6.7	108,265	76.8	8.5
Upper South	30,158	—	5.5	30,158	88.5	8.1	94,085	65.5	10.4
Lower South	2,199	—	1.6	4,386	99.5	2.1	14,180	223.3	3.9
Maryland	8,043	—	7.2	19,587	143.5	15.6	33,927	73.5	23.3
Baltimore	323	—	11.7	2,771	757.9	49.4	5,671	104.7	54.8

Source: U.S. Bureau of the Census, *Negro Population of the United States, 1790–1915*, 35–37.

Table 5. White, Slave, and Free Black Populations in Maryland by Region, 1790 and 1820

	1790			1820		
	White	Slave	Free Black	White	Slave	Free Black
Eastern Shore	65,141	37,591	3,907	70,706	35,303	15,700
Southern Maryland	55,898	48,711	2,145	46,757	47,016	7,555
Northern Maryland	87,610	15,734	1,991	142,760	25,078	16,475
Baltimore[a]	11,925	1,255	323	48,055	4,357	10,326

a. Included in figures for northern Maryland

Sources: Berlin, Slaves without Masters, 46–47; U.S. Bureau of the Census, Population of the United States in 1860, 600–601; McSherry, History of Maryland, 403–4; Wright, Free Negro in Maryland, 86–88.

Table 6. White and Black Populations of Baltimore as a Percentage of Total, 1790–1830

	White		Black	
Year	Population	Percentage	Population	Percentage
1790	11,925	88.3	1,578	11.7
1800	20,900	78.8	5,614	21.2
1810	36,212	77.8	10,343	22.2
1820	48,055	76.6	14,683	23.4
1830	61,710	76.5	18,910	23.5

Sources: Fairbanks, Statistical Analysis of the Population of Maryland, 105; McSherry, History of Maryland, 403–4; Fields, Slavery and Freedom on the Middle Ground, 62, 70.

viewed free blacks as threats to the social order. Though not legally disfranchised until 1805, their voting clout was always severely limited since so few were eligible to vote because of the property qualification.[5] Moreover, in a predominantly rural culture, free Negroes in early Maryland were afforded few economic opportunities; some farmed, but most hired themselves out, most often as farm laborers. In 1790 less than 4 percent of landholders in Baltimore County were listed as free and nonwhite.[6] Small in number, politically neutered, and limited economically, Maryland's free black population during the era of the Revolution gave the state's white residents little reason to see them as a menace to social stability.

Yet neither were free Negroes accepted as equals with whites. In a 1692 statute, which decreed that offspring of white women and slave men should no longer be considered free at birth, the Maryland General Assembly made mention of "negroes and other slaves," a curious phrase that includes yet separates unfree peoples of black and red skin but also illuminates the slight distinction white Marylanders made between black people, whether slave or free. In 1776, while the Continental Congress met temporarily in Baltimore because of a British threat against Philadelphia, the Massachusetts delegate John Adams grumbled that Baltimoreans "hold their Negroes and convicts, that is, all laboring people and tradesmen, in such contempt, that they think themselves a distinct order of beings." While such sentiment existed, a significant number of Baltimore residents do not appear to have held such a view.[7]

In the early decades of the nineteenth century Baltimore City attracted from all parts of the state newly freed black people seeking employment and a break from the oppression of their rural slave past. Most in those years, however, traveled there from close to home—Baltimore County. Although large planters on the Eastern Shore and in southern Maryland often resorted to slave traders to rid themselves of unneeded slaves, strong Quaker and Methodist influence in the northern counties of Maryland, closest to southeastern Pennsylvania and Philadelphia, acted to discourage such activity in that region. Small farmers in northern and western Maryland felt the not-so-gentle persuasion of their pious neighbors and usually liberated their slaves instead of selling them. As a result, Baltimore's early black population came primarily from those counties closest to the city itself, especially those to the north. Of the five counties contributing most to Baltimore County's free blacks, three claimed fewer slave residents in 1800 than in 1790.[8]

Despite Baltimore's promise of regular employment in nonagricultural occupations—with adequate wages and without contracts—as well as the city liberties born of anonymity, most freedpeople were reluctant to move great distances from their home counties. The decision to leave family and friends in the wake of freedom for the unknown of a faraway city proved difficult, though obviously not impossible, for rural African Americans, even in such a small state as Maryland. Although moving away offered the chance for a life free from the encumbrances and stigma of their former bondage from which they would never fully escape by remaining near their erstwhile masters and white neighbors, freedpeople in Maryland found compelling reasons to remain close to their birthplaces. Complex family structures of rural black families, interlaced regularly with both slave and free members, anchored both groups of black people close to their former plantation homes.[9]

This early rootedness is documented in Baltimore County's freedom certificates. Of the 468 free blacks who applied for certificates of freedom in Baltimore County between 1806 and 1816, nearly half had been born in Baltimore City or in the county. Each of the three counties with the next highest totals—Harford, Anne Arundel, and Calvert, respectively—border on or are close to Baltimore County. Most migrants from outside Baltimore County and those counties closest to it came from counties in southern Maryland rather than from the Eastern Shore.[10] Only sixty-one had been born in Eastern Shore counties, separated from Baltimore by the bay, and none was from the state's easternmost county, Worcester, both geographically and logistically the farthest removed from Baltimore.[11]

Though reluctant to leave family and friends, many skilled and semiskilled freedpeople did leave the countryside for Baltimore rather than work the same fields they had during slavery. Moreover, free Negroes did not move to Baltimore County to live in the countryside; they came in great numbers to live in the city. Prior to 1851, when Baltimore City was officially separated from Baltimore County, figures for the city and county were reported together. From 1790 to 1800 Baltimore County's free black population increased more than threefold, from 927 to 4,307. During the same period the number of Baltimore City's free people of color grew from 323 to 2,771, representing more than 72 percent of the county's overall growth. The figures from 1800 to 1810 are more dramatic; the growth of the free black population in Baltimore City constituted the entire increase of the county's free Negroes. Of the 4,307 free blacks residing in the county in 1800, approximately 65 percent lived in Baltimore City. By 1810 that percentage had increased to more than 78 percent.[12]

The method by which Marylanders freed slaves (legal and not) proves crucial to the development of a black populace in Baltimore, which itself was wholly unlike that of any other slave-state city. Nearly two-thirds were African (meaning dark-skinned) rather than mulatto because manumissions in much of Maryland during the postrevolutionary era were made without regard to white ancestry or status. In 1755 mulattoes constituted less than 9 percent of the state's black residents, and as late as 1860 only 14.6 percent.[13] Similarly, Baltimore's free black population appears always to have contained a small number of mulattoes. While in 1755 more than four of ten of Maryland's mixed-blooded persons had been free, a half century later this figure, at least in Baltimore, had declined substantially. Of 110 freeborn black persons who applied for certificates of freedom in the city between 1806 and 1816, only 24 (21.8 percent) were mulattoes, while just 84 (23.5 percent) of the 358 manumitted during the same period were light-skinned.[14]

Conversely, in the Lower South, where masters often bestowed freedom on the offspring of illicit liaisons with slaves, the pattern of manumissions had created a free people of color who were mainly light-skinned. In the Lower South more than three of every four free African Americans were of mixed parentage, requiring colonial planters to employ an array of racial terminology to delineate such people according to hue, parentage, and even cultural antecedents. Mulattoes constituted two-thirds of Charleston's free Negroes and more than three-fourths of the free black population of New Orleans.[15]

In keeping with the general pattern in the Upper South, the freedpeople who traveled to Baltimore were more often dark-skinned rather than light-skinned. The certificates of freedom registered with the Baltimore County Court for these newly freedpeople provide evidence of this. Of 352 persons for whom skin color was registered (the notation provided solely by the white clerk's perception of skin shading, rather than ancestry, and thus inherently subjective), two-thirds were registered as "dark" or "black," while the remaining third were listed as "yellow," "light," or simply "mulatto." Interestingly, slightly more light-skinned women than men were freed, perhaps reflecting masters' preference for mulatto women when granting freedom.[16]

Dark skin was predominant among freeborn Baltimore County Negroes to an even greater extent than in Baltimore City. Of those applying for freedom certificates between 1806 and 1816, 86 of 110 (78.2 percent) were characterized as black rather than mulatto. This figure appears to have held steady throughout the antebellum period; by 1860 mulattoes would account for only 22.3 percent of Baltimore City free blacks. As many of these recently freed black men and women made their way to Baltimore, the city's black population was considerably darker than in those cities farther south in the slave states. In contrast to free Negroes in Charleston and New Orleans, Baltimore's were far more black than brown.[17]

Not only were they brown, but the freedmen who came to Baltimore appear to have been both physically small and youthful. The average freedman was just under five feet six inches tall, while freedwomen generally stood slightly over five feet two inches.[18] Of 326 free blacks who applied for certificates of freedom in Baltimore County between 1806 and 1816, the oldest male was forty-nine when manumitted, one of only four applicants past the age of forty; the oldest female was just forty-seven. No slaves, male or female, applied for a freedom certificate while in their fifties.[19]

These early freed blacks who traveled to Baltimore City appear to have been younger than commonly thought. From such statements as those made by Hezekiah Niles in 1830, historians generally have concluded that former slaves who went to Baltimore were "aged and infirmed and *worn-out*" at the time of their manumission. Since they were unable to provide profitable labor on the plantation but their masters were required to pay property taxes on them, owners purportedly set loose these superannuated slaves, who then trudged in desperation to Baltimore "to live if they can, or die if they must."[20] Data from Baltimore County show that nearly 50 percent of freedmen were over the age of thirty when granted their freedom, and nearly 40 percent of women were at least thirty when freed.[21] While they might have been past their prime, their age hardly qualifies them as infirm or superannuated.

A number of those freed who moved to Baltimore received that freedom without due process; their masters simply emancipated their slaves instead of formally manumitting them. In other words, some masters verbally gave their slaves their freedom and sent them on their way, rather than provide them a more formal, and legal, manumission. In Maryland, where term slavery had already blurred the lines of bondage and freedom, masters appear to have felt relatively comfortable that their slaves, though legally bound, could live as free—without penalty to either party. The distinction between formal (meaning legal) manumissions and informal emancipations proves crucial, not only for understanding the slave experience in Maryland but also for interpreting the transition from slavery in Maryland to quasi-freedom in Baltimore.

James Rigbie's 1768 deed of manumission serves as an excellent example of the informal emancipations in Baltimore. Though he gradually freed all of his slaves, Rigbie provided special stipulation for the freedom of Nanny and Hager at age twenty-five, "Both at Liberty some years ago." In 1822 Peter Hoffman, a merchant of Baltimore City, freed his slave Charity, then thirty-six, though "in fact released by me from servitude in May, 1819." Some benevolent masters allowed these interim years of freedom (called by one contemporary "a species of *quasi* emancipation") so that their bondpeople could adjust to a new life and even acquire property before they gained legal freedom. Others, too, opted to avoid the legal process, creating a significant population of Negroes with a contingent right to freedom, whom various historians have referred to as "free-slaves" and "slaves virtually free."[22]

The prevalence of "deferred manumission" and the corresponding existence of simple emancipation in Maryland suggest that at least in early Baltimore freedom papers held little importance. In the bustling city, where a black person could find an anonymity unknown in the countryside, written proof of freedom was required only sporadically, and because Maryland had not standardized its manumission forms, counterfeits were easily obtained. Moreover, free Negroes in Maryland, unlike in North Carolina, were not forced to renew freedom certificates annually. Indeed, the legislature rejected such a bill in 1835 on the grounds that greater numbers of such certificates in circulation increased proportionately the chances for slaves to obtain them fraudulently. Free Negroes were required to register only once during their lifetime, unless they lost their original freedom papers. Urban ambivalence forced the state legislature in 1805 to require the inclusion of physical features on certificates of freedom to prevent their fraudulent usage, primarily by slaves passing as free and living "at liberty" in the city. Such surviving certificates suggest wide variance in both form and degree of detail, often failing even to include those physical features.[23]

Evidence such as this suggests the laxness with which Baltimore authorities enforced racial control measures. Since 1752 Maryland law had required that any black person claiming to be free yet without freedom papers was subject to arrest. Baltimoreans appear to have disregarded the statute since the state's attorney general, Luther Martin, in 1810 appealed to constables to execute the "old practice of arrests" and incarcerate all free blacks without papers, on the traditional presumption that they were escaped slaves. Even Baltimore courts appear to have been ambivalent. That same year John Scott, the circuit court judge, released two free blacks arrested without papers, demanding evidence or witnesses that the accused were indeed runaways, thus overturning the prevailing notion in slave states that black persons were presumed guilty until proven innocent.[24] Without pressure from city officials, ambitious Baltimore businesspeople could hardly be expected to turn away cheap, available laborers, especially since no state law held them responsible if their employees should prove to be escaped slaves.

Free-labor Baltimore, with its small slave population working primarily in unskilled positions and as domestics, had a much reduced sense of need or desire for slave control. The city never enacted a badge law like that of Charleston, which required slaveowners to purchase work permits annually for those slave laborers they hired out. Such a law not only limited slave hiring, which appeased Charleston's white artisans who competed with a large number of skilled slaves in the workplace, but also, by requiring slaves to carry their badges, restricted the movements of those slaves who were not hired out.[25]

Because of these policies and economic opportunities that were largely unavailable in a rural setting, Baltimore attracted thousands of free black migrants of both sexes in its early years. Though unwitting agents of change, former masters had actually increased many of their once-slaves' chances for success in Baltimore. Moreover, small country towns that developed in conjunction with the plantation system provided only limited employment opportunities for recently freed black folk. Agricultural labor was usually the most readily available employment for freedpeople in the country, yet such labor involved annual or semiannual contracts all too reminiscent of slavery. Many former slaves, particularly those who had acquired a modicum of trade skills, opted to take the chance that they would find employment in Baltimore. More often than not, however, their knowledge of such skills was at best marginal. A sizable number of ex-slaves possessed minor skills, but the largest portion of former slaves who traveled to Baltimore had emerged from slavery unskilled.[26]

Baltimore, with its diverse economic base, offered a variety of employment opportunities for unskilled and semiskilled workers. Lacking capital, most freedpeople stood little chance of farming independently, and if they chose to stay in the country, they were forced to hire themselves out to white landowners as agricultural laborers. Their wages were generally so meager (less than forty cents per day before 1790) that the chances of saving enough of their earnings to acquire land for themselves were dismal. Seeking the higher wages and regular work that did not resemble the slave routine, free black people moved to Baltimore in substantial numbers during the four decades following the Revolution.[27]

Many who fled to Baltimore were fugitives from bondage who sought sanctuary. Runaway slave advertisements in Maryland newspapers suggest that slave escapes soared in the years immediately following the Revolution. As the largest urban center in the Upper South (and often the nearest), Baltimore offered anonymity to fugitives, a luxury unavailable anywhere in the cloistered atmosphere of the Maryland or northern Virginia countryside. One historian of Baltimore has estimated that from 1773 to 1819 nearly 20 percent of runaway slaves in the region escaped to Baltimore (increasing to nearly three in ten during the 1810s), whereas just 7 percent went to Pennsylvania, a nonslave state but farther away.[28] Passing as free, many escaped slaves ran to the city knowing that among its large, concentrated free black population they stood a good chance to find both shelter and protection from their masters.[29]

Many slaves who escaped to the city sought free black relatives living there, whom they knew would provide them such shelter. Richard Mason of Charles County advertised for his escaped man, Phill Carter, observing that "it is very possible that he is gone to Baltimore, as his father is living there on Howard's hill, and is a dray man, his name is James Carter." Similarly, Dorson Summers of Talbot County called for Baltimore residents to be on the lookout for John, whose "father, a free negro man, lives in Baltimore, and it is supposed that he might have gone there."[30] Other fugitives sought spouses from whom they had been separated as a result of sale or the settlement of the estate of their deceased owner. The rural owner of Adnah

Douglas, who "calls herself Adnah Pierce," believed his property to be "lurking in or about Baltimore," where her free black husband, Henry Pierce, lived. In September 1804 William Osgood advertised for his bondman, Bill, whom he "supposed to be about Pratt street, where his old master, Mr. Stewart, lives, as his wife lives with Mr. S." Similarly, Samuel Smith believed that his mulatto slave, Allick, was in Baltimore, along with "a Negro woman for a wife, named Barbara, belonging to Mr. Job Smith, who also ran away some considerable time since, and they may probably have got together."[31]

Still others, in more complicated scenarios, stole their slave families and escaped to the refuge of the city. Caroline Hammond recalled that her father, an Anne Arundel County free Negro, had been working to pay for the freedom of his wife and daughter when the widow of their owner reneged on the agreement that Hammond had made with her late husband. A desperate Hammond bribed the local sheriff and absconded with his family to Baltimore, where a sympathetic white family on Ross Street gave them shelter.[32]

Even if fugitives left Baltimore for other locales, it would appear that the connections made there sometimes drew them back to the city for visits—often at considerable risk. In January 1805 Sam C. Hunt of Baltimore County advertised that his slave Robert, who had escaped nearly two years earlier, was reported to have been living near Joppa, and "likely he will be in Town or at the Point in the holidays to see his acquaintances." Similarly, George Wilson believed his fugitive slave woman, Rose, to be harbored by "relations in Harford county . . . [because] she has been brought from thence to Baltimore several times, when she had run-away." Luke Tiernan, a Baltimore owner, advertised that he would pay a thirty dollar reward for the return of his mulatto slave, Joe Smith, but cautioned that "having numerous acquaintance of free negroes they will furnish him with other cloathing." Both slaves and whites knew that free black people harbored innumerable fugitives in Baltimore and the surrounding countryside and that the city acted as a magnet.[33]

Not all escaped slaves chose Baltimore as a permanent place of refuge. Many fugitives looked to the city as merely a way station on their journey to other destinations. The thriving seaport, with dozens of ships arriving and leaving its harbor each day, served as a powerful inducement for runaways to secret themselves to Baltimore to find passage by water—often to former homes. Charles Jessop advertised that his slave Batt "was raised on the Eastern Shore, near Cambridge, and will probably make that way, as he has been seen in town, on the wharf, trying to get a passage." O. H. Williams gave notice that his servant Clyde had "gone to Baltimore, with an intention of going from thence to Charleston, where he is from."[34]

Baltimore's location, just over forty miles from Pennsylvania, induced many other fugitive slaves to travel there in an effort to make their way to the free states. Ezekiel John Dorsey advised city residents to watch for his escapee, Jonathan, who most likely "will endeavor to get to Pennsylvania or New-Jersey, where, he says, he has been repeatedly advised to go." Similarly, Richard Dorsey of Anne Arundel County had heard that his two escaped males, Tom and Ben, "were seen in Baltimore-town . . . [and] it is supposed said fellows are going toward Pennsylvania."[35]

That escaped slaves were able to find residence and employment fairly easily in Baltimore suggests an atmosphere of relaxed control in the city during the late eighteenth and early nineteenth centuries. Black people appear to have found a measure of liberty unavailable in the countryside, where suspicious rural residents regularly accosted black wanderers. At the least, free blacks assisted escaped slaves by offering bogus freedom papers, or so was the opinion of Prince George's County planter Rinaldo Johnson, who advertised in 1793 for his fugitive slave, Nace, whom he suspected "has obtained an original certificate from some of those free negroes, lately liberated by the courts of law of this state."[36] An urban white population accustomed to having black people in its midst, coupled with the anonymity offered by the city, enabled fugitive slaves to find a haven unsurpassed elsewhere in the state. Though Baltimore's population in 1810 was still less than fifty thousand—hardly a sprawling city—its white residents were seemingly ambivalent about black strangers, which generated confidence among fugitives that they would find safety in the city. Indeed, the product of one of American history's infamous (if debated) trysts went to the city as a runaway slave; one of Sally Hemings's sons (whispered to have been Thomas Jefferson's illegitimate son) escaped from Monticello, went to Baltimore, and passed as white. Ironically, tradition maintains that he married into one of the city's eminent white families. Likely apocryphal, the story nonetheless sparks our imagination that had they known, the family might have welcomed the young man in spite of his race, given Baltimore's Republican leanings and its devotion to Jefferson.[37]

Many fugitives found employment in the shipyards or the hundreds of other businesses and industries in the city. Fells Point appears to have been especially attractive to fugitives, where both shipbuilders and ship captains appear to have hired slaves readily. In 1790 John Granberry advertised for his escaped bondman, Lancaster, who "has been used to the business of a Ship-Carpenter, . . . I expect, he may be employed on board vessels in the harbour as a Carpenter, passing as a freeman." Similarly, four years later John Jonson speculated that his escaped male slave, Peter, was "at Fell's Point, working or harboring on board of some vessel."[38]

Escaped slaves used skills they had acquired on the plantation to find employment, and they accumulated wages to pay for forged freedom papers, clothing, food, and transportation, as well as perhaps housing once they reached freedom. They also learned by observing (as only slaves could) or from knowledgeable residents exactly how they might gain sea passage to more distant destinations without being discovered. Possibly they made contacts with sympathetic residents—especially the region's numerous Quakers—who would help them on their perilous journey northward. As one urban historian has written, Baltimore at the turn of the nineteenth century often served "as a springboard to freedom," because of its proximity to the North and its access to the sea. Although the city's reputation as a place of refuge would diminish considerably several decades before the Civil War, such a distinction was yet unblemished during the early years of the nineteenth century.[39]

The runaway slaves who escaped to Baltimore in the late eighteenth century appear to have shared a number of characteristics with their free black counterparts. In his study of Baltimore fugitives between 1747 and 1790, one historian has found that most runaways, like recent freedmen, were young and male. Eighty percent of those fugitives were male, and of them 75.8 percent were between the ages of fifteen and thirty-four. Similarly, six out of ten slave females who fled their masters were in the same age group.[40] A sample of fifty-eight fugitive slave advertisements placed in four newspapers in Baltimore and Annapolis between 1789 and 1805 reveals that slightly less than a quarter of the escaped slaves for whom their masters advertised were listed as having skills, ranging from ship carpentry, to blacksmithing, to midwifery. Doubtless others possessed skills not listed in the advertisements. Southern cities generally boasted a higher percentage of skilled slaves than did rural areas, and Baltimore appears to have been no exception. By trying to increase the worth of their slave investment, slaveowners had—however unwittingly—furnished their human property with psychological buttresses crucial to a successful escape: a heightened sense of expectation and a confidence in self-improvement as the means to their own future advancement.[41]

While most fugitives escaped to Baltimore on foot from Baltimore County or nearby counties, Baltimore's connections with the sea allowed the city to attract runaways from much farther away. Samuel Ellis, of Surry County, Virginia, just west of Norfolk, advertised that his slave Tom had escaped from the sloop *Phoenix*, on which he worked, once it had reached Baltimore and docked at the city's Cheapside wharf. Similarly, one Portsmouth, Virginia, master offered a twenty dollar reward for the return of his slave Lancaster, who "went off in some vessel from hence to Baltimore, about two months ago." While relatives of these fugitives sometimes lived in Baltimore, inducing them to travel there, most escaped slaves from such great distances found their way to the city simply because of the sea traffic.[42]

Baltimore was by no means solely a locus to which slaves outside the city migrated; many resident bondpeople used the city streets and alleys as avenues of escape within the city limits. Particularly intriguing is the great number of fugitive slaves who escaped from Baltimore City residents and apparently remained in the city after their escape. John Tagart, who operated a mill less than a mile from Baltimore, advertised that his hired out slave, Jim, had escaped from his Baltimore employer, yet he still "supposed [him] to be lurking in or about Town."[43] Of the fifty-eight fugitive slave advertisements mentioned earlier, more than half were taken out by city, rather than country, masters. Nearly a third of those thirty-one city masters who advertised for their escaped property specifically said that their slaves had most likely remained in the city. A Monsieur Bidetrenoulleau, recently emigrated from Saint-Domingue, offered a six dollar reward for his "French Negro, named FRANCOIS, . . . [who] calls himself a freeman, assumes the name of *Prince Coyaux*, and . . . frequents the Point and Old-Town, and intends going to sea." Even in such a small community as Fells Point, slaves could evade their masters. George Wilson, a ship joiner living on Ann Street, advertised for the return of his slave woman Rose, who "has been seen frequently skulking about the Point."[44]

In his work on urban slavery, the historian Richard C. Wade has shown the difficulties urbanites faced in trying to establish the same "web of restraints" for their slaves that their rural counterparts had. The exact conditions of the urban setting that attracted slaves from the country—a dense population, a diverse economic base (based on free, not slave, labor), and relatively large slave and free black populations—posed enormous problems to the enforcement of slave discipline. Slaves found it fairly easy to slip away, "beyond the master's eye," to seek out acquaintances in the city.[45]

A significant number of Baltimore slaves who escaped from their city owners had pasts quite different from those of most slaves living in the city. These bondpeople were of French heritage, brought to Baltimore as part of a large contingent of refugees from the island of Saint-Domingue. In the autumn of 1791 a slave insurrection involving several thousand slaves erupted near Le Cap-François, which in the next fifteen years spread throughout the small colony and involved an estimated 100,000 slaves. By the late spring of 1793 a coalition of slaves and Spanish forces from Santo Domingo were rumored to be converging on the port stronghold of Cap-François, the island's urban center and residence of the colony's greatest concentration of slaveowners. Thousands of white and mulatto residents of the prosperous port, fearful of both the imminent invasion and a general slave emancipation, hastily gathered their belongings—often including their slave property—and left the island for asylum in America. During the month of July some fifteen hundred of those émigrés arrived in the Baltimore harbor—five hundred of whom were mulattoes and Negroes—aboard fifty-three ships. More émigrés, black and white, followed this initial migration. Between 1793 and 1805 white émigrés from Saint-Domingue declared entrance for 168 slaves; of those, 113 arrived from 1793 to 1795 alone.[46] Hoping to reestablish their plantations and planter status, many of those with capital left the city for rural lands in Maryland, but a large portion stayed in Baltimore to engage in trade in the flourishing seaport similar to Cap-François.

In Baltimore free and slave expatriates saw an opportunity to start their lives afresh. For many of the slaves this meant escape and freedom. The large influx of black French people to Baltimore prompted one white resident—alarmed about the growth of Baltimore's free black population and the possibility that the violent heritage of the islanders might spread to the city—to remark that Baltimore had "become the headquarters of free blacks and people of Colour, not only from other states of the Union, but from the islands."[47]

By all indications the majority of the black migrants to Baltimore from Saint-Domingue were Negro slaves. A much higher percent of the white émigrés had slaves than did their native counterparts, and on average they possessed many more slaves. The 1798 tax assessment for Baltimore City lists fifty-eight white immigrant property owners, thirty-seven (63.8 percent) of whom owned a total of 143 slaves, 52.4 percent of them males. Most of these refugees seem to have arrived in Baltimore cash-poor but slave-rich. Benjamin DeSobry, who found residence on Commerce Street, owned just £12 sterling worth of personal property, yet he possessed five male slaves assessed at £225. Similarly, Lewis Voyart, a grocer, owned no taxable property other than his six slaves, worth £210.[48]

While some owners desperate for cash sold their slave property to natives, many of the larger, more affluent white French slaveholders settled at Fells Point, where they used their slaves in their homes or businesses or hired them out to the various shipyards and maritime industries. After leaving Cap-François, the shipbuilder Joseph Despeaux settled first in Philadelphia, but migrated to Baltimore because Pennsylvania laws discouraged the importation of slaves. In a climate that encouraged slave ownership, Despeaux acquired four slaves in 1798, all of them working-age males. Two years later he owned twice that number.[49]

Many of the Saint-Dominguan slaves took advantage of their masters' temporary difficulties when they first arrived in Baltimore and, like their native counterparts, escaped from bondage. Of a sample of twenty-five runaway slave advertisements placed in the *Baltimore Daily Intelligencer* between October 1793 and October 1794, 60 percent were for French-speaking slaves from Saint-Domingue. Of those, nearly three out of four were young males. Given the brutality of slavery in the Caribbean (especially compared with that in the Upper South) and the difficulty of successful escape on the cloistered island, these slaves no doubt perceived their transportation to the American mainland as a long-awaited portal to freedom. Branded on either breast with the name of their island owner and able to speak little or no English, the French fugitives would appear to have stood very little chance of evading capture. Yet if the frequency of their escapes (no doubt aided by resident free blacks) is any indication, most French emigrant slaves considered the uncertainties of flight into a foreign land far more appealing than the oppression of continued enslavement under their French masters.[50]

Although black French émigrés to Baltimore were slaves who accompanied their white masters, a small number of free mulattoes did migrate from Saint-Domingue, and some of them brought slaves themselves. The federal manuscript census for 1800 lists seven black householders, four designated as "Monsieur" and three as "Madame," a strong indication that they had come from the island. Another dozen have French surnames, suggesting that they might also have been émigrés. Of the seven identifiable mulatto immigrants, three had from three to six slaves living in their households in 1800.[51]

Yet it would appear that these "people of color," a term introduced to Baltimoreans as a result of the French migration, were by no means as well off as their white French counterparts, the once *grands blancs*. The city's tax records for 1798 list no black property holders from Saint-Domingue or with French surnames. A committee of merchants, appointed by the city's populace to suggest measures to aid the refugees, boarded the vessels off Fells Point and interviewed the passengers, concluding that "the Distresses of those unhappy People have not been exaggerated" and recommending "a great exertion of humanity" for their aid. Their interviews, however, were conducted among the white passengers, "exclusive of people of color and negroes." Doubtless those benevolent whites who furnished beds and who "politely furnished them with the Participation of their Tables" did not lend such unqualified succor to free mulattoes in need.[52]

Moreover, their once-privileged free status based on their white heritage quickly disappeared in the new milieu of the revolutionary era. An 1810 duty list for Saint Mary's parish, written in French and containing the names of those who attended confession in preparation for receiving communion on Easter Sunday, lists ninety-eight people of color, eighty-four of whom were women. Fifty-two of those (just under 62 percent) were listed as Negroes rather than mulattoes. Seventeen years earlier most of these black French Catholic women had probably migrated as slaves.[53]

Whether slave or free, French or native, thousands of Negroes were lured to Baltimore, and unless coerced they traveled there believing that the city offered a wider variety of trades and more numerous opportunities for employment than those available in the countryside. Men sought out the shipyards and manufactories of Baltimore, as well as the peripheral services and trades that complemented such industries, where they could obtain higher wages than they could by hiring themselves out to farmers. There free blacks, hired slaves, and unskilled whites often worked side by side. Though largely untrained for industrial occupations, many former slaves possessed skills learned in slavery that enabled them to find employment in the burgeoning city and realize the dream of an autonomous existence. Moreover, they experienced, most likely for the first time, the freedom to seek the best possible employment or to leave present jobs for better opportunities. Women, as much as men, could hope for employment, especially in domestic service in the homes of genteel whites—employment that was difficult to obtain in a countryside filled with slaves. In general, the diverse opportunities of Baltimore offered to many Maryland free Negroes and slaves the hope for a better life, and while most found reason not to move there in the two decades after 1790, thousands more found compelling reasons to do just that.[54]

The free Negroes who began to crowd into Baltimore after 1790 came from similar backgrounds; nearly all had emerged recently from slavery. Of the 470 who applied for freedom certificates between 1806 and 1816, over 75 percent had been manumitted.[55] Although most ex-slaves traveled to the city from farms and plantations in Maryland, especially Baltimore County, a significant number came from more distant and even exotic places. Most of those outside Maryland had been born in Virginia, but others came from Delaware, Pennsylvania, New York, and the West Indies, particularly Saint-Domingue, and Jamaica. One had been born in Surinam and one in Africa, most likely brought to the state while still slaves and then liberated. While this could account for the rest of those ex-slaves as well, a check of the birthplaces of free blacks who were born free reveals that a number of them had been born in the same places as the freedpeople and in other locales as well, including Massachusetts, Connecticut, Rhode Island, North Carolina, and New Orleans. What becomes clear is that both freed Negroes and those born free migrated to Baltimore from a variety of homelands, lending parts of the city a modestly cosmopolitan air.[56]

Free Negro laborers quickly became the backbone of the maturing Baltimore economy. Many employers preferred free black men and women to slaves in their households and businesses because they were readily available and less expensive. The free labor system offered employers the flexibility to hire and lay off wage laborers according to the vagaries of the market. As a result, Baltimore industries employed far more free blacks than slaves to maintain elasticity in labor costs. Hiring a slave often involved not only paying the going wage but also feeding, clothing, and being responsible for the health of that slave during the term of contract, as well as making sure that the bondperson did not run off while out of the master's charge. Hiring a free Negro or unskilled white simply involved paying the wage, which made far more sense financially than hiring a slave. Moreover, ambitious employers often wanted more incentive for productive labor than a master's lash—one they often could not wield themselves. As the editor J. D. B. DeBow observed, many capitalists preferred "the well-trained free black," readily available in Baltimore and "subject to dismissal for misconduct," to "the slothful slave, who has no fear of loss of place."[57] In a city in which slavery was never an economic foundation, which was tied increasingly to the fluctuations of the world market, and which had a prodigious substitute labor force available to it in free blacks and working whites, slavery declined rapidly after 1810, shedding the veneer of importance it had enjoyed only briefly and even then had survived largely to enhance the remaining owners' nouveau genteel status.

Because of free Negroes' availability and flexibility for employment purposes in Baltimore, the demand for them increased as the city grew. In 1793 John Conrad Zollicoffer advertised in the newspaper for "a FEW small honest NEGRO BOYS, English or French, from 8 to 14 years of age to be employed in the Chimney Sweeping Business." Some weeks later Zollicoffer advertised for either black or white boys and promised "reasonable wages will be granted them, according to their activity and knowledge."[58] Free blacks themselves realized that opportunities for their services were available; many solicited door-to-door, while still more congregated at the city's three public markets, erected in 1784, and waited for white employers who needed a day's labor, knowing that they could find a ready supply of laborers there.[59] Occasionally, prospective black workers even advertised their services in the newspaper, such as that in a 1793 *Baltimore Daily Intelligencer*, which read "*Wants Employment*, a NEGRO MAN, who can drive carriage, wait on table, or attend on a single gentleman." In 1810, 829 white households, representing 17 percent of the city's white households, employed free blacks as personal servants.[60]

Because of the variety of labor sources available in Baltimore, many slave-owning families also hired free blacks and slaves to supplement the labor provided by their own slave property. William Smith, a rope manufacturer in Argyle Alley at Fells Point, owned five males between the ages of twenty-one and fifty but hired three more working-age males from one Widow Nichols. These additional hands would augment his work force during periods of increased demand for his product, without substantially increasing his permanent overhead, which would be the case if he purchased them. The shipwright James Biays owned twenty slaves in 1810, while keeping an additional seven free blacks in his household, many or all of whom probably worked in his business.[61]

Not all white slaveholding employers of free blacks had large businesses; in fact, far more did not. Christian Mayer, a merchant; William Jessop, a flour merchant; and John Isett, who owned the Columbian Inn, were more representative—generally tradespeople and servicers who employed free blacks and slaves in their shops, inns, and homes while also owning slaves. The English visitor Alfred Pairpont noted that in Baltimore, "the more genteel of [slaves] are here employed principally as waiters."[62] In 1810 one in four of the white slaveholding households employed free blacks in addition to holding slave property. Few of these free Negroes appear to have resided with their employers; in 1810 only 6 percent of the total white households in Baltimore housed both slaves and free Negroes. While slaves most often lived in the quarters in the rear of a master's house, free blacks generally lived elsewhere—though relatively close by—and traveled to their place of employment.[63]

With ever-increasing numbers of free blacks and slaves coming to the city, there was an ample supply of black laborers from which to choose, not only for domestic service but for other types of labor as well. Business owners hired free black and slave men regularly as carters, draymen, wagoners, and stevedores. From 1790 to 1805 Henry Nagle, a Baltimore brickmaker, hired numerous black workers, both slave and free, on a regular monthly basis to provide labor, and he hired specific individuals regularly—Little Tom, Sall, Old Tom, and Sandy—to cart bricks for him on certain days each month.[64] Frederick Douglass recalled a free Negro named Lawson who hired himself to James Ramsey, the owner of a ropewalk at Fells Point. Aside from domestics, individual homeowners employed free black laborers as ditch-, cellar-, and well-diggers, as well as gardeners, carpenters, and washers. In 1796 Ambrose Clarke, a sugar importer, received a bill from his hired laborers, "Thomas pitt and Moses gerall black men [who] has finished diging your Cellar and it Contains Eighty-four yards at one shilling and six pence."[65]

Because Baltimore's city directories do not differentiate between blacks and whites before 1808, obtaining an accurate assessment of the number of black laborers in the work force prior to that year is a difficult task. Yet existing scraps of evidence suggest that free black workers provided vital labor to both the private and public sectors of the growing community. The city frequently hired black laborers, generally for menial tasks, such as digging ditches, wells, gutters, and sewers; paving, repairing, and cleaning streets; and sinking pumps, as well as for larger public works projects. Moreover, free Negroes appear to have received no less than whites did for similar labor. From June to September 1796 a Negro named Samson worked for the city on various labor crews, cleaning ditches on Howard Hill and opening drains on Conoway Street, Pratt Street, and South Street. Samson was the only black crew member and regularly received the same daily wage as every other member: six shillings.[66] In September 1796 "Ben Jefferis a Negro," listed in that year's city directory as an Old Town drayman, received ten shillings per day for three and a half days of work carting. Benjamin Wells, a white carter, received the same pay as Ben Jeffries for the same amount of work. In May of 1797 a Negro named Peck, the only black carter of thirteen employed by the city to pave the streets, received precisely what the white carters received: thirteen shillings per day.[67]

Slaves and freedpeople worked much like common whites in Baltimore. The city hired slaves as well as free Negroes and paid them the same wages that they paid white laborers. In August of 1790 Brittingham Dickinson, a Fells Point resident, hired out "his Negro Man" to the city for four days, for which he received the going rate for unskilled labor, three shillings and nine pence per day, and was reimbursed at the end of the month by the city's special commissioners. James and Sam, free Negroes, hired themselves to the city in May 1791, as did Joseph Osborn and Richard Beazo, whites, and each received the same compensation as Dickinson's slave. In early Baltimore, where work was plentiful and competition low, unskilled white laborers received no more pay than Negroes, either slave or free, simply because of their light skin. Moreover, there is no record of animosity on the part of white laborers at this time for receiving the same pay as hired slaves and free blacks.[68]

Consequently, black residents moved rapidly into a number of positions in the city's economy. While hired slaves were mainly limited to a small number of menial occupations in which they could readily find employment, primarily as domestics and unskilled laborers, free blacks were occasionally able to branch out into a number of trades and occupations, even some that were skilled and semiskilled. The 1817–18 Baltimore city directory lists 402 "free householders of colour," who engaged collectively in fifty-five different occupations. Though the largest single occupation was laborer, significant numbers of free Negroes also took up such semiskilled trades as carting, draying, sawing, driving hacks, coaches, and stages, whitewashing, brickmaking, bricklaying, nailmaking, boot and shoe blacking, brushmaking, harnessmaking, baking, cigarmaking, dying, comb making, potting, stonecutting, and gluemaking. Moreover, a number of others acquired enough expertise to engage in such highly skilled trades as blacksmithing, tanning, barbering, coopering, shoemaking, carpentry, and butchering. One, Alex Haley, even managed to become a ship's captain. Many of these skilled and semiskilled artisans managed to open their own stores and shops, while still others without special skills did likewise, running oyster houses, cook shops (diners), and various retail shops.[69]

Still others pursued their livelihood through more illicit means. Black grogshops and tippling houses, located in cellars and the rear of groceries in Baltimore's backstreets and alleys, appear to have been fairly common, selling liquor and offering gambling and even prostitutes to free blacks, slaves, and poor whites alike. Later, in the 1830s and 1840s, one Baltimore newspaper complained that the local police should break up the "filthy little groggeries, where the most debased and abject of our black and white population assemble to drink and gamble" and engage in "obscene language and drunken orgies."[70] Despite a Baltimore grand jury's pronouncement that such places were "evil, destructive to the morals of the poorer class of people, . . . the rendezvous of the worthless white and slave [and] are the fruitful source of . . . the most disorderly and riotous conduct," local officials apparently did not make a concerted effort to close them until the 1850s. Neither did they restrict black people from running them, even though some considered these places notorious for "entertaining slaves on the Sabbath" and rural southern whites feared that slaves and free blacks would hatch whiskey-induced schemes of rebellion during such unsupervised interaction. Accustomed to close contact between the races, white Baltimoreans appeared less concerned with such notions than were their rural counterparts.[71]

Not all black people who migrated to Baltimore went into the traditional service trades. Some found opportunities to take less traditional routes to success. A wave of black showmen came to the city in the mid-1790s, performing most likely for mixed audiences. In January 1795 the city charged one such "Negro Rope Dancer" four dollars, and that December it received eight dollars for a month's license from "Wm. Nisbitt a bl[ac]k man to Exhibit on the Slack Rope, Tumbling, &c." The next fall Nisbitt returned for another engagement, and the city granted licenses to other black performers, such as Robert Wilson, a free Negro, "for Exhibiting a Show to 1st Jany next," and another exhibitionist, "a Negro turned White as a Show."[72] Still other entrepreneurs provided professional services to the city's growing population; the city directory for 1817 lists four such professionals—a teacher, a minister, a musician, and even a portrait painter, Joshua Johnston, whose deftness with a brush and pallet had allowed him to maintain this unique though financially precarious business since 1796, attracting clientele from some of the city's leading white families. Johnston, reputedly an immigrant from the West Indies, was quite likely the first black professional portrait painter in the United States.[73]

Not all such black entrepreneurs were free; on occasion, slaves, too, earned their living in Baltimore by means other than domestic service or manual labor. In 1805 Stephen Comte requested permission from the city's mayor, Thorowgood Smith, "for his servant and Negro-man *Sansnom*, to open an academy school for dancing, in the precincts of this city, *Reister's Town road*; where shall only be admitted free people or such as shall have leave from their masters." To placate any white disapprobation over a bondman plying a trade, Comte took care to assure the mayor and other uneasy whites "that nothing contrary to the rules and tranquility of the city will take place" and that he was "convinced of the faithfulness and good behavior of said servant."[74]

Maritime occupations and industries attracted a growing number of both unskilled and skilled free blacks to Baltimore. The city's wharves and shipyards, with their ready availability of menial and skilled jobs—carrying cargo to warehouses, loading and unloading ships, as well as repairing them—employed many of those identified in the city directories as "labourers," while the more skilled could find higher-paying positions as ship caulkers and ship carpenters. Black men dominated the caulking trade early on; the 1822 city directory lists twenty caulkers in the city, nineteen of whom were free Negroes. These workers, proud of their skill and status, eventually formed an early trade union, the Association of Black Caulkers, the only such organization known to have existed in the city.[75] Other black laborers, especially those who had worked on the bay or the ocean during slavery, sought work as seamen, cooks, and deckhands on the numerous ships, sloops, and fishing and oyster boats that docked at Baltimore's busy wharves or anchored in its harbor. The peripheral trades and services in Baltimore's maritime industry engaged still others as sawyers, stevedores, porters, ropemakers, and riggers and provided steady and potentially lucrative work for carters and draymen.

A look at one of the city's busiest shipyards, that of Joseph Despeaux, suggests the intricate involvement of whites, free blacks, and slaves—men and women alike—in the yard's operation. Yet it also suggests a subtle racial occupational structure, which probably existed in most Baltimore industries and which maintained reasonably relaxed race relations in the city. The trade that paid the highest wages (generally $2.00 per day) and offered the steadiest work—carpentry—Despeaux appears to have reserved exclusively for whites. No black men broke into this privileged elite. Immediately below the carpenters were the caulkers, a trade that offered less consistent work but paid well, generally $1.50 per day and even more when the yard was particularly busy, such as just before the War of 1812. Black men dominated this semiskilled occupation, and both free Negroes and slaves engaged in it. Slave caulkers commanded wages slightly lower than those of free black caulkers, earning $1.25 per day. Beneath the caulkers was a wide variety of unskilled workers, both black and white and male and female: women spinning oakum, men boiling pitch, and young apprentices assisting the carpenters and the caulkers. While the unskilled workers appear to have worked the same jobs and earned the same wages whether white or black, skilled workers had a decided hierarchy based on color. By reserving wages and steady work mostly for white workers, owners preserved racial harmony in their yards. Because in Baltimore the mass of free Negroes filled the occupational slot normally reserved for slaves and whites were employed largely in the skilled and semiskilled trades, racial harmony prevailed in the city.[76]

The sea became an increasingly important source of employment for free blacks in the city after 1817; in the ensuing decade the number of black workers listed in the city directories as being engaged specifically in maritime trades increased by nearly 143 percent. By 1850, 112 of the 168 employed black males living in the city's second ward (which included Fells Point) made their living in the shipping trades. Moreover, the dramatic increase of the free black population at Fells Point, the center of shipbuilding, reflects the importance of the industry to black employment. Between 1817 and 1819 alone the number of free black households in the Fells Point area listed in the city directories grew more than threefold, from 37 to 164.[77] The city's docks were so crowded with black faces that one English visitor, Alfred Pairpont, recalled that being in Baltimore's harbor area "seemed, at first, as if I had been transplanted to some unknown land." The black folk were "yelling and shouting to one another from numerous fishing vessels at the wharf, while others—driving teams, carrying loads—" created "such a din in their nigger tongue" that the entire scene seemed nearly foreign. Adam Hodgson, an English visitor to the United States in 1824, observed that most labor done around the docks in Norfolk, Virginia, was performed by slaves, either hired out or living out, but most of the black dock workers in Baltimore were free.[78]

In addition to attracting dock workers, Baltimore's status as a thriving seaport brought to its harbor innumerable slave sailors from all over the hemisphere. Black sailors, both slave and free, served regularly on sailing vessels. A random sampling of twenty ships entering the port of Baltimore between January and June 1806 and between March and October 1835, with crew sizes ranging from four to seventeen, reveals that all but four carried black sailors. Although the majority of the crew was white on all but three of the ships studied, 32 of the 143 crew members on all twenty ships (22.4 percent) were black. On one ship, the brig *Potomac*, six of the seven crew members were black (two of them slaves), and on another, the schooner *Rochambeau*, three of five crewmen were free Negroes. Like their landlocked brethren, most of the black sailors were young (their average age was just over twenty-six) and had been born in rural Maryland counties. All but six resided in Baltimore.[79]

Although most black sailors on the various sloops, brigs, and schooners that harbored at Baltimore appear to have been freemen, bondmen working on board ships often took advantage of the city's size and relaxed racial climate to make good their escape. In November of 1804 William Smith, captain of the Danish schooner *Esther*, reported that two slave seamen, "but a few months from the coast of Africa," had escaped into the city, and he had "reason to believe the above negroes are harbored on the Point." Moreover, frequent warnings in newspaper advertisements suggest that ship captains in need of crewmen to set sail were not above impressing African Americans whom they suspected of being escaped slaves—or, perhaps, offering freedom in return for serving on board their vessels as seamen. In 1793 Thomas Jones warned that his escaped slave, Sam, "will endeavor to get over to Dorset county, on the Eastern Shore. All Skippers of vessels, and others, are forbid to hire or assist him in any manner." A year later William Rhea advertised a reward of eight dollars for the capture and return of his escaped man servant, James, who had come from the West Indies only a few days earlier and "will probably endeavor to get employment . . . 'till he can find an opportunity of returning to the West-Indies. . . . All masters of vessels and others, are forbid harboring or carrying him off at their peril." In 1804 Peter August Guestier, a local merchant, believed his "Guinea Negro man, named Major, . . . has been carried away by some of the armed vessels, which have sailed some days ago." Major and many other escaped bondmen—as well as their masters—realized that Baltimore's access to the sea afforded slaves the most available route to freedom. Ships' captains in rural counties were reluctant to hire free blacks because they feared they might be runaways, but the number of black seamen in Baltimore suggests that such proscriptions went largely unheeded in the city's ambivalent, profit-driven atmosphere.[80]

Like free black men, free women of color found work in the cities with increasing regularity, as indicated by the number of female-headed households in Baltimore. Between 1817 and 1827 the portion of the entire work force made up of women household heads with occupations grew significantly. In 1817, 61 (15.6 percent) of the 391 households included in the city directory, for which the head listed an occupation, were headed by women. By 1819 the number of employed female heads of households had risen to 126, constituting nearly 37 percent of the working householders. In 1827 the number had fallen again to 23.7 percent. The high rate in 1819 probably occurred because of the economic downturn the entire country experienced beginning that year. The ensuing panic hit Baltimore's laboring black community particularly hard and probably forced male heads of households to leave the city in search of work. Many of those wives left behind found employment themselves in an attempt to support their families.[81]

❖   ❖   ❖

Slaves and free blacks had remarkable confidence in their futures in Baltimore, both individually and collectively. Hundreds, perhaps even thousands, of escaped slaves, both native and French, remained in Baltimore and risked capture by masters or their masters' acquaintances who lived only a mile or two away. Thousands of freedpeople from all over the state and region left the oppression of slavery in the countryside and came to Baltimore rather than move to the free states. Free blacks accepted the occupational hierarchy, even though they doubtless desired greater access to trades. Each attests to black people's perception of the redemptive powers of the city of refuge by the bay.[82]

Free blacks and slaves remained in Baltimore instead of traveling farther north for a number of reasons: employment opportunities, proximity to family (both in the city and on their former plantations), and, perhaps most important, the pervasive yet unspoken sentiment that no matter the hardships, their lot in Baltimore was considerably better than on the plantation as a slave or a hired laborer. A mature Frederick Douglass recalled eloquently his youthful sentiment that "life, in Baltimore, when most oppressive, was a paradise" when compared with the hardships of the plantation. Douglass punctuated his recollection with a wry analogy, one that bespeaks the aspirations and the ultimate realities of most of those who staked their futures in the growing city. Recalling that because he "had endured much in this line on Lloyd's plantation," Douglass declared that he "could endure as much elsewhere, and especially at Baltimore; for I had something of the feeling about that city which is expressed in the saying, that being 'hanged in England, is better than dying a natural death in Ireland.'" As an ironic postscript to Frederick Douglass's somber analogy, as early as 1817 a few respectable black residents resided in the largely tradesmen-occupied neighborhood known as Gallows Hill at the northern edge of Old Town.[83]

4

The Contours of Quasi-Freedom

In the spring of 1792 Thomas Brown, a Baltimore resident, decided he would run for one of the city's two allotted seats in the Maryland House of Delegates in the upcoming October election. Brown, a local horse doctor, had fought for his home state in the Revolution and had experience in public service, having been appointed to a minor position in local government. A staunch Federalist and supporter of the Constitution, a respected tradesman and family man, and with a slave in his household, Brown believed he not only was qualified for the job but also would attract a broad constituency.

Vowing, if elected, to flush out any remaining Tories or Anti-Federalists currently in office, Brown officially announced his campaign to the people of Baltimore on September 24 by placing an advertisement that ran two days later in the *Baltimore Daily Repository*. In it he stated his platform and his reasons for wanting to serve: "justice and equality will excite you to choose one Man of Colour to represent so many hundreds of poor Blacks as inhabit this town, as well as several thousands in the different parts of the state."[1] In 1810 (the year that Maryland last amended its constitution to limit the right of suffrage to whites), another Baltimore free Negro, apparently unaware that his race barred him from voting until informed of the new law at the polling place, publicly denounced the legislation. Addressing a crowd of white onlookers and voters "in a strain of true and passionate eloquence," he condemned the glaring inequities of a society that could, solely on the basis of his dark skin, withdraw a right that the state constitution of 1776—the year of independence—guaranteed to all free property holders, regardless of skin color.[2]

Such bold and even brazen challenges to the status quo of a slave state in early national America might appear startling to observers of early American history, especially those of the American South. Recent scholarship has focused on the autonomy African Americans—slaves and free alike—exerted within what has generally been considered a rigid slave system, but the actions of Thomas Brown, who ultimately lost his bid for election, and the unnamed free black appear extreme even by the fairly liberal standards of the Upper South, at least compared with those of the Lower South. Yet incidents such as these hint at something more than aberrant (and risky) challenges to white authority. Together they represent a nascent yet identifiable black consciousness in Baltimore, remarkable not so much for its existence at such an early date but for such vigorous demonstration in a slave state.

In Baltimore such pronounced autonomy bore heavy fruit by the middle of the nineteenth century, where one of the nation's most unique demographic mixes and anomalous racial atmospheres existed. Looking on Baltimore as a "city of refuge," just as they once had the more distant Philadelphia, free black men and women from a multitude of backgrounds came to the port city from all over the Upper South in hopes of creating lives that would prove better than what they could make for themselves, or be allowed to make, elsewhere. During the three decades following Thomas Brown's unsuccessful bid for election, the contours of black life took shape in Baltimore, where its residents enjoyed liberties already known by many during slavery: establishing households, making families, and finding employment.

Yet Baltimore offered immigrant freedpeople and slaves far more than just an augmentation of their slave lives on different, if not completely free, ground. They found the liberty to create small yet vibrant neighborhoods, diversified by an expanding populace, both black and white, as in other developing southern cities. These neighborhoods provided assistance and comfort during times of hardship to both freedpeople and slaves. Just as important, if not more so, in literally hundreds of ways these new black Baltimoreans quietly reshaped their individual lives that had been dominated by plantation culture, defining themselves as a people who had come from different though similar pasts and, if yet unknowingly, ultimately staking their claims to one collective future. These black itinerants who flocked to Baltimore in the first decades of the century took their first small yet determined steps in the slow process of building a community. For several brief but vital decades the new people of Baltimore possessed a narrow window through which many, like Thomas Brown, exerted themselves not only as free Negroes but also as free men and women.

No matter how purgative former slaves might have viewed their move to Baltimore to be or how ameliorative the city's racial climate might have seemed compared with that of the countryside, a sizable number of freedpeople who came to the city brought with them remains of their slave past.

Because so many of the new black residents of Baltimore had come directly from slavery, a great number carried with them physical vestiges of their bondage. While the extent of psychological debilitation as a result of slavery is difficult for the historian to measure, one can assess—and cannot help but be struck by—the remarkably high number of former slaves who moved to Baltimore bearing permanent physical disfigurements, both major and minor, as a result of injuries or punishment suffered during their enslavement.

For identification purposes, freedom certificates listed noticeable physical features of all sorts, including height, skin color, and any disfigurements, such as scars and burns, most of which were limited to those areas of the body generally not covered by clothing. It is therefore likely that some scarred backs went unrecorded. Of the 143 former slaves, both male and female, who applied for freedom certificates in Baltimore County between 1806 and 1810, nearly a third were listed as having disfigurements noticeable enough for the individual to be recognized by them. Nearly 42 percent of males bore such scars, as opposed to just over 25 percent of females, and males suffered all but one of the major disfigurements listed on the certificates. While this could be a result of the more physical—and often dangerous—nature of male work assignments on the plantation, historians have shown that slave women regularly provided field work and even more regularly subjected themselves to physical danger by such daily tasks as hefting iron cook pots over open fires in plantation cook houses and cabins. No evidence exists that would suggest such exertions were any less prevalent among slaves on Maryland plantations and farms than with slaves elsewhere in the South.[3]

Most disfigurements listed in the certificates were minor, with scars and small burns making up the largest proportion. A Negro named Alice, manumitted by Sarah Rogers in September 1806, bore a scar over her right eye, while Charles Nelson, freed by Jane Crockett in June 1809, had a two-inch scar on the outside of his ankle. Yet some freedmen suffered major disfigurements, such as a Negro named Jerry, manumitted by Mary Ridgely in November 1808, whose right knee was permanently out of joint; Samuel Hudson, freed by Sarah Ferguson in 1805, who had lost two fingers of his left hand; and a Negro named Jacob, who sometime before 1806 had had one of his little fingers burned off while a slave of Sarah Rogers. Although Baltimore free Negroes who had been born free also carried scars, only 13.8 percent of those who applied for freedom certificates between 1806 and 1814 were listed as bearing any disfigurements—none considered major. Such figures bear stark witness to a most visible motivation for freedom: the physical brutality slaves often endured in simply performing their daily tasks.[4]

For virtually all newly freed black people, scarred or not, the move to Baltimore represented an attempt to escape all vestiges of slavery and create a new identity for themselves. Perhaps the most immediate and expressive step this first generation of Maryland free men and women took in exercising their newfound freedom was the act of naming, both themselves and their children. For most African Americans their name held considerable social significance or reflected unique personal circumstances. The historians Eugene D. Genovese and Herbert G. Gutman, among others, have written of the importance of naming practices in understanding what the anthropologist M. Meyers Fortes has termed the "personal experiences, historical happenings, attitudes of life, and cultural ideas and values" of societies.[5] African American naming practices provide the historian a window to the mentality of those who left little literary evidence of their lives and serve as an index to acculturation. By examining the names and naming practices of those former slaves who came to Baltimore as free people, one can find evidence of as much pride in their present status and confidence in their future as they had in their new home itself.[6]

Renaming was an act of personal liberation and individual defiance, as is evident in examining the names of Baltimore's slaves and free people of color. Because so many former slaves, for the first time in their lives, were able to choose for themselves the name by which they presented themselves to the world, an analysis of slave and free names is vitally important in understanding the transition from slavery to freedom. The act represents more than mere choice; naming is an act of cultural self-definition. A new name symbolically eradicated the vestiges of an oppressive past (ironically similar to the act of earlier whites, who renamed African slaves to expunge their cultural franchise) and created a singular personal and African American identity.[7]

The 1798 tax assessment, the earliest one for black residents of the city of Baltimore, reveals a rich mixture of names among those slaves owned by city masters (see table 7). It also reveals discernible patterns of slave naming that differ from those of the deeper South. Purely African names (or those clearly of African origin), fairly common on colonial plantations in the Lower South—such as Juba, Cuff, Minta, Cato, and Mingo—were infrequent in Baltimore. Only 27 (approximately 2 percent) of the 1,446 slaves named in the tax assessment had African names, perhaps reflecting the ban on African importations that Maryland imposed, unlike those states in the lower seaboard South. Similarly, few English place-names and day-names, common among plantation slaves named by white owners, appeared among Baltimore's slaves; just twenty-one (1.4 percent) had such names as London, Fairfax, York, Limerick, and Easter.

Table 7. Given Names for Baltimore Slaves, 1798

	Number			Percentage		
Origin of Name	Male	Female	Total	Male	Female	Total
African	14	13	27	1.0	0.9	1.9
Place-name	9	4	13	0.6	0.3	0.9
Day-name	0	8	8	0.0	0.6	0.6
Classical/literary	38	40	78	2.6	2.8	5.4
French/Italian	43	67	110	3.0	4.6	7.6
Biblical	244	157	401	16.9	10.9	27.8
Anglo-American[a]	275	472	747	19.0	32.6	51.6
(short or						
diminutive)	(116)	(203)	(319)	(42.2)	(43.0)	(42.7)
Other	23	39	62	1.6	2.7	4.3
Total	646	800	1,446	44.6	55.4	100.1

a. Includes shortened or diminutive.
Source: BC Tax, Series 1: General Property Tax Books, 1798–1915, microfilm reel BCA 177, BCA.

Judging by the names of Baltimore's slaves, it would appear that urban owners cared little for re-creating the classic, slave-based patriarchal societies of ancient Greece and Rome that some plantation owners fancied themselves to be perpetuating in the rural South. Slightly more numerous, but still infrequent, were classical names, such as Pompey, Alexander, Daphne, Sampson, Caesar, Venus, Hercules, and Apollo. Only seventy-eight (5.4 percent) of Baltimore's slaves carried these names in 1798, a figure well below that which the historian Cheryll A. Cody found on a South Carolina plantation during the same period. More likely, slaves themselves had exerted their influence on their Maryland masters, since they had assumed the responsibility for naming their own children during the colonial period. Consequently, few classical names existed among slave children in Baltimore on the eve of the nineteenth century. Of the eighty-six slave children under the age of twelve listed in the 1798 tax assessment, just two carried classical names.[8]

Because of the influx of émigrés from Saint-Domingue during the 1790s, a significant number of Baltimore slaves in 1798 carried given names that were foreign. Like their native counterparts, these French slaves rarely had surnames, at least ones their owners cared to recognize. One hundred and ten slaves in the tax assessment (slightly less than 8 percent of the total slave population) carried discernible French names or, as appears to have been fashionable among the white Saint-Dominguan owners, Italian names. Only three of these names were duplicated; no one name, either male or female, appears particularly popular, unlike certain Anglo-American names. The Saint-Dominguan male slaves had such diverse and unique French names as Baptiste, Maurice, Justin, Ferdinande, Cassointe, and Valentine, while the females were known by such names as Felicité, Delphine, Gogo, Elizenne, and Charmante. Perhaps harking back to the classical societies of the ancient Mediterranean, some Caribbean slaves in Baltimore were known by such romantic names as Feneore, Fegaro, Femisso, Lizetto, Mantacello, and Lazere and such classical Mediterranean names as Polidore, Marcellan, Westavis, and Reticles.[9]

The names most prevalent among Baltimore's slaves were either Anglo-American, biblical, or both. In 1798, 1,148 slaves (79 percent) carried these names. Because slaves themselves had for years virtually controlled naming their children and because slave importations were so limited in the Upper South, by 1798 nearly eight of ten slaves in Baltimore bore names of English origin, indicative of the acculturation of many slaves to the dominant white American culture. The most popular names for slave women were Hannah, Rachel, Sally, Betty, Fanny, and Polly, and for men they were James, Charles, John, George, William, Benjamin, Thomas, Samuel, and Henry.

Several more purely biblical names appear in the slave assessments, such as Hezekiah, Elijah, Moses, Saul, Tamer, and Hagar, but they were far less popular. Particularly striking is the number of the English slave names, both male and female, that were shortened—such as William to Will or Bill, Richard to Dick, James to Jim, Samuel to Sam, Hester to Hetty or Het, Elizabeth to Betsy or Bess, and Priscilla to Prissy or Prissas—as well as the remarkable number of shortened, diminutive given names, especially among slave women—such as Cate, Beck, Jin, Nace, Biddy, Co, Letty, Penny or Penn, Lise, and Kitt. Of the 747 purely Anglo-American names in the 1798 tax assessment, 324 were shortened versions of full Christian names. A full 43 percent of slave women's names and over 42 percent of men's names were diminutive. Of the sixty-six different names given for slaves under the age of twelve, twenty-two (approximately 33 percent) were shortened or diminutive. The frequency with which masters ascribed these shortened names serves as clear evidence of whites' subtle, yet perceptible, daily imposition of the master-slave relationship. Their penchant for shortening names that slaves had often chosen for themselves suggests the secondary status that white Baltimoreans regularly ascribed to slaves and free Negroes.[10]

Once freed, former slaves in Baltimore appear to have wasted little time naming themselves yet again, thus fashioning their own social identity. While classical slave names, diminutive names, as well as day-names and place-names—so characteristic of Baltimore's slaves—were still used, their numbers fell dramatically when compared with the 1798 tax list of slave names. Only 111 such names were included in those 1,008 free Negro heads of households with given names listed in the censuses, constituting just over 11 percent of the total. Freedmen even more than women adopted Anglo-American names once out of slavery; while in 1798, 42.6 percent of slave men in Baltimore carried Anglo-American names, in 1810 more than 53 percent had adopted such names. Freedwomen with Anglo-American names increased from 59 percent to nearly 65 percent of the total, a rate half that of men. Moreover, some changed classical names to shortened versions that were far more Anglo-American (or, perhaps more accurately, far less slave). Negro Sampson, for instance, referred to himself as Sam Davis when he was freed. By contrast, while seventy-eight slaves (5.4 percent) in the 1798 tax records were listed as having classical names, only fourteen free persons of color (1.4 percent) listed in the censuses went by such names between 1790 and 1810 (see tables 7 and 8).[11]

More dramatic still is the small number of Baltimore free black household heads who assumed or retained shortened or diminutive names. Only

Table 8. Given Names for Baltimore Free Black Heads of Household, 1790–1810

Origin of Name	Number			Percentage		
	Male	Female	Total	Male	Female	Total
African	8	9	17	0.8	0.9	1.7
Place-name	1	0	1	0.1	0.0	0.1
Day-name	0	1	1	0.0	0.1	0.1
Classical/literary	11	3	14	1.1	0.3	1.4
French	4	1	5	0.4	0.1	0.5
Biblical	267	80	347	26.5	7.9	34.4
Anglo-American[a]	372	201	573	36.9	19.9	56.8
(short or						
diminutive)	(47)	(64)	(111)	(4.7)	(6.3)	(11.0)
Slave	19	4	23	1.9	0.4	2.3
Other	16	11	27	1.6	1.1	2.7
Total	698	310	1,008	69.1	30.7	100.0

a. Includes shortened or diminutive.
Sources: First, Second, and Third U.S. Census, 1790, 1800, 1810, Population Schedule, Baltimore City, NA.

111 of 573 heads of households with Anglo-American given names (just over 19 percent) retained the shortened forms of Anglo-American names so prevalent among slaves. This was especially true of males, who, judging by their names, exerted their newfound status as free men most vigorously. Of the 372 male heads of households with Anglo-American names, more than 90 percent responded to the census taker's knock with full given names. In slavery many had been forced to be Charlie, Jim, Bill, and Ben, but in freedom the overwhelming majority referred to themselves proudly as Charles, James, William, and Benjamin. Occasionally, one can find remnants of the slave past in the names of Baltimore free blacks, such as Primus Johns, Caesar Augustus, Pompy Smith, and Sukey Hill, but usually their names in freedom were indiscernible from those of their white neighbors.[12]

Yet the majority of former slaves did not limit themselves to altering or assuming different given names; nearly all also took surnames, a privilege not often extended by their erstwhile owners. Of the 1,446 slave male and females listed in the tax records in 1798, only 6 (a mere four-tenths of 1 percent) listed surnames. Similarly, of the 415 deeds of manumission registered in Baltimore County between 1789 and 1805, just 68 (16.4 percent) listed surnames. This is not surprising since white owners rarely gave their slaves surnames and usually refused to recognize the surnames slaves gave themselves.[13]

That so many Baltimore freedpeople assumed surnames suggests the rapidity with which they exerted their independence. At the same time, however, it also highlights their conscious acculturation to white societal norms. Slaves often took as their surnames the names of former masters and used them despite their present owners' objections. Of 358 manumitted slaves who applied for freedom certificates in Baltimore between 1806 and 1816, more than 40 percent listed surnames. Of those with surnames, only 10 percent bore the same last name as their manumitter. In advertising for his escaped mulatto slave woman, Charity, Nicholas Darnall of Prince George's County warned that "she is in or near Baltimore-Town, passes for a free woman, practices midwifery, and goes by the name of SARAH DORSEY, or DAWSON, the GRANNY." Similarly, George French of Georgetown advertised for his mulatto runaway, Charles, and had "no doubt of his being possessed of a pass, calling himself *Charles Pointer* or *Saunders*."[14] Of the 1,008 free black heads of households listed in the censuses between 1790 and 1810, more than 92 percent possessed surnames. Dramatically, more than 99 percent of Baltimore slaves listed in the 1798 tax assessment were listed without such surnames. Judging by the frequency with which one can find such surnames as Howard, Carroll, Tilghman, Dashiell, and Dorsey—all prominent slaveholding families of early Maryland—among black household heads in Baltimore, many freedpersons obviously kept the names of former owners.[15]

Most Baltimore freedpeople, however, assumed completely new surnames as legitimate identification. Generally, freedmen took simple surnames commonly found among whites: Johnson, Bailey, Smith, Jones, Brown, Jackson, Robinson, Williams, and the like. Occasionally, however, they assumed names that made statements about themselves as individuals—such as John Fortune, Elisha Caution, and Charles Togood—names that bespoke their faith in (or skepticism about) their future in their American homeland, or names emulative of famous Americans—such as Freeborn Garrettson, George Washington Taylor, and Thomas Jefferson. Most often free persons of color chose correct-sounding names that simply expressed their desire for respect as men and women and, perhaps more important, reflected their respect for themselves as individuals who had attained membership in Baltimore society.[16]

Renaming themselves was only the beginning of the freedpeople's efforts to define freedom. Soon after moving to Baltimore, generally singly and newly emancipated, free persons of color set about building new lives not only by securing work but also by establishing households and beginning families. Especially striking in the records of early black households and families in Baltimore is the overwhelming number of households that were male-headed. Judging by the household makeup of the city's free persons of color, the transition from slavery to freedom generally included the establishment of male-headed, two-parent families. Moreover, as time passed, the number and percentage of such households increased (see table 9). In 1790 males headed two-thirds of the forty-two Baltimore households listed in the census and identifiable by sex. It remained virtually identical in 1800,

Table 9. Free Black Household Heads in Baltimore Identifiable by Sex, 1790–1830

Year	Total	Male-Headed	Percentage	Female-Headed	Percentage
1790	42	28	66.7	14	33.3
1800	305	204	66.9	101	33.1
1810	681	475	69.8	206	30.2
1820	1,300	923	71.0	377	29.0
1830	2,423	1,833	75.7	590	24.3

Sources: First, Second, Third, Fourth, and Fifth U.S. Census, 1790, 1800, 1810, 1820, 1830, Population Schedule, Baltimore City, NA.

when 204 of the 305 households were male-headed, after which the percentage began to rise steadily. By 1810 nearly 70 percent of the free black households were headed by males, and in 1820 males headed 71 percent of the households in Baltimore. By 1830 more than 75 percent of the black households in Baltimore were headed by men, an even higher figure than in neighboring Philadelphia a full seven years later, where just 71 percent of free black households were male-headed.[17]

The large number of male-headed households in Baltimore attests to the strength of black men's commitment to preserving traditional family structure, not only as an integral element of the slave experience but also after African Americans attained their freedom. White society considered a stable family to be an indication of a man's moral fiber and personal virtue; it was an essential component of social standing and often financial success. Slaves, too, valued cohesive families but recognized that the stability of their families was determined not so much by the strength of their own character as by the caprices of an outsider: namely, the white master. Though slaves succeeded in forming traditional families, members of such households knew that in time of economic need or as punishment any one of them could be sold and the family broken up.[18]

Baltimore's black households most commonly included two parents. In his study of Philadelphia's antebellum black community, the historian Theodore Hershberg has found that in 1838, 78 percent of free black households in Philadelphia were two-parent. Interestingly, two-parent households existed in even higher proportions among ex-slave families than among freeborn households, 80 percent to 77 percent, respectively, suggesting the tenacity with which former bondpeople adhered to stable family relationships once they were allowed to pursue such arrangements without hindrance. While no figures are available for Baltimore prior to 1850, and even then are not broken down by former slave and freeborn status, a sampling of 333 families in four city wards in 1850 reveals that 82 percent of free black households in Baltimore were two-parent, an even higher percentage than in Philadelphia a dozen years earlier. This discrepancy may, however, be the result of a higher number of families in Baltimore that originated in slavery or the time factor, which allowed for a fuller development of such familial arrangements.[19]

Former slaves in Baltimore assumed their newfound legal rights and married, confident that their families could not now be broken up by anyone but themselves. The historian Herbert Gutman suggests that this immediate proliferation of two-parent, male-headed households demonstrates not only the adaptability of black familial arrangements but also the powerful social value African Americans attached to familial ties and kin networks in both slavery and freedom. From the beginning but especially immediately after gaining freedom, a high percentage of free families of color in Baltimore structured themselves according to traditional social norms. Baltimore's African Americans assumed that, at least for the record, these families should be male-headed and two-parent.[20]

In Baltimore, located in a state that in 1810 still maintained one of the largest slave populations in the country,[21] free black residents could not escape the intrusions of slavery in their households. Many female heads of households in Baltimore were quite likely spouses of slave men who lived elsewhere, either on plantations or with their owners or employers somewhere in the city. Similarly, free black men were often forced to live without their spouses while working to pay for their freedom as well as that of their families. Caroline Hammond, born in Baltimore in 1844, recalled that her father, George Berry, a free Negro, gained permission to marry her mother, then a slave owned by Thomas Davidson of Anne Arundel County, with the stipulation that he purchase her within three years of the wedding. Berry worked diligently as a carpenter in Baltimore, making partial payments until he had fulfilled the $750 purchase price of his bride.[22] Similarly, in 1832 Moses Lynch purchased his wife, Cornelia, and son, George, from James Smith, a Baltimore physician residing on Franklin Street, and then manumitted them the same year.[23]

Because of slavery, black families in Baltimore were subject to a wide variety of spatial and legal interruptions to traditional nuclear, single-dwelling households. In 1832 Anthony Parks, a twenty-two-year-old free shoemaker, lived with his free wife and one free child, but he had two other children who were slaves to David Walters and another who was owned by a Mr. Owings. Parks had most likely managed to purchase his wife from her former owner, and the two had had a child since she received her freedom, but they had not yet mustered the purchase price for the remaining children, who had been born while the woman was still in bondage. Fanny Johnson, who worked as a nurse at St. Mary's College after being manumitted by Alexander Claxton in 1832, had two children who were the property of James Swan. The husband or father was not listed. Despite the strain that separation placed on family cohesion, the great desire of African Americans to establish and maintain strong family units not only allowed such fractured families to exist but also likely gave them strength in their effort to live together as free people.[24]

While most black domestics did live with their owners or employers, the blurred ties between slaves and free blacks in the city, as well as the prevalence of hiring slaves for labor, forced more flexible living arrangements for black residents in Baltimore than in other slave cities. Because slavery in Baltimore centered on domestic service, nontraditional arrangements were common. Harriet Stokes, a twenty-four-year-old house servant of Daniel Parrish, was allowed to live "near the spring with her father," a free Negro who resided on Eden Street. Similarly, Marceline Nicholas, a freed servant of Louis Seger, lived with her free husband on Chatsworth Street. Though empirical evidence is scant, the nature of urban domestic work in Baltimore appears not to have necessitated the permanent separation of black families.[25]

Evidence of slave living arrangements may be sketchy because few free black families in Baltimore housed slaves at all and still fewer owned them (see table 10), particularly compared with free black families in cities in the Lower South. In Charleston more than three out of four free persons of color worked as artisans and small businesspeople, and they were better able to afford skilled slaves to assist them in their various business enterprises—allowing them to profit even more. As a result, as early as 1790, 49 (32 percent) of the 155 free Negro families in Charleston had entered the slaveowning class; by 1830 nearly 75 percent of Charleston's free Negro households contained slaves.[26] Conversely, free blacks in cities in the Upper South, who worked primarily as unskilled laborers, generally lacked the economic resources to acquire slaves. In 1813 just five free blacks were assessed taxes for a total of six slaves in Baltimore (all were women), and in 1830 slaves resided in only 89 (just under 4 percent) of the city's 2,423 black households.[27] Even in 1820, when the slave population of Baltimore reached its peak, slaves could be found in only slightly more than 5 percent of free black households, and then rarely more than one or two at a time. Likely, most of those slaves listed in free black households

Table 10. Free Black Households with Slaves in Baltimore, 1790–1830

Year	Total	With Slaves	Percentage	Slaves in Free Black Households	Average
1790	47	1	2.1	1	1.0
1800	305	13	4.3	32	2.4
1810	681	18	2.6	42	2.3
1820	1,488	77	5.2	131	1.7
1830	2,423	89	3.7	149	1.7

Sources: First, Second, Third, Fourth, and Fifth U.S. Census, 1790, 1800, 1810, 1820, 1830, Population Schedule, Baltimore City, NA; Curry, Free Black in Urban America, 44–47; Clayton, Black Baltimore, 11–16.

were not owned by any member of that household. Many of these slaves were probably bondpeople whose masters had allowed them to live out, and they found lodging as boarders in the lofts, garrets, cellars, and attics of free Negro households throughout the city.[28]

While free black slaveholding was obviously infrequent, Baltimore's records do provide evidence that the practice did exist in the city. Some black Baltimoreans did hold slaves as laborers, just as they did in the Lower South. In 1791 Ben Jefferies, a black carter, hired out "his Man"—presumably his slave—to the city for nine and a half days of labor, receiving the regular daily wage of three shillings and nine pence. Similarly, in 1795 Jacob Gilliard, an Old Town blacksmith, advertised for his escaped bondman, "a Mulatto boy, named John Chapman, about 5 feet 7 or 8 inches high, round shouldered, and has a slovenly walk, down look, and is apt to stammer when sharply spoken to."[29]

Although income-oriented free Negro slave ownership existed in Baltimore, far more owners in the city held slaves who were their own family members. In 1798 only one free Negro slaveowner was listed in the tax records, Anthony Jackson of Frederick Street, listed as a "black man," who owned his wife, Cloe, and his two young children, Harriet and George, aged four and two, respectively. Harriet Williams lived with her seven children on South Howard Street, until she and her husband, Philip, a slave waiter on board an independent steamboat, were able to afford his purchase price in 1832; technically her husband's master, Harriet then legally manumitted him. In general, free Negro slaveholders in the Upper South owned slaves who were members of their own families or loved ones instead of holding them as laborers.[30]

The larger-scale manumissions of the Upper South contributed to the relative absence of slave ownership among Baltimore's free Negroes. More slaves had access to manumission there than in the Deep South, where slavery continued to be a bulwark of its economic system. Because slaves owned by whites were more likely to be manumitted in the Upper South, often as whole families and without regard for skin color, fewer free Negroes needed to purchase family members to effect their escape from white masters and, given the racial atmosphere of Baltimore, had even less reason to keep them in slavery, thus perhaps explaining the low number of free black slaveowners in the city.

Moreover, with the prevalence of term slavery, where manumission had already been made but was to be delayed, free blacks often preferred to wait for the designated date of manumission rather than arrange to pay for their own freedom or that of loved ones who remained in bondage. Nonetheless, manumission records attest to the fact that free blacks did manumit their own family members. In 1805 John Cooper, a free Negro, freed "Charity Cooper aged about Sixteen years the daughter of Rachel Bantam now Rachel Cooper, whom I purchased of Henrietta Birckhead." In the same year Samuel Norwood sold two mulatto boys, "children of Charles Parraway and Hat[ti]e his wife who has been heretofore sold to the said Charles Parraway by me." In 1809 Mingo Jackson freed his twenty-six-year-old wife, Rebecca, who lived outside the city in Baltimore County. The previous year Jacob Gilliard, an early leader of the city's black residents, set free his two sons, Jacob Jr. and Nicholas, after laboring for some years to purchase them from their (and, probably, his previous) owner.[31]

Gilliard's unique case suggests that "benevolent" slave ownership could suffer problems not unlike those of more conventional master-slave relationships. In 1805 Gilliard's own slave son ran away from his father-master, who still owed $510 for his purchase and for which he had, as he put it, "given my bond and entered security, in order to extricate him from bondage." Forced to advertise in the newspapers for his bondman's return as any other owner would, the blacksmith described his son as "a brownish yellow Man, named Jacob Cokkey: he sometimes calls himself *Jacob Vanlear*, at other times *Jacob Guillard*." The wording of Gilliard's solicitation did not hide the bitter irony the situation engendered: "I leave it to a generous public to judge, whether such base ingratitude in a young man towards an aged father, can pass unnoticed—who, in his declining days, is obliged to pay a sum of money which he is unable to raise without selling part of that property which he labored hard to procure against old age."[32]

Because of the relatively low economic position of most free Negroes in Baltimore, other free blacks and slaves who lived in the same households were often family members. Few could afford to purchase slaves for servants, pay taxes for them, or even to employ them. Overall, Baltimore, when compared with cities in the Lower South, had few slaves residing in the homes of free blacks, even as family members. In Baltimore by 1860, as Leonard Curry writes of the Upper South in general, "the phenomenon of free blacks owning slaves had nearly disappeared"; in 1856, not one free black property holder was assessed taxes for ownership of a slave.[33]

Because so many free Negroes had come so recently from slavery, the transition to autonomy often required a short tenure as an employee in the home of one of the city's white families. The purpose was to accumulate capital to fashion their independent existences. Migrating with virtually no property or savings, many were forced to seek such arrangements for several years before establishing their own households. In 1790 over 43 percent of the 325 free blacks enumerated in the census resided in white house-holds, working as domestics or indentured laborers. George A. Hackett, who would become one of the city's most respected and influential black busi-nessmen and church leaders, started out as a coal digger living in the im-proved attic of Joseph Griffith at his residence on Stirling Street.[34]

For many free blacks, temporary residence in a white household in Bal-timore provided only a transitional step between bondage and autonomy. Free Negroes appear to have wasted little time leaving white residences for dwellings of their own. Once they gained economic security, the city expe-rienced a dramatic increase of households headed by free persons of color. From 1790 to 1810 the number of free Negro households rose from 47 to 683, an increase of 1,353.2 percent, proportionately even greater than the overall free black population increase of 1,123.7 percent during the same period.[35] In 1800, 1,004 (36.2 percent) of the city's 2,771 free blacks lived in households headed by whites, and in 1810 just 1,184 (29.8 percent) of the 3,974 free Negroes resided with a white family. While still high, the per-centage steadily decreased as black people in greater numbers sought to exert their independence and fashion their own existence without white assistance or, more important, interference.[36]

Despite the rise in black-headed households, few of these free Negro heads of household owned their dwellings. Luther P. Jackson has suggested it often took a generation of freedom for former slaves in the Upper South to gain the economic independence represented by real property.[37] Balti-more's early property tax records appear to support such a claim, because the 1798 tax assessment indicates that of over 2,100 homeowners in the city, only 8 were black (see table 11). Invariably, the dwellings these few free blacks owned were small, frame tenements or row houses, generally one- or two-

Table 11. Baltimore Free Black Property Ownership, 1798, 1804, 1813, and 1815

Year	Number of Free Black Owners	Percentage of Total Owners	Average Value of Free Black Property[a]	Average Value of White Property[a]
1798	8	3.3	$226	$1,479
1804	8	0.2	227	1,117
1813	41	1.9	208	770
1815	58	1.4	150	800

a. Rounded to nearest dollar.
Sources: BC Tax, Series 1: General Property Tax Books, 1798–1915, microfilm reel BCA 177, BCA; Baltimore Assessment Record Book, 1815, Ms. 55, MHS; Baltimore County Com-missioners of the Tax, 1804 and 1813 Assessments, Baltimore City, MSA C226, MdHR.

story, with street fronts usually twelve feet in width and depths ranging from twenty to forty feet. The assessor specifically noted that several of the dwellings were "small." Fire proved to be a constant threat, as indicated by the frequency of such reports in the newspapers. These few free black property holders were scattered throughout the city, a pattern that would prevail until after the Civil War. Moreover, they held property valued at far less than that of whites. None of the black property holders in 1798 held property assessed at more than £75 sterling ($333). While the average property assessment for whites in the city was nearly £333 sterling (roughly $1,479), the average for free blacks was less than a sixth of that at £51 (just over $226).[38]

During the early decades of the nineteenth century, as the number of black homeowners increased slowly, their percentage of ownership of the city's real property decreased dramatically. The tax assessment for 1815 reveals several noticeable changes. In that year, while the number of black persons holding property in the city had grown to fifty-eight (an increase even greater than the increase of the city's free black population during the period), this increase did not match the percentage of growth of white property ownership. The average size of black holdings fell by just over a third, to just over $150, still over five times less than the valuation of the average white holding.[39]

Baltimore's black real property ownership was noticeably lower than that in other antebellum seaboard cities. Though more than one-fourth of Maryland's two hundred black property owners between 1783 and 1818 lived in Baltimore, the average value of the holdings of those Baltimore property owners in 1815 was just $150. The Maryland average was $104, meaning that even in Baltimore, where city property commanded higher assessments than those in the countryside, the valuation of a typical free black's real property was only slightly higher than in the countryside. Though in 1832 the drayman George Douglass owned three lots of property, including a brick house valued at nearly $2,000, Harriet Berry's property proved more typical. Her old twenty-by-twenty-two-foot frame shack was so dilapidated that in 1831 the city assessed it at just $13.75, and she was not required to pay taxes on it. In direct contrast, Charleston's free persons of color, with access to skilled trades, had begun to acquire property well before the American Revolution and by the 1790s boasted a number of black craftpeople who possessed impressive amounts of property. Because most propertied black Baltimoreans were in the service occupations rather than the more lucrative skilled trades, the number of black people acquiring real property, as well as the value of property held, was low.[40]

A comparison of property ownership in Baltimore and Philadelphia reveals that Baltimore's free Negroes were far less likely to acquire property than were the black residents of its neighboring city to the north. In 1820 property ownership among Philadelphia black residents stood at 11.6 percent; in Baltimore in 1815 the percentage was a modest 5.3 percent. This percentage would be the highest either city would experience during the decades before the Civil War. As late as 1850, while 0.72 percent of Philadelphia's black people owned property, just 0.40 percent of those in Baltimore did, a figure that was not only the lowest of any major city in the slave states but also the lowest in the nation.[41]

Moreover, no individual black property owners in Baltimore ever approached the level of the wealthiest African Americans in Philadelphia. In 1837 dozens of Philadelphia's black householders owned property in excess of $3,000. No less than 282 black residents of that city possessed property valued in excess of $1,000, of which at least three, including the sailmaker James Forten, held estates in excess of $40,000. In Baltimore as late as 1850 only 101 free blacks owned any real property whatsoever, while in 1860 only 75 possessed as much as $1,000 worth, one-fourth the number in Philadelphia twenty years earlier. The total wealth mirrored that figure: in 1856 black Philadelphians owned some $800,000 in taxable property, while Baltimoreans had just over $250,000.[42] That year, a total of only 104, including those above-mentioned property holders, owned a combination of real and personal property estimated to be worth at least that much. Several remarkably wealthy black individuals did reside in Baltimore: the barbers Thomas Green (whose Light Street home and business were located just west of the basin, in the fashionable merchant district, and who became so prominent that his was the only black entry in the city directories to be listed boldly in capital letters), Henry Jakes, and Francis M. Turner, with $18,910, $16,000, and $6,045 worth of real and personal property, respectively, as well as Henrietta Gun, with $18,000 worth of real property and $500 worth of personal property. Yet such successes could not rival the wealth many of the free blacks in Philadelphia had acquired some three decades earlier.[43]

In even greater contrast, in 1860 Charleston's free Negro elite (those fifty-five persons who possessed $2,000 in real estate) constituted 8.00 percent of the city's free black population. In Baltimore in 1850 and 1860 only fifty-one such owners existed, constituting only 0.02 percent of the free black population. In fact, only slightly over 1.00 percent of the free black population in Baltimore owned as much as $500 worth of real property during those years.[44] Of fourteen antebellum cities, Baltimore had the lowest percentage of property owners. Philadelphia had twice as many, and Charleston had three times as many, while only Washington witnessed a smaller average size of holdings than Baltimore's $1,327 in 1850.[45] Free Negroes in Baltimore

were uniformly less prosperous than those in either Philadelphia, their northern free state neighbor, or Charleston in the Deep South—a reflection of
the social origins of the communities and regions as much as the occupational structure.[46]

Free Negroes in Baltimore did not achieve autonomous living arrangements, whatever their condition and whether owned or rented, without cost
to their standard of living. At the same time more of them were finding independent housing, their dwellings became increasingly crowded. Between
1790 and 1830 the average size of individual free black households grew from
just under four to just over six persons per household (see table 12). Because
Maryland tenant laws required renters to be responsible for a third of the
taxes on property, the city's poor—both white and black—tended to live in
tiny, squalid dwellings.[47]

As the black migration to the city became heavier, free Negroes found
their already small living spaces increasingly cramped. While most Baltimore
free black households held close to the average family size for free Negroes
nationwide, a significant number had far more individuals residing with
them. Although many of these were either immediate family members or
close relatives, Baltimore's free Negroes appear to have given sanctuary to
distant kin and acquaintances from the country. One newspaper advertisement placed by Thomas Jones, who lived in Baltimore County, remarked
that his escaped hired out slave, Sam, "was seen . . . travelling toward Baltimore-Town, where he has several relations (manumitted blacks), who will
conceal and assist him to make his escape." Such arrangements, whether
surreptitious or not, extended the city's partial-kin networks already established among slave families on plantations.[48]

In addition to taking in other black boarders, free Negroes appear to have
taken in whites occasionally. Often, such households included single white
adults and children; many of the adults likely were runaway apprentices who
had traveled to the city with little knowledge of urban ways, almost invariably in search of what their black benefactors had found—a free and autonomous existence. The federal censuses list numerous free black households
in Baltimore in which white children resided. In 1820 a white girl under the
age of ten lived with Fells Point gardener Augustine Burgoine's family of
five. In the same year an elderly white man roomed with Elizabeth Clarke
and her family of three at their residence on South Bond Street at Fells Point.
It is possible these white children were orphans, runaways, or those with
physical or mental impairments for whom the child's family paid a black
family to provide care. In an atmosphere of race and class tolerance, such
cross-racial, lower-class cooperation could and did exist in Baltimore.[49]

Table 12. Average Size of Baltimore Households, 1790–1830

	White		Free Black[a]	
Year	Number	Average	Number	Average
1790	1,686	7.07	47	3.94
1800	3,594	5.81	305	5.89
1810	4,858	7.45	681	4.16
1820	7,846	6.12	1,488	5.04
1830	9,946	6.20	2,423	6.10

a. Including slaves living in free black households.
Sources: First, Second, Third, and Fourth U.S. Census, 1790, 1800, 1810, 1820, Population Schedule, Baltimore City, NA.

As poverty-ridden freedmen and freedwomen crowded into the city in search of work, more residences housed unusually large numbers of solely black occupants. The federal census for 1790 lists five of its forty-seven free black households as made up simply of "Free Negroes"—quite likely black boardinghouses. Such dwellings persisted throughout the first decades of the century. In 1800 John Antony, a hairdresser, reported to the census taker that he was one of fourteen free blacks residing in his dwelling at 64 Charles Street. Similarly, that same year Benjamin Cooper, a stevedore living in a small dwelling next to 157 Bond Street at Fells Point, housed sixteen free Negroes in his home. In 1820 John Berryman, a Fells Point blacksmith, had twenty-six free people of color living in his home on South Bond Street, twenty-one of whom were working-age males. Presumably, several labored for Berryman in his shop.[50]

Despite the rapid increase in the number of free Negroes in Baltimore, prior to 1830 their households were generally smaller than those of whites. Between 1820 and 1850 an average of 29.3 percent of white Baltimore families and 26.7 percent of free Negro families had children under the age of fourteen in the household. A shortage of males in the city as a result of occupations that took them away from Baltimore, such as sailoring, mining, or road building, might well have contributed to a lower birthrate than that of whites in the city, though such a conclusion is largely speculative. Whatever the case, the percentage of children among free black families remained lower than that of whites throughout the early antebellum period. Maryland whites in later decades would sound the alarm of swelling numbers of free Negroes, perceived as a result of the Negro's innate lasciviousness (a belief regaining wide acceptance in the Upper South at the turn of the nineteenth century), but the average household size of free persons of color in Baltimore does not support such beliefs.[51]

The Baltimore property records also indicate that many free blacks, like working-class whites, turned their property into multifamily dwellings to maintain their economic independence. Some built small structures in the rear of the main dwelling house and rented them out. William Briscoe, a drayman, let out a one-and-a-half-story brick house in back of his residence at 134 North Howard Street to Jane Isaac. Others rented parts of their own dwellings, especially attics and basements, to tenants and even entire families, such as Charles Cornish, who rented the basement of his dwelling at 47 Frederick Street to Alexander Christie, a laborer. Such arrangements were often made between those having the same occupations, such as John Amour and Joseph LeClaire, hairdressers, who shared a dwelling at 34 Market Space. Often, too, single women shared dwellings, such as the widow Aba Waters and the washerwoman Charlotte White, who lived together at 82 North Charles Street. Black Baltimoreans readily adapted their living arrangements to ensure and protect their hard-won autonomy. Without economic security their freedom was fragile.[52]

Baltimore was similar to other southern cities in that no overt racial segregation emerged in its residential patterns. The nature of slaveowning and slave hiring in Baltimore alone dictated that this would be so, because slaves who lived with their wealthy owners, as well as those living close to (if not with) their middle-class masters, were dispersed throughout the city. By 1820 none of the city's eight wards had less than 250 slaves. Though nearly three-quarters of Baltimore slaveowners owned just one slave, noticeable clusters of slave ownership surfaced in the city.[53] Because affluent white Baltimoreans tended to live in the same neighborhoods, slave ownership in the urban setting tended to exist in blocks. Genteel residents on the same street, wanting similar servants, often owned slaves, hired slaves or free blacks, or both.

While slave ownership was the most desirable demonstration of affluence, white homeowners often hired black domestics, both for economic practicality and to keep up appearances for their equally status-conscious neighbors, sometimes until they were able to afford a slave of their own. In 1840 George Litting, a hatter, hired a free black, Elizabeth Bebee, paying her five dollars a month to serve as a housekeeper. Three years later, upon Bebee's departure, Litting hired a free black woman, Mary, whom he paid four dollars a month, and a slave woman, Sarah, whose term of service would last two years in return "for her victuals and clothes." A month later he purchased a slave woman, Juliet, from Archibald Dorsey, a local physician. In moving from hired black labor into slaveowning, Litting enhanced his respectability by white genteel southern urban standards.[54]

Ownership of slaves and hiring of slaves and free blacks as domestics was especially concentrated in the city's commercial core, stretching from Jones' Falls on the east to Howard Street on the west and running north from the basin to Saratoga Street. There one could find the city's banks, insurance brokerages, and fashionable shops as well as the homes of most of the city's white elite: namely, its merchants. In 1810 on one stretch in the affluent central section of the city, twenty-five of twenty-seven residents listed consecutively in the census owned anywhere from one to forty-five slaves. John Gadsby, the owner of forty-five slaves, also owned the Indian Queen Inn, one of early Baltimore's poshest hotels. Most of these slaves undoubtedly worked at the inn, yet, as in the homes of most of Gadsby's neighbors, some simply worked in the household.[55]

While rural white Marylanders derived economic and social status from the labor of slaves, for Baltimore's white residents (many of whom, ironically, gained their wealth by trading slave-produced goods) slaves enhanced such standing more by their presence than by their labor. Residents acquired black domestics by any means possible. In 1798 one Dr. Lancaze, a physician living on Commerce Street, owned a young slave woman, Rose, while hiring two other young female slaves. In that same year, Solomon Etting, a prosperous Jewish merchant who was himself denied the right to hold political office, held four slaves. In 1810, on one block facing Baltimore Street, nine neighbors owned slaves. One of them (William Cook, a bank president) held six, while four others (including Cook), who might well not have been able to afford to own slaves yet likely needed to keep up appearances in their fashionable neighborhood, hired free blacks who worked and lived in their homes.[56]

The disparate living patterns of slaves also held true for free blacks, whose lodgings were likewise spread throughout the city. Occupational proximity, rather than social cohesion (including racial), played the greatest role in residential patterns. Workers in early nineteenth-century American cities, before public transportation, most often lived close to their work, which spread free Negro laborers throughout the city. Economics rather than color thus dictated where individuals lived. Free blacks, slaves, and whites, especially those of the lower stratum, lived side by side, even sharing the same households. The Baltimore city directory for 1810 reveals that free black households were fairly evenly represented in all eight of the city's wards. A look at the residential patterns in the city during the early decades of the nineteenth century reveals, as was also true of Philadelphia, a growing residential segregation based on class more than race. Of the 135 free black household heads listed in the 1810 city directory, the largest number—over 42 percent—resided in Baltimore's five central wards, the area in which the city's most affluent whites lived as well. Another 37 percent lived in Ward 1, to the far west of the city. The smallest number of free blacks listed in the directory lived in the wards east of Jones' Falls, either in Old Town or at Fells Point, representing just over 14 and 6 percent, respectively. In 1815 all but twelve of fifty-eight property holders owned their homes in one of those two areas. At this time no dense clusters of black families appear to have existed as they would only a decade later, although more free Negroes lived on certain streets—North Street, Green Street, South Charles Street—and in specific areas—the streets, alleys, and courts near Federal Hill on the far south side of the city across the basin from Fells Point.[57]

In the decades following 1810 a perceptible shift of residential patterns for thousands of free blacks occurred in Baltimore. As the commercial core of the city became an area made up almost exclusively of affluent white families, black and white laborers were pushed toward the periphery of the city. Although as late as 1810 nearly half of the city's free Negroes lived in the central wards, by 1830 less than 10 percent resided in that part of the city.[58] The largest number moved to the western precincts, where developers had responded to the population boom by laying out new streets and erecting cheap tenement housing. The rest of the city's displaced free blacks relocated east of the commercial core, either across from Jones' Falls in Old Town, an area of the city where most were craftspeople and laborers, or into the narrow streets and alleys in and around Fells Point, where older, cheaper housing was merging with new row-house construction.[59]

Unlike many cities in the Deep South, where high walls enclosed yards containing slave quarters (thus often precluding the incorporation of alleys into the municipal design), Baltimore had a maze of alleyways and courtyards in which most of the city's free blacks soon came to make their homes. Invariably narrow (municipal codes required them to be no more than twelve feet wide) and lined with small, tightly wedged houses, the alleys of north and east Baltimore and Fells Point became densely populated corridors of black life. In 1820 such places as Happy Alley, Argyle Alley, Strawberry Alley, Petticoat Alley, and Apple Alley in or near Fells Point; Union Alley and Liberty Alley in Old Town; Bottle Alley, Whiskey Alley, and Brandy Alley in the core city; and Welcome Alley, Waggon Alley, Dutch Alley, Sugar Alley, and Honey Alley just to the west of the central city and to the south of it in the Federal Hill area were lined with small row houses in which multiple free black and slave families lived. The 1820 census lists eight consecutive free black households, consisting of twenty-eight free blacks and nine slaves, on Happy Alley. A similar cluster of twenty consecutive free black families, collectively containing 118 members, lived on Strawberry Alley.

White families still maintained residences in the alleys at this time, but their numbers declined rapidly. In 1810 less than a fifth of the free black household heads listed in the city directory made their homes in the city's alleys; by 1835 nearly four in ten black residents listed in the city directory resided in dwellings situated in alleys, a figure that excludes those families living in courtyards and in the yards in the rear of buildings. By 1835 ten times as many blacks as whites lived on alleys. In one part of Old Town in 1830, constituting several blocks between Forrest, East, and Douglass streets, the federal census lists fifty-one free black households out of the fifty-five dwellings, including twenty-six in a row. A decade later a similar cluster appeared in South Baltimore (the fastest-growing black residential area in the city at that time); fifty-six of sixty-one households were free black—including two separate blocks of twenty-five consecutive black households.[60]

While alleys early on became predominantly black areas of residence in Baltimore, the city as a whole did not so quickly exhibit such segregation. Similar racial clustering existed outside the alleyways in the various streets, lanes, and courtyards scattered throughout the city, but the degree of segregation remained low through the first three decades of the nineteenth century. As in other southern cities, no legal segregation existed in antebellum Baltimore, and all residential streets (and even the alleys) had black family dwellings interspersed with those of laboring and poor whites. Yet segregation emerged to some degree, only marginally because of white prejudice. Black Baltimoreans over time tended to create neighborhoods of their own, seeking out one another as neighbors for solidarity and security. Only after 1830 did large corridors of residential clustering proliferate, reflecting the economic segregation of Baltimore's working-class populace. In that sense, the city's black population itself remained relatively unsegregated. Unlike in Charleston, where free Negroes differentiated themselves according to the lightness of their skin, no such segregated black community appears to have developed in Baltimore. Neighborhoods were mixed by race and occupation, as lower-class blacks and mulattoes, slave and free, lived in austere dwellings in close proximity to one another and to working-class and poorer whites, in the city's courtyards and alleys.[61]

Because the federal censuses did not designate blacks and mulattoes prior to 1850, obtaining an accurate picture of the interaction between those of different hue is difficult. Few other records exist that indicate this distinction, perhaps reflecting the lack of emphasis the society at large placed on the skin color of its black population. In such Deep South places as South Carolina, Louisiana, and Alabama large black populations forced whites to view mixed-blacks as allies, but Maryland's demographics engendered no such perceived threat to the racial order. Thus prior to 1850, when the national government mandated recording such distinctions, Marylanders appear to have been relatively unconcerned about registering color differentiations. By cross-referencing the 1850 federal census, which provides ages and skin colors, among other information, with the Baltimore city directory, which lists the addresses and occupations of the city's inhabitants, a rich mixture of hues emerges in the city's growing neighborhoods, which likely reflects the situation in the years prior to 1830.

Along Slemmer's Alley, which ran for only four city blocks just east of Jones' Falls in the southernmost part of Old Town (created in the early 1820s when the city filled in a large section of the basin just to the west of Fells Point), one can find a cross section of the city's free Negroes.[62] A survey of the residences along Slemmer's Alley illustrates the pockets of black households on such minor streets. The 1827 city directory, the first to include Slemmer's Alley, registered just eight households—five white and three black. Just over two decades later, in 1849 and 1850, the ratio of black and white families remained largely the same, but now at least fifteen black families (compared with twenty-nine white households) resided on Slemmer's Alley, including five consecutive households of free blacks clustered midway along the narrow street. At No. 30 Emile Dubois, a forty-year-old mulatto barber, lived with his thirty-year-old mulatto wife, Amelia, both of whom were literate, and their two mulatto daughters, eight-year-old Phillipa (who attended one of the city's black primary schools) and two-year-old Scoconde. Barbering was a potentially lucrative occupation, and free black "tonsorial artists" had a virtual monopoly on the trade in Baltimore as well as in many other antebellum cities. Though he did not own property, Dubois appears to have been reasonably successful at his craft, for in his home lived two apprentices, his younger brother, Samuel, a twenty-year-old mulatto, and Patrick Taylor, a sixteen-year-old black. Also residing in the house were Dubois's mother, Louisa, a fifty-five-year-old mulatto.

Next door to Dubois, at 28 Slemmer's Alley, Evans Tubman, a thirty-year-old mulatto seaman, lived with his mulatto family, including his wife, Emily, aged twenty-five, and their two children, William and James, aged six and three. Two other families lived in Tubman's dwelling: Eliza L. Bennett, a twenty-eight-year-old illiterate mulatto who was very likely the mother of the two mulatto children in the household, six-year-old Nathaniel and four-year-old John; and George and Mary Cornish, aged fifty and thirty, respectively, who were black and illiterate.

On Dubois's other side, at 32 Slemmer's Alley, lived Theodore Johnson, a thirty-year-old black laborer; his wife, Nancy, aged thirty-one and black, who, like her husband, was illiterate; two mulatto children, who do not appear to have been their own, Charles Purnell, aged twelve and in school, and Sarah A. Johnson, ten months old; and Anne Wilson, an illiterate black laundress, aged forty, and her two children, Harriet and Gilbert, aged six and four months, respectively. Like Charles Purnell, Harriet Wilson attended school. Across the street, at 29 Slemmer's Alley, lived Evan Gaines, a forty-year-old black stevedore, with his thirty-five-year-old black wife, Nancy. Living in the same dwelling were twenty-nine-year-old Susan Egleston and her five-year-old daughter, Mary, both black. All of the members of the five households has been born in Maryland.

This pocket of black households in Slemmer's Alley was wedged between the white households and nine black households interspersed along the four-block concourse. Its ratio of black and white was typical of most working-class neighborhoods in the outlying areas of Baltimore in the 1820s and 1830s. Many of these neighborhoods' white residents occupied the same occupational and economic positions as their black neighbors—seamstresses, laborers, and small tradespeople—and rented their houses from largely white landlords. Sir Charles Lyell, visiting Baltimore in 1841 as part of a tour of the nation, observed the working people of the city and was "reminded for the first time of the poorer inhabitants of a large European city by the mean dwellings and dress of the labouring class, both coloured and white."[63]

Yet, as can be seen in the case of Slemmer's Alley, occupational distinctions had begun to create subtle yet discernible residential patterns in the Baltimore streets. Although in Baltimore during the first half of the nineteenth century many free blacks, mulattoes, working-class whites, and even slaves coexisted in similar social and economic conditions, generally without significant class and racial tensions, as early as the 1820s its occupational hierarchy (which reserved trades largely for whites and unskilled labor largely for blacks) had noticeably affected the composition of those people living with one another. In 1819, of the ninety-four white household heads listed in the city directory as living on Happy Alley (located in the eastern part of Fells Point), nearly 80 percent plied some form of trade, either skilled or semiskilled (such as blacksmiths, pilots, seamstresses, and carters), or owned a small business. Conversely, just 16 percent were unskilled laborers or laundresses. Just 5 percent listed no occupation, signifying unemployment or the inability to work. Among twenty black residents, 30 percent had skilled or semiskilled occupations, while the remaining 70 percent were unskilled. By 1827 the black percentages remained similar; approximately 34 percent possessed trades, 60 percent were unskilled, and the remaining 6 percent did not list an occupation. The occupational profile of whites living in the alley, however, appears somewhat different. Of the fifty-nine white households in the alley, just over 60 percent held trades, 15 percent were unskilled, and nearly 25 percent listed no occupation.[64]

The occupational and racial transformation of Honey Alley, or later Little Hughes Street (located near Federal Hill in the south part of town) was even more dramatic than Happy Alley's. Eleven white household heads resided in Honey Alley in 1819; of them, eight were skilled or semiskilled, two were unskilled, and one listed no occupation. In the same year, of the fifteen black household heads, seven had trades, and eight were unskilled. In 1827 ten whites were listed; of them, just three had trades, one was unskilled, and the remaining six listed no occupations. Of the ten black residents listed, six were skilled or semiskilled, three were unskilled, and one listed no occupation. A canvass of Montgomery Street, near Federal Hill, confirms the trend for white tradespeople to move away from alleys onto main thoroughfares. In 1819, of the forty-two who were listed, more than three-fourths had trades, while just one-fourth was unskilled. In 1827, of the forty-five listings, thirty were tradespeople, two were unskilled, and thirteen listed no occupations, ten of those being married women. If Happy Alley and Honey Alley are any indication, the whites who continued to reside on such secondary streets tended to hold unskilled occupations, suggesting a gradual yet noticeable migration away from alleys to main streets that was based more on occupational than racial distinctions.[65]

The entwinement of occupational and residential patterns in Baltimore owed its tight weave largely to the city's employment trends. For free black men and women in Baltimore, an equally noticeable pattern of occupational exclusion emerged in the decades immediately following the turn of the century. Just as free blacks appear to have been able to find ready employment in the city, so did whites begin to restrict them to the most unskilled positions in Baltimore's work force. Prior to the great influx of foreign immigrants to the city in the 1840s and 1850s, free blacks had little competition from whites and even hired slaves for those low-paying, menial positions, especially as wage laborers, who generally were hired by the day or week and earned between fifty and seventy-five cents per day. The federal census for 1820 lists only 1,359 foreign-born whites of a total of 48,055 whites in the city, constituting just 2.8 percent of the population.[66]

Driven by a quest for economic and social advancement, native whites who migrated to the city aspired to better forms of employment, particularly the mechanical trades. Consequently, between 1796 and 1814 the proportion of white unskilled laborers in the city's occupational structure decreased substantially. The total number of mechanics, or skilled craftsmen, increased by nearly 73 percent, and their proportion of the total white work force grew from 45.3 percent to 48.6 percent. During the same period the number of unskilled white laborers decreased by just under 10 percent, while its proportion of the city's workers decreased even more dramatically, from 18.4 percent to 10.3 percent.[67]

As Baltimore attracted skilled laborers, many formerly unskilled whites acquired trade skills that allowed them to move into the ranks of the more desirable skilled trades—trades that largely excluded black workers. Consequently, fewer whites during the years prior to 1830 were engaging in common labor. As black men increasingly filled these positions, many native whites refused to consider taking them, even in times of dire need, characterizing them increasingly as "nigger work." Though Ira Berlin has contended that in the Upper South "racial prejudice relegated most free Negroes to the meanest drudgery at the lowest pay," it would seem that white ambition, as well as racial prejudice, helped plant the seeds of the free black occupational caste.[68]

The occupational structure of Baltimore's free blacks was totally unlike that of free blacks in the Deep South cities of New Orleans and Charleston some years later. In 1850 more than nine in ten free black workers in New Orleans were in the skilled trades; a decade later in Charleston, three-fourths of free black men worked as skilled tradesmen. Fewer than one in five free men of color in the South Carolina port worked as common laborers, and just one in twenty held nonmanual occupations as shopkeepers. Similarly, six out of ten free black women in Charleston worked as semiskilled dressmakers, mantua makers (used in caulking ships), and seamstresses; less than one-fourth worked as laundresses and even fewer as domestic workers. Slaves, outnumbering free Negroes more than four to one, served as the primary source of unskilled labor in Charleston, where, with a relatively small white population, an even smaller number of free blacks held an important niche in the city's skilled occupational structure. In Baltimore a large and growing population of free blacks and a dwindling number of slaves proved the inverse of the New Orleans and Charleston experiences.[69]

One can find the role of free blacks as laborers in Baltimore, both actual and assumed in the minds of whites, nowhere more evident than during the city's defense in the War of 1812. In 1814, during the crisis of an approaching British invasion, Baltimore's Committee of Vigilance supervised the erection of defensive earthworks around the city's perimeter. Baltimore's "able bodied free men of colour," barred from the state militia (though having served in the Revolutionary War and currently on privateering vessels), were required "to turn out and labour on the Fortifications or other works;

and in case of refusal to call on the commanders of the several companies of exempts to assist in enforcing such persons to turn out and labour." The city had acted similarly in 1794, when David Stoddard, a Fells Point shipbuilder, assembled free black work crews each morning to repair the fort guarding the basin in the wake of the Saint-Domingue rebellion. Though Baltimore's ambitious community accepted free Negroes into its ranks in its pursuit of progress, the white majority found ways to preserve the racial ordering of its society. Black people were regarded as laborers first, and any ambitions on their part were not to interfere with that assigned role. Imposing labor restrictions on free Negroes, whether forced in time of crisis or tacit in time of peace, served such purposes quite well.[70]

The opportunities for free black women in Baltimore were even more limited than they were for black men. Even more so than their male counterparts, black women were largely unskilled during slavery.[71] Once free, the overwhelming majority of women who found employment outside domestic service made their livings by providing services traditionally associated with household duties. After 1817 more than nine out of ten women household heads were employed as laundresses, washing clothes for the city's upper- and middle-class whites. In 1819 nearly a third of the city's washerwomen lived at Fells Point. They were most likely women whose husbands had gone to sea as sailors—a particularly poor-paying occupation. These women were thus forced to provide an income for themselves and their families during their spouses' numerous and often lengthy absences. Most of those other few worked as cooks, seamstresses, midwives, and spinsters. A growing number of women made their livings as hucksters, or street vendors, who hawked various goods—fruits, vegetables, oysters, clothing, handmade items—from small stands on the streets and near the markets. A few managed to open their own businesses, generally small shops, oyster cellars, cook houses, and one in 1819 ran a boardinghouse. These few black businesswomen's achievements are particularly remarkable considering that the capital outlay required to open and maintain such a venture was exorbitant for women who received extremely low pay for long hours of washing and mending clothes and cooking meals.[72]

Occasionally, free blacks in the city operated joint ventures with whites to pool capital to open a business and perhaps to obtain as wide a clientele as possible. One raid on a Baltimore gambling den revealed that it was run by three white men and a free Negro. Such partnerships, however, appear to have been limited in number, and as the century progressed, fewer black Baltimoreans, both men and women, found themselves able to open their own businesses. More went into occupations that did not involve such a high initial cost. The overwhelming majority of free Negroes found work as common laborers.[73]

That Baltimore free blacks were being forced into unskilled occupations before 1830 can be seen nowhere better than in the city directories. Between 1817 and 1827 the number of free black householders increased by more than 150 percent, from 402 to 1,012. In 1810 those who held the most unskilled positions—laborers and laundresses—constituted 32.3 percent of the total number of householders with listed occupations (see table 13). By 1827 that number had risen to 57.4 percent, meaning that well over half of all employed free black householders earned their livings as either unskilled laborers or laundresses. Although in 1810, 22 household heads had worked in the most menial of occupations, by 1827, 410 did so, a more than eighteenfold increase, far outstripping the growth of householders as a whole. While the number of occupations in which free Negroes were employed rose from twenty-nine in 1810 to seventy in 1827, an increasingly smaller percentage of black workers engaged in those trades. Baltimore free blacks

Table 13. Free Black Occupations in Baltimore, 1810, 1819, and 1827

Occupation	1810 No.	%	1819 No.	%	1827 No.	%
Laborer	19	27.9	188	38.5	221	30.9
Barber	13	19.1	25	5.1	24	3.4
Cook shop	8	11.8	5	1.0	0	0.0
Carter	5	7.4	32	6.6	25	3.5
Mariner	5	7.4	15	3.1	15	2.1
Oyster house	4	5.9	10	2.0	0	0.0
Laundress	3	4.4	118	24.2	189	26.5
Waiter	3	4.4	10	2.0	32	4.5
Drayman	3	4.4	6	1.2	47	6.6
Blacksmith	3	4.4	10	2.0	16	2.2
Boot black	1	1.5	25	5.1	7	1.0
Sawyer	0	0.0	5	1.0	75	10.5
Caulker	0	0.0	15	3.1	24	3.4
Brickmaker	0	0.0	10	2.0	14	2.0
Porter	1	1.5	9	1.8	2	0.3
Whitewasher	0	0.0	1	0.2	7	1.0
Hack Driver	0	0.0	0	0.0	8	1.1
Huckster	0	0.0	4	0.8	8	1.1

Sources: Fry, *Baltimore Directory for 1810*, passim; Jackson, *Baltimore Directory, Corrected up to June, 1819*; Matchett, *Baltimore Directory for 1827*.

constituted a significant part of the city's laboring population, but they did so by occupying its lower stratum, a level that engaged proportionally fewer of the city's whites as the century progressed.[74]

By 1810 black laborers in Baltimore were already experiencing difficulty maintaining their grasp on even the lowest rung of the city's economic ladder. When economic times soured, desperate white workers supplanted black laborers in even the meanest laboring positions. Because its economic base was so heavily dependent on shipping and export, Baltimore became especially sensitive to the vagaries of national and international market fluctuations. The rise and fall of the demand for grain, and concomitantly its price, produced numerous downturns in the local economy, which were often not felt as keenly by the rest of the nation. International political and economic events of the Jeffersonian and Jacksonian eras affected the Baltimore economy acutely; the grain embargo of 1808, the Napoleonic conflicts, the War of 1812, and the panics of 1819 and 1837 caused especially great hardships in the city.[75] As businesses and shipyards hired and released laborers in response to market fluctuations, day laborers often were put out of work for extended periods of time and scrambled for income. Unemployment soared, felt most keenly by black workers (especially by the growing number of black women in the work force), who found employment difficult to obtain in the face of sharpened racial prejudice. The city directories provide some indication of growing black unemployment, which accelerated especially after 1820. In 1819 only fourteen free black householders were listed without occupation, six of whom were women. By 1827 the total number had grown more than tenfold, to 143, approximately 47 of whom were women. By 1835 the free black heads of households without occupations had again more than doubled, to 320, more than 56 percent of whom were women. While some of these householders without occupations might have been elderly or recent arrivals to the city, they could not have accounted for such a dramatic increase over the course of nearly two decades.[76]

❖   ❖   ❖

By the end of the 1820s free black residents of Baltimore had experienced the best of times but were beginning to see the worst of times. The city offered an astonishing variety of employment opportunities for black people, which had brought both freedpeople and slaves in large numbers from the countryside to fill them. During the three decades following the Constitution's ratification, while the nation began to build itself politically, economically, and ideologically, Baltimore's black people fashioned their new lives as well, moving quickly into a wide array of occupations made available by the city's booming economy and finding their own independence in an environment that was secure enough to allow them to do so. Yet just as the nation was jolted out of its euphoria of liberty by encountering the grim realities of a harsh world market, Baltimore would find itself plagued now by the same foreign trade that had created its looming stature only decades earlier. Black workers, finding their employment opportunities restricted largely to unskilled occupations, witnessed even their tenuous position at the lower end of the economic strata threatened, both by an unstable economy and the resultant heightening of racial prejudice. Historians normally attribute this hardened racism to Nat Turner's 1831 slave rebellion in Southampton County, Virginia, but in Baltimore the process began earlier and involved forces far more varied and complex.[77]

Despite such hardships, Baltimore's black residents clung tenaciously to their place in a city that many believed would provide true freedom. Precisely as black Baltimoreans' economic situation deteriorated, they began to forge a web of social institutions and organizations that would allow many of them to achieve extraordinary social progress. In many ways the economic hardships experienced by the city's free Negroes and slaves solidified them into a unified people. In their struggle to maintain their autonomous existences, black Baltimoreans created a social shield that would protect them as Baltimore's once-liberal racial mood worsened in the face of a host of problems that beset the city during the three decades before the Civil War. In the process Baltimore's African Americans built a community.

PART 2

A Community of Commitment, ca. 1820–60

5

Climbing Jacob's Ladder

In June of 1793 Thomas Jones advertised in the *Maryland Journal and Baltimore Advertiser*, offering a forty dollar reward for the return of his slave Sam, who had recently escaped from the Baltimore County planter to whom Jones had hired him. In addition to a physical description of his escaped chattel, the circumstances of his escape, and his possible destination (in this case, Baltimore Town), all of which were customary in such advertisements, Jones included what he considered the primary motivation for his bondman's flight. "He was raised in a family of religious persons, commonly called Methodists," wrote Jones, "and has lived with some of them for years past, on terms of perfect equality; . . . he has been in the use of instructing and exhorting his fellow-creatures, of all colours, in matters of religious duty. . . . the refusal to continue him on these terms, the subscriber is instructed, has given him offence, and is the sole cause of his absconding."[1]

Thomas Jones's illuminating advertisement does far more than suggest the fears of many late eighteenth-century Marylanders who found little good in the Methodists' equal treatment of Negroes within their denomination. Jones provides evidence of the importance of religion in his slave's life, as well as the hopes and aspirations the tenets of Methodism raised among black people for their own futures, both in this life and beyond. Those Maryland whites who viewed the spiritual freedom allowed to black members of the church as dangerous to the maintenance of the social order feared such leveling of the races, especially when it involved slaves. Treating Africans as the spiritual equals of whites would not only ruin slave members but also cause free persons of color to expect more liberties than those to which they should be entitled. One of those liberties would soon cause great anxiety among many white Marylanders: the development of autonomous black churches.

For nineteenth-century black Americans, slaves and former slaves, rural and urban alike, no single guiding force provided more motivation and hope for the future in their daily lives than religion. The spiritual inspiration provided by, in Sterling Stuckey's words, "the African version of Christianity marked by an awareness of the limits of the religion of whites" formed a foundation for black people's daily search for the more secular gratifications of self-respect and dignity in an oppressive, demeaning existence.[2] Scripture relieved the suffering by giving them hope not only for this world but also for the everlasting. As a source of inspiration and, perhaps most important, perseverance, the black church was without peer. As Martin R. Delany, a Harvard-educated physician, intellectual, and civil rights activist, wrote in 1849 in *North Star* (the abolitionist newspaper founded by the most famous black ex-Baltimorean, Frederick Douglass), "As among our people, generally, the Church is the Alpha and the Omega of all things."[3]

Once established, black churches quickly became the social, political, economic, educational, and even cultural centers of the Baltimore black community. Black Baltimoreans' earliest organized efforts at economic self-help, education, and political organization revolved around black churches. Lacking the wide class stratification based on wealth that characterized white society, Baltimore's African Americans found other means by which to attain social status. In that vein, black churches were crucial, for they often served as proving grounds for aspiring leaders of the black community and provided an essential rostrum for the development of oratorical skills. Though the Methodist church had by far the largest number of the city's black communicants, by mid-century four other major denominations—Baptist, Episcopalian, Presbyterian, and Catholic—provided centers of black worship in the city. By 1850 Baltimore had the greatest denominational variety of black churches of any city in the nation, and on the eve of the Civil War a Baltimore correspondent to New York's *Weekly Anglo-African* reported confidently that "no city where I have been can boast of better churches among our people. Baltimore churches are not a whit behind, either in beauty or attendance, for our people are a church going people."[4] Obtaining and maintaining religious independence, however, proved a long, difficult process for many of these Baltimore congregations. Once established, however, the African churches as centers of organization served as anchors for what would become a mature black community in the growing city and for the formation of a distinctly urban, Baltimore, and African American consciousness.

The seed of the independent black church movement in the Upper South, and ultimately Baltimore, sprang in many ways during the era of the American Revolution. Ironically, as the founding fathers tried to justify on intellectual grounds the obvious contradiction of establishing a government based on republican egalitarianism while maintaining a society based on racial exclusion, black Americans took advantage of the ideological climate of political independence and individual liberty to form their own religious communities. Obtaining enough freedom to establish black churches and ultimately congregations that were independent of white control, however, proved a long and tortuous effort. Although some southern evangelicals might have once been willing to accept black residents as Christian brethren, few by the turn of the nineteenth century were inclined to grant them any liberty that had such a potentially dangerous consequence: the freedom to interpret the Bible—and thus their ultimate destinies—for themselves.

The postrevolutionary era brought especially large numbers of black people onto the membership rolls of organized churches. The process started earlier in the century, when the Great Awakening spawned waves of evangelical revivals, which introduced many slaves and former slaves to Christianity. As the established denominations splintered in the face of the movement's emotionalism, new evangelical sects sprang up and quickly gained adherents. Those sects that saw the most dramatic growth in the Upper South were Methodists, Baptists, and, for a time, Presbyterians. Eschewing the formalism that had characterized the Anglican church and emphasizing individual salvation, these dissident groups took advantage of postrevolutionary egalitarianism and welcomed black members into their congregations, asking only that they accept Christ as their savior as the requirement for acceptance. The Methodists and Baptists consequently absorbed the great majority of black Christians, and their ranks swelled with the influx of both slaves and free blacks, as postwar emancipations in the Upper South created a sizable class of black people capable of choosing their own denomination and congregation.[5]

Baptists, who found especial strength in the colonies and states of the Deep South, were the first of the southern denominations to accept black Christians formally into their fold.[6] In Maryland, however, Methodism had the greatest initial impact of the evangelical sects. A reform movement against the Anglican church led by the Anglican dissident John Wesley, Methodism stressed spiritualism over ritual and emotional faith over rote liturgy.[7] The first Methodist society in America was organized in 1764 by Robert Strawbridge at Sam's Creek in rural Frederick County, Maryland. That the fledgling denomination, which scorned vanity or inequality of any kind, included African Americans as charter members made no small contribution to the wide appeal of Methodism in the state, as well as in neighboring Pennsylvania and Delaware. The powerful black orator "Black Harry" Hosier, who traveled and preached with such early Methodist leaders as

Francis Asbury and Thomas Coke, also helped attract many slaves and free blacks to the new faith. Within a year two churches opened in the yet small community of Baltimore Town, at Lovely Lane and Strawberry Alley. Of the eleven denominations that maintained churches or meetinghouses in the city in 1801, Methodists had opened the most churches—three. By 1815 one out of every fourteen Baltimoreans was a Methodist; among the earliest members of each of those congregations were a number of city residents who were black.[8]

Methodism held particularly great appeal for those of African heritage. In many ways a product of the Revolution itself, the church exhibited a republican spirit that contributed much to the demise of the Anglican church in the South and attracted former slaves, as well as common whites, to its ranks. Its simplicity and informality, characterized by its emotional, often extemporaneous preaching rather than highly intellectual sermons, as well as its genuine warmth and evangelical fervor, led many black people into the fold. The plain, often untrained itinerant preachers, scorned by seminary-trained ministers from other denominations, found their message welcomed by those of similar low economic positions, both white and black.[9]

The church's emphasis on class meetings—small groups of ten to twenty parishioners generally meeting weekly in private homes and forming the basis of active membership in the congregation—created an appealing informal setting in which black men and women could discuss as equals a particular scriptural passage selected by the leader, share individual concerns, or spend time in prayer. Class meetings promoted scriptural understanding not always available at regular church services and offered the opportunity for the free exchange of ideas, a liberty southern whites rarely granted to black people. In 1792 there were nearly 14,000 black Methodists nationwide; by 1815 there were over 43,000, representing a quarter of the total number of Methodists in the United States. Virtually all of these black members were in the southern states.[10]

Perhaps the greatest contributing factor in this move of thousands of African Americans into the Methodist church was the church's early opposition to the institution of slavery. As early as 1743 John Wesley, Methodism's spiritual father, had included in the General Rules the prohibition of "the buying or selling the bodies and souls of men, women, and children, with an intention to enslave them." Wesley's position had not mellowed thirty years later when he wrote in his *Thoughts upon Slavery* that "no circumstances can make it necessary for a man to burst asunder all the ties of humanity" by justifying a "Villainy" such as slavery. With such precedent, nourished by the recent Revolution, the Quakers' antislavery stance, and the reformist Methodist "conscience," it is little wonder that American Methodists felt pressured to take an official stance against the practice.[11]

In the 1780s (especially after 1784, when American Methodist church leaders officially severed ties with the Church of England and established the Methodist Episcopal Church of America) Methodist preachers vigorously denounced the institution of slavery as contrary to both natural law and the Christian religion. Led by such notable examples as the itinerant preacher Freeborn Garrettson (who between 1775 and 1783 freed his own slaves and became one of the earliest and most widely traveled of the antislavery preachers and, in the words of his biographer, "endeavoured frequently to inculcate the doctrine of freedom in a private way" to his black converts), such Maryland ministers as Thomas Haskins sermonized that "perpetual bondage and slavery is repugnant to the pure precepts of the Gospel of Jesus Christ." At the 1780 General Conference Methodists required that all traveling preachers set their slaves free. At the 1796 General Conference, held at Christmastide in Baltimore, Methodist leaders pronounced African slavery a "great evil" and ruled that *all* those who attained official positions in the church must emancipate their slaves, that those members of the laity of the church who sold their slaves would be excluded from the church, and that they could purchase slaves only on the condition that they and their offspring be freed after a term of service. By that time thousands of newly emancipated slaves had joined and regularly attended the Methodist church, attracted by numerous revivals and inspired by its stance against their former bondage. Baltimore's autonomous freedpeople and slaves were in the vanguard of such a movement.[12]

Initially, Baltimore's white Methodists did nothing to discourage black residents from participating in their faith, partly because they needed bodies in their upstart churches but far more important because their belief in spiritual equality served as a bulwark to their faith. White and black Methodists together built the chapels at Lovely Lane and Strawberry Alley, and at least in the beginning it appears that members of the small congregations worshiped in nearly complete equality. Seating arrangements appear to have been nondiscriminatory, and deceased black members were buried in the same Methodist burial grounds where white members were interred.[13]

Among Baltimore's white Methodists, church membership came predominantly from the city's "middling classes": small merchants and shopkeepers, especially artisans. They accepted a more democratized doctrine of salvation than that offered by the older churches, one that eschewed the idea of predestination and offered to all social classes the hope for grace. The autonomy granted local congregations by the church hierarchy offered the

Methodist laity the opportunity to aspire to posts of authority. Positions of leadership in the local church appealed to status-conscious mechanics as an important avenue for social mobility. Guided by the church's official Doctrine and Discipline, mechanics fused religious notions with their personal ambition to form a creed of self-discipline, thrift, industry, and sobriety, with which they would separate themselves from the lower-class subculture, where drinking, gambling, rioting, and carousing prevailed. Benevolent whites believed they could work great benefit for society by taking black members into the church and by teaching those members—especially those who were free—to practice such doctrines as well, particularly by instilling in them a strong work ethic (ironically, something slaveholding whites thought former field workers lacked). Thus, in free labor Baltimore, beneath the veneer of a quest for conversion, lay the belief of even "levelling" Methodists that such religious instruction not only would assist in racial control but also would ensure dutiful and diligent laborers—a concern of nearly all white business-people, regardless of denomination or "enthusiasm."[14]

For a few years the Baltimore Methodist church enforced the denomination's stance against slavery. Between 1799 and 1801 parishioners made eight purchases of slaves, all of whom the conference manumitted gradually, establishing individual terms of bondage from four and a half to sixteen years in length. On 8 August 1799 James McCannon purchased Caesar, "a boy . . . about 14 years old . . . to serve 4½ years." Similarly, on 14 September 1801 "James Ives having a female black child in his poss[ess]ion about four years old he submitted to the Quarterly Meeting Conference the time she ou[gh]t to serve him to pay for her raising—and the Conference determined that she should serve him till she is twenty-one years old. She is the[re]fore to be free in the year of our Lord 1817." Although the church ultimately found it necessary to retreat considerably from its stance against slavery and restrictions imposed by the General Conference grew less frequent, Methodists continued to convert slaves and to plead for the amelioration of slavery's brutality.[15]

Church membership was particularly important to African Americans. The Methodist church provided an essential social undergirding upon which black Christians could build their lives in the new urban setting. By performing certain secular services, such as marriages, funerals, and baptisms, the church legitimized—though by white standards—black people's seemingly nebulous existences, which were by no means ensured even after their often hard-won independence. The Baltimore Methodist churches accepted both slaves and free blacks into their congregations, apparently not differentiating between the two. Between 1799 and 1802, 287 black residents—

both slave and free—were approved for trial membership (in contrast to 690 whites) and were listed as members of the various classes.[16]

Black members, both slave and free, were married in the city's Methodist churches. Because slave marriages were not recognized by law and because formal ceremonies on the plantation occurred only rarely, perhaps nowhere existed a more telling example of the freedoms available to black people in the city (as opposed to the slavery of the countryside) than the ability to be pronounced husband and wife in a Baltimore church, with the same formal ceremony that whites enjoyed, and by an ordained minister. As William Wells Brown remarked, "It must be admitted that the blacks always preferred being married by a clergyman."[17]

Between 1806 and 1809 Methodist ministers in the churches of the Baltimore City Station performed at least thirty-two marriage ceremonies for black parishioners. Most weddings involved free persons of color, but occasionally ministers joined together free blacks and slaves—only after receiving permission from the slave's master. On 2 January 1808 the Reverend Michael Coate married James Batten, a free man, and Sylvia Mackrel, a slave woman, with "liberty from her master J. Gitchel." Occasionally, two slaves were married in a formal church ceremony, such as on 10 December 1807 when the white minister Seely Bunn married Peter and Lucy, with "liberty from Mr. H. Fischer master of sd. persons." That the Methodist church would perform such services for black Methodists as they did for whites no doubt added to the growth of the denomination's black ranks. By 1800 black people made up over 35 percent of Baltimore's Methodist population, and in 1815 nearly half of the city's 6,600 parishioners had dark skin.[18]

In addition to its spiritual value a church contributed greatly to the concept of self-control. Black parishioners gathered on Sundays to worship for their own spiritual fulfillment and for the image that regular attendance engendered, both among their own people and among whites attending the same worship services. The Methodist creed of thrift, diligence, and sobriety as keys to success, which white churchgoers expected of the black members, also included piety and regular devotions. Ambitious black Baltimoreans realized that in a society where whites dictated norms and mores, their hope for advancement often hinged on public conformity to such behavior.[19]

Because the church served as a springboard for social status within the black community and offered the chance to learn to read, conspicuous attendance—especially at class meetings—was essential. In 1799, in the Baltimore Methodist churches, there were 290 black members enrolled in twelve classes, all of which were led by white men. By 1803 the number had grown to 482 in sixteen classes, representing 36 percent of the members who attended classes in the city. Included were many free blacks who would later establish themselves as some of the most influential in the city's black community: Jacob Gilliard, William Watkins, Nero Graves, Benjamin Lynch, George Hackett, and Stephen Hill, among others.[20]

Despite the support black members gave to their congregations (or perhaps in response to it), Baltimore's white Methodists increasingly found reason to segregate their Sabbaths. Even those who were most liberal on the issue of slavery took care to exert and maintain control over anything or anyone they thought might potentially be unruly. At the same time that they encouraged participation in the Christian religion, they wished to avoid the disruptive, distinctly Africanized version of religion so prevalent on the plantation and for which their black members still had a penchant (no matter how appealing the antislavery stance of early Quakers might have been, few Africans found the Quakers' quiet, introspective meetings compelling). White Methodists appear to have had only limited success. After observing a Baltimore mixed service, the European visitor Frances Trollope sneered that she was "much amused . . . by the vehemence of the negro part of the congregation; they seemed determined to bellow louder than all the rest, to show at once their piety and their equality." Frederick Law Olmsted labeled it more simply, calling black worship practices a "mockery of religion."[21] Neither of the observers appears to have noticed that many southern whites behaved similarly in their own evangelical services.

White Methodists kept close watch on the religious practices of their black communicants. Seating already segregated by class now became further divided by race, in part to preserve peace within churches as well as to safeguard the caste structure of Maryland society. Wayward black members were expelled for moral offenses against the church. On 29 July 1801 Jane Hall was removed for "evil speaking," while on the same day Ann Lemmon was censured for "marrying an unawakened person." Some sympathetic observers believed that such vigilance (aimed at white members as well but particularly at black communicants) was largely unwarranted. The Baltimore-based Maryland Society for Promoting the Abolition of Slavery reported to the American Convention of Antislavery Societies in Philadelphia in 1796 that "a large number of them appear religiously disposed as is manifested by their attachment to places of Worship—numbers of them Zealously attending the same, particularly amongst the Society of Methodists— which Society have liberally appropriated a part of one of their Meeting houses, for their religious Instructions, some of their Number attending with them for that purpose, & to see that good order & decorum is preserved in their Meetings, which appear for the most part to be reputedly conducted."[22]

Non-Methodists in Maryland found ample reason to condemn the social leveling that they attributed to the Wesleyan faith above all others. Many blamed all slave misbehavior and racial unrest—especially slave escapes—on the Methodists. In 1790 George French of Georgetown advertised for his fugitive bondman, Charles, who left on Christmas eve, claiming that "he pretends to be a Methodist, and can deliver many text of Scripture, which he is fond of doing." Similarly, the Baltimorean Samuel Smith claimed that his escaped slave man, Allick, "affects to be a Methodist, and may probably be furnished with a forged pass as a freeman." Fearing the Methodists' democratic tendencies threatened the social order, Marylanders pressured them to refrain from treating black members as equals.[23]

In Baltimore, as in the Upper South in general, white members of mixed churches suffered increased tensions from the conflict between Christian fellowship and the southern racial system. As one historian has observed, fellowship required that all church members be treated alike, yet the maintenance of slavery in Maryland inclined white parishioners to treat all black members, slave as well as free, differently.[24] By the final decade of the eighteenth century, once they had welcomed thousands of new converts to their chapels and the fervor of the Revolution's legacy had cooled, white Baltimore Methodists began to withdraw from their earlier commitment to racial equality before God. Black Methodist parishioners now found their status in the churches circumscribed as sorely as in society itself. Although some urban slaveowners continued to allow their bondpeople to sit with them in the family pew, more often white parishioners assigned black worshipers, both free and slave, to seats in the rear of the church and the loft, commonly called the "African corner," or the "Nigger pews." This would ensure social decorum and protect the pecuniary value of those coveted white pews at the front of the chapel, farthest from the black seats.[25]

Black Methodists had no decision-making power in the various churches, were forced to wait for white members to receive communion before being allowed to do so themselves, and were not considered for ordination as ministers in the faith prior to 1800. While white Methodists might have espoused the doctrines of the equality of souls before God and maintained a stance opposing slavery, they were unable to offer black Methodists opportunity for positions of leadership in their churches. Moreover, evening and Sabbath school classes were segregated by both race and sex and were rarely taught by any but whites. Not until 1809 did a black man, Daniel Coker, achieve the status of class leader in the Baltimore City Station Methodist churches.[26]

Finally, black Christians in Baltimore were quickly denied the privilege of being buried in church cemeteries. Throughout the city's early history, white Baltimore masters on occasion buried their most beloved black servants and slaves on the grounds of their homes or with them in burial plots and crypts. Since the city made no provision for public slave cemeteries, free blacks and slaves alike were buried in the city's unpaved streets. Although initially Baltimore's mixed Methodist churches allowed their black members to be buried in the church grounds (much as the Catholics did), once large numbers of black and white residents had outgrown the space available for common burial, white churches began to refrain from burying black members in the increasingly crowded churchyards. Consequently, just before the turn of the nineteenth century the city purchased land for potter's fields, or public burying grounds, to bury its poor at public expense. Starting in the 1820s black residents who could afford to bury their own could do so in various black churchyards or in one of the two independent African cemeteries established as early as 1822.[27]

Any form of Christianity that even entertained the notion of racial inequality or the desirability of worship along racial lines struck black Americans as a repudiation of the tenets of the religion and an abomination to be avoided. Yet racial discrimination alone did not prompt the movement for black ecclesiastical independence that carried thousands of African Americans from the ranks of white churches into their own centers of worship. The primary motivation grew from reasons far deeper and more spiritual. Whites dictated the decorum at church services, and despite the evangelicalism of the Methodist church, there was little room for the spontaneity, singing, choral responses, and communal interplay vital to the religious life of the slave community. White hymns were the rule; black spirituals were unacceptable. Whites disdained the animated style of black worship. Even Bishop Francis Asbury, a friend of black Methodists, lamented while visiting friends that an "apparently thoughtless young lady, Gough Hollady, a niece to Mrs. Gough, found the Lord among the black people last night, and this morning leaped and shouted in the family pew at morning prayer."[28]

The restrictions placed on black behavior at church services no doubt caused many black parishioners to feel their worship was compromised and incomplete. Moreover, the message gained from the mixed services was completely from a white perspective, with little room for the interpretation of Scripture that slaves had fashioned and spread at secret prayer meetings during years of servitude while on the plantation. Similarly, the white-dominated power structure of the church was all too reminiscent of the repression of slavery itself. In a social situation that was too often inequitable, the afterlife was a realm black people could not allow whites to restrict. The need for cultural uplift and spiritual freedom and the reaction to white parishioners' limited Christian fellowship now combined to inspire Baltimore's black Christians to separate from white churches and to form their own religious communities. As one historian has written, "In the church, with their own kind, amid songs of redemption and the promises of Paradise, a life-line could be thrown into the future."[29]

The final motivation for black separation from mixed churches stemmed from a growing racial identification among those who had emerged from slavery. Ironically, just as the church had promoted spiritual equality, so had it prompted an awareness of black identity and a movement for religious independence in its attempts to curb the liberties of its black parishioners. The message of personal liberation essential to evangelical Christianity provided for many black people a psychological edifice with which to justify their feelings of dissatisfaction for the white-controlled church and to reinterpret personal interests as communal interests. This as yet nascent feeling of racial identification, which provided initiative for a response to the ecclesiastical separation that swept the white and mixed churches, would soon expand beyond the realm of the churches to the whole of Baltimore's African American population.[30]

The Baltimore independence movement followed closely on the heels of a similar movement in the neighboring city to the north, Philadelphia. Prompted by many of the same motivations as the free blacks in Baltimore, a small group of black Philadelphians, led by Richard Allen, organized prayer meetings as early as 1786. The next year some of these same freedpeople organized the Free African Society, a quasi-religious group patterned along the lines of African age set societies and white mutual aid societies, which attempted to ease the transition from slavery to freedom and to define by collective experience the emergence of a black community in Philadelphia. In 1794 black people in that city opened the doors to two of their own churches, one Methodist and one Presbyterian, both still under denominational control.[31]

A close line of communication between black residents of Philadelphia and Baltimore inspired those in the southern city to follow the lead of the northern city and gradually move toward autonomy. Yet the very motivation that pushed them toward ecclesiastical independence also hindered their efforts. The racial controls, cardinal to the slave system, led whites to have grave suspicions about any freedoms black people might obtain. Well aware that Maryland whites possessed powerful legal protections with which they might have prevented any unchecked exodus from the city's mixed churches, Baltimore's black people were forced to be somewhat circumspect in their

efforts to separate from white churches. Moreover, black Christians aban-
doned white churches only reluctantly. Baltimore's black churchgoers faced
a longer wait for the ecclesiastical liberties available to their free neighbors
to the north, for physical separation was the last logical step after spiritual
separation.[32]

Soon after news of the separation in Philadelphia reached Baltimore,
Jacob Fortie began leading prayer meetings among a small group of free
Negroes in a downtown boot black cellar operated by Caleb Hyland, also a
church member. During the next several years, as more black Methodists
dissociated themselves from the integrated Lovely Lane and Strawberry
Alley Methodist churches, the number of black people attending Fortie's
meetings grew until the group—soon known as the Colored Methodist
Society—began meeting at the homes of various members. The consolation,
mutual aid, and solidarity experienced during these sessions only whetted
the appetites of those dissidents who longed for a church of their own, a
church based on shared experiences and heritages that would minister to the
needs of free blacks and slaves alike.[33]

In the spring of 1795, a year after Philadelphia's black Christians had
opened two separated churches, some of Baltimore's Colored Methodist
Society's leaders met with Bishop Francis Asbury in an effort to obtain a
separate building and form "a distinct African, yet Methodist Church." Asbury was sympathetic to the formation of black Methodist churches, because
he believed that the "more houses the more people; and the more preaching, and the more converted," but he appears to have dragged his feet. By
fall, however, the requests of the Colored Methodist Society had expanded.
"The Africans of this town desire a church," wrote Asbury, "which, in tem-
porals, shall be altogether under their own direction, and ask greater privileges than the white stewards and trustees ever had a right to claim." The
bishop rejected this plan outright. An independent black Methodist church
in a slave state might easily provoke opposition among the slaveowning elite,
uncomfortable about extending black people too many privileges. The first
bishop of the still-young Methodist Episcopal Church of America was unwilling to undertake such a risk.[34]

Despite such setbacks, the small group of black Methodists continued to
press for an all-black congregation in Baltimore. In 1797 some of the leaders leased a building on Fish Street and drew up a resolution stating their
reasons for doing so and advertising for members: "In view of the many
inconveniences arising from the white and colored people assembling in
public-meeting, especially in public worship of Almighty God, we have
thought it best to procure for ourselves a separate place in which to assem-

ble, therefore, we invite all our Methodist brethren, who think as we do, to worship with us."[35]

No opposition to the effort appears to have surfaced, and with the help of members of the city's Abolition Society, Baltimore's Colored Methodist Society advertised for a teacher "to instruct such black children & children of any color as may be entrusted to his care." After a few months, however, a lack of funds forced the group to vacate the building. Without adequate membership and support, the group was forced to face the secular reality that the inability to pay rent superseded the spiritual quest for solidarity.[36]

The setback was only temporary, however. Within four years, in 1801, Jacob Gilliard, a blacksmith, and Richard Russell, a carpenter, probably using funds obtained from the group, purchased for $870 two parcels of land on "Forrest Lane" (probably Forrest Street). The sale of the land would fund a "convenient house for the accommodation of the members of the African Methodist Episcopal Church in the city of Baltimore, to be occupied by them as a house of worship or to such other purposes as the trustees to be appointed on behalf of the said church shall and may direct."[37] A year later Gilliard, Russell, and seven others purchased for the dissident group a lot on Sharp Street, owned by the Quaker James Carey, "for the use, benefit, and behoof of the Affricans in the city of Baltimore and belonging to and in common with the society of Christians commonly known by the name of the Methodist Episcopal Church in the United States of America. . . ." The lot also provided a burial ground for the members, something now denied to black members of mixed churches. Not a church in the strict sense of the term, the building was to serve dually as a religious and educational center for "black children of every persuasion" and was bound only in that "such ministers and preachers belonging to the said church or society of Christians as shall time to time be duly authorized by the General Conference to preach."[38]

According to the wording of the land deed, black Methodists established the meetinghouse on Sharp Street—soon known as the African Academy—with the sanction of the white Methodist clergy. What caused Bishop Asbury's apparent change of stance between 1795 and 1801 is unclear. From an ecclesiastical standpoint, so long as the black churches remained under the pastorate of white ministers and were regulated by state laws and, perhaps more important, Methodist authority, separate black houses of worship posed little threat to the religious order of things. Moreover, with the rapid growth of the city itself and the concomitant increase of membership in the Baltimore Methodist churches, both white and black, the presiding elders were probably more willing to allow black Methodists to establish branch churches to free up the pews that might otherwise seat white members who could present more substantial tithes. Removal of blacks' disruptive presence no doubt was a welcome relief for many white parishioners.

Ultimately, enough black members remained in and continued to join the mixed churches that white Methodists might even have seen the need for relieving the overcrowding of the city's four small chapels. As late as 1809–10, 149 blacks were admitted on trial membership to the Baltimore mixed churches (compared with 330 whites). In 1802 there were mixed Methodist churches on Light Street, Wilk Street, Exeter Street, and Dallas Street (formerly Strawberry Alley). The number of black members at the Dallas Street church was so large that in 1802 Bishop Asbury concluded it could be considered colored; eight years later black Baltimoreans were doing just that.[39]

To ensure control of the separated Africans, white clergymen chose carefully the Sunday sermons they would present to the black congregation. Understanding that many in the audiences at the "African house" were slaves, ministers (including the bishop himself) offered scriptural lessons that stressed those social aspects whites found most desirable for black ears: docility, diligence, and submission. From Ephesians 4:1–6, Asbury read, "I therefore, the prisoner of the Lord, beseech you that ye walk worthy of the vocation wherewith ye are called, With all lowliness and meekness, with longsuffering, forbearing one another in love; Endeavoring to keep the unity of the Spirit in the bond of peace." From Colossians 1:9–12, he exhorted them, "That ye might walk worthy of the Lord unto all pleasing, being fruitful in every good work, and increasing in the knowledge of God." And from I Peter 5:5–7, he read, "Likewise, ye younger, submit yourselves unto the elder. Yea, all of *you* be subject one to another. . . ." Similarly, Freeborn Garrettson's sermon to the Baltimore Africans in 1818 quoted Paul in Philippians 3:16: "Nevertheless, whereto we have already attained, let us walk by the same rule, let us mind the same thing." The ministers' choices of scriptural passages were obviously deliberate. Three of them they found in the letters of the apostle Paul, who, at the time of his writing, was himself held in bondage, languishing in a Roman prison cell.[40]

Though for several years the African Academy served some of the needs of Baltimore's black Methodists quite well, providing a host of services beyond those that were strictly religious or educational, the facility did not satisfy their need for a church of their own. The use of white ministers only exacerbated this yearning. Each Sunday the white face and effete message of that day's minister reminded them of their exclusion from church decision making and their inferior status in society in general. As one black Baltimore Methodist saw it, "It is evident, that there was a difference made between the coloured members and those of a superior colour (vulgarly so called) in point of church privileges; and it is evident that all this distinction was made on account of the complexion."[41]

The demeanor of many of the visiting ministers toward Baltimore's African Academy no doubt only exacerbated the situation. A number of them appear to have viewed preaching to the Africans as merely a bother. Jacob Gruber recalled that he "did not consider it a very great favor" being sent to preach at the Sharp Street church. Francis Asbury rebuked some of the Baltimore Methodists for ridiculing the white church's ministration of black parishioners. "It was mean, it was childish," he wrote, "to compare our preachers, and presiding elders, to Africans, and African overseers. . . ." For a time black Methodists were willing to accept such terms, because they controlled virtually all of the academy's activities except for the delivery of the Sunday sermons. Moreover, it would appear that the presiding elders backed off of their stance against black preachers. By 1810 at least seven black lay ministers preached to the city's African Methodists. Despite such successes, the zeal for a church of their own did not diminish for many of Baltimore's black Methodists.[42]

The individual most responsible for the independent black church movement in Baltimore was Daniel Coker, a young mulatto minister born in 1780 in Frederick County to a white English indentured servant mother and a slave father. Coker was decidedly light-skinned and reputedly learned to read and write from the son of his parents' master, with whom Coker was friends. While still in his teens, Coker escaped to New York State, where he obtained more education and was converted to Methodism. Ambitious and willing to take risks, he rose in prominence in his local congregation and was ordained deacon by Asbury himself. In 1801 he decided to leave the relative safety of the northern free state and return to his native Maryland to preach. Coker lived in Baltimore, reputedly working as a day laborer, while friends attempted to arrange for his purchase from his still-legal master.[43] Little is known of Coker's activities in Baltimore until 1807, when he began operating a school associated with the Colored Methodist Society and the African meetinghouse on Sharp Street.[44]

Coker's Methodist deacon's orders quickly earned him stature in the Sharp Street church, so much so that in 1810 he referred to himself as a "Minister of the African Methodist Episcopal Church in Baltimore," though he was never officially ordained. By becoming a leader of both the church and the school, Coker held two powerful avenues by which to gain prominence among the city's black churchgoers, as well as those with the financial wherewithal to provide for their children's education.[45]

Coker's inability to be ordained as a minister in the Methodist faith tempered his hard-won status as a leader in the Baltimore black community. Though he knew personally of as many as eight African Americans who had received such orders in the free states, Coker no doubt believed he was unable to be rewarded similarly for his efforts in a slave state because of his skin color. Although he did have the distinction of becoming the first black Methodist class leader in the Baltimore City Station, this was hardly ministerial status. Coker was keenly aware of the limitations of his separated black church, which went beyond access to pastoral ordination. The white conference leadership controlled representation in denominational governance, pastoral services, and ownership and use of church property, as well as participation in congregational discipline. Moreover, Coker realized that the conference considered "the coloured societies . . . nothing but an unprofitable trouble." While many of Sharp Street's black members accepted their separation as virtual independence, Coker saw that little ecclesiastical authority rested in the hands of the African Methodists.[46]

Partly out of personal frustration and religious persuasion and partly in an effort to solidify his community status, Coker became an outspoken critic of slavery and its attendant racial prejudice. Taking advantage of Baltimore's relaxed racial climate, he was not afraid to use either his school or his church as a rostrum for his antislavery beliefs. In January of 1810, after a public recitation at his school, Coker "made a few observations on the extra-ordinary opinion of some philosophers, that the Africans are inferior to the whites in the organization of body and mind; and concluded by recommending to the attention of the audience, the addresses which were to be delivered by his pupils."[47]

Later that same year Coker went even further; he published *A Dialogue between a Virginian and an African Minister*, one of the earliest antislavery tracts published by a black man in the United States. Written in dialogue, the pamphlet makes skilled use of both Scripture and Lockean natural rights philosophy to argue against any defense of slavery fashioned on moral grounds as well as to support legal emancipation. Each of the Virginian's arguments in support of slavery—biblical sanction, fear of amalgamation, natural inferiority, and environmentalism—the minister parries with reasoned response, until the Virginian is so overwhelmed by the African's sagacity that he agrees to liberate his own fifty-five slaves. To conclude his pamphlet, Coker uses the same quote from Peter that the founders of St. Thomas African Episcopal Church in Philadelphia drew on for the side wall of their church in 1794: "But ye are a chosen generation, a royal priesthood, and an holy nation, a peculiar people; that ye should shew forth the praise of him who hath called you out of darkness into his marvellous light: which in time past were not a people, but are now the people of God. . . ."[48]

Coker's obvious allusion to racial solidarity, fashioned on the same biblical grounds that many Americans used to justify enslavement based on black skin, forms a backdrop for his efforts to achieve independence from the white-dominated Methodist church. By 1810 Coker was well-connected within black Methodist circles and was in close communication with the Philadelphia congregation. Coker knew about the effort on the part of Richard Allen and the northern congregation to achieve ecclesiastical independence and the long court battle to gain legal legitimacy for the "African Supplement" at St. George's Methodist Episcopal Church because he and Allen corresponded regularly. Since its grievances were similar to those of the Baltimore congregation, Coker found the Philadelphians' movement quite useful in organizing his own such effort. Finding a number of willing ears in the congregation, he led what became a radical faction of several hundred Baltimore black Methodists, both free and slave, who were dissatisfied with the direction the Sharp Street church was moving, and in May 1815 he instigated a withdrawal from the church. Calling themselves the African Methodist Bethel Society, Coker, Gilliard, Stephen Hill, Don Carlos Hall, George Douglass, and David Brister rented a lot and building that once housed the Zion Lutheran church and established a small church, independent of the Baltimore General Conference.[49]

Unrecognized by the denomination and initially supported by only a small number of Baltimore's black parishioners, Daniel Coker risked a great deal to test the limits of white tolerance for black autonomy. Yet he had a vision. His choice of the name Bethel, from the biblical meaning "House of God," held a deeper meaning, one that heralded the rise of a strong, unified black people. In Genesis 28:10–16 Jacob is said to have slept one night along the road from Beer-sheba to Haran, where he had a dream of a great ladder reaching from earth to heaven. After climbing the ladder, Jacob met the Lord, who told him that "the land whereon thou liest, to thee will I give it, and to thy seed; And thy seed shall be as the dust of the earth, and thou shalt spread abroad to the west, and to the east, and to the north, and to the south: and in thee and in thy seed shall all the families of the earth be blessed." Upon awakening, Jacob named the place Bethel. The story of Jacob's seed took root in Baltimore by growth of another type: the development of the first independent black church in the slave states.[50]

On Sunday 21 January 1816 Daniel Coker's sermon to the Baltimore Bethel congregation had particular emotional charge. Learning earlier that week that the Supreme Court of Pennsylvania had ruled in favor of the legal independence of the African Bethel congregation in Philadelphia, Coker delivered a celebratory message. He compared the victory of the Philadelphia brethren with the return of the Jews from captivity in Babylon. "May the time speedily come," Coker exulted, "when we shall see our brethren come flocking to us like doves to their windows. And we as a band of brethren, shall sit down under our own vine to worship, and none to make us afraid." As the only ordained black Methodist deacon in Baltimore, Coker had particular reason to celebrate the supreme court's decision, for he now became the undisputed leader of the city's independent church. Within months he would even be recognized briefly as the leader of the African Methodist Episcopal Church in America.[51]

That the black independent church leaders in both Philadelphia and Baltimore, and later in Wilmington, New York, and other cities and towns, should take the name "African" for their free societies and ultimately their denominations was more than a signal act of self-assertiveness; it represented a proud identification with their ancestral past, unscarred by the yoke of servility. While the demeaning and degrading oppression of slavery and its attendant white racism inflicted undeniable scars on slaves, freedpeople found inspiration in images harking back to the proud days of the Mandingo, the Ashanti, the Ibo, and the Bantu—noble warriors and free people, masters of their destinies. By establishing an "African" church, as opposed to a "Negro" church, Baltimore's black Christians sought to rekindle the pride of their ancestors. They acted, as the trustees of the Baltimore church had written in 1805, "in behalf of our brethren of color, . . . of the African race, . . . [who] have long suffered under the influence of ignorance, and device, its invariable concomitant." The name African provided a positive identification for a cultural institution separate from whites that would enhance their own lives, educate those ignorant of their rich cultural heritage, and ultimately benefit the lives of their children, the future Mandingo.[52]

Buoyed by their recent successes and eager to capitalize on reports of conflicts between black and white Methodists in other locales, in early 1816 Richard Allen issued a call for African Methodist leaders to meet in Philadelphia "in order to secure their privileges and promote union and harmony among themselves." In April sixteen delegates from five cities—six of whom came from Baltimore, the largest delegation present—arrived in the city to participate in the meeting. Resolving "that the people of Philadelphia, Baltimore, and all other places, who should unite with them, shall become one body under the name and style of the African Methodist Episcopal Church," the convention delegates elected Coker and Allen the first bishops of the independent African Methodist Episcopal (A.M.E.) church.

Allen had been absent on the day of the nominations, but he returned the following day and immediately voiced objection to them, claiming that the new church was still too small to justify two bishops. Such a move would make the church appear ambitious for status. Moreover, some of the delegation appear to have objected to Coker's light skin on the grounds that an African church should be led by someone who would best portray such a heritage. The delegates consequently reversed themselves and elected Allen the sole bishop. After formulating the rules, governing structure, and by-laws of the new church, patterned after the Doctrine and Discipline of the white Methodist church (but reinstating the legislation prohibiting slave-owning by members), the convention adjourned, and the Baltimore delegation returned to their newly legitimized church.[53]

In Baltimore the Bethel leaders drew up a constitution and elected trustees "to regulate the temporal concerns of the church and hold all property in trust." In planning for their own governance, the black Methodists soon fell victim to some of the same discriminations that plagued white congregations. No woman achieved the rank of class leader in the church, even though Bethel's women members outnumbered men more than two to one and such leadership roles appear to have been common in neighboring Philadelphia's black Methodist churches. Similarly, no women were licensed as ministers or exhorters in the city's black churches during the antebellum years.[54] Moreover, although slaves were included in the church's care (and continued to be taken in as members until the 1850s), the free black leaders granted them no leadership rights. Bethel's constitution stipulated that the church's five elected trustees were to be "Africans; and free; and should have been in the society for at least one year." Delegates to future A.M.E. conventions of "colored ministers and lay members, [would be] chosen by the male member of this church." Though their membership was crucial to the church's life in these early years, neither slaves nor women had any leadership role in its hierarchy.[55]

The first few years of its independent existence proved exceedingly difficult for the Bethel congregation, forcing it to turn often to friendly whites for various forms of assistance. Because only a small number left the relative security of the Sharp Street church for the new radical church, the congregation faced immediate financial hardships. As the leaders had done a decade earlier in attempting to enlarge their African meetinghouse, in July 1815 the Bethel trustees appealed to sympathetic whites in newspaper advertisements for contributions to help pay the expenses of the church, hoping "that the motives by which they [the trustees] are influenced will be correctly estimated by all those that believe the most inconsiderable individual shares the bounty and interest of God." That Coker and the other leaders should make such a plea suggests that they probably had already received encouragement from some of the city's whites to form their own independent church.[56]

To gain new members, Coker as minister organized and conducted camp meetings and revivals for both blacks and whites, even soliciting "any friendly white minister of any religious denomination [who should] feel disposed to aid in promoting the salvation of this description of mankind . . . [and promising] that they will have an opportunity of speaking to thousands of the sable sons of Africa, that they might never otherwise have an opportunity of speaking to." Freeborn Garrettson wrote that revivalists would often travel as many as fifty or sixty miles to attend one of these camp meetings and that the black participants were by far the most boisterous. "Extravagance was carried to the greatest height among the blacks," Garrettson regretted, "for many of them continued . . . jumping, dancing . . . for hours together. . . . The poor blacks seemed almost ready to fly."[57]

The revivals were generally held on the property of white owners outside the Baltimore city limits, both to appease white fears of the congregation of such large groups of black people and to ensure their protection in the event of white harassment. Sometimes these disrupters were local authorities or individuals searching for fugitive slaves who used Methodist camp meetings as a means of making good their escape. In 1840 one Baltimore master offered five hundred dollars for the return of his "Negro boy JOHN MURPHY, who left my premises on Sunday, 30th August, under the pretense of going to the Camp Meeting on the Liberty Road, 6 or 7 miles out." Most often, however, the intruders were simply hecklers intent on disrupting the meeting. Such disruptions were frequent enough that newspaper advertisements promoting the meetings often included warnings against such behavior.[58]

Despite the support some whites gave him, Coker had good cause for vigilance during his church's early years; its very existence had engendered suspicion and even hostility among many nonsympathetic whites. In September of 1817, after a camp meeting held about five miles outside Baltimore on the Washington Road, some black Methodists were accused of assisting in the escape of two black runaways in attendance. Fearful of white reprisal against the African Methodist church, Coker was forced to curry favor in a local newspaper. "That an affair such as related, took place," he affirmed, "we have strong reasons to doubt and . . . we are satisfied that none of our members would have any hand in a crime of such magnitude, as that of causing the guilty to escape the hand of justice." Then, in a measured effort to allay white fears, Coker stated that "hundreds of our respectable white citizens were at the meeting on the Sabbath day . . . and they are of the opinion, that the report is false, and justify us in contradicting the same."[59]

While white Methodists rewarded some loyal black parishioners, such as John Mingo, a local blacksmith who remained in the church, with a recommendation for deacon's orders, the "recalcitrant" Africans who left the church stood to receive little other than ostracism. Moreover, Baltimore's white Methodist Episcopal church leaders appear to have regarded most of their remaining black members almost with contempt. At a meeting of the city's elders on 9 April 1817 those in attendance "resolved that the Coloured people be requested to retire from the Light Street, Eutaw and old Town churches." Later that fall Samuel Krebs, a local white combmaker, was censured by the quarterly conference of the Baltimore Station for having "attended a Camp meeting held by Danl Coker and preached there." Accordingly, the conference resolved to "disapprove of any of our Official Members or Members of our Society attending D. Coker's meetings."[60]

The Bethel church grew rapidly and by 1817 had outgrown its small rented building. With over six hundred members, the congregation not only needed more room but also was now better able to afford it. In 1817 the trustees rented a three-story brick building on the south side of Fish Street "for a Meeting house of Worship . . . the inside finished in a convenient manner with Pulpit, Pews & Galleries, having large boards." Though austere by the standards of all but the newest of white churches, the building represented hard work and a bright future to Bethel's members. Taking out an insurance policy on the building worth four thousand dollars, Bethel soon became Baltimore's largest and most influential black congregation, the driving force—and host—of the first Annual Conference in 1818. Between 1818 and 1826 membership in the Baltimore A.M.E. conference doubled, most of this from the spectacular growth of Bethel. By 1848 the church had over 1,200 members.[61]

The lion's share of Bethel's growth and development would occur largely without the guidance of its spiritual and political leader, Daniel Coker. In April 1818 a member of the conference brought charges against the Baltimore minister for reasons that remain unclear but prompted a committee to submit a resolution "that no business of a secret nature referred to a committee shall be taken out of the Conference. . . ." The committee found Coker guilty of misconduct and ruled that he "shall forfeit all [his] official functions for one year, and shall not obtain [his] license until [he] give[s] proper satisfaction to the Annual Conference." Obviously ambitious, Coker might well have resented his removal as bishop, thus souring his connections with the A.M.E. conference. Upon his application the following year, the conference reinstated him but allowed him to preach only with the permission of the elder in charge.[62]

Coker's personal finances had also plummeted. Preaching offered little remuneration for even the most established ministers, and an expelled, unordained African Methodist preacher could expect even less. His school, while successful and well respected, failed to provide an adequate source of income, and in 1818 Coker applied to the city of Baltimore for insolvency. Ironically, on 4 July of that year, the day when most of the city celebrated their independence from Britain, Daniel Coker stood before a judge asking for independence from his debts. Coker's father-in-law, Nicholas Gilliard (son of one of the independence movement's founder), agreed to act as trustee for his son-in-law's troubled finances, and Coker received a personal discharge. In addition to his personal problems, Coker believed that bitter squabbling between Bethel and the Sharp Street church—which remained governed by the white-controlled Methodist Episcopal conference—divided the city's black church community and robbed both churches of ecclesiastical strength. All of these problems contributed to what became Coker's apparent disgust at the lack of opportunities for a man of his color in the land of his birth. Disaffected and demoralized, in February 1820 Coker opted to "leave all these divisions in America" for the land of his ancestors' birth; he emigrated to Liberia under the aegis of the American Colonization Society, the most prominent American to be relocated in this way.[63]

The divisions to which Coker referred stem largely from the unwillingness of a great many Baltimore black parishioners to leave the white-controlled Methodist church for the Bethel congregation, even after the establishment of the A.M.E. denomination. Freeborn Garrettson recalled preaching a Sunday sermon in 1818 "in the afternoon to nearly 1,000 Africans—many stood at the doors, and windows, as their church would not contain them all. . . ." In 1831, the year before the Sharp Street church would be incorporated into the Methodist Episcopal conference, 1,919 black people retained their memberships in the church. Within a dozen years that number had more than doubled.[64]

Those who had achieved leadership positions at the Sharp Street or Strawberry Alley churches obviously were reluctant to forfeit such stature and probably considered their positions of authority in an older, established church and denomination more respectable than those in such an upstart church as Bethel. Being a class leader appears to have been an important first step to elevation in the church hierarchy. Of the forty-three class leaders listed for the Sharp Street church in 1826, twelve were by 1831 lay ministers for black congregations in the city's Methodist Episcopal churches. Many probably saw the white churches as the best avenue available to them for social and economic advancement. They were willing to accept that no black preacher would receive ordination as a member of the conference in return for the social benefits they sought in remaining in the older churches and some promotions in the Methodist Episcopal churches.

Though class distinctions appear to have had little to do with Bethel's separation from Sharp Street, they did play a part in members' advancement in both churches. In 1826 just five of the eighteen class leaders at Sharp Street (like those of Bethel, all men) with identifiable occupations were unskilled laborers, and only two of them had risen to lay minister in 1831. Not surprisingly, Lewis G. Wells, recommended for deacon's orders in 1828, was a well-known local black carter and part-time physician, the former a respectable trade, the latter nearly unheard of among black people.[65] Moreover, of the thirty-three class leaders at Bethel between 1825 and 1853 with identifiable occupations, just five were laborers. The rest held skilled or semi-skilled jobs, such as waiter, porter, "wall colorer" (painter), tailor, and cordwainer. Only one was a lay minister. Unskilled black men could become class leaders because black parishioners were able to choose such leaders for themselves, but advancement to higher roles in the church proved far more difficult. At both Bethel and Sharp Street (where white elders controlled promotions), leaders imposed their own standards, which invariably were predicated on factors other than service and piety—namely, achieving such desirable black goals as literacy, articulateness, and respectable occupations.[66]

Although the individual black Methodist congregations strove for harmony and solidarity, internal divisions inevitably shook the seemingly stable foundation of this social edifice. Black Methodists squabbled over issues ranging from theological doctrines for the whole congregation to personal disagreements between individuals. In February 1839 Perry Armstrong appeared in Baltimore's city court to answer charges of wielding an axe, "with which he intended to assault the sexton" after being "turned out of the Sharp street meeting house, for disturbing the worship."[67] Bethel's membership roll indicates that a significant chasm erupted in its congregation during the winter of 1848–49, apparently at the General Conference meeting in Philadelphia, which led to the expulsion of both leaders and laity for "rebellion," including the lay minister Nathaniel Peck and four class leaders. The incident ultimately led to violence inside the congregational walls. In February of 1849 Eliza Peters and Serena Richfield were expelled for "attempting to kill Rev. D[arius] Stokes in the very altar." The exact nature of both the dispute and the individual attack is unclear, but Stokes himself was expelled two years later.[68]

Though the motivations for such outbursts varied, one particularly violent incident provides insight into the nature of spiritual debate that racked the Bethel church. In 1850 the minister Daniel Payne, later bishop of the A.M.E. church, tried to prohibit the singing of spirituals in the church, claiming they were "Corn-field Ditties" and disorderly "extravagances in worship." Two women rose from the front row of pews and attacked Payne and his assistant pastor with clubs. Payne escaped serious injury with a blow glancing off his shoulder, but the unfortunate assistant minister suffered a serious blow to the head and lay unconscious and bleeding on the dais. The congregation expelled Payne from their church, and he subsequently refused to return to his ministration of it, despite the bishop's urgings.[69]

The incident suggests far more than any penchant for violent behavior that Baltimore's black Methodists might have possessed. The attack reflects the depth of black Baltimoreans' commitment to spiritual autonomy and the lengths to which the community would go to preserve it. Yet perhaps more significant is the importance Baltimore's African Americans attached to the maintenance of African traditions in their most important social institution: the church. Though Payne condemned such activities as the ring shout, hand clapping, swaying, exaltative singing, and other "heathenish mode[s] of worship," the startling opposition of the Bethel congregation offers strong evidence of black parishioners' literal understanding of their denominations' self-assumed title of "African Methodist" church, as well as the solemn pride with which they preserved the cultural vestiges of their own distant past.[70]

By 1832, when the Sharp Street Methodist Episcopal Church was incorporated into the Annual Conference, with black trustees and with black lay preachers as well as white ministers assigned to it, four black Methodist houses of worship served the needs of the city's black churchgoers. The St. James Protestant Episcopal Church, established in 1824, became the first black church in the slave states to exercise complete local autonomy within the framework of affiliation with a white national church organization. Unlike Bethel, St. James took particular care to involve both slave and free parishioners in the operation of the church, specifying in its articles of association that "all the male members of the Church above the age of 21 years whether bond or free, holding seats in the church are entitled to vote." By 1860 sixteen black churches and missions—of a total of 148 churches in the city—had been established in Baltimore, representing six denominations and located in twelve of the twenty municipal wards, of which Sharp Street, Bethel, and St. James were valued at $25,000, $11,000, and $10,000, respectively. At least 6,400 black worshipers were enrolled as active members of these churches, representing more than one-fifth of the city's total black population, a rate of attendance far higher than that of the city's whites.[71] The services were so well attended that one resident complained to the mayor in 1831 that "the Negroe's which visit Sharp St meeting on Sunday are a great nuisance to our citizens. . . . The crowd being so great and the Negro's so ungentlmanly that Ladies have to go arround them by way of the Street."[72] These churches drew from more than just the city population. Charles Torrey, a minister, recalled that "the colored people, for ten miles round, are induced to come to Baltimore on the Sabbath, to see their friends, and attend church."[73]

Perhaps most apparent in the development of the city's black churches was the freedom of the black congregations to practice religion in a distinctive African American style. Unburdened by many of the devotional restrictions that white elders and parishioners once placed on them, many of the city's black halls of worship—at least among the evangelical denominations—literally rang with exhortations, shouts, and song. The Englishman William Faux recalled that "at a half a mile distant, we could distinctly hear their devotional songs. . . . The pious prayers, and sensible, cheerful singing of the poor negroes, (who are, however, apt to rise into wild enthusiasm), are very honourable to black capabilities, and exonerate them from the charge of natural and moral inferiority."[74] Ethan Allen Andrews reflected similarly on what he saw at a Sharp Street service. "There is, in some of the African voices," he observed, "a wild and touching pathos, which art can never reach." Andrews concluded that the extemporaneous style of the minister and the emotional response of the congregation were elements inseparable from one another: "The responses of the Methodist church seem to be especially adapted to such an audience as were there assembled. They serve to fix the attention of such hearers, and to cheer and animate the preacher, by the interest they evince in his performance. Were the preacher engaged in pursuing a connected train of thought, the responses might perhaps interrupt the attention of his audience, but with such a preacher no effect of that kind is likely to occur."[75]

Although Faux and Andrews as visitors could make somewhat favorable observations, many local residents regarded the African services far less favorably. One annoyed white resident recalled the shouts, wails, laughter, measured stamping of feet, and songs that exuded from Bethel's windows and doors on a summer night as part of their emotional style of worship:

Many and many a harmless street stroller has been dragged off to the watchhouse for singing a song or bawling in the streets at unseasonable hours—while here are hundreds of negroes assembled together for the purpose of "worship" making night hideous with their howls, dancing to the *merry* song of some double-lunged fellow, who glories the more his *congregation* yells. . . . Is an entire neighborhood to be disturbed day after day and night after night by these *rioters*—because some well meaning persons choose to say they are free to worship?[76]

This expression of deep spirit affected some white observers more positively. Jacob Gruber, a minister who had once looked on duty at the black churches with little relish, admitted that although "there was no religion in their appearance, or dress; it was in their souls, and could not be seen, no. I never found as large a number of members as plain as Sharp-street and Asbury Methodists. I preferred trying to preach to them above any other congregation in Baltimore." Gruber's enthusiasm was no doubt enhanced by the large attendances guaranteed to him when he preached to black Methodist audiences.[77]

Equally important to the parishioners at the city's independent black churches was the freedom of black preachers to interpret and impart scripture uniquely. In "carrying on the good work," ministers became unquestionably the most important and influential figures in the lives of the congregations and exercised a powerful social and moral influence. Their success was based on something more than preaching sermons with a more acceptable interpretation of the Bible than that which whites had traditionally foisted on black Christians. While this skill had long played an important part in a black minister's repertoire, the attraction of a black as opposed to a white minister was most often far more basic. No matter how liberal or sympathetic they might be, few if any white ministers could communicate their message to a black audience as effectively as could an exhorter of African descent because they had not shared their audiences' experiences, their aspect, or, in many ways, even their language. At the Sharp Street church in 1835 Ethan Allen Andrews listened with silent amusement to a black preacher's fractured rendition of Philip's meeting with and conversion of an Ethiopian in Samaria (Acts 8:26–40). Andrews condescendingly recalled that "Philip, according to the preacher, was told to 'go and *cotch* right hold of the chariot,' (for so he interpreted the direction 'to go and join himself to it,'). . . . An apology was made for the seeming impropriety of Philip's being 'so bold as to cotch hold of the chariot and to ask a *gemman* such a question.'" Despite the preacher's grammatical failings, Andrews was impressed with his ability to interpret the essential meaning of the passage and relate it to the congregation through metaphors unmistakable to his black audience:

> With all his quaintness and ignorance of letters, the preacher evidently possessed respectable talents, and uncommon skill in illustration. He warned his hearers against supposing that they could enter heaven without love to Christ in their

hearts; this he told them was the only *"free pass."* "If they wanted to go from the south to Philadelphia or New York, they knew very well that they would be stopped on the way if they had not a free pass, and so it would be if they should try to enter heaven without a pass containing the name and broad seal of Christ." All this was perfectly intelligible to his hearers, who showed in their countenances and by their animated responses, how thoroughly they entered into the spirit of his remarks.[78]

✣   ✣   ✣

The churches established in Baltimore soon stood as centers of the black community, not so much as centers around which the population developed but as centers of political and social organization as well as religious activity. Barred by legal disfranchisement in 1802 from traditional political participation, Baltimore's black residents achieved political organization even without the vote. Each church, irrespective of denomination, served as a focal point for the black residents in the immediate vicinity and beyond, affording a vehicle for collective action for the congregations and the population at large. Churches provided innumerable services to the community as educational centers, libraries, meetinghalls, community recreational centers, and social centers. Each conducted Sabbath schools, sponsored benevolent societies, and held fairs, exhibits, Christmas pageants, and concerts for the financial benefit of the church, the moral and cultural improvement of parishioners, and the future of the children. Moreover, by providing burial sites for black parishioners—which few white churches and private burying grounds would now permit—the African churches conferred respectability even in the afterlife. In 1818, 105 black people were buried in the African Methodist churchyard, while another 42 were placed in various church cemeteries around the city, most of which were black churches. For many black Americans, death held great promise of a release from the travails and inequities of the secular world. When the city's slaves and free blacks gathered at church graveyards on Sundays and holidays to pay respects to their departed by singing and dancing, they celebrated—rather than mourned—not only what had been but also what would be.[79]

In offering spiritual and social uplift, the churches succeeded in regularly bringing together from all parts of the city people with diverse occupations and backgrounds, who shared and found pride in a common heritage. More than simply those residing in the immediate vicinities attended the churches. Of the eighteen identifiable class leaders of the Sharp Street church in 1826, only two lived within five blocks of the church; the rest traveled as far as twenty blocks, nearly three-quarters of a mile, at least twice a week. Through individual congregations and ultimately through the network of Christian fellowship, the churches enabled much of the city's black population, as one historian has written, "to celebrate themselves as a collectivity, and they provided the protective space whereby each could contend with the other about common concerns."[80]

For most black residents in Baltimore, the activities of the black churches served a deeper purpose; they fostered a sense of racial unity—that there was among the city's black Christians one, rather than many, people of color. In addition to demonstrating to parents the success of the First Presbyterian Church's school in educating their children, the juvenile concert scheduled for 29 May 1840 intended to "bespeak the dawn of the latter days' glory, when the abodes of the suffering sons and daughters of Africa, whose very aspect utters forth the sadness of the heart of the indweller, shall resound with praise to God for the return of their former lustre."[81]

Latent in the advent of Baltimore's black churches was their role as the cradles of black consciousness and organization. As the achievement of ecclesiastical independence gave black Baltimoreans the opportunity to exercise control over the salient aspects of their daily lives, the successes of the various churches spawned among black people throughout the city a new sense of self-respect and racial pride. Despite the criticisms of those such as Frederick Douglass, who castigated separate black churches as perpetuating racial caste and white perceptions of black inferiority ("negro pews, on a higher and larger scale," as he termed them), in Baltimore they provided the foundation for the maturation of the black community by means of the various social organizations that often sprang from the church polity and structure itself. By constructing ideological supports—a sense of unity and common purpose—the African American churches in essence became the collective soul of Baltimore's maturing black community.

Thomas Waterman Wood's 1858 oil painting "Market Woman," portraying a free black street vendor in Baltimore. Many African American women were vendors, or "hucksters," in the antebellum years.
Courtesy of the Fine Arts Museums of San Francisco, Mildred Anna
Williams Collection, 1944.8.

W. H. Bartlett's 1838 *Battle Monument, Baltimore* depicts black street life in antebellum Baltimore. The city's numerous monuments were sites for regular black gatherings. Courtesy of the National Archives, Washington, D.C.

Freedpeople and their families arrive in Baltimore. The city offered refuge for former slaves throughout the nineteenth century. From *Frank Leslie's Illustrated Newspaper*, September 30, 1865. Courtesy of the Maryland Historical Society, Baltimore.

The Slave Dandy, sketched by an artist for the *Illustrated London News.* Balti-more slaves often dressed in "genteel" fashion. Courtesy of the Maryland Historical Society, Baltimore.

Interior of the Bethel A.M.E. church in 1845, depicted in an artist's lithograph entitled "The presentation of a gold snuff box to the Reverend Darius Stokes on behalf of the colored people of Baltimore as a gift of gratitude, December 18, 1845." Courtesy of the Maryland Historical Society, Baltimore.

Baltimore's African Americans celebrate the Fifteenth Amendment, which established the right of suffrage, near the city's Battle Monument. Courtesy of the Maryland Historical Society, Baltimore.

6

The Maturation of a Black Community

The middle antebellum decades of the nineteenth century in many ways proved a watershed for Baltimore's people of color. The city's African Americans evolved from a formless aggregate of transients who had wended their way from the countryside and still lacked social cohesion and, to some degree, collective vision, to a society that coalesced around the affirmation of racial distinctions—differences that grew increasingly important to both the black and white residents of the city. The creation of independent black churches in Baltimore had created a spiritual and psychological bedrock on which to construct the social foundation of a community. Yet this edifice still needed frames, joists, transoms, and windows. Urban black Baltimoreans would finish their community structure in ways both infinitesimal and perceptible, fashioning a culture different from their rural counterparts and to some extent from other urban black communities.

The liberties available in the city, relatively unhindered by the constant white suspicions of the cloistered countryside, coupled with the multitude of black people in the unique urban milieu who lived and worked in relatively close proximity, nurtured a vibrant social life and singular cultural style among Baltimore's black residents. By 1850 almost 90 percent of these people were free; some families were able to trace their freeborn standing three generations or more. As these residents moved further from slavery, so did they create a more tangible, and collective, definition of freedom. In this collectivity, so too did the populace begin to construct a more mature community. Divisions were inextricable, but a sense of place emerged that bound these once-transients to this city, this experience, and this future.

The process of community-building did not mean complete intraracial equality or harmony. The essence of freedom, while providing impetus to the development of group consciousness, also allowed room for individual aspirations and created social stratification. As black Baltimoreans created a self-identity born of the urban experience and the common plight of being black in a southern state and city, they diversified internally along economic, social, and ideological lines. Just as the urban setting of Baltimore became for black residents an intersection of race and social class, so did it become a means by which they layered the very community they built. The community that matured in the years after 1830 was thus diverse, multi-leveled, and sometimes divided.

Yet the black community in Baltimore proved less divided internally than did Baltimore's white society and was less fractious than comparable black communities in other cities, North and South. Although by the 1830s Philadelphia's black society had become nearly as stratified as white society, Baltimore's community of color was far less divided than its neighbor to the north. So pronounced were these differences between the communities that in 1841 Joseph W. Wilson, a Baltimore resident, leveled trenchant criticisms against the black society of Philadelphia for its "liberal share of animadversion, on account of the numerous divisions which exist among [the] . . . distinct social circles, even among those equally respectable and of equal merit and pretensions, [and] are carried into most of the relations of life, and in some cases are kept up with the most bitter and relentless rancor." Wilson reserved his harshest admonishment for the city's black "higher classes" for their conscious withdrawal from the mainstream of Philadelphia's black life in favor of an independent, self-sustaining existence, in which its connections through business and antislavery groups were directed toward whites rather than the common black residents, and the resultant failure of black Philadelphians to work as a united force against racial prejudice.[1]

That Wilson was a black Baltimorean was no coincidence, for in 1841 Baltimore's black populace had not yet seen the "rancorous" divisions of its society into higher and lower classes. Ironically, the same nearly ineluctable poverty that dragged Baltimore's black people down below nearly all other urban black societies of the day mortared the walls of their embryonic community. Only during the last antebellum decades did its societal edifice begin to show cracks.

The emergent self-identity of Baltimore's people of color was partly determined by the dynamic nature of the city's populace. The majority of black people in the city prior to 1816 had come to the city as recently freed slaves from rural counties; however, by the 1850s the free black population had changed dramatically. While natural increase, which continued to accelerate as the century progressed, augmented an already large black population, after 1830 Baltimore's black population was composed largely of those who not only were free but had been born free. According to the certificates of freedom for free blacks in Baltimore City registered between 1852 and 1860, 399 out of 710 (56.2 percent) had been born free, as opposed to having been manumitted. Just over four decades earlier, more than 75 percent had been manumitted.[2]

The same generational change that had created a mass of people inured of freedom from birth had also produced a populace that had been raised solely in the urban setting. Of the 351 who registered freedom certificates in the city between 1848 and 1857 and listed their birthplaces, 241 (68.7 percent) had been born in Baltimore City. Only three of those registered had been born outside the state of Maryland.[3] Black Baltimoreans appear to have not only recognized their urban-born status but even flaunted it, especially to those who lived in the countryside. Upon first arriving in Baltimore as a young slave, Frederick Douglass recalled that the local free black boys "chased me, and called me '*Eastern Shore man*,' till really I almost wished myself back on the Eastern Shore."[4] Just as Philadelphia black residents seem to have looked down on black immigrants from Baltimore (Alexander Mackay recalled that a black porter in Philadelphia who was competing for his business told Mackay to "neber mind him, Sa; he's only a nigga from Baltimore. . . . Dat ere negga not seen good society yet—knows nuffin—habn't got de polish on yet"[5]), so did Baltimore-born free blacks hold country-born immigrants, free and slave.

African Americans throughout Maryland appear to have acceded to such an image as well. Levi Coppin, a Methodist minister, recalled proud amazement as a young slave on the Eastern Shore when he was told the story of how his plantation slave father, rather than city suitor, had won the hand of his Baltimore-educated mother, "the foremost young woman in Cecil County." "Why not be wooed and won by a Baltimore lad," Coppin queried, "who could boast at least of having 'city ways,' a thing quite unknown to a 'country clodhopper.'" Coppin, whose own social advancement occurred through his involvement with the Baltimore church, reckoned the long-standing "presumtiousness" of Baltimore society "may even be inherited."[6] Such communal identification, even if prejudicial, and the growth of a large free black population in Baltimore that was both freeborn and urban-born signified far more than mere adaptation to the city landscape; they provided an essential undergirding for the development of a unique urban culture and a cohesive community in Baltimore.

In forging the contours of their collective existence in Baltimore, urban black men and women exerted themselves as individuals in innumerable ways, none more immediately recognizable than their apparel. One of the earliest indicators of the emergence of an urban black image was the clothing antebellum black Baltimoreans wore. In a class- and caste-bound urban society, in which personal image was not yet wholly dictated by mass marketing and assumed particular importance as an index of social position, free Negroes were especially sensitive to the detail of dress.[7]

The dress habits of Baltimore's free blacks reflect a combination of white and black urban present, as well as the plantation past. In a city proud of its place in the growing web of commerce, and with mass textile production making a wide variety of affordable manufactured clothing readily available, Baltimore white residents sought stylish machine-made and machine-printed clothing over the homespun or coarse articles of the country because it was cheaper and a sign of genteel aspiration. A number of historians have found that plantation slaves, drawing on African traditions, obtained special, often brightly colored garments either to supplement or to replace to their coarse "osnaburgs" (cheap, mass-produced, cotton clothing designed for slave usage) and other traditional slave garb. They dressed up regularly for church and parties as a means of "assert[ing] themselves as proud men and women."[8]

In the urban setting Baltimore's free blacks found additional motivation—and opportunities—for using dress as an encoded indication of communal affiliation and autonomous existence. As early as the 1790s whites had acknowledged how quickly free Negroes used appearances to separate themselves from their former slavery. In 1793 Rinaldo Johnson advertised for his escaped slave, Nace, noting that "he has nothing of that cleanliness about him, which is common (from pride) among those who set up a claim of freedom." Just as many urban whites strove to separate themselves from those of "laborers' dress," urban free blacks sought to distinguish themselves from their slave past by their manner of dress.[9]

Such pressure started early; even as slaves, many urban black people were better dressed than their rural counterparts because urban whites simply did not want shabbily dressed servants in their households. Frederick Douglass recalled his mistress making preparations for the youngster's impending move to Baltimore, replacing his knee-length tow shirt (ubiquitous on the plantation) with trousers, which both recognized as more befitting the "refinement" of urban bondage. In 1794 William Rhea described his escaped servant, James, as wearing "a gold ring in one of his ears, and his hair in a small tie; he had on, a second hand, superfine broadcloth coat, of a very light ash color; a red colored cotton waistcoat, close white linen trousers; a white shirt, with torn sleeves; a round hat, with a string of yellow lace, and tassels." Christian Fleetwood, a young free black, remembered a white benefactor insisting that he be "elegantly dressed in embroidered jacket with silk hose." With domestic slaves so well dressed, fashionable free men and women of color would not be caught dead in the garb of plantation slaves.[10]

Far from exhibiting humility, later urban black residents used high fashion to exert nonthreatening defiance, which whites permitted, most likely because they did not completely understand its implications. On her visit to Baltimore in 1832 Frances Trollope, an Englishwoman, observed that black women getting water at the public fountains were "all dressed with that strict attention to . . . smartness which seems the distinguishing characteristic of the Baltimore females of all ranks."[11] While riding through Baltimore on a train several years later, Alfred Pairpont observed "numerous sable grinning Dianas, with grotesque looking turbans on their heads of nearly every colour and design, with little black piccaninnies capering round them." Two historians of slave hair styling as an indicator of black self-identity have found that brightly colored turbans, or bandannas, were prevalent on eighteenth- and nineteenth-century plantations and that such self-adornment and aesthetic display held great cultural significance as acts of defiance against the dominant white culture.[12] Similarly, Theresa Pulszky, a Hungarian visitor, found that black women were observant of the latest fashions of not only whites but also other black people and, like slaves on the plantation, generally dressed in the brightest, most vivid colors. "The negro women cluster together," she noted, "talking and glancing around, obviously delighted at the pageantry—the topic of the day. They form the gaudiest portion of the varied objects before us; their dress, though poor in material, is of brilliant hue; none wears a dark shirt or a sable handkerchief; all are adorned with purple, yellow and blue."[13] Each of these observers, all of them white and foreign, overlooked an important aspect of free blacks' dress: it was in essence African.

Baltimore's black people, especially women, dressed gaily and fashionably throughout the week, rather than just for Sunday church meetings. Yet like plantation slaves, they appear to have reserved their best finery for Sundays. Church-going prompted the week's sartorial height. Men smoothed and parted their hair, women adorned themselves with makeup, and, as the Methodist minister Jacob Gruber recalled of the revivals held at the city's various black churches, these "gay and fashionable persons . . . joined the church with all their gayety and frippery—lace, ruffles, curls, rings, lockets—hanging about them, like Jacob's flock, spotted, speckled, ring-streaked, and grizzled."[14] Similarly, Frances Trollope recalled that one black female church member, upon seeing another parishioner fall from the gallery of the church in a paroxysm of conversion, remarked that "she 'liked religion right well, but that she never took fits in it, 'cause she was always fixed in her best when she went to chapel, and she did not like to have all her best clothes broke up.'"[15] Ridiculed by whites, Baltimore free persons of color exerted their independence and individuality through habits of dress that not only drew on their own African and slave heritage but also reflected their present status and aspirations as free urban citizens.[16]

Like dress habits, public gatherings, both organized and impromptu, reflected and fostered the development of black cultural identification. As early as the eighteenth century, African Americans in Baltimore and Fells Point had such meetings. Those few slave residents in the two towns then lived in white homes, and drawn by the need for social congregation, they gathered in alleys and on street corners, as well as at the wharves, at Jones' Falls, and at the courthouse. Black residents exchanged pleasantries, made fashion comparisons, and, more important, renewed kinship ties and gained information about relatives and friends with whom, because of the dislocations that slavery and gaining freedom had inflicted on African Americans, they had lost touch. Alfred Pairpont, a visitor from England, observed "crowds of coloured people that were catering here for their masters and mistresses [who] curtsey and bow to each other half a dozen times, and then come a series of giggles and shakings of the hand, interspersed with questions about uncle Johnson, cousin Jackson, and twenty other darkeys of their acquaintance, whose history and welfare seem to afford to both a vast deal of merriment."[17] Just as rural slaves had their grapevine, urban black residents had their street corner telegraph.

These meeting practices only flourished as the city's black population grew during the nineteenth century. When touring Baltimore in 1856, Pairpont noted that "along the road might be seen various groups of coloured men, who were playing at foot-ball and other games that gave the swarthy players ample opportunity for laughing, jumping, leaping, capering, and the thousand other antics which blacks are so fond of exhibiting." Pairpont also observed numerous black street-corner musicians who regularly drew crowds, particularly banjo players, who "may daily be heard strumming, when not too busy, in the barber-saloons attached to the hotels, or in the streets."[18] Street corners and sidewalks were regular sites for black gatherings, because many were attracted by the growing number of hucksters in the city who hawked goods there. Theresa Pulszky, visiting the city in 1851, noted that "'none but the coloured people loiter about corners of the avenues, staring idly with their large, dazzling dark eyes and walking lazily but a few steps to stop and stare again.'" Twenty-seven years earlier three Old Town merchants complained to the mayor that they were "annoyed of late with the . . . introduction of a class of hucksters who occupy the west side of

Harrison street in the sale of old cloathing &c—it has become a mere harbour for drunken disorderly persons & crowds of people of color." Despite
such remonstrances, street corners continued to be constant sites of black
interaction and culture.[19]

With the erection of public facilities, the city's various fountains, monuments, and markets became regular sites for black congregation. Frances
Trollope recalled in 1832 that the Baltimore fountains "were never without
groups of negro girls, some carrying the water on their heads . . . some trip-
ping gaily with their yet unfilled pitchers; many of them singing in that soft
rich voice, peculiar to their race."[20] As markets attracted more black residents on a daily basis, increasingly intolerant white Baltimoreans found reason to condemn, as one woman complained to the mayor, the number of
"filthy looking negroes forcing themselves through the market, and you will
meet them at almost every turn."[21]

With white opinions of free black Baltimoreans growing harsher as the
antebellum years wore on, black residents' brushes with the law became more
regular. Yet such legal entanglements appear not to have blemished respectability among the black population in the same way they did in white society. All Maryland Negroes (or southern Negroes, for that matter) understood
that the laws of the state and city were white men's laws and that black people—even free ones—had only limited legal or political recourse. Baltimore's
black residents understood well that white authorities quickly suspected them
for suspicious fires, thefts, and vandalism. Black people recognized that by
law slaves and even free Negroes could be and were treated differently than
whites for similar offenses. An 1828 ordinance changed a thirty-year-old law
stipulating that slaves and white servants "guilty of offences against the laws
and ordinances of the corporation of the city of Baltimore" be punished with
a lashing "not exceeding thirty-nine stripes" so that now only slaves received
such treatment.[22] Even free blacks unable to pay fines incurred for such
minor infractions as throwing stones, fighting in the markets, breaking curfew, and not observing the Sabbath regularly received such punishment,
while white offenders received jail terms.[23] Free blacks' tacit recognition of
their status and their legal definition as "Negroes and other slaves" led them
to regard laws quite differently than whites did. While Baltimore black residents generally upheld and obeyed local and state laws (in many ways more
assiduously than lower-class whites), they believed occasional infractions
were inevitable under such conditions, moving a group of white petitioners
in 1828 to remark that the city's black population was "less fearful of the
operation of the law than the white population." Such incidents did not
detract from their capacity for, or attractiveness in, leadership positions.[24]

Many of the later leaders of the community suffered various legal and financial misfortunes on their arduous journey to respectability. While city whites, with Protestant rectitude, condemned their own leaders for any such fall from grace as unvirtuous moral degenerates, incapable of leadership, Baltimore's black people appear always to have been far more tolerant of the failings of their respectable folk and dwelled on their accomplishments rather than their foibles. In 1790 Jacob Gilliard, a blacksmith who was later a leader of the independent African church movement, was tried for bastardy charges brought by Philip Rogers, master of "one Sarah Coil." Fifteen years later, as we saw in chapter 4, Gilliard dared to advertise his own family troubles in the city's newspapers by offering a reward for the return of his slave son, Jacob Jr., who had escaped from his master, even portraying him as an addicted gambler for whom Gilliard was about to be forced to pay more than five hundred dollars that he had promised the master as bonded security so the young man could live at large. Daniel Coker applied to the city for insolvency while he was the minister of Bethel without losing his position, as did George A. Hackett, an even later leader of the African Methodist church and a successful coal yard operator, without losing the respect and support of the black community.[25]

Though the city's black people accepted the Protestant ethic of acquisition of worldly goods through hard work, apparently they did not measure themselves completely by such standards. Unlike whites, black people appear to have accepted adversity and possible failure as part and parcel of the process of advancement. In many ways black community leaders with flaws might well been more attractive to their followers because they had fought the same battles (perhaps best expressed in a phrase common among African Methodist congregations, "like priests, like people") and were different from those white leaders who neither considered nor understood black struggles.[26]

Birthplaces, freeborn status, and dress and meeting patterns offer a few stands of the complex social fabric woven in Baltimore's black community during the middle antebellum decades. Within the emergent communal culture that offered them racial identity lay a pattern of social experience that somewhat dichotomized moral identities. Alongside widening economic and social differences grew cultural and even spatial boundaries between the "rough" and the "respectable" worlds of the black community. Yet such distinctions were not drawn as sharply as they were in other contemporary black communities. Most black Baltimoreans lived very much within both worlds, moved between them, and used each of them to negotiate their survival and autonomy. As the community itself flowered, it witnessed at once the dual developments of social cohesion and social division; their mutual existence created for its members agency both within and outside its ranks.

Property ownership also provides evidence of a maturing African American community in the late antebellum decades. The acquisition of property was particularly important to free Negroes, not only socially (as an indication of upward mobility) but also psychologically (as evidence of their separation from a slave past when they themselves were considered property). During the final three antebellum decades, the number of black property holders in Baltimore rose substantially, both indicating and contributing to a growing sense of community among the city's people of color. In 1832, 207 individuals held a total of $157,100 worth of property, both real and personal. By 1856, 236 such owners held more than $250,000 in property, and in 1860, 348 free blacks in Baltimore held property valued at $449,138, making the average black property holding $1,291, nearly double what it had been a quarter of a century earlier and nearly ten times what it had been four decades earlier. Though there were only ten black women property owners in 1850, there were nearly seventy by 1860.[27]

When compared with the amount of property owned by free blacks in the Maryland countryside, the magnitude of the property held by black Baltimoreans takes on even greater significance. In 1850 the average black Baltimore owner of real estate held $1,327 worth of real property, while the average rural black owner possessed just more than $450 worth of property. Moreover, ten of the twelve free persons of color in the state who held property valued at more than $5,000 resided in Baltimore.[28] Maryland's most affluent black resident, Thomas Green, called Baltimore his home. After emigrating from Barbados around 1813, Green opened a small barbershop on Light Street and built a large clientele that included white and black customers. He began to acquire rental property in South Baltimore as early as 1838, and within two decades Green owned ten city lots and seven buildings, which he rented out, mostly to black tenants. By the early 1840s Green had become so well-to-do that he could take his family on extended vacations to fashionable Saratoga Springs, New York, a resort town frequented largely by aristocratic white vacationers. Green became so prominent in the community that by the 1850s his name was listed boldly and in capital letters in the city directories—one of the city's only African American to be afforded such a privilege. At his death in 1858, at age seventy-one, Green's net worth exceeded $17,000, nearly $6,000 of which he kept in cash.[29] The increase of real property value among Baltimore's free Negroes appears particularly striking. Although the 1813 city tax records list only thirty-nine black owners of real property (who held less than $8,500 worth of property collectively), by 1850 that number had more than doubled, behind only New Orleans and Washington among cities in the slave states.[30]

Free blacks accumulated property almost solely through their own efforts; few Maryland masters gave their former bondpeople gifts upon granting them their freedom. Rare indeed was the benevolence exhibited by William Matthews, a Baltimorean who in his 1829 will manumitted his three slaves, James Dawson, Edward Dawson, and Rachel Robinson, providing the two men with $500 each and the woman with an annuity of $32 for the duration of her life. Rarer still was the generous endowment of another Baltimore master who in 1859 provided his former slave with a house and lot worth more than $12,000.[31] While such gifts occurred, occasionally involving the transfer of slaves to free blacks, allowing for the reconstruction of families, most property accumulation among Baltimore's people of color resulted from years of enterprise, frugality, and sacrifice.[32]

By the 1850s the majority of black homeowners resided in brick homes, generally two-story row houses characteristic of working-class neighborhoods in many cities of the Northeast. These row houses sprang up on Baltimore's periphery, replacing the frame dwellings that had predominated among black property owners only decades earlier. Such appearances led rural black people to believe that Baltimore was a gateway to their future prosperity, and the chance to acquire property in Baltimore not only continued to attract blacks to the city but also enhanced the solidarity of its emerging black community.[33]

While the increase in the number of free black property holders in Baltimore is significant, such growth proves deceptive, especially when compared with that of other black communities of the era. Despite the huge black migration to the city, the 236 property holders in Baltimore in 1856 is just one-third that of New Orleans, which counted 650 Negro property owners as early as 1850. Moreover, the $254,697 of assessed property owned by black residents of Baltimore that year represented just under a quarter of the total property that black people held in the entire state of Maryland, though just under 8 percent of the state's black property owners lived in Baltimore.[34] The limited amount of property acquired by Baltimore's people of color becomes even more apparent when compared with that of the city's white residents. Though the number of property holders in Baltimore doubled between 1818 and 1850, the population as a whole became so large that by 1850 black owners of real property constituted only four-tenths of 1.00 percent of the city's free black population. Moreover, in 1850 propertied free blacks made up a minute 0.06 percent of the city's population as a whole. In 1860 the numbers were about the same; only 0.91 percent of free

Negroes in Baltimore owned any real property at all, and its combined value constituted not more than 3.5 percent of the total value of property owned in the city.[35]

Of the free black populations of fourteen major cities in the nation in 1850, Baltimore free blacks were least likely to own property. The majority of whites in Baltimore also failed to acquire real property, but one historian has determined that black people in his study were less than half as likely as whites to own real property, and what property they did own was generally far less valuable than that owned by whites. In 1860 the per capita average holding for whites was $690.71; for black people, it was just $17.49. Many if not most of the continually increasing number of black Baltimoreans remained in the city's poorest housing—wooden shacks in alleys—just as they had decades earlier. Although rural Negroes still believed that Baltimore held their best chance for property holding, the reality proved their faith was chimera.[36]

Moreover, a black propertied elite did not emerge in Baltimore as it did in Philadelphia. In 1837 dozens of Philadelphia's black householders possessed property in excess of $3,000, and no less than 282 black residents of that city possessed property valued in excess of $1,000, of which at least three held estates in excess of $40,000. In Baltimore as late as 1850 only 101 free blacks owned any taxable property whatsoever, while in 1856 only 75 owned as much as $1,000 worth, one-fourth the number in Philadelphia twenty years earlier. The total wealth mirrored that figure; in 1856 black Baltimoreans owned just over $250,000 worth of taxable property, while black Philadelphians owned some $800,000 worth. Of major antebellum cities only Washington's free Negroes boasted a smaller average holding than Baltimore's $1,079 in 1856.[37]

By even greater contrast, in 1860 Charleston's free Negro elite (meaning those fifty-five persons who possessed $2,000 in real estate) made up 8 percent of the city's free black population. In Baltimore in both 1850 and 1860 only fifty-one such owners existed, each year constituting only 0.20 percent of the free black population. Only slightly over 1.00 percent of the free black population owned as much as $500 worth of real property during those years.[38] Of fourteen antebellum cities in the North and South, Baltimore's percentage of property owners was lowest; Philadelphia's, New Orleans's, and Charleston's percentages were more than twice, three, and four times higher, respectively. Only Washington's free blacks had a smaller average size of holdings than Baltimore's $1,327 in 1850. The small amount of property ownership in Baltimore offered a source of cohesion, albeit through virtual poverty, which few cities shared.[39]

Like property holding, skin color afforded Baltimore's free blacks more cohesion than stratification. The black population of Baltimore was especially unlike Charleston's in that it was not dominated by a free mulatto class. Property ownership in the city suggests that Baltimore's mulattoes never did form an elite economic group. While terminology offers ample room for debate, in 1815 thirty-nine out of fifty-eight Negro property holders were identified as being "colored" rather than "black." Yet two of the three free black residents who held the most property were listed as "Negroes" (most likely, meaning dark-skinned) as opposed to "colored," including Richard Russell, a carpenter who led the list with $1,345 worth of property. Moreover, the third who were dark-skinned owned nearly half of the property held by the city's free Negroes. Of the forty-two free black property holders one historian has identified by color in 1850 and 1860, only thirteen are designated as mulattoes. Moreover, while more than half of the free mulatto elite owned slaves in Charleston, no such brown master class emerged in Baltimore.[40]

Baltimore's mulattoes did not draw on the heritage of the Caribbean, as did those in Charleston, to form a "middle class" with which they distanced themselves from the mass of slaves in an effort to court favor with the city's whites. While those few free mulattoes who emigrated from Saint-Domingue appear to have reaped benefits from their former status among the white French émigrés, their influence was limited to that group of people. In Baltimore no Brown Fellowship Society distinguished those of brown skin from those of a darker hue, who were considered inferior. The attitudes of black Baltimoreans ran so contrary to the attitudes of black Charlestonians in matters of complexion that one contemporary source has suggested that Daniel Coker, a leader of the Baltimore black Methodists, was replaced as the first bishop of the fledgling African Methodist Episcopal church in part because his skin was too light. Called by one contemporary "nearly white," Coker appears to have been, in one historian's opinion, "tormented his entire life by his middle position as a free Negro and a person of mixed racial heritage." Perhaps because he had rankled a number of Baltimore's black residents by considering himself privileged as a result of his light skin, the perceived discrimination caused him to condemn racial amalgamation as "truly disgraceful to both colours" and to declare that black men with white wives were "generally of the lowest class, and are despised by their own people."[41]

Judging by the words of late antebellum white Baltimoreans, white society offered those of light skin as few advantages as those granted by the black community. The majority of Baltimore whites appear to have regarded mulattoes and Negroes about the same. Alexander Mackay, who toured the

United States in 1846, related an incident on a Baltimore train ride in which the conductor ordered a "very respectably dressed" free mulatto to the "negro crib" (an unheated box car reserved for black passengers), an action that drew approval from several of the passengers. Remarked the conductor to Mackay, "Blow me, if you can't reg'late a thousand of your out-and-out onpretendin' niggers much more easier than one of these composition gentry; they think because they have got a little whitewash on their ugly mugs, that they're the real china, and no mistake." From such observations, one might speculate that Baltimore's best-known fugitive, Frederick Douglass, might well have been escaping more than slavery in his flight to the North; he might also have been fleeing prejudice against his own light skin.[42]

A maturing black Baltimore society had indeed found ways to divide itself internally by the mid-antebellum period, beyond property holding, slaveowning, and mulatto standing. As one white Baltimore minister observed in 1834 (judging by standards he could understand and, more important, accept), the city's free Negroes tended to "look upwards, not downwards . . . constantly seeking, and acquiring, the privileges of whites."[43] Although the degree of differentiation in Baltimore was slight compared with that of other antebellum black communities, these distinctions among African Americans were every bit as important in defining community leadership as they were in Philadelphia, Charleston, or New Orleans. Perhaps in their minuteness, they became all the more prominent. In the years following the 1820s Baltimore's African Americans created their own, if subtle, brand of elitism, but they employed their own blend of ingredients by which to define and measure such standing. By the later antebellum years such once-minute differentiations gave way to a more recognizable brand of stratification that had characterized other black communities much earlier.

Perhaps more important than wealth in Baltimore's black society was occupation. Occupations plied by black Baltimoreans could prove lucrative and thus could be connected directly with material wealth. Yet the two measures were not uniform, nor were they a requirement for status in the black community in the same way that they were in white society. Craftspeople and traders, especially those who managed to acquire their own shops, stood tall in the black community, no matter the size or financial success of their businesses. The importance of occupation to elite status in Baltimore's black community becomes readily discernible when looking at the Baltimore contingent at a convention held in the city in 1852 to determine the matter of colonization. Of the forty-two delegates, eighteen were Baltimoreans; of those, fifteen are listed with occupations in the city directories for 1851 and 1853. Of those fifteen, all but one are listed as plying a trade, either skilled or semiskilled, or a profession. Four were draymen, three were porters, two were teachers (both also listed as ministers), and one operated a bar on a steamboat. Only one was listed as a laborer. Charged with representing the city's black people, these leaders reflected the "respectable" aspirations of those who selected them to leadership.[44]

Fathers with the knowledge of skilled trades, especially those that were steady and lucrative (such as ship caulking and barbering), considered it essential to pass on their skills to their sons. The censuses for 1850 and 1860 are replete with examples of this, such as James Mingo, a caulker who taught the trade to his teenage sons, James Jr. and Charles, who then found gainful employment.[45] Moreover, without a public system of education for black children, many black Baltimore parents without trades sought out respected black tradespeople as indispensable to their offspring's future success. Borrowing on colonial Maryland law and tradition that charged county courts with apprenticing orphans and poor free blacks to produce a marginally trained labor force (as well as to prevent the proliferation of public charges), many black parents sought out such tradespeople, to whom they apprenticed their sons and daughters so that they might learn a trade.[46] Urban and rural free blacks indentured themselves and their children voluntarily to both free black and white tradespeople in Baltimore to learn a trade, an essential component in their children's personal and professional advancement.

Generally unable to provide their children with property and standing, free Negro parents felt keenly that the greatest tool for their progenies' advancement was a skill with which they could carve better lives for themselves. By the later antebellum years apprenticeship served as a particularly important way station on the arduous road to this autonomous life. In 1827 James Campbell of Baltimore County indentured his fourteen-year-old son, Richard, to Alexis Silvie, a white barber on Gay Street, for four years, during which he would learn the trade and receive "such necessary night schooling, with a French teacher, as he the said Alexis Silvie may see proper." While later enactments on apprenticeship in Maryland would target free black children specifically, in Baltimore the practice was apparently already confined largely to black adolescents.[47]

Although apprenticeship laws contained an educational provision requiring a limited period of formal schooling, it had never been enforced, and white masters largely ignored any such stipulation with their black apprentices.[48] Yet black masters appear to have consistently provided at least a rudimentary education for their charges (and generally better than that), reflecting their conscious commitment to the future advancement of the city's black community and increasing their attractiveness as trainers for the city's future respectable black residents. In 1826 Isaac Watts, a boot black, achieved a real coup when he indentured his thirteen-year-old son, Samuel, to Thomas Green (regarded as the best, and certainly the richest, barber in the city) until the age of twenty-one, not only to learn barbering but also "to have one years schooling." John Fernandis, a Brazilian immigrant, had taken on various apprentices since as early as 1826, one of whose contracts stipulated that the elder Fernandis would "by the best way . . . have his apprentice William Adams taught to read and write."[49]

Not all apprentices came from the lower classes of Baltimore's black society; often the opportunity to learn a trade from one of the city's more prominent tradespeople was tied to family and intraclass standing. In 1860 the barber Jonathan A. Fernandis maintained two young apprentices, Joshua Boone and Samuel Locks, the latter Fernandis's nephew and son of John W. Locks, a caulker, hackman, and funeral director who was becoming one of the city's social leaders.[50] Occupational skills served as an especially valuable avenue to respectability, or bourgeois status, in Baltimore's black community. Its members, whether lower- or middle-class, regarded apprenticeship, which provided both occupation and education, as essential.[51]

Another avenue to social advancement was leadership activity in the local churches. Because the Methodist and Baptist churches were such important centers of black culture, the leaders of the city's churches ranked as pillars of the community. Despite such status, black ministers of all denominations often suffered chronic economic woes. Since they received no regular pay, were sustained by performing weddings, baptisms, and other services to society, and had poor, often itinerant congregations whose contributions were perforce small and irregular, black ministers—whether ordained or lay—were almost invariably forced to find additional employment to supplement their church income. Noah Davis, a former slave and Baptist preacher who arrived in the city from Virginia in 1847, rented a small room in a private home and there held a Sabbath school (despite "never [having] had a day's schooling") to provide income to sustain his call to preach. Of the nineteen black ministers ordained in the city between 1816 and 1850 identifiable in the city directories, fifteen had other occupations, such as teaching, blacksmithing, and driving a cart. All of the lay ministers listed among the class leaders in 1825 in the Bethel records were listed in the 1831 city directory as also plying a trade.[52]

Consistent with Baltimore's social structure, such ordinations and lay appointments appear to have been closely tied to having one of the city's more "respectable" trades, not necessarily skilled but above the status of a common laborer. None of the ordained black ministers in the city between.

1816 and 1850 worked as an unskilled laborer. The plan of appointments of the Methodist Episcopal churches in the Baltimore City Station for 1831 lists twenty-four lay ministers, who serviced the various black churches in the city; of those, seventeen were listed in that year's city directory. Only three of the seventeen were listed either without a trade or as a laborer; the rest were employed as porters, waiters, blacksmiths, teachers, draymen, and shopkeepers. Each of the six original trustees of the Sharp Street Methodist Episcopal Church identifiable in the city directory had similar trades. Finally, only five of the thirty-four class leaders at Bethel between 1825 and 1853 were listed in the city directories as laborers; the rest had trades similar to those of the ministers and trustees—all of whom were respected as members of the black "elite." Such status in black Baltimore society did not necessarily require financial position or membership in one denomination, though it would appear that membership in one of the more respectable occupations enhanced such standing.[53]

Baltimore's black elites appear to have consciously maintained their hard-won social status through intermarriage. In a society that largely lacked wealth transferable through marriage ties and did not reward light skin, family name proved extremely important in separating the elite of Baltimore's black society from those of humbler stature. Marriage to a member of one of the city's respectable families could solidify or even enhance the family name. Moreover, an aspiring young man could significantly improve his chances for social advancement by marrying into one of those respected families. Just as they were among the most available means by which to advance in black society, the churches appear to have served as the most direct conduits to such family unions. Both Daniel Coker and George Hackett married daughters of Nicholas Gilliard, the son of Jacob Gilliard, one of the leaders of the city's independent African church movement. Similarly, William Watkins, a teacher who was soon to become one of the city's most prominent religious and educational black leaders, married the daughter of Richard Russell, a blacksmith who was one of the original trustees of the Sharp Street church. Unlike Hackett and Coker, Watkins married into property and standing; in 1813 Russell was the wealthiest black man in the city.[54]

Such marriages even extended to respectable families from other neighboring cities. In December 1846 John A. Jones, a local barber with a thriving business on busy Baltimore Street, married Mary Ann Dickerson, the daughter of a former slave, Martin Dickerson, now a propertied Philadelphia valet, at the St. Thomas African Episcopal Church—famed as the first independent black church in the country. The ceremony was performed by the Reverend William Douglass, one of the most respected religious leaders in the city, who was a freeborn native of Baltimore, had attended Daniel Coker's school, and before moving to Philadelphia had been ordained in the A.M.E. church and had worked with William Watkins in opposition to colonization. Dickerson had been educated at the notable female academy of Sarah Douglass, who was active in both the antislavery and woman's rights movements. During their brief marriage the couple resided in Baltimore but maintained ties with Philadelphia's black elite; Mary Ann compiled a scrapbook, in which she incorporated poems written to her from various black Philadelphia community and antislavery leaders, including the Douglasses, James Forten, and Robert Douglass Jr. Connections such as these, in this case not with the wealthiest of Philadelphia's elite but with those whose standing mirrored that of Baltimore's most respectable families, helped cement the community standing that Baltimore's elite coveted yet could not achieve by wealth alone.[55]

The weight that family name carried for many such young, aspiring leaders is evident in the similar scenarios of William Watkins and John Fortie, both local teachers and ministers. Watkins's father, William, had been a successful, though illiterate, boot and shoe maker and an original trustee for the Sharp Street church. The Watkins family name went far in his son's becoming a lay minister in the church and then, at the age of nineteen, taking over the most established, respected black school in the city.[56] Similarly, Fortie's father, Jacob, had organized the city's first Colored Methodist Society and had played an instrumental role in the early formation of Bethel. Partly because of his family's prominence, the younger Reverend Fortie was named president of the Banneker Monument Committee, a group organized in the city's black community to provide a monument to Benjamin Banneker, Baltimore County's famed free black scientist, mathematician, and almanac writer.[57]

This unique formula for class standing had by the final antebellum decade given way to one that mirrored those established in other urban black communities much earlier in the antebellum period. A look at the marriage patterns of black Baltimore families suggests that by 1850 color and class differentiation had worked its way into nuptial decisions. A sampling of 360 black husbands and wives drawn from four different wards of the city in 1850 reveals that most marriages were endogamous, or between spouses of the same color. Mulatto husbands were more than four times more likely to have mulatto wives than black wives, while black husbands were nine times more likely to have black wives than mulatto wives.[58] Similar marriage patterns held true when class and color were examined; nine in ten skilled mulatto tradesmen and eight in ten mulatto males who held service occupations had mulatto wives, while more than three-fourths of unskilled mulatto male laborers had light-skinned spouses (see table 14). Male workers of a darker hue were equally as likely to have black wives; more than 91 percent of unskilled male laborers had dark-skinned spouses. Though free black Baltimoreans were as a group less affluent than their neighbors in Philadelphia or Charleston, by the final antebellum decade they appear to have been exhibiting their own brand of color-consciousness that would become far more prevalent after the end of slavery.[59]

As skin color became an increasingly defining characteristic of social standing in late antebellum Baltimore, some black residents appear to have sought and even perpetuated interracial unions. Interracial marriages, while not numerous, did occur in late antebellum Baltimore, even though they were prohibited by law. In February 1841 the *Baltimore Sun* reported the arrest of Thomas Brown, described as a "light mulatto," for the assault and battery of his white wife, Margaret. The city court confined Brown to jail for having threatened her life and for tying her up, until he posted a security against harming her again. The *Sun* concluded its report by denouncing the incident as merely "evidence of the cursed results of amalgamation."[60] Such relatively mild censure suggests that interracial marriages in the city were fairly common; the example of one black family suggests its frequen-

Table 14. Marriage Patterns among Baltimore Free Blacks, by Occupational Status, 1850

Occupational Status	Percentage with Black Wives	Percentage with Mulatto Wives	Total Number
MULATTO MALES			
Skilled tradesmen	7.7	92.3	13
Semiskilled tradesmen	0.0	100.0	5
Service occupations	20.0	80.0	30
Unskilled	22.2	77.8	36
Total	18.6	81.4	84
BLACK MALES			
Skilled tradesmen	83.3	16.7	48
Semiskilled tradesmen	100.0	0.0	10
Service occupations	87.0	13.0	54
Unskilled	91.4	8.6	152
Total	89.6	10.4	264

Source: Seventh U.S. Census, 1850, Population Schedule, Ward 1, 2, 3, and 10, Baltimore City, NA.

cy, as well as the importance of environment in forming racial perceptions. In 1860 the Conaway family lived in five separate dwellings on or near Johnson Street. The census for that year lists each of the five brothers, Perry, John, James, Eli, and William, as mulatto; remarkably, each of them had a white wife, one of whom, Catherine, William's spouse, had been born in Germany. The men, who plied such trades as caulking, carpentering, and fishing and ranged in age from twenty-four to forty-nine, must have been extremely light skinned, for all of the thirteen children born of the various unions were listed as white. Moreover, the family matriarch, Elizabeth Conaway, who resided with her son John, was listed as white as well, meaning that the five brothers were likely all products of an interracial marriage.[61]

Another element that both unified and stratified Baltimore's black population was education. Upon arriving in Baltimore in 1847, Noah Davis, a black Baptist minister, was astounded (even after having spent several months in northern cities) that Baltimore's black residents were so "advanced in education." Davis found that the city's "colored people had the advantages of schools, and . . . their pulpits were occupied, Sabbath after Sabbath, by comparatively intelligent colored ministers" and that because he had not had such advantages, he "was far behind the people."[62] Davis's observations are particularly germane to the advent of black schools in Baltimore, for the city's churches played an essential role in their founding and black congregations worked in tandem with the schools to provide education not only to the community's youth but also to its unlettered adults. More important, Davis's observations attest to the success of the city's black schools in providing at least basic literacy to a people who lacked such a skill only three decades earlier.

With the opening of the African Academy on Sharp Street in 1802, established as a dual educational and religious center, the African church became the primary vehicle of education for most of those black community members who received formal schooling. Because the African church had available rooms in which to conduct classes and functioned as the focal point for black life in the city, the black church affiliated naturally with the nascent movement for black education. Yet Baltimore's first Sabbath school provided such unsatisfactory instruction even by the standards of the learning-starved members of the African church (most likely because it lacked a teacher with sufficient education) that some parents withdrew their children to enroll them in some of the city's white private schools, most of which, they quickly found, barred them. Not until 1809 did Daniel Coker begin teaching classes at the African Academy, which attracted large numbers of students. Starting as a leader of Sabbath school classes, Coker proved himself more than able and within the year had opened a day school that operated out of the church. With seventeen initial pupils, Coker's school soon became the most celebrated black school in the city.[63]

Coker offered his students more than just classical literature and history. Coker's school provided an intellectual foundation for the development of racial consciousness. As he would soon demonstrate from the pulpit, Coker used his school as a rostrum from which to oppose slavery and advocate emancipation, as well as to foster pride in the history and accomplishments of black people, both African and American—beliefs he published later that year in his antislavery pamphlet, *A Dialogue between a Virginian and an African Minister.* Despite potential white antagonism, Coker even dared to make such philosophies public at his students' exhibition, a testament to Baltimore's then-relaxed racial climate and Coker's courage, since his new school was hardly on sound footing. "An Observer" reported that before introducing his pupils for recitations, Coker praised the recent abolition of the international slave trade and "made a few observations on the extraordinary opinion of some philosophers, that the Africans are inferior to the Whites in the organization of body and mind," confident that the students would refute such beliefs. Following the exercises, Coker's assistant, George Collins, concluded by giving a stirring speech that adeptly couched the concept of black liberation in patriotic terms, praising the founding fathers for establishing a spirit of freedom in his nation and city that "declared that man was by nature equal, and entitled to the privileges of life, liberty and property," for which "the trembling captive lifted up his hands, bound with the galling fetters of slavery, and exclaimed, *I too am a man.*" Coker's school became so popular that he soon offered night classes to adults in the community. By 1820, when Coker closed the school, as many as 150 students were enrolled, some from as far away as Washington City.[64]

Coker's emphasis on racial equality and cultural affinity spread to other private schools that new churches of various denominations opened in the city after the 1820s. Yet as more black churches began to hold classes, with black teachers, black students—like the parishioners themselves—gravitated to them. Plagued by financial hardships because many black Baltimoreans could not afford the tuition, insufficient materials, and even white interference in the curriculum, the black church schools had precarious existences and frequently closed. Nonetheless, these schools continued to grow with their churches and provided the bulk of educational opportunities for the city's black residents.[65]

Baltimore's black people were committed to "the improvement and happiness of the present and future generations," and education—either formal or technical—was an essential mechanism for improvement. Reflecting the city's free trade ideology, some white employers found that literacy made for better black employees and encouraged it. While Frederick Douglass recalled vividly the harsh rebuke his Baltimore master, Hugh Auld, gave his wife, Sophia, for teaching the young slave to read (telling her that "if you teach that nigger . . . how to read the bible, there will be no keeping him," thus forcing Frederick to turn to more clandestine means of learning letters), no such caution needed to be given to free Negroes. In nearly all trades and businesses, the ability to read even rudimentary words and letters—such as the letters Douglass noticed on the timbers and boards used in shipbuilding, labeled for correct placement during construction of the ship's frame—proved essential in achieving maximum efficiency. Some employers actually required literacy and even mathematical ability of their black workers. One newspaper advertisement read, "WANTED—A COLORED MAN, to act as Porter. None need apply unless they can read, write, and understand figures." Instead of being suspicious, many Baltimore employers, acting in their own economic interests, demanded educated free black workers. More important, free blacks understood well that literacy was a direct avenue to economic advancement.[66]

Parents capable of doing so eagerly enrolled their children in the city's Sabbath schools. Within a year of its opening, the Asbury Methodist Society had three hundred black students enrolled in its night classes alone. Less than three months after taking charge of the Bethel church, Daniel Payne (once a schoolmaster in his native South Carolina, who had arrived in Baltimore in 1844 from Philadelphia, having fled Charleston a decade earlier after the state prohibited teaching black children to read and write)[67] received a request from the wife of one of the lay ministers to tutor her children. "As soon as it became known that I was receiving her children," recalled the minister, "I was besieged by other parishioners, so that within twelve months I found myself at the head of a school of about 50 pupils." Baltimore's black children attended schools, both black and mixed, in such numbers that one visiting clergyman concluded after touring a lower-class district of the city that black residents appeared "more desirous of instruction than the whites; for when it is gratuitous to both, the same portion of each is found at the school, although the physical condition of the blacks, has been shown to be worse than that of the whites, and the obstacle to attendance of schools, therefore comparatively greater to them."[68] In 1860 less than 23 percent of school-age white children were enrolled in the city's public schools. A year earlier, one contemporary estimated that 2,665 black students attended the city's fifteen African schools, which was more than 10 percent of Baltimore's entire free Negro population.[69]

Though all black schools appear to have been well attended, the quality of the various schools and teachers in Baltimore, whether private or church-sponsored, varied widely. William Watkins (who took many of Daniel Coker's students when Coker departed) was such a demanding taskmaster with the sixty to seventy students in his academy that one contemporary wrote, "A year in his school was all the recommendation a boy or girl of that day needed." Besides daily instruction in traditional subjects, William Lively's Union Seminary at Fells Point offered an ambitious curriculum that included lessons in French and Latin and provided classes "for female adults every sabbath . . . taught gratuitously."[70] In 1838 Bethel's Sabbath school had more than a thousand books in its library, and in addition to teaching scripture it used John Conley's *Speller*.[71] The Asbury Society classified its students in categories ranging from "those who are unacquainted with letters" to "those who begin to read the Bible."[72] In 1835 Ethan Allen Andrews, who was forced to trudge through "a narrow and dirty lane" and climb over dozing hogs to get to the Sharp Street Sabbath school, concluded that he had "seldom been equally gratified by the appearance of any Sabbath school. In the teachers I found not only a degree of intelligence far superior to what I had expected, but a conscientious devotedness to their employment . . . and I have never seen, among pupils of any Sabbath school, more countenances indicative of respectable talents, or of good dispositions." Later Andrews visited the St. James Protestant Episcopal Church school, where he found a full class "greatly in want of more extended accommodations. Most of the children are learning to read; a few, however, are receiving instruction in catechisms. . . . This school is less perfectly organized than that in Sharp street; but the teachers have a good spirit, and many of the children are very promising."[73]

Such diversity of facilities, teachers, and students was only augmented by the fact that Baltimore's black schools took in slaves as well as free Negroes. In some instances they even taught. Ethan Allen Andrews reported that during his visit to the Sharp Street school he "inquired of one of the teachers whether there were any slaves in the school. He replied that there were a good many, and that he himself was one." Because Maryland had no legal proscriptions against slave literacy and because of the fervor for education among Baltimore's free blacks, many slaves in the city probably were lettered or obtained at least the rudiments of literacy while living in the city. Frederick Douglass recalled carrying around a copy of Webster's spelling book in his pocket when he was a young slave, even though his master had forbidden his wife to teach the boy to read. When Douglass returned to the city after an interruption of several years on the Eastern Shore, he remembered feeling that he was "once more in a favorable condition to increase

my little stock of education, which had been at a dead stand since my removal from Baltimore."[74]

Through newspapers, books, street signs and placards, and close proximity to many free blacks and sympathetic whites who were literate and
helped them learn, slaves in the city had access to literacy and training largely
unavailable in the countryside. According to Levi Coppin his slave mother
"was sent [from Cecil County] to Baltimore, ostensibly to live with her aunt,
Lucy Harding, but, in fact, it was that her Aunt Lucy might find some one
who would teach her to read and write; and so she did." Similarly, Lucy
Brooks recalled that her mistress, Ann Garner of Anne Arundel County, was
"gwine to sen me to Baltimo to learn to be a nurse. . . . I thought that would
be fine."[75]

The federal censuses for 1850 and 1860 confirm that Baltimore's church
schools took advantage of such an atmosphere of learning and contributed
greatly to the education of slaves and the eventual high literacy rate of free
Negroes when those slaves became free. Although literacy rates for slaves
(and for free blacks prior to 1850, when the census allowed for such enumeration) in the city are difficult to assess, the number of free Negroes capable of reading not only appears to be remarkably high but also increased
appreciably during the final decade of the antebellum period. According to
the 1850 census, of the 25,442 free Negroes living in Baltimore, 9,318 (36.6
percent) claimed to be literate; a decade later, nearly 19,500 black residents
claimed literacy, more than three-fourths of the black populace.[76]

A close look at three of the city's wards in 1850 and 1860, each with
particularly dense free black populations, reveals the increased importance
of the city's schools to the overall growth of literacy among Baltimore's black
people, especially among those of school age (see table 15). By separating
those black Baltimoreans literate in 1850 and 1860 into two groups, one that

Table 15. Literacy among Free Blacks in Baltimore by Age, 1850 and 1860

Age Group	1850[a]			1860[b]			Percent Increase
	Total	Literate	%	Total	Literate	%	
13–29	893	500	56.0	1,031	721	69.9	13.9
30 and over	766	204	26.6	1,097	448	40.8	14.2
Total (13+)	1,659	704	42.4	2,128	1,169	54.9	12.5

a. Includes Ward 1, 2, and 10.
b. Includes Ward 1, 2, and 17.
Sources: Seventh U.S. Census, 1850, Population Schedule, Baltimore City, Ward 1, 2, and 10;
    Eighth U.S. Census, 1860, Population Schedule, Baltimore City, Ward 1, 2, and 17, NA.

includes individuals between the ages of thirteen and twenty-nine, and the other that includes those individuals thirty years of age and older, one finds not only a notable increase in literacy for both groups but also a striking disparity of literacy between them. In 1850, 56 percent of the free Negroes between thirteen and twenty-nine in the three wards were literate, more than twice the rate for those aged thirty or older, among whom only 26.6 percent were able to read. By 1860 almost 70 percent of black residents under the age of thirty were capable of reading, while more than 40 percent aged thirty or more were literate. The availability of educational facilities appears to have influenced substantially the level of literacy among free blacks.[77]

Despite such a high rate of literacy, the level of literacy varied widely among those who listed themselves as literate. Such distinctions emerge clearly when considering the low level of writing skills Baltimore's free Negroes possessed in the decades preceding the Civil War. However literate the city's black people might have considered themselves, an amazingly small number of them appear to have mastered the ability to write, a skill decidedly different from reading. Because the census does not differentiate the two and because census records are often riddled with inaccuracies, assessing such skills is tricky.

In Baltimore, however, the court records offer a relatively reliable indication of the level of literacy black residents attained by the middle of the antebellum period. As part of the 1831 legislation, free blacks who wished to leave the state were required to file a petition, stating their intended destination and providing such personal information as name, age, and sex. The standardized forms also required petitioners to provide their signature. Between 1832 and 1845, 1,430 individuals ten years of age or over filled out such forms, of whom only 394 (27.6 percent) were capable of signing their own names. That figure alone is remarkable, but the disparity between genders is even more striking. Whereas 319 (40.8 percent) of the 782 male petitioners could write, only 75 (11.6 percent) of the 648 women were able to do so.[78] This reflects the lack of available formal schooling and probably the practice of providing male but not female apprentices with reading and writing skills. It does not, however, detract from the remarkable fact that more than half of the city's black adults, many of whom had emerged from slavery unlettered or barely so and without provision for public education, had at least learned to read.

While individual incentive no doubt contributed significantly to the increase of literacy during the decade, the dramatically higher number of literate blacks under the age of thirty (from whose ranks would have come the bulk of those attending schools opened during the final four decades of the period) suggests that Baltimore's free blacks understood well the importance of schools in the development of the black population. As William Watkins declared in a speech to Philadelphia's Moral Reform Society in 1836, "Give the rising generation a good education and you instruct them in and qualify them for all the duties of life. . . . give them a good education, and then when liberty, in the full sense of the term, shall be conferred upon them, they will thoroughly understand its nature, duly appreciate its value, and contribute efficiently to its . . . preservation."[79]

The education William Watkins advocated did not come without cost to Baltimore's black community. Education came to be viewed as essential to black advancement, but it transformed Negroes into citizens acceptable to a white-dominated society. In the very early decades of the century literacy was not a very important mark of distinction. In 1816, when Bethel broke from the City Station Methodist Conference and applied for incorporation as an independent Methodist church, four of the six trustees were unable to write their names on the charter application. In 1832, when Sharp Street did the same, seven of the nine trustees were literate.[80] Literacy appears to have become viewed as indispensable to advancement, a signpost toward uplift, which, as black Baltimoreans saw it, was or should be available to all.

Moreover, the growth of private schools furthered division in the black community by creating additional means of identifying those who had ascended—or eventually would—into that small group of community elites who, though not always financially far removed from the mass of the black population, recognized themselves as elites and who, either as parents or students, were able to afford the tuition necessary to attend such schools. In 1850 two-thirds of those black residents who managed to become propertied were able to read and write.[81]

The intersection between occupation, literacy, property ownership, and skin color can be seen clearly in the signers of a black-initiated petition sent to the Baltimore mayor and city council in 1850 to protest the exclusion of black children from the city's public schools. It was signed collectively by such respected leaders as the Reverend Moses Clayton, the Reverend Lewis Lee, Daniel Myers, Solomon McCabe, Samuel Hines, Nathaniel Peck, Samuel Trusty, Osbourn Burley, John Jordan, John Fortie, and Thomas Green, who provide a clear cross section of the black elite of Baltimore. Most, but not all, owned property, and those who did, with the notable exception of Thomas Green, held modest amounts. All but one were in the skilled or semiskilled trades or service occupations, and roughly two-thirds were black, while the remainder were mulatto. All appear to have been literate, and all unquestionably were free. None was a slaveholder.[82]

In a society such as Baltimore's, in which income alone only rarely determined social status, visible adherence to such bourgeois values as thrift and moral virtue proved ever more important to class stratification. Because the mass of black residents had uniformly low levels of material wealth, conspicuous middle-class behavior was the key to distinguishing one's self. To offer support for such class definition, black organizations brought together those black bourgeoisie with the same moral and behavioral practices into socially cohesive, self-conscious groups.[83] Amid a wave of reform throughout the eastern cities, black people in Baltimore organized societies designed to provide social and cultural support, economic advancement, and mutual relief for those with dark skin, who were excluded from similar white organizations. Various black spokespeople in Baltimore had begun in the 1820s and 1830s to extol the virtues of self-help as a foundation of the free black community, including trust in the "philanthropy of . . . humane and influential white citizens," the necessity of conducting themselves "in a peaceable and orderly manner," and the importance of honest toil as prevention against becoming public charges.[84]

Such vision was not limited to maintaining the fruits of liberty for current free blacks alone. Theirs was an even more weighty charge: to protect the potential freedom of current and future generations of slaves. In February 1824 the famed local abolitionist Elisha Tyson issued a "farewell address" to Baltimore's people of color, for whom he had labored so long in pursuit of justice. In it he admonished the city's free blacks to remain vigilant

> to the importance of the relation in which such of you as are at liberty stand, to those who are in bondage. I desire to convince you, that your conduct, whether good or evil, will have a powerful influence in loosening, or in riveting the chains of such of your oppressed fellow descendants of Africa as may yet remain in slavery. How lamentable is the reflection that the misconduct of some amongst you, who are enjoying the rights and privileges of freemen, should afford ground for the assertion that you are unworthy of liberty, and that this abuse of your privileges should furnish a pretext for perpetuating the sufferings and oppressions of your brethren who remain under the galling yoke of bondage![85]

Heeding Tyson's words, many of Baltimore's free blacks aspiring to respectability demonstrated their commitment to self-help by organizing, joining, and in various ways sustaining a wide array of black fraternal societies, benevolent associations, mutual aid and relief societies, and literary and debating societies. Like Negro schools, black social organizations were often inextricably tied to the church. The black societies in Baltimore fulfilled a multitude of purposes. Benevolent societies provided assistance to those less fortunate by soliciting contributions from the more affluent black residents. As early as 1821 one such benevolent society existed in Baltimore, the Baltimore Bethel Benevolent Society of the Young Men of Color; by 1835 a committee of Negro ministers reported that there were at least thirty-five, with memberships of as many as 150 each. Many of these organizations had money in the city's banks, including the African Friendship Benevolent Society for Social Relief, which had four hundred dollars in funds when it was incorporated in 1833. By 1858 forty-four separate black institutions had accounts in Baltimore's Eutaw Savings Bank.[86]

Similarly, beneficial societies utilized the regular dues paid by members of various trades to provide for the mutual support of members and former members and their families who were ill, unemployed, or deceased (in which case the beneficial society provided for the burial of the former member). The city's black caulkers, coachmen, porters, mechanics, barbers, and bricklayers organized such benevolent associations. The Free African Civilization Society provided a sick pension for its members and mandated that upon the death of a member, "his widow or children, or relatives, shall receive 25 cents per member out of the funds, and 25 cents from each member."[87]

Black women established at least as many societies as men did, and as late as 1838 they had more. That year women in the city counted nine such associations, out of a total of fifteen in the city, including the Star in the East Association, the Female Ebenezer Association, and the Daughters of Jerusalem. In the winter of 1859 and 1860 the Ladies' Sewing Circle of Bethel provided clothing, food, and firewood for nearly two hundred of the city's poor, in addition to hosting regular dinners and addresses that drew hundreds.[88]

Not all of Baltimore's free blacks could, or chose to, share in the relief efforts of the black-sponsored mutual aid societies. Some, either because they were not affiliated with the societies or because they sought a larger and more guaranteed form of disability insurance than that offered by charitable organizations, subscribed to policies provided by independent agencies. Such organizations as the People's Union Association offered financial relief to black Baltimoreans in the event they were "rendered wholly incapable, by sickness common to both sexes, or bodily injury, of pursuing, superintending, or overseeing . . . usual or ordinary business." For an initial installment of $3.50 and an annual payment of between $2.00 and $10.00, participants would receive weekly benefits equal to their annual contribution during their incapacitation, with women receiving a maximum of $4.00 per week and men a maximum of $10.00 per week. Participation was limited to applicants between the ages of fourteen and seventy, with an additional charge of twenty-five cents for those over the age of fifty. Likely directed specifically at working-class black and white subscribers—and signaling the company's high-risk clientele—the association's contract stated that such benefits would be sustained only if "such sickness or bodily injury shall have occurred while in the prosecution of a lawful, peaceable and honest pursuit, and be not the result of immoral or improper conduct."[89]

At least one organization performed in a dual capacity, as a beneficial society and an early trade union. Baltimore's Caulker's Association, organized as early as 1838, secured a right that was rare among black workers in the antebellum United States—collective bargaining with the city's shipyard owners. The organization used this power to gain better labor conditions and remarkably high wages—as much as $1.75 per day—and used the threat of strikes as leverage. Black caulkers commanded wages so high that owners in 1858 claimed they were fifty cents higher than those paid to the average white caulker. Because black caulkers dominated the semiskilled trade prior to the late 1850s, whites tolerated the organization despite its successes.[90]

Free blacks in Baltimore shared in the intellectual, cultural, and moral growth that characterized white society during the second quarter of the nineteenth century by forming a number of literary societies, debating societies, and lyceums. Established generally later than other organizations, these societies strove to provide moral and mental uplift to their members by engaging in such activities as reading and critiquing famous and contemporary works of literature, declamatory speaking, and writing prose and poetry, as well as sponsoring lectures on current issues and instruction in grammar, rhetoric, logic, and composition. Occasionally, the speakers were white, but most often they were members of the society itself or respected members of the black community. By disseminating knowledge, the societies prompted many illiterate or marginally literate black residents to improve their reading skills so that they could get the most from the discussions, lectures, and debates.[91]

Formed in the early 1830s, the first two such societies in Baltimore were the Young Men's Mental Improvement Society (for the Discussion of Moral and Philosophical Questions of All Kinds) and the Phoenix Society. By 1860 there were at least six, including the Galbreath Lyceum, which printed a newspaper, the *Lyceum Observer*, and boasted one of the city's finest libraries. Members enjoyed such lectures as "Natural History—the Habits and Instincts of Insects." The Mental and Moral Improvement Society of Bethel stated in its 1859 annual report that it had provided funds for one member to study for the ministry at Oberlin College. In pursuit of moral improvement several bible societies sprang up in the city during the period, and at least fifteen hundred black residents belonged to three black temperance societies in the second quarter of the century.[92]

Black fraternal organizations, like the literary and intellectual societies in Baltimore, reflected the interlocking nature of the city's black social institutions. Emerging late in the antebellum period and working in tandem with churches, they resembled the beneficial and literary societies. These organizations emulated similar white societies in that they provided for burial of former members and the relief of their widows and children, as well as assistance for infirm members of the various black orders. More important, the powerful institutional manifestation of self-improvement (offered more widely by these organizations than by any others in the community) allowed their leaders, who served simultaneously as leaders of other black organizations in the city, to develop oratorical and organizational skills and to gain a wide base of support in the city by demonstrating the ability to achieve collective goals. Such involvement, like leadership of the church and schools, served as springboards to political activity for the leaders and for the community at large.[93]

The first such fraternal organization established in Baltimore appears to have been the Friendship Lodge, a society of freemasons founded in 1825. Black Masons in Baltimore founded two other such local lodges of the "higher degrees" of freemasonry, similar to those that flourished nationally among whites and blacks during the period. In 1848 local residents established the Zion Lodge No. 4, Prince Hall Lodge of Free and Accepted Masons, bringing to the city the oldest black Masonic fraternity in the nation, which had been founded in Boston in 1775 and had been active among the Philadelphia black elite since 1797.[94]

During the next two years, a period ripe for establishing similar lodges in Baltimore, lodges of the Royal Arch masonry, Good Samaritans, and the Order of Odd Fellows began in Baltimore. The Order of Odd Fellows was another national fraternal order that chartered black lodges in several of the northern cities and soon became the most popular such black lodge in the Baltimore. In providing burials for deceased members, these societies took great care to demonstrate the great respect they had for their departed brothers by holding elaborate funeral ceremonies and orchestrating dignified processions in full regalia through the streets to the city's black burial grounds. Moreover, members of these groups were instrumental in the establishment in 1852 of Laurel Cemetery, the first nonsectarian burial ground exclusively "for the benefit of the colored people of the city and county of Baltimore." Until then all black corpses in the city were placed by law either in church cemeteries, at the almshouse, or in one of the two Potter's Fields established to bury the poor after city streets began to be paved. In 1818, 427 of a total of 574 reported Negro burials in the city took place in the Potter's Fields.[95]

Black fraternal organizations sponsored social events that provided members of the black community with leisure activities, including picnics, camp meetings, periodic parties, "fancy balls," cakewalks, and outings for its members. These were in addition to their regular meetings, which proved a vital source of recreation. Because the work week was six days long, the various organizations held the bulk of such activities on Sundays, usually in the afternoon after church services. The Odd Fellows sponsored various parades and picnics, Bethel's Ladies Sewing Circle did likewise, and the Barbers' Association had more than a thousand at its 1859 outing. Moreover, the community held a "family pic-nic," which drew families from all over the city and outstripped all others in its attendance.[96]

Such recreational activities were often designed for more than simple leisure; they fostered among Baltimore black people both group identification and racial solidarity and helped develop black self-awareness outside the boundaries of their own city. The Odd Fellows held their celebration on the first day of August to commemorate the British emancipation of slaves in Jamaica in 1833. Though not necessarily understood by whites, the significance of both the day and the celebration was unmistakable to black people, who drew together to "remember the morn when eight hundred thousand immortal beings stood up freemen." In 1859 a number of Baltimore free blacks traveled to Harrisburg, Pennsylvania, to join in that community's celebration of the event and to hear a speech given by Henry Highland Garnet, once a Maryland runaway slave who had since become a leading abolitionist writer and speaker in the northern states.[97]

Rather than celebrate the Fourth of July, a holiday that commemorated the independence of white Americans, black Baltimoreans often honored an event that held far greater import to those of their own race. As early as 1825 Baltimore's free Negroes gathered to celebrate Haitian independence day, a tradition that soon spread to other southern cities. It was a celebration of not only Haiti's independence but also what they hoped would be their own future as a people. In one issue of the *Genius of Universal Emancipation*, a black Baltimore writer, "whose colour subjects him to the sneers of pride and prejudice," was "persuaded that it [the Fourth of July] should not . . . be spent in frivolity and unprofitable recreation" by black people, for he "knew not whether we were included or not . . . [in] the inestimable privileges which they [white citizens of the United States] enjoy."[98]

Black organizations both reflected and contributed to the divisions of the mature black community in Baltimore. By encouraging the moral uplift and intellectual advancement of their members, these agencies inherently separated those black community members who had demonstrated—and succeeded with—bourgeois morals from those more bereft members who still needed such guidance. Moreover, these societies sought to encourage progress and individual achievements in order to promote good standing among whites, who were indispensable to the ultimate progress of the black bourgeois who made up their membership.[99] Free status appears to have been an important criterion of membership. The Free African Civilization Society, along with other groups, was made up exclusively of freemen and required that each of its members "be free from all bodily affliction that would have a tendency to render him burthensom to the society; he must possess a good moral character; he must be a free man . . . and shall not exceed forty-five years of age."[100]

Evincing a decidedly Protestant—and middle-class—ethic of work and social standing, most organizations came to be made up of respectable tradesmen and shopkeepers rather than common wage earners. Most black community leaders belonged to one or more of the city's black societies, and the organizational leaders were often prominent members of the various churches as well. Hiram Revels, minister at the Madison Street Presbyterian Church and a future Mississippi senator, was a leader of the Galbreath Lyceum; similarly, Bethel's minister John M. Brown served as president of the church's Mental and Moral Improvement Society. James A. Handy, another minister at Bethel, was also a grand master of a lodge of Masons as well as a founder of an order of Nazarites in the city. Francis J. Peck, a minister, and Isaac Scott, a barber, represented the Baltimore chapter of Odd Fellows at the national conference in Toronto in 1859, and the Lone Star Lyceum was well represented by barbers, porters, and other elite tradesmen.[101]

✜   ✜   ✜

The middle and late antebellum decades witnessed the complex development of Baltimore's black community. The city's residents staked out the parameters of their own communal identity: free, urban, and decidedly unique to the marginality they found in Baltimore's social and economic community structure. Such marginality fostered the growth of an African American consciousness that rested on common racial identity born of collective struggle. Baltimore's African Americans' social identity proved far more multifaceted than W. E. B. Du Bois's famed "double consciousness" or "two-ness" paradigm of the African American psychological construct.[102] Their social identity was simultaneously advanced and retarded by the strong self-help organizations that signified the structural maturity of a community. While trumpeting the notion of community advancement, these organizations—born of stratification that separated its members from much of the black community at large—represented a broad tear in the social fabric itself. Yet this split, mirroring that of other comparable black urban communities, occurred later and proved far less divisive in Baltimore. Baltimore's black community, still not far removed from slavery, remained a people more cohesive than divided, struggling individually and collectively to distance themselves from the oppressive yoke of bondage. As this community would find as the antebellum years wore on, white Marylanders would create an ideological atmosphere that would make it increasingly difficult, if not impossible, for the black community to escape its slave past.

7

"Cursed with Freedom"

There is nothing which the curse of slavery has not tainted. It rests on every herb, and every tree, and every field, and on the people, and on the morals.

William Lloyd Garrison, Baltimore city jail, 12 May 1830

It is not the negro's fault that he is cursed with freedom: it is the fault of the State.

Curtis W. Jacobs, Maryland House of Delegates, 1860

Although Baltimore was not subservient to Maryland's slave economy, the city did not carry on independent of the institution. As Barbara Fields has written so trenchantly, "Varied services of marketing, processing, exchange of information, purchase and sale of slaves, and provision of food, supplies, and legal advice linked Baltimore with slave society in Maryland and with the rest of the slave South." Moreover, a complex network of family connections, friendships, and other personal relationships inextricably fused the worlds of urban and rural white elites, networks that proved ironically similar to those maintained by rural and urban black Marylanders.[1] Beyond these economic, social, and legal ties that bound Baltimore to the slaveholding South lay perhaps the two locales' most important nexus: Baltimore occupied a political and ideological position in a state whose entire social system was predicated on the maintenance of white supremacy.

Commencing as early as the 1820s, many of the states of the South enacted laws designed to curb the growth of their free Negro populations. Although Maryland was once a bastion of revolutionary egalitarian sentiment in the nation (enough so that a former Maryland free Negro living in South Carolina publicly boasted that "Maryland was an abolition state"),[2] slavery's powerful ideological heritage never relinquished its hold on the state. Fundamental socioeconomic changes—emancipation, economic diversification, urbanization, and industrialization—sharpened white Marylanders' commitment to white supremacy, which swept up a reluctant Baltimore, significantly constricting the city's once liberal racial climate. Baltimore, more than any other single locale, provided the focus of those intent on rectifying what they perceived as Maryland's greatest error: the unchecked proliferation of free blacks within its borders.

Beginning in the 1820s, following a series of depressions and economic downturns that were aftershocks of the nation's first great panic in 1819, Baltimore experienced nearly four decades of uneven growth and limited periods of prosperity. Although city leaders hailed these years as evidence. of Jacksonian progress, citing real estate values that rose at unprecedented rates and expanding industries, such growth belied the true state of the city's economy for much of the period. Rampant inflation, frequent bank failures, and the overextension of businesses (resulting in numerous failures and bankruptcies) revealed the fallacy of these boasts of a booming economy. Foreign markets dwindled during the years of peace, resulting in a stagnate economy throughout the middle decades of the prewar era, with contracting credit, lowered prices, and declining business activity of all types.[3]

Moreover, as all types of shipping and manufacturing slowed, renewed only occasionally by economic upswings (such as during the mid- to late 1840s), national banking crises compounded Baltimore's economic woes. The Panic of 1837 created nationwide credit shortages, which ground new construction to a halt and created great hardships for small merchants and manufacturers. Maryland invested heavily in internal improvements, in canals but especially in railroads, in an ambitious attempt to make Baltimore the principal center of grain export for the entire West. In so doing, the state nearly bankrupted itself, forcing higher taxation and limiting its ability to provide relief during the frequent periods of economic distress. Even though the value of industrial products in Maryland more than tripled during the final three decades of the antebellum period, Baltimore lost considerable ground to New York and Philadelphia in its race for commercial supremacy in the nation.[4]

All classes of people in Baltimore suffered, but the city's economic misfortunes had the greatest effect on its wage laborers, who found themselves regularly struggling to maintain their already fragile economic standing. As the spasmodic downturns gripped the city's economy, frequent periods of high unemployment took their toll on the city's laboring class. Tax increases imposed to subsidize the state's internal improvements amounted annually to nearly a week's wages for the average day laborer, and the city's working families often were forced to use their meager savings simply to weather the recurring financial tempests.[5]

Because free blacks made up such a large percentage of the city's laborers, they were particularly hard hit. Anchored at the lowest economic level, few free blacks possessed adequate savings to carry them through periods of unemployment. The Panic of 1837 forced thousands of free Negroes to plead for public relief, though in earlier years black people had applied for and received only a fraction of such available funds. In 1810 black Baltimoreans constituted just over 4 percent of those receiving public relief in the first district; in 1827, 20 percent of those in the city's almshouse were black (many of whom were vagrants, subject to confinement to the almshouse "at hard labor for any term not exceeding three months"). By 1841, following the panic, black paupers made up almost 25 percent of those residing at the almshouse.[6]

Less able to obtain credit than whites, who could often go into debt to meet their payments, other black indigents resorted to petty theft—especially of food and clothing—in an effort to survive. One such offender, arrested in 1838 for stealing meat, pleaded that "he was hungry, and he merely took a small piece to eat." The daily newspapers were replete with such incidents, as well as other signs of great deprivation among black residents. In 1840 the *Baltimore Sun* reported the abandonment of a "newly born colored child . . . in the sink in the rear of a dwelling in N. Charles street . . . placed there by some wretch, who doubtless could not afford to keep her." The child was taken to the almshouse. Many of those too proud to accept relief were jailed for vagrancy, 138 in 1851 alone, and were sent to the almshouse.[7] After 1850, largely because the trustees of the almshouse determined who should be admitted there, fewer black vagrants were committed to the almshouse and instead were sentenced to the penitentiary. Unlike white inmates at the city jail, who could choose to labor to reduce their sentences, black inmates were forced to work without the possibility of shortening their terms of incarceration. At the state penitentiary labor was compulsory for all inmates. After 1858 few black convicts were sentenced to the penitentiary and instead were sold as term slaves.[8]

The applications for insolvency in Baltimore provide an indication of the hardships black residents were suffering in the decades before the Civil War. In 1817 and 1818 a total of 954 city residents applied to the commissioners for relief of their debts. Of those applicants, just 10 (slightly more than 1 percent) were free Negroes. By 1849 black applicants constituted more than 17 percent of those who applied for insolvency in Baltimore. Moreover, because debt reflects an individual's apparent capacity both to borrow and to repay, the great disparity between the average values of the debts of white and black applicants (as well as the exceedingly low value of black debts) indicates the fragile economic standing of most free blacks in the city. White applicants had average debts of nearly a thousand dollars, while black applicants who asked for relief carried an average debt of less than forty-seven dollars. Only three black applicants held debts of more than a hundred dollars, and one James Robinson, a laborer, was unable to pay his debt of just seven dollars, a week's wages. Between 1835 and 1850, 90 percent of black debtors imprisoned for their debts had obligations of less than ten dollars, as opposed to 67 percent of whites.[9]

For free Negroes, Baltimore's economic downturn meant far more than a worsening of their already precarious financial situation. Free blacks in the city suffered substantially higher mortality rates than whites during the period. Unable to afford private health care, most free Negroes in the city failed to obtain adequate and regular medical attention; they had even less than poor whites and slaves. The mortality rate of Baltimore's free Negroes was even higher than for free African Americans in the countryside, because of poor and crowded housing and recurring epidemics. The New England observer Ethan Allen Andrews noted in 1835 that "the moral and physical condition of the free negroes in Baltimore is . . . represented as more depressed than it was while they were slaves," and he estimated that slave deaths in the city were "only about two-thirds as great as among the free people of color."[10]

Baltimore was not an anomaly in this regard. During the 1820s free blacks suffered higher death rates than whites and slaves in nearly all of nine comparable antebellum cities.[11] However, Baltimore's free black population proved an exception to the other cities in that its mortality rate did not improve substantially during the ensuing decades. The city's Board of Health was baffled about why free Negroes in the city appeared reluctant "to receive the proffered services of the vaccine physicians," but this "reluctance" probably stemmed from fear and distrust.[12] White Baltimore authorities do not appear to have made much of an effort to educate free blacks and poor whites about the available health services and the importance of inoculation. Moreover, the black hospital at the almshouse sat on low ground, directly adjacent to a pigsty and overflowing cesspool, "two to three feet deep . . . contain[ing] one or two dead pigs, and seemed to be in a state of rank and pestilent fermentation," as well as "the overflowing contents of the men's privy and the washings from the dead house." In 1849 Thomas Buckler, the city physician, determined that this filthy pool was a leading source of that summer's cholera outbreak in Baltimore, which was particularly deadly to the black community, no doubt spread from those black residents who sought care at the almshouse.[13]

Epidemics always proved especially deadly to the black residents of Baltimore. The city's narrow alleys and courtyards that so many free blacks inhabited were generally ignored by city health officials and were often notoriously dirty, with stagnant pools of water and uncollected garbage, manure, and other refuse festering in the summer heat and humidity. Under such conditions, contagious diseases flourished in the city. During a cholera outbreak in 1832 a city health official reported that half of the newly reported cholera victims were black. Free blacks suffered 998 fatalities in that epidemic, 28 percent of the deaths in the city that year. One third of those who died during an 1849 cholera epidemic were black, while a typhus epidemic the same year killed 791 more, 17 percent of the city's total deaths. During that outbreak Buckler observed that although the areas of the city most plagued were occupied by working-class whites as well as free blacks, the disease attacked the blacks almost exclusively. He blamed the outbreak of the disease on "a number of pig-styes . . . kept by some free negroes, whose houses were only accessible by narrow alleys running into St. Paul street. The filthy condition of these places beggars description. . . . L alley, near the centre of the city and directly back of the public stores, was entirely depopulated." Similarly, the 1832 cholera epidemic first appeared in Ruxton Lane, judged "one of the filthiest parts of town." Both outbreaks occurred in areas of dense black residence, and free Negroes suffered disproportionately.[14]

After 1840 progressively fewer Baltimore free blacks received inoculations to prevent contagious diseases or sought treatment at those public services available to them for such purposes. In 1844 just over 21 percent of those Baltimoreans who were admitted to the almshouse for medical treatment were black; by 1860 that figure had fallen to 12 percent. In 1857 less than 14 percent of those persons treated at the city's Eastern Dispensary were black.[15] As a result, between 1824 and 1860 the percentage of free black deaths as part of the city's whole was higher than its share of the city's population in all but eight years; conversely, during the same thirty-six-year period, the proportion of white deaths exceeded the corresponding white share of the population only once.[16]

Commenting on the poor health of free blacks in Baltimore, Hezekiah Niles wrote in the *Niles' Weekly Register* in 1825, "It is well called 'evidence of improvidence'; and the fact certainly is, that the free blacks in Baltimore are not only less abundantly supplied with the necessaries and comforts of life than the slaves, but they are also much less moral and virtuous." In 1832 Niles attributed the high number of fatalities among free blacks during that year's cholera epidemic to their "sloth and indisposition to arduous work," which led to destitution and an inability to afford proper medical care, though he suspected they were also "less carefully attended."[17] Similarly, the city's consulting physician concluded in his 1829 report that the high mortality rate of black residents "can only be lessened by regular habits, by which . . . they will avoid unnecessary exposure and intemperance, the usual pandora of this class of people."[18]

Observations such as these reveal far more than a mere concern over the poor health of free blacks in Baltimore. They suggest a perceptible shift of white opinion about free Negroes in Maryland society by the middle antebellum years. This change was particularly noticeable in Baltimore. Although the city's economic opportunities and liberal racial climate had once attracted free blacks and had allowed for relatively relaxed relations between the races, rapid economic changes during and following the 1820s, in combination with the haunting specter of an uncontrollably huge free black population, prompted whites to have a less tolerant attitude toward black residents. This change soon altered dramatically the ideologically moderate racial temperament of the state. Starting in the late 1820s Maryland became far more like its neighbors in the Deep South in terms of racial ideology and even less tolerant than other slave states in its actions regarding free Negro residents. Though Baltimore resisted some of these radical measures, it too was swept up in the state's maelstrom of racial hostility.[19]

Such harshened ideology in Baltimore was ushered in by a repressive wave of legislation enacted by the state of Maryland and directed at black people. Like other slave states, after 1830 Maryland implemented a complex web of laws designed to regulate the behavior of slaves. By their very nature, however, they ineluctably restricted the liberties of free Negroes as well. These laws included the registration of manumissions, written proof of freedom, the prohibition of their testifying against a white in court, disfranchisement, the codification of the legal status of the offspring of free black–slave unions, the restraint of free black trade in plantation staples (which were presumed stolen), restriction of their use of firearms, licensed ownership of dogs (which they used for hunting), and a ban on "disorderly assembly," as well as those attempting to curb "idleness" and vagrancy (punishable by forced labor, since whites regarded Negroes as valuable only insofar as they served as productive workers).[20]

Yet even these restrictive laws proved far less severe in practice than in theory, especially in Baltimore. During the first quarter of the century, most laws passed regarding Negroes dealt with slaves rather than free blacks. Prior to 1830 Maryland's pattern of restraint was no more strict toward free Negroes than those of other slave states, and some laws were actually closer to those enacted in the North. The state did enact certain laws designed specifically to control free blacks, such as the 1808 law that empowered justices of the peace to indenture all "roving free negroes" between the ages of eight and twenty-one, and the 1818 law that allowed punishments other than imprisonment—such as flogging, banishment, or sale into term servitude—for serious noncapital offenses committed by free Negroes. But these laws dealt with "nonproductive" free persons of color and did not deter most working people. Even the 1805 law that required free blacks manumitted henceforth to apply for certificates of freedom was designed to control slaves more than to restrict free Negroes. Because state law still made few distinctions between the legal status of free blacks and whites, especially concerning property rights and the pursuit of trade (canons too sacred to the American creed of individual liberty to abrogate for any free person, even those who were black), most free Negroes enjoyed a relatively high level of freedom.[21]

As the nineteenth century progressed, this ambivalence toward free Negroes diminished sharply. Marylanders grew increasingly uneasy about the anomaly of "free Negroism" in a social system designed for but two classes: free white people and unfree black people. Maryland's proportion of free Negroes to slaves rose from nearly one in thirteen in 1790 to less than one in three in 1820, attributable almost wholly to the increase of free blacks rather than any decrease of slaves. The small state's unique agricultural situation only compounded the apprehensions of much of its white populace, many of whom were voicing increased concern about the decline of slavery and the growth of a free Negro population that by 1820 was the highest of any state in the entire nation (see table 16).[22]

In contemplating gaining control of the state's large population of free Negroes in an attempt to protect its system of chattel bondage, Marylanders had much to consider. The state's economic practices caused public opinion to be uniform neither in opposition to free blacks nor in support of slavery. Maryland free blacks had long formed an essential labor force, both rural and urban, and were not controlled significantly for a long while. Because so many of the freedpeople had moved from the countryside to Baltimore, where they made up an important source of cheap labor for the burgeoning industries (appeasing both rural slaveholders, fearful of losing control of their slaves because of the large number of free blacks, and urban employers, desirous of high profit margins), rural and urban residents alike were for a long while tolerant of the proliferation of their troublesome presence.[23]

Holding considerable sway in defining the parameters of freedom outside Baltimore, planters (using the term carefully, for slaveholdings were small and

Table 16. Slave State Free Negro Populations, 1820, 1840, 1850, and 1860

	1820	1830	1840	1850	1860
Alabama	571	1,572	2,039	2,265	2,690
Arkansas	59	141	465	608	144
Delaware	12,958	15,855	16,919	18,073	19,829
District of Columbia	4,048	6,152	8,361	10,059	11,131
Florida	—	844	817	932	932
Georgia	1,763	2,486	2,753	2,931	3,500
Kentucky	2,759	4,917	7,317	10,011	10,684
Louisiana	10,476	16,710	25,502	17,462	18,647
Maryland	**39,730**	**52,938**	**62,078**	**74,723**	**83,942**
Mississippi	458	519	1,366	930	773
Missouri	347	569	1,574	2,618	3,572
North Carolina	14,612	19,543	22,732	27,463	30,463
South Carolina	6,826	7,921	8,276	8,960	9,914
Tennessee	2,727	4,555	5,524	6,422	7,300
Texas	—	—	—	397	355
Virginia	36,889	47,348	49,852	54,333	58,042
Totals	134,223	182,589	215,575	238,187	261,918

Sources: U.S. Bureau of the Census, Population of the United States in 1860, 598–99; Berlin, Slaves without Masters, 136.

planters thus few in Maryland; in 1860, 90 percent of all owners held less than fifteen slaves, and only sixteen individuals owned as many as a hundred slaves) wanted it both ways. In turning from slave labor to free labor, they tried to maintain not only the low labor costs associated with slavery but also racial control. Like Baltimore industrialists, planters turned routinely to free blacks to provide labor and insisted that they sign yearly labor contracts with lower wages than those demanded by whites. Rural free blacks, however, resisted such contracts, bargaining for better terms or refusing to work (something those slaveowners who liberated their slaves earlier in the century did not plan for) and burdening white farmers desperate for labor during peak seasons. More ominous, the autonomy free Negroes exerted made clear that black and white conceptions of independence were not the same. Embarrassed about their dependence on free black labor as well as the obvious loss of control of their labor force, rural white farmers bemoaned the critical labor "shortage" in the countryside, punctuating their laments with the argument that free Negroes were a people sorely in need of greater white control. The clamor easily reached the ears of those rural planter delegates in the Maryland General Assembly.[24]

Such debate foreshadowed more widespread anti–free Negro sentiment that flowered in Baltimore during the decades after 1830. The combination of a swollen free black population and severe economic downturns in the previous decade caused the state's crisis of "free Negroism" to become a source of particular concern for white Baltimoreans. In 1820 nearly a fourth of the state's free blacks resided in the city, and that proportion would continue to increase for the next three decades, until it had grown to just under a third. The size of the free Negro population of Baltimore unsettled even Hezekiah Niles, a staunch opponent of colonization, forcing him to comment somewhat pragmatically that "we *have* the blacks, and must make the best of the unhappy condition in which we are placed that we can."[25]

Many in Baltimore disagreed with Niles's apparently acquiescent stance. Instead of evoking empathy from Baltimore's whites, the dire effects of the recurring economic downturns only began to harden their once-tolerant convictions. While some white Baltimoreans continued to view free Negroes as "honest, industrious and peaceable," whose social organizations provided valuable services to "the destitute of their own color,"[26] many more either ignored or were unaware of the successes of the city's black community, or quite possibly were threatened by them. Rather than identify slavery as the problem, as did Niles, far more Marylanders believed that instead of having too many slaves, Maryland housed too many blacks who were not in bondage. Baltimore became the focus of this startling anomaly.

As the nation struggled with the rapid growth of the free Negro population, white Marylanders quickly moved to the fore in lending support to various schemes for reducing its free black class. As early as 1817 such concerns manifested themselves in Baltimore in support for the newly formed American Colonization Society. That year Robert Goodloe Harper, a former congressman from South Carolina who had recently moved to Baltimore, published a lengthy public letter supporting colonization. Free blacks, according to Harper, were "condemned to a state of . . . degradation" partly because of their "idle and vicious" habits, attributable to slavery; consequently, whites were unable "to help . . . treating them as our inferiors . . . since we cannot help . . . associating them with the slaves." Even if a free black person were to "follow some regular course of industry," Harper concluded that those "habits of thoughtless improvidence which he contracted while a slave" would prevent him from providing for himself adequately and consistently enough to avoid becoming a public charge. "You may manumit the slave," Harper wrote grimly, "but you cannot make him a white man." More ominous, free blacks were a most undesirable influence on, and potential accomplices to, those held in bondage. They were "a nuisance and a burden . . . [they] encourage the slaves to theft, because they partake in its fruits. They furnish places of meeting and hiding, for the idle and vicious slaves." Harper and others supported efforts designed to arrest the growth this "idle, worthless and thievish race."[27]

Robert Goodloe Harper was not the only Baltimorean to draw attention to the city and state's free black problem. Joseph D. Learned, an attorney, proposed a scheme of forced relocation of African Americans—not just from Maryland but from all southern states—to trans-Mississippi Missouri. There, in isolation, they would develop social and trade skills that would allow them to survive and even compete once white settlement in the region grew—a plan that presaged Andrew Jackson's "final solution" for Native Americans. Such Baltimore leaders as John Pendleton Kennedy trumpeted the evils of free blacks' anomalous status. In 1821 he told the Maryland House of Delegates that the "free black population [was] too high for communion with slaves, . . . too low for the associates of freemen," and unable to "compete for work with . . . whites." Echoing Harper's pronouncement, Kennedy declared that without options, free blacks turned naturally to vice, contaminating slaves in the process.[28]

Even Hezekiah Niles, who stridently opposed slavery and colonization and supported gradual emancipation in his Baltimore publication, found ample room in his editorials to demean free blacks. He argued in 1819 that the "free blacks among us are less honest and correct, less industrious and not so much to be depended upon . . . as the well-treated slaves. They will make a thousand shifts rather than seek employment, unless pinched by instant necessity." Niles charged that the "indolence and improvidence" of free blacks "slackens the zeal of the friends of emancipation, and is the source of great triumph to those who totally reject the expediency of it."[29]

In cooperation with the Washington-based American Colonization Society, whites organized several state-level efforts to rid Maryland of its free Negroes.[30] In the mid-1820s respectable white Baltimoreans, such as the attorneys John H. B. Latrobe and Charles C. Harper (son of Robert Goodloe Harper), carried the standard, undertaking the daunting dual task of convincing the state legislature of the need for state appropriations to the effort and garnering financial support within the city and state. In 1827 an anxious Harper wrote to his dearest friend Latrobe that "we must not die until we find some place of refuge for the blacks," despairing that "a fearful conflict is in preparation for posterity."[31] The following year the group ushered about town Abd Rahman Ibrahima, a West African prince sold into slavery in Mississippi nearly forty years earlier and released through the intercession of President John Quincy Adams. Garbed "in Moorish costume," Ibrahima visited various city sights and solicited contributions to enable him return to his homeland. Even the indefatigable antislavery activist Benjamin Lundy, editor of the *Genius of Universal Emancipation* that had recently moved to Baltimore, supported a Haitian emigration plan as early as 1824 and acted as an agent, promoting the society's efforts in his paper the following year, though adamantly maintaining that his efforts were not to remove blacks from the United States but rather to free slaves.[32] By 1832 such efforts had resulted in the state government's appropriating annual funds to the Maryland State Colonization Society, an auxiliary of the American Colonization Society, the first such state to do so.[33]

In conjunction with this change of mood, white constables began seeking black suspects for most petty crimes perpetrated in the city. The French visitor François La Rochefoucauld-Liancourt observed that "the judges attribute the multiplicity of robberies to the free negroes."[34] The percentage of black people incarcerated rapidly outstripped the proportion of free Negroes in the population. By 1853 black inmates made up 34.7 percent of those confined in the city jail, while free blacks constituted less than half that percentage of the city's population. William Lloyd Garrison noted the change of attitude toward blacks as early as 1830, writing in the *Genius of Universal Emancipation* that "there is a prevalent disposition among all classes to traduce the habits and morals of our free blacks. The most scandalous exaggerations in regard to their condition are circulated by a thousand mischevious tongues, and no reproach seems to them too deep or unmerited."[35]

Not surprisingly, disparagement of free blacks in Maryland increased along with the rise of the proslavery defense, beginning in the 1830s. In one historian's words, "It was no accident that an articulate defense of slavery appeared with the emergence of the free Negro caste." When abolitionist speakers and writers in both the North and South (including several even in Baltimore) launched their crusade to expunge the blight of slavery from the American utopia, white southerners moved to protect the institution. Proslavery polemicists subsequently bombarded Baltimoreans and other white southerners not only with justifications for the positive good of slavery as the natural lot for innately inferior people (free Negroes created an obvious contradiction) but also with the opinions of learned and respected southern leaders attesting to the inherent inferiority of the Negro.[36]

As early as 1832 Attorney General Roger B. Taney, a former Baltimore slaveowner and supporter of colonization who in five years would be named chief justice of the U.S. Supreme Court, wrote that "the African race in the United States even when free are everywhere a degraded class. . . . The privileges they are allowed to enjoy, are accorded to them as a matter of kindness and benevolence rather than of right." Presaging his famous ruling on the *Dred Scott* case of 1857, Taney concluded that Negroes "were not looked upon as citizens by the contracting parties who formed the Constitution" and that the lowly condition of their race suggested they deserved no change in their legal status. Free blacks, possessing the same economic privileges and opportunities as whites, demonstrated unmistakably by their poverty and ignorance that their race was naturally unfit for freedom. Ignorant themselves of the reality of Baltimore's free Negro community, advocates of this belief pointed to Baltimore, where they insisted that miserable health conditions, squalid housing, and widespread unemployment among free blacks served as no better proof of the veracity of their opinion.[37]

Marylanders did not direct their frustration solely at free blacks. Much of the hostility evinced by rural residents had become centered on the city of Baltimore itself. The growth of Baltimore's free black and working-class white population only exacerbated suspicion of the city itself among rural whites, especially slaveholders. With classic Jeffersonian dualism, planters found industry and urban ways inherently evil and debilitating to the noble pursuit of farming but enjoyed the fruits of progress made possible largely by Baltimore's huge contribution to the state's tax base.[38] To ruralites, city people simply thought differently than they did. Susanna Warfield, daughter of a prosperous Carroll County planter, charged that Baltimoreans "live very much within themselves" as a result of their unbridled devotion to business. As early as 1786 rural legislators had blocked efforts to move the state government to Baltimore from Annapolis, where the slow pace and prevailing conservative ideology seemed more appropriate to the country delegates.[39] As Baltimore grew, however, it received progressively larger shares of the state's appropriations, further rankling planters who paid increasing land taxes, while its flour- and grain-based economy moved continually further from the tobacco and cotton interests of Maryland's southernmost counties.

Finally, planters feared that Baltimore's phenomenal growth and its free labor inclinations undermined the foundations on which slavery was built in Maryland. Had not the state's antislavery movement originated there? Was it not still the locus for it, with those "hot abolitionists"—Benjamin Lundy and William Lloyd Garrison—publishing their seditious, even libelous, antislavery literature in the city?[40] Had not a Baltimore lawyer, Daniel Raymond, the president of the Maryland Abolition Society, run a strong campaign in 1825 for election to the first branch of the city council on a platform based solely on antislavery, garnering most of his support from the city's white mechanics?[41] Rural slaveowners viewed the ever-increasing labor force in Baltimore as a threat to the value of their slave property. To them, white mechanics in the city, who had odd notions of republicanism (including a hostility to slave competition) and whose numbers were rapidly increasing, would use their vote to dominate slave interests in the state. All of these factors exacerbated their innate suspicion and even fear of the city. This fear was articulated no more clearly than in an 1859 editorial in the *Planter's Advocate*, which expressed a preference for the state's numerous free blacks over "a class of free white labor that would be hostile to slavery, would be entitled to vote, and might finally dictate terms to slavery itself."[42]

Finally, the weakening of the plantation economy in Maryland and the growth of industry in Baltimore sparked debate over the efficacy of slavery as a labor system, which stirred both anger and even more fear of Baltimore among planter aristocrats. According to its critics (many of whom, like Hezekiah Niles, were Baltimoreans), slavery was a fetter to industry and economic progress in the state. Competition with slaves devalued all labor in Maryland, which was detrimental to both white workers and employers in the state. "Slavery is no longer compatible with progress," charged the Baltimorean Robert S. Steuart in 1845, "it is a dead weight and worse; it has become a wasting disease, . . . a leprous distillment into the life blood of the commonwealth." Steuart calculated on the basis of the latest census returns that had it not been for the great increase in the population of Baltimore, Maryland's population would have stagnated completely during the preceding decade—contrasting unfavorably with the progress of several northern and even western states, whose population increases and industrial outputs now far exceeded those of Maryland.[43]

Baltimore appeared to have little stake in the social institution that not only assured planter aristocrats of social legitimacy and political dominance but also preserved racial control in an atmosphere of fragile social harmony. Planters needed no further proof of Baltimore's threat to their hegemony than the rapid decline of slavery in that city. In 1830 only 4 percent of the state's slaves resided in Baltimore, a figure that fell by nearly half during the remaining antebellum years. The small percentage of Maryland slaves in Baltimore was eclipsed by the small number of slaves in the city's population. The decline of the institution in the city moved C. W. Arfwedson, a foreign visitor, to remark in 1832, "Any person, ignorant that slaves exist, would never be able to discover it, nothing in the houses or streets giving the slightest indications of it." The fears of planters, intensified by economic difficulties and shifts of political power, caused such ruralites as Susanna Warfield to conclude that "Baltimore is a wicked city."[44]

In a conscious effort to maintain the primacy of planter interests in Maryland, state legislators had consistently denied Baltimore representation commensurate with its population. Under the state constitution of 1776 each county was entitled to four seats in the House of Delegates, while Baltimore and Annapolis each received two. Not until 1838, when Baltimore comprised more than one-fifth of state's population, did the legislature amend its constitution and begrudgingly grant Baltimore the same number of representatives that the largest county received. Even at its representational height in 1851, when it separated from Baltimore County and received ten delegates, the Baltimore contingent constituted only one-seventh of the House of Delegates' members. This underrepresentation proved crucial because those delegates from the city generally opposed Maryland's rural legislators' conservative attempt to preserve traditional values in the face of Baltimore's progressivism. The Baltimorean John Pendleton Kennedy recognized the countryside's mistrust of the city when he concluded that "from the many symptoms already manifested of the temper of the present Legislature against our city, I am disposed to believe that the [upcoming 1822] session will be marked by more than one act of unequivocal hostility." This hostility stemmed from Baltimore's free blacks as much as from its whites.[45]

Supporters of slavery—many of whom served in the legislature—had grown anxious about the potentially dire consequences of the unimpeded growth of a huge free Negro population that was inextricably entangled with the state's slaves. Increasingly, state legislators moved to protect slavery in Maryland by curbing the growth of its free black population, prompting one legislative committee member to remark in 1843 that "hardly a session of the Legislature passes that some law is not enacted restricting them [free Negroes] in their rights and privileges." The legislator's observation proved not far from the truth, for beginning in the 1820s and accelerating thereafter, the Maryland legislature instituted a series of enactments, unprecedented in their severity, designed not only to check the growth of this unwanted class but also to restrict free Negroes' already limited liberties.[46]

As early as 1807 Maryland lawmakers had acted to curb its rapidly growing free Negro population by prohibiting further immigration into Maryland from other states. At best, this act proved difficult to enforce, especially in Baltimore, and to render the enactment even less effective, in the ensuing years the legislature itself granted exceptions to a number of individual petitions. Knowing that county constables were not vigilant in enforcing the law, in 1822 Eastern Shore Dorchester County residents petitioned that fines and whippings be administered to illegal black immigrants, prompting the General Assembly to reaffirm the law publicly and order magistrates and officers to arrest such miscreants under threat of fine for neglect.[47] Moreover, in response to the complaints of labor-starved farmers, in 1825 lawmakers passed laws forcing free Negroes to show proof of gainful employment or be banished from the state. Free black convicts would be banished upon their release, and if they remained for more than two months, they could be sold as slaves. Prior to the 1830s the state acted to prevent new black immigration and expel its most undesirable black residents, but the start of the new decade would find it targeting the whole of the Maryland free black population.[48]

In the autumn of 1831 the Maryland General Assembly reconvened amid reports of the Nat Turner slave insurrection in Southampton County, Virginia. Fear of a similar incident in Maryland gripped white residents. During the next two years slave sales in Baltimore more than doubled, from 65 in 1831 to 145 in 1832 and 147 in 1833.[49] In the rebellion's aftermath, while delegates learned the details of the insurrection, they were deluged with petitions and statements from Baltimore and elsewhere in the state calling for the abolition of slavery to forestall any such violence in Maryland. Proslavery legislators were fearful that such sentiment signaled the ascendance of an antislavery movement, which had long been apparent in Maryland but which had grown into a sectional fervor. By the end of the 1820s the Upper South boasted more antislavery societies than the northern states had. A strong abolition movement in Maryland could bring the end of the institution in the state, where it was already dying, as it was in neighboring Delaware and had in Pennsylvania. As early as 1823 the governor of nearby Delaware had conceded that within a generation forced manumission would be inevitable in that state. Even in slave-rich Virginia, lawmakers, prompted by Nat Turner's bloody uprising, were debating hotly the issue of legislative emancipation.[50]

The white hysteria that emerged in response to the Southampton rebellion soon implicated Baltimore's black residents as being part of a wider conspiracy that included free Negroes. In September, just a month after the Turner insurrection, the mayor of Baltimore received ominous warnings of at least two imminent rebellions in and near the city. In one case Mayor Jacob Small received a dubious correspondence, purportedly intercepted as it passed between conspirators, that outlined a plot involving "eight hundred peple in town that were going to help murder the damd white people." The scheme invoked "all of our colur to rise and murder our master . . . [and] butcher all other men woman and children . . . although the constables have taken our guns away yet by God now we can do our buisnes with the knife," but it implored that "in gods name do not hurt Quakers. . . . Quakers we can make work for us when we gin possession of the country." Less than a week later the editors of one of the city's newspapers received an anonymous warning that "a number of Blacks have been in the habit for several nights past, of Assembling in Military Unifor[m] . . . putting them through their Military exercise—Citizens of Baltimore be on your guard."[51]

Not all such talk of black rebellion in Baltimore appears to have been contrived. In November 1831 Mayor Small received a note from James Christian, a Baltimore County black resident, who reported that "the colerd peple intend risin here on satarday next to go to buttemur [Baltimore]. i was at preching on sundy whin 234 Jind them[.] I hav gred to go wid dem but hop dis notis wil sav me as i will strive to stop dem[.] when we gets to the sity you will mimber i tuld you 1st as i am a preacher among dem and my wif and chldrn will be saf. . . . be redy and de Lord prusuve you all." Baltimore's free Negroes, recognized for their autonomous demeanor, seemed to white Marylanders to be the epicenter of a widespread racial upheaval. In the midst of such an unsettling climate (and perhaps taking advantage of it), jittery proslavery legislators in Annapolis acted quickly to preserve racial order in Maryland.[52]

In late 1831, abandoning the state's long-standing toleration, the Maryland legislature, citing Old Southampton's slave insurrection, enacted legislation designed not only to control slaves but also, more pointedly, to codify a uniform legal status for free Negroes. The preamble to enactment, which denotes white Marylanders' heightened fear in the aftermath of Nat Turner's shocking rebellion, reveals more strikingly the deeper hostility those same whites had begun to evince toward resident free blacks, a hostility born of motivations entirely separate from the Virginia slave uprising: "Resolved, that the increased proportion of the free people of color, in this State, to the white population—the evils growing out of their connection and unrestrained association with the slaves, their habits and manner of obtaining a subsistence, and their withdrawing a large portion of employment from the laboring class of the white population, are subjects of momentous and grave consideration."[53]

Though one of the law's provisions targeted slave control by forbidding further importations of slaves into the state either for residence or for sale, the bulk of the law proscribed the liberties of free blacks. Drawing on the 1829 opinion of a special committee on colonization that free blacks were a national evil and an embarrassment to the wholesome operations of government, lawmakers attempted to limit the growth of the state's "troublesome presence" by prohibiting free blacks from entering the state and subjected migrants remaining in Maryland more than ten days to fines or, if they defaulted, sale into slavery. Maryland free blacks who left the state for more than thirty days were considered nonresidents and liable to this law upon their return.[54]

Courts were granted the authority to banish from the state free blacks convicted of noncapital offenses. Outside Baltimore and Annapolis (where lawmakers acceded to the provision's impracticality), blacks were forbidden to assemble or attend religious services not conducted by white clergymen or "respectable" proxies, and even in Baltimore and Annapolis such meetings were forced to end by ten o'clock at night. Free blacks were forbidden from purchasing liquor without a special permit, and the law prohibited whites from purchasing sundry produce (including corn, wheat, and tobacco, staples of the southern and Eastern Shore counties) from black vendors, ostensibly to prevent theft from white fields but more specifically to inhibit prosperous black farmers. Finally, in conjunction with the creation and state support of the Maryland State Colonization Society, all further manumissions were to be reported to the state's board of colonization, and sheriffs were charged with the task of enumerating all potential free black emigrants in their respective counties. White advocates of colonization appear to have been particularly vigilant against black anticolonizationists; in the summer of 1832 Baltimore colonizationists effected the arrest of a Philadelphia black preacher, Charles W. Gardiner, known to have spoken against the scheme, on charges that he had remained in the state longer than ten days, a violation of the 1831 legislation.[55]

During the subsequent decade, although Maryland legislators focused on constructing railroads and other efforts to boost the state's lagging economy, they continued their assault on the state's free Negroes. Although no slave insurrections emerged in Maryland and the specter of Nat Turner had faded from people's memory, the General Assembly still passed a succession of bills designed to restrict further the freedoms of free Negroes. In 1835 lawmakers empowered criminal courts to sell out of state those free blacks previously convicted and sentenced to the Maryland penitentiary. In 1840 the legislature passed a supplement to the 1831 law that empowered county sheriffs to arrest free blacks without visible means of support for sale as term slaves, while free Negro children would be indentured, males until the age of eighteen, females until age twenty-one. In 1841 legislators made it a felony, punishable by no less than ten years of imprisonment, for a free Negro to "knowingly call for, receive, or demand from any Post Office" abolitionist literature. This resulted in immediate arrests in Baltimore. In 1842 the General Assembly forbade all black societies, and three years later it outlawed all meetings of black residents "for religious purposes except those held at regular houses of worship," targeting camp meetings and lengthy outdoor meetings. In addition, representatives unsuccessfully introduced additional bills forbidding free blacks from acquiring and holding real estate, compelling them to move to the free states to "Advance the Interests of Tradesmen, Mechanics, and Other Laboring Persons," and forcing them to hire out by the year.[56]

Though generally resistant to such anti-Negro legislation, even Baltimore succumbed to pressure to curb the growth of the free Negro caste. White residents, aware of the large population in their midst, heard the warnings of state leaders opposing free blacks. In 1819, in response to the large number of free black felons confined in the state penitentiary, which was located in the city, a Baltimore grand jury had recommended passage of a municipal ordinance allowing such convicts to be sold into term slavery. Later that year the city council enacted the recommended law without significant debate. The state followed suit six years later. Ironically, now the state was following Baltimore's lead in repressing free Negroes.[57]

After two decades in which Baltimoreans felt no need to restrict further its black residents, the city again began to constrain free Negroes. In 1838 Baltimore imposed a curfew on free Negroes, requiring that all gatherings be broken up and individuals in their homes by ten o'clock each night. Local officials appear to have enforced this ordinance rigorously, even among the black churches, for the Reverend Jacob Gruber lamented having "to conclude our meetings by ten o'clock at night, so that all might keep good houses, according to law."[58] The city also required free Negroes to obtain written permission from the mayor for gatherings and insisted that a white male patron submit the request, along with his recommendation. Not even black schools were exempt from this ordinance; they were required to obtain permits to hold student exhibitions. In the summer of 1853 the state's attorney for Baltimore County instructed the sheriff to summon a posse to arrest all black people at camp meetings held outside the city. Black passengers on the Philadelphia, Wilmington, and Baltimore Railroad were required "to apply for tickets at the [Pratt Street] office before 8 o'clock" in the morning, so that company agents would have ample time to inspect their free papers before departure, or they were barred from traveling. Though Baltimore's restrictions on free blacks were generally later and far less stringent than those enacted by the Maryland legislature, the city found its racial middle ground shrinking rapidly in the face of growing antipathy in the state toward its free Negro population.[59]

By the 1840s and 1850s that middle ground had all but vanished as a result of the economic and demographic changes buffeting the city. Beginning in the 1830s, in the midst of the deepening economic crisis made worse by huge state appropriations for internal improvements, Maryland experienced an unprecedented surge of immigration from abroad. Though in 1834 just 759 paying foreign passengers arrived in Baltimore aboard 113 ships, by the end of the decade 55,000 more immigrants had arrived in the city, increasing its number of foreign-born by more than fourfold over the previous decade. Most of these early arrivals were Germans, fleeing principalities they feared would soon lose their autonomy in the face of nationalism. Some also came from Ireland, Britain, and other nations of western Europe. By 1839 the German-speaking population of Baltimore stood at nearly 20,000, constituting one-fifth of the city's population. As they crowded into Baltimore and scrambled for jobs, these immigrants sharpened the competition for employment. Though their numbers were already prodigious, the heaviest immigration to the city had not yet commenced.[60]

During the 1840s and 1850s as many as 170,000 foreigners arrived in Maryland, 100,000 in the 1850s alone. More than three-fourths of those immigrants arrived in Baltimore. In 1847 alone just two persons short of 11,000 passengers landed in the city; in 1854 more than 10,000 arrived; and in 1857 9,000 immigrants came. In 1839 more vessels cleared Bremen destined for Baltimore than for New York. Buoyed by the sudden influx of foreign immigrants into the city, Baltimore experienced yet another phenomenal growth spurt. Between 1830 and 1860 the city's white population increased by 132,810, much of which resulted from immigration. In 1820 less than 3 percent of the city's 48,055 residents were foreign-born, but by 1850 nearly 40,000 (28 percent) of Baltimore's 140,000 residents had been born in another country.[61]

While Germans continued to make up Baltimore's largest foreign contingent, during the famine years of the late 1840s and early 1850s the number of immigrants from Ireland rose until they constituted nearly half of the yearly immigration. During his travels abroad Bishop John Carroll, the first bishop of the Catholic church in the United States, promoted Maryland as a haven for persecuted Catholics, stressing the cultural and religious diversity of America. When famine plagued their homeland, tens of thousands of Irish embarked for the United States, thousands of them destined for Baltimore, attracted by the promise of employment as laborers on the various railroads, canals, and turnpikes. By 1860 the city housed more than two-thirds of the state's foreign-born residents. Largely unskilled and illiterate, the new Irish arrivals crowded into tenements on the northern and western outskirts of the city and, like their German predecessors, struggled to find employment in the city's soured economy. Hiring for the cheapest wages, they immediately competed with those residents already providing Baltimore with most of its unskilled labor: working-class whites and, especially, free blacks.[62]

Though slavery in Baltimore was already in decline, the massive influx of white immigrants into the city accelerated the institution's demise. As industrialists opted for unskilled immigrant laborers willing to accept work for low pay and without contracts, they virtually drove hired slaves out of the city's labor market. For the most part slaves remained in the city's labor force only as domestics (most affluent white homeowners preferred the more traditional service of blacks and mulattoes to the unfamiliar habits and tongue of Irish and German immigrants). More ominous for resident free blacks, these latest arrivals began pushing them out of the unskilled labor market, one they had only recently come to dominate.[63]

The labor competition caused by European immigration quickly revealed the fragile position free Negroes occupied in Baltimore's economic structure. Baltimore's free blacks played no role so vital to the city's economy that they could not be replaced by unskilled whites. This was unlike the situation in Charleston, where the city's small number of free blacks (as part of a large black population) served as skilled tradespeople and artisans, and even rural Maryland, where small plantation owners relied on free Negroes as vital laborers for their grain fields in the absence of large slaveholdings and an influx of immigrants, who remained largely in Baltimore. The city had always had ample whites to fill necessary petit bourgeois occupations (as free Negroes did in Charleston), and most black people were resigned to laboring jobs. With the arrival of so many immigrants, the majority white population became even larger, outstripping even the growth of the city's free Negro population between 1830 and 1860 more than elevenfold and by 1860 lowering the free black share of the city's population to just over 12 percent.[64] Such developments rendered even less necessary the labor of most of Baltimore's free blacks, who were by now looked on as anathema to a progressive—and stable—Maryland society. Ethan Allen Andrews observed as early as 1835, "Irish and other foreigners are, to a considerable extent, taking the place of colored laborers. . . . [They] are found in public as well as in private houses, mingled with the blacks, and performing the same offices; and the great public works are executed by them exclusively."[65]

At precisely the same time that Baltimore became home to thousands of new European immigrants, the city suffered its most severe economic downturn. After a decade of prosperity, during the early years of 1850s (even before the panic and national depression experienced in 1857) Baltimore was stricken by industrial stagnation and economic depression that engulfed all levels of society. All manufacturers suffered, particularly small-shop craftworkers, who often lacked the capital to survive the loss of business. More than two of every three manufacturing establishments open in 1850 had failed by 1860, with such traditional handicraft manufacturers as blacksmiths, carpenters, and brickmakers bearing the brunt of these closings. With the closing of 2,625 such establishments and as other manufacturers scrambled to save their businesses, more than 43 percent of the hands employed in Baltimore's manufactories, both male and female, lost their jobs during the decade.[66]

Having once controlled most of Baltimore's unskilled and some of its semiskilled trades, during the 1850s free blacks found themselves replaced by native whites and European immigrants, signaling what was becoming a general exclusion of black laborers, both skilled and unskilled, from the city's trades. In an environment that now painted blacks as improvident people and slothful workers, white employers exercised their racial prejudices without fear of a lack of labor by hiring immigrant workers who often demanded less pay. An 1845 petition of workingmen employed by the city protesting working conditions provides an indication of this trend: thirteen of the fifteen signatures carried Irish surnames, while five of the remaining six were German. Charles Mackay, a Scotsman visiting Baltimore in the late 1840s, noticed that white workers were replacing black workers in most occupations other than as domestic servants, barbers, and drivers. Still others noticed that black workers "monopolized [only] the work in hotels."[67]

This trend of occupational discrimination, similar to that witnessed in most northern cities at the time, had become so pronounced in Baltimore and the surrounding countryside that in 1845 Robert S. Steuart commented, "Already . . . white labor had driven the black from many employments . . . and even on Fells Point may be witnessed the same result, in consequence of the late rapid increase of German and Irish immigrants."[68] In 1851 John H. B. Latrobe was moved to recall that only a decade earlier, "the shipping at Fells Point was loaded by free colored stevedores. The labor at the coal yards was free colored labor. . . . Now all this is changed." He saw "every European arrival as a sign and a warning to free black workers," for as foreigners "enter into competition with the black man in all avenues of labor— in most of them [they] drive him to the wall. . . . The white man stands in the black man's shoes; or else is fast getting into them."[69]

Fierce competition for employment forced free blacks to accept lower wages and work longer hours as the most effective recourse against being undercut by immigrant workers. In a climate of economic uncertainty sharpened by intensified competition, native workers in the city believed that free black competition kept wages artificially low, and slaveowners despised free

Negroes as the primary deterrent to hiring out their slaves. Baltimore's laboring whites sought reasons for their economic deprivation, and free Negroes proved a convenient target. The continued employment of such black workers as caulkers and barbers was a glaring affront to white artisans who had lost work and those unskilled workers who found their own opportunities for employment limited. Where once, as one resident observed, "the citizens of Baltimore did not look with a jealous eye at free Negro labor" and white workers had tolerated black labor so long as white craftworkers possessed the privileged positions in the work place, heightened competition and economic insecurity now reigned. James F. W. Johnston, a visiting English observer, put Baltimore's situation in succinct terms in 1851 when he wrote that "whenever the interests of the white man and the black come into collision in the United States, the black man goes to the wall. . . . It is certain that, wherever labour is scarce, there he is readily employed; when it becomes plentiful, he is the first to be discharged."[70]

Foregoing their own prejudices against the Irish, Baltimore's laboring whites used their organizational strength to force free black laborers from many positions in the city. White artisans, facing the destruction of premodern industrial paternalism and limited opportunity for advancement because of rapid industrialization, were particularly vulnerable to antiblack rhetoric, highly publicized in the state since the advent of antislavery and the colonization issue. Faced with the prospect of equating themselves with blacks working alongside them, white workers united to oppose them in many trades, despite having voiced no such opposition earlier in the century (in 1794 many craftworkers had even resisted a black disfranchisement provision in the proposed city charter on the grounds that it ran "contrary to reason and good policy, to the spirit of equal liberty and our free constitution").[71] By the later antebellum years black laborers were routinely barred from workers' associations in Baltimore, and the dearth of similar black organizations allowed a relatively unified white opposition to begin the process of excluding black laborers from the trades, even many of those long considered "nigger work."[72]

In 1828 sixty city residents signed a petition that they submitted to the mayor and city council requesting that blacks be prohibited from driving hacks, carts, and drays in the city. Claiming "difficulties and inconveniences" resulting from granting such licenses, the petitioners charged that "persons employed as common carriers have greater facilities to steal or commit depredations on the property with which they are entrusted" and were "generally persons without property, frequently slaves and therefore incapable of meeting the responsibilities of their occupation." This opposition was probably because of the prevalence of blacks in this trade; by 1850, 613 free black draymen and carters labored in the city, a figure that was five times that in any northern city and represented nearly 10 percent of the total number of free Negro men employed in Baltimore. The city failed to pass the ordinance, and the petition reached the legislature, which tabled debate indefinitely.[73]

In 1841 Baltimore whites petitioned the legislature to forbid black employment in the state tobacco warehouse, and six years later a number of citizens submitted a petition to prevent free blacks from huckstering hay and straw. Neither of these measures passed. Three years later the newly incorporated Baltimore Cemetery included in its rules and regulations a statement that "proprietors shall not allow the interment of colored persons to be made in their lots." In 1858 residents petitioned the city council unsuccessfully to prohibit "colored persons from renting and licensing stalls in the several market houses." In 1860 a large number of Baltimore tradespeople petitioned the city council to bar free blacks in the city from pursuing any mechanical branch of trade.[74]

Racial tensions were now a part of daily life in Baltimore. Having established a reputation for mob violence during the American Revolution that would only increase as the nineteenth century progressed, Baltimore's rowdies (or "plug-uglies," as they would come to be called) first turned their wrath on the city's free blacks in the summer of 1812, when during a series of anti-British mob actions they destroyed free Negro homes, ostensibly on reports that at least one freedman had expressed hope that an English victory would bring an end to slavery, as promised by the British during the American Revolution. Similarly, in 1822 a city newspaper reported a white mob destroyed the *"Africa theatre* in Mercer street, with full intent, as is understood, to break it up root and branch." Although before the late 1820s examples of white vigilantism were rare, during the ensuing years incidents of such extralegal violence and terrorism against Baltimore free Negroes increased dramatically.[75]

As the recognized center of the black community, both physically and spiritually, Baltimore's African churches became natural targets for racially motivated harassment and violence. In 1837, partly motivated by the financial panic that began that year, a gang of whites was arrested for being "in the habit of lounging about the aisles and interrupting the worship of the congregation of the colored church in Sharp street." By 1840 harassment of black Methodists at camp meetings had grown so prevalent that the newspaper advertisement announcing an upcoming meeting saw need to include the admonishment that "all persons are forewarned against intruding on said limits."[76]

The writer had good reason for caution, for harassment had already turned to mob violence. Late in the evening of 23 August 1838 near the Sharp Street Methodist Episcopal Church, a group of black men severely assaulted a white member of the city's night watch, apparently in response to the watchman's recent badgering of the group. For the next several nights small bands of whites, believing the men were connected with the black church, threatened retaliation against the Sharp Street church. Waiting until its next regular gathering, on Sunday the twenty-sixth, a "considerable mob . . . commenced an attack on the house, by throwing stones and breaking the doors and windows. Great alarm among the congregation there assembled was the consequence, and they made their exit by rushing through the doors, jumping out of the windows, &c." Many churchgoers were injured both by flying stones and in trying to escape the mob's assault before police arrived to establish order. The mob dispersed too quickly for the police to make any arrests.[77] Such violence, as yet sporadic, would grow in scope and frequency as the antebellum years drew to a close.

The large influx of Irish and other foreigners into Baltimore and the resulting occupational competition frequently tinged the city's racial violence with ethnic overtones. Relations between Irish and black residents of Baltimore had not always been strained; at one time they even appear to have been fairly amicable. Black apprentices, such as George Pinter, frequently ran off "in company with a couple of Irish servants [from] where they had been at work together for some time past." As late as 1832 Frederick Douglass (who later characterized the Irish as the most bigoted element in American society) met with "good Irishmen," who "expressed the deepest sympathy with [him], and the most decided hatred of slavery."[78] Within just a few years, once immigration and the depression had shifted Baltimore's ethnic and labor landscapes dramatically (and once he had imbibed Massachusetts's unique brand of prejudice), Douglass would change his views of the Irish, as the racial mood of the city itself changed.

An indication of this change surfaced as early as 1836, when Douglass was working in a Baltimore shipyard. Douglass recalled that "until a very little while before I went there, white and black ship carpenters worked side by side, in the ship yards. . . . To outward seeming, all hands were well satisfied." Yet such harmony appeared all but ended by the time of Douglass's employment, when white mechanic sentiment had been transformed: "The feeling was, *really*, against having their labor brought into competition with that of the colored people at all; . . . they dealt their blows on the poor, colored freeman, and aimed to prevent *him* from serving himself. . . . Had they succeeded in driving the black freemen out of the ship yard, they would have determined also upon the removal of the black slaves." As a result, on more than one occasion white apprentices assaulted Douglass, and, as he recounted, "they came near killing me, in broad day light." At least half the assailants Douglass named were Irish lads, competing at the same level as the teen-aged male slave.[79]

As the years progressed, such violence grew worse and expanded beyond the work place. In the autumn of 1856, as a large group of free blacks from the city returned to town on several wagons after a picnic, they passed a party of Irishmen on foot. The two groups exchanged racial slurs, and a fight ensued. The black combatants quickly drove off their Irish assailants, who gathered reinforcements in nearby saloons and returned, only to find that the black people had "armed themselves with stones and drove the white men entirely off." Douglass laconically concluded that "the whole sentiment of Baltimore was murderous."[80]

Such violence soon spilled over into the trades, without regard for ethnicity. In 1858 violence against black workers reached its zenith. As Baltimore struggled through the economic depression that had beset the nation the previous year, in May more than two dozen whites organized to drive off black workers from two Federal Hill brickyards, owned by Darington Thomas and by Daniel Donnelly. In the ensuing struggle one of the black workers was shot to death, and the incident so terrorized the other black employees that the brickyard owners reported "that many of the workers were so disturbed by this incident that it was difficult to get some of them to return to work." The incident forced police to remain on patrol in the area for several days, and the *Baltimore Sun* reported that the "yards of Thomas and Donnelly were mostly idle."[81]

Later that summer racially motivated labor riots erupted in Fells Point between white and black ship caulkers. Black caulkers had long dominated the semiskilled trade, prompting the *Baltimore American*, in its coverage of the riots, to comment that "until the riot Baltimoreans were not aware that any white caulkers even existed." Although the free Negroes' skill and traditional ties with their employers had previously precluded their exclusion from the lucrative trade, such buffers proved insufficient in the city's new racial atmosphere. By 1858 whites not only had gained access to the profession in the boat yards in the Whitestone Point area south of the harbor but also had used violence to dominate employment there and gain access to the larger, more established yards in Fells Point. Gangs of white "Tigers" roamed the Baltimore docks, beating black caulkers and pressuring white shipyard owners from employing them. The riots forced the temporary closing of the Skinner and Sons shipyard, and the owner of the yard, William

Skinner, quickly succumbed to the marauders' pressure and replaced twelve black caulkers with whites. Skinner allowed other black workers to continue in his yard only if they obtained a permit from the Society of Employing Shipwrights, an exclusively white organization. When the Association of Black Caulkers attempted to protect its members' right to work, a local court ordered the group to dissolve. The *Baltimore Sun* reported that "so great is the fear excited in the minds of the colored caulkers by the frequent attacks made upon them that a number have deserted the city and sought labor in other seaboard cities."[82]

Similar incidents occurred the next year, both in and outside the shipbuilding trades. In June a group of between sixty and seventy whites stormed a city railroad work site on Broadway between Pratt and Lombard and demanded employment. Informed that the daily wage was $1.00, the white crowd (many members of a local labor society) cried that they would work for no less than $1.25 per day and would allow no one else to do so either. They targeted the black workers on the job, claiming they were laboring for artificially low wages and were keeping white wages down as well. The gang forced the black workers to stop working. Later that month whites attacked a group of black workers sheeting a ship's hull with copper in a Fells Point shipyard when they refused to stop work. When no white witnesses would come forward, the culprits were released.[83] The acceleration of such incidents substantiates one historian's claim for Maryland that "no other slave state in the 1850's experienced quite the same degree of white labor militancy, and in no other slave city, even including New Orleans, was there such a virile trade union movement as in Baltimore."[84]

Inevitably, the result of this occupational discrimination, job-busting, exclusion, and racial violence was a precipitous rise of black unemployment in Baltimore by the final decade of the antebellum period. As one historian has discovered, between 1850 and 1860 only seven of the twenty-five trades in which black workers were most frequently engaged experienced an increase (see table 17). Of those, four were unskilled occupations, the sole exceptions being bricklaying and barbering—both traditionally black occupations. In each of the remaining occupations black participation, both male and female, declined. In such traditional black occupations as carting, washing, and sawing the declines were dramatic; sawyers alone declined by more than two-thirds in the 1850s.

The deterioration of black workers in positions as common laborers proved especially telling in this crisis of Negro labor. Although native whites had only recently conceded such unskilled occupations to free blacks, between 1850 and 1860 the number of Negro laborers in the city shrank by

Table 17. Leading Black Occupations in Baltimore, 1850 and 1860[a]

Occupation	1850	1860	Total Difference	Percentage Difference
Barber	91	96	+5	+5.5
Blacksmith	31	27	-4	-12.9
Bricklayer	63	93	+30	+47.6
Butcher	16	9	-7	-43.8
Carriage driver	33	34	+1	+3.0
Carter, drayman, etc.	385	331	-54	-14.0
Carpenter	26	13	-13	-50.0
Caulker	75	63	-12	-16.0
Cook	22	26	+4	+18.2
Grain measurer	27	17	-10	-37.0
Hod carrier	14	10	-4	-28.6
Huckster	19	28	+9	+47.4
Laborer	799	571	-228	-28.5
Ostler	11	9	-2	-18.2
Oysterman	24	50	+26	+108.3
Porter, waiter, etc.	236	226	-10	-4.2
Ropemaker	12	1	-11	-91.7
Sawyer	146	47	-99	-67.8
Seaman	94	107	+13	+13.8
Seamstress	20	4	-16	-80.0
Shoemaker	24	11	-13	-54.2
Shopkeeper	21	13	-8	-38.1
Stevedore	35	34	-1	-2.9
Washer	260	142	-118	-45.4
Whitewasher	70	62	-8	-11.4

a. Occupations with at least ten entries in the 1850 Census.
Sources: Della, "Problems of Negro Labor in the 1850's," 28; Matchett, *Baltimore Directory for 1849–50*, 439–73; Woods, *Woods' Baltimore City Directory*, 427–59.

228, or more than 28.0 percent. Overall, Negro labor declined by at least 20.8 percent in the final antebellum decade. Each of those few occupations that experienced increases required little capital, but they also were poorly remunerated. For some, such as seamen and cooks, the pay or profit was uniformly low, while others, such as hucksters and oystermen, suffered from either seasonal labor restrictions or meager and uncertain profits. Indeed, in 1855 Frederick Douglass, still keenly aware of the Baltimore situation, wrote from faraway Rochester, New York, "Every hour sees the black man elbowed out of the employment by some newly arrived emigrant whose hunger and color are thought to give him a better title to the place." At all levels, and with only rare exceptions, during the 1850s black laborers were being forced from employment in Baltimore at a frightening rate.[85]

In 1850 nearly half of the city's free blacks were engaged in unskilled occupations, such as common labor and washing (nearly nine out of ten women were employed as washers), while just 14 percent held skilled or semiskilled trades, such as barbering, blacksmithing, ship caulking, and carpentry. The remaining 37 percent worked in semiskilled service occupations, such as carting and waiting, instead of plying the more lucrative skilled trades, which offered generally modest remuneration. The largest percentage of black persons who held property in 1856 and whose occupation could be identified were employed in those service occupations (44 percent); only slightly more than a third were engaged in skilled or semiskilled trades.[86]

In the 1850s a decades-long process of tightening legislative proscriptions against free Negroes in Maryland intensified. In 1854 state lawmakers included in one enactment a provision·requiring free blacks to enter into written labor contracts and to serve the entire term; if they failed to fulfill the terms of the contract, they forfeited wages for the time lost and were liable for trial costs.[87] In 1858, in an effort to reduce the state's free black population, the legislature banned all future manumissions of slaves under the age of ten and over the age of forty-five, even if they were able to earn a living. It also mandated that slaves manumitted by a deed or will that stipulated they must leave the state would not be freed until they actually departed.[88]

Finally, ostensibly to alleviate the overcrowded condition of the state penitentiary, the legislature radically altered its method of punishing free Negro lawbreakers. If convicted of petty thefts valued at less than five dollars or breaking and entering and stealing goods worth less than one dollar, free blacks would be sold as slaves for terms of from two to five years. For arson, instead of being hanged or imprisoned for at least twenty years, free Negro convicts could be hanged or sold into slavery for life, either in or out of the state. For grand larceny, the court had the discretion of selling the black convict as a slave for a term of up to ten years. The proceeds of such sales, after the costs of prosecution were remitted to the city or county government, went to the family of the convict.[89]

In Baltimore the results were immediate. During the ensuing two years eighty-nine free blacks in Maryland were sold as slaves, twenty-four of them in Baltimore. Although as late as 1850 more than half of the inmates at the penitentiary were black, in 1860 just one Negro was sentenced to the penitentiary (as opposed to fifty-three whites). That same year the state's Committee on Colored Population reported that without the 1858 law the number of black inmates in the penitentiary, which stood at 121, would have been nearly twice that. Indeed, in 1860 there were six times as many whites as blacks in the penitentiary. Similarly, the number of black inmates at the Baltimore city jail fell from 879 in 1858 to 794 in 1860.[90]

Despite such harsh enactments, many Marylanders remained unhappy about the elevated status of the state's free Negro class. Such sentiment was hardly unique to Maryland; a wave of repression of free blacks was sweeping the entire nation, north and south. Southern states sought actively to protect the institution of slavery in the face of what they perceived as a concerted attempt on the part of Republicans and northerners in general to destroy it. As the two sides fought verbal duels over the issue of slavery on the national level, one issue seemed to enjoy uniform white support: free Negroes were either unpleasant nuisances or dangerous presences that needed to be removed.[91]

Their anxieties whipped up by the fray, slaveowning Marylanders sought a solution. Following the examples of similar meetings held in Annapolis in 1842 and in Cambridge in the autumn of 1858, slaveowners held a statewide convention in Baltimore during the summer of 1859 to deal with a problem that many now blamed on their forebears: the unchecked growth of the state's free black population. Though the city proved far from welcoming to the collection of wealthy slaveowners (providing no official delegation to greet the distinguished group and even attempting to move the convention to Frederick), the delegates were undeterred in their resolve to protect "the industrial and social interests of this State." Drawing on the sentiment expressed at the Constitutional Convention of 1850–51, which called for more stringent regulation of free blacks in Maryland, many among the large turn-out of delegates (most of whom were from outside Baltimore City) arrived determined to support the resolution of the Cambridge convention, which stated that "free negroism and slavery are incompatible . . . and should not be permitted longer to exist in their present relations."[92]

Despite such sentiment, most delegates proved unwilling to support the drastic proposal that Maryland free blacks be presented with the choice "of going into slavery, or leaving the state." Some, like James Alfred Pearce, reminded the group that "the removal of the free Negroes would deduct nearly fifty percent from the household and agricultural labor furnished by the people of color . . . [and] would produce a great discomfort and inconvenience."[93] Echoing the complaints of Eastern Shore residents that their severe labor shortages were caused by those "unproducing" Negroes their parents freed, the Baltimore delegation resolved after tremendous debate that "the free black population should be well and thoroughly controlled by efficient laws to the end that they may be orderly, industrious, and productive." Opting against the removal of free blacks, the majority urged the state to enforce more strictly the 1832 provision that emancipation be conditional on removal through colonization and recommended that a committee consisting of one member from each county submit to the legislature the views of the convention.[94]

More ominous was the minority opinion of the convention, which above all else became a forum for the radical views of Curtis W. Jacobs, a wealthy Eastern Shore planter who shortly would be elected to the House of Delegates from Worcester County. Prior to the convention Jacobs—an owner of twenty-two slaves—had served as the chairman of a committee at the 1850 Constitutional Convention charged with making recommendations on the "negro question." Jacobs presented a report asking the state to "terminate free negroism in Maryland at an early day, and on the most advantageous terms to our white population." Jacobs called for a provision in the new constitution authorizing banishment or reenslavement of free Negroes. "Sir, the negro knows what slavery means, because it is natural to him," Jacobs argued. "But when you set him free, and then pass laws to restrain that freedom, it is all jargon and moonshine to him . . . hence the necessity of re-enslaving our free negroes." Though his recommendation was not included in the new constitution, he influenced passage of an amendment allowing the legislature to regulate and dispose of the black population "as they may see fit." Opponents of free Negroes in Maryland had found an indefatigable champion.[95]

In January 1859 Jacobs published a lengthy pamphlet entitled *The Free Negro Question in Maryland*, a composite of arguments he posed in 1851 that expressed opposition to the presence of free blacks not only in Maryland but also in the nation. Laden with the rhetoric of Negro inferiority, Jacobs's pamphlet argued that black people "make good slaves, because the principle of slavery is the predominant element in their nature; they abuse freedom, because they have no rational concept of its uses. . . . Slavery, then, being the true normal condition of the negro, his happiness lies only in that direction. To free him is to inflict the greatest possible injury, for by that you expose him to the higher cares, duties and responsibilities pertaining to citizenship, and for which he cannot attain by practice."[96]

Jacobs amplified the belief of a growing number of white Marylanders that free Negroes were the primary cause of the state's economic distress. He punctuated his rhetoric with the fanciful claims that black workers were monopolizing urban occupations, thus forcing white workers from the state, and that "it would not be long before other occupations would also be threatened by free black laborers." Affirming Maryland's right to do whatever necessary to protect the interests of slaveowners, Jacobs called for an end to "free Negroism" in Maryland, forcing emigration on free blacks and, for those who refused to leave, allowing the state to sell them into slavery for life at prices low enough to guarantee quick and complete purchase.[97]

After John Brown's raid in western Virginia in October of 1859, the hysteria in neighboring Maryland allowed conservative proslavery candidates to carry the statewide elections held just weeks later. More important, some of those legislators were vocal opponents of the presence of free Negroes in the state. An incident that occurred in December in Baltimore merely exacerbated the already volatile situation. When police interrupted the annual caulkers' ball, they discovered numerous pictures of John Brown, with a bust inscribed "The martyr—God bless him." Drawn on the floor was a chalk outline of Governor Henry Wise of Virginia, straddled by "a huge Ethiopian," amid, as the *Baltimore Sun* reported, "inscriptions unfit for publication." The newspaper coverage of the incident heightened the Upper South's prevailing paranoia, deflecting it in Maryland away from northern Republicans and slaves and toward those by now considered the state's true menace: free Negroes.[98]

The timing of the Harper's Ferry raid proved most fortuitous for Curtis Jacobs. Not only did the sweep of Democratic proslavery candidates in the fall elections carry him into office, as well as a number of the most vocal members of the minority of the Baltimore convention, but also Jacobs's wide reputation quickly garnered him an appointment as chairman of the House of Delegates' Committee on Colored Population. As the committee's chair, Jacobs could advertise his by now well-formulated opinions (which the editor of the *Easton Gazette* regarded disdainfully as "peculiar and extreme views") as the committee's. Because six of its seven members were wealthy slaveowners, including five who owned at least seventeen slaves (decidedly atypical of most Maryland slaveowners), Jacobs—the wealthiest of the group—spoke well for the personal interests of the committee.[99]

Buoyed by a number of petitions submitted to the legislature (where more than half of the seats were held by representatives from counties of southern Maryland and the Eastern Shore) calling for more stringent restrictions of free blacks, Jacobs submitted a lengthy report on behalf of the committee that called the 1831 act a failure and introduced drastic recommendations for legislative proscriptions of the state's free black population. "Nothing short of an ultimate extinguishment of the free negro element," Jacobs read to the House of Delegates, "will cure the evils we labor under or meet the emergencies besetting the peculiar condition of Maryland." Because Negroes were "an inferior class of our population," Jacobs continued, "we owe to them the enactment of such laws as will restrain them from self-destruction and make them subordinate and useful to our citizen population and the industrial interests of our State." For the future good of the state, free black people must be "held in complete subordination to the citizen population, and made to work under the direction and control of our citizens."[100]

To accomplish this, the committee submitted a bill to the General Assembly, largely Jacobs's work, which proved one of the most prohibitive introduced in any of the nation's legislatures. The Jacobs bill, as it came to be known, closely resembled a bill the South Carolina legislature had considered and ultimately rejected the previous year.[101] It recommended that the legislature forbid all future manumissions and that all black people already free be enslaved and compulsorily hired out for renewable terms of ten years. Children under the age of twelve would be bound out until the age of thirty-five. Any children born to such bound Negroes would become property of the owner of the mother's term of service. All free Negroes were allowed to choose their masters if they entered into slavery voluntarily, a clause obviously designed to encourage such actions. Further, any blacks who had been manumitted prior to the act on the condition that they leave the state and who had failed to do so would have their freedom and their children's revoked and would be restored to the former owner or heirs.

Additional stipulations of the Jacobs bill were directed largely at suppressing the free black population of Baltimore. One provided for the prohibition of separate assemblages of Negroes, even for religious purposes (going so far as to initiate the auction of black churches "for the benefit of the white congregation to which the property so sold belonged or was attached"), and required that constables "visit once a week in the night, or oftener upon information, all places . . . where it is suspected unlawful assemblages of colored persons—slave and free—are held." Further, the bill recommended the "suppression of stragglers and venders of small wares and notions." Finally, a provision aimed directly at what Jacobs believed to be the pediment of Baltimore's vibrant black community prohibited free blacks from either acquiring or holding property and specified that "should any free negro refuse so to sell and convey, the county commissioners, or mayor of Baltimore shall do it, and apply the proceeds to the school fund."[102]

When the House of Delegates began debate on the committee's bill, Jacobs revealed a deep hatred of free blacks that went far beyond simple concern for the future economic growth of the state of Maryland. Criticizing the amount of property owned by free Negroes, he lamented "that the free negroes in Annapolis were building more houses, and owned as much property as any other persons," and he was incredulous that in Baltimore "it did not take long to raise the wind [money] among the colored population."[103] Ridiculing the laws passed by the state in earlier years yet not enforced, Jacobs proclaimed that "the free negro is an alien to the government of this State; . . . the negro knows what slavery means, because it is natural to him; but when you set him free, and then pass laws to restrain that freedom, it is all jargon and moonshine to him. . . . It is as natural for a negro to steal as for the sparks to fly upwards. . . . The wrong consists in setting him free at all, for which the negro is not to blame." Responding to criticism for his strong stance, Jacobs retorted harshly, "Sir—Free-negroism is an excrescence, a blight, a mildew, a fungus—hanging on to and corrupting the social and moral elements of our people in Maryland." Jacobs believed that people in Maryland thought likewise, and he was determined to allow voters to decide the issue.[104]

James Hall, the agent of the Maryland State Colonization Society, attempted to revitalize the near-moribund colonization effort in the light of the recent efforts against free Negroes in Maryland. Claiming to be "intimate with people of color, . . . and almost all the acts of his life have been, more of less, intimately connected with them" and "mainly devoted to their interests," Hall targeted Baltimore's black population in a pamphlet published in 1859. Motivated by "feelings engendered by long and agreeable intercourse, from repeated acts of kindness and hospitality . . . experienced at their hands," Hall believed his voice to be a sympathetic voice of reason the city and state's free black people would naturally heed. He warned them:

> The more you advance in intelligence, the more you elevate yourselves, the nearer you assume an erect, independent position, the more obnoxious you become to the dominant race. . . . As you can never be *citizens*, you must be considered *aliens*, although born on the soil, and the Legislature of the State consider your residence in it prejudicial to its interest; . . . Individually you may say, you have a *right* to remain, that your local attachments and your indolence overbalance the spirit of manhood in you, and you *will* remain. . . . You all must know that the Legislation of the State, in regard to the "free people of color," is becoming more and more stringent, that every session of the Legislature adds one or more chapters to the statute book, curtailing, in some degree, your shadowy rights and privileges. And is there any prospect that this policy of the State will soon be changed? None.[105]

✢ ✢ ✢

As James Hall and Curtis W. Jacobs would soon learn, the bulk of Baltimore's black residents did not share the two men's views of their inevitable social demise. As witnessed by the swift and organized reaction of the free people of color to such efforts to rid the state of their presence in 1859 and 1860, their past would provide structure to their resistance to this heightened institutional menace, a structure that had emerged from more than half a century of commitment to making the abstraction of freedom real, both individually and collectively.

8

"Freedom Shall Not Perish"

In late March 1832 the managers of the Maryland State Colonization Society met at the Baltimore courthouse to formalize the body's organization. Earlier that month the state legislature had passed a law empowering the society's board of managers to remove from the state all persons of color already free and those freed henceforth. To facilitate the relocation of Maryland's people of color to the African continent, the legislature had appropriated $200,000, which it placed at the society's disposal for use over the next twenty years. Stable underwriting thus secured, the task of the Colonization Society's managers then lay in convincing the state's free black people that they, too, should embrace the opportunity to leave the state. At the meeting Moses Sheppard, one of the managers who was a successful grocer and cotton twine manufacturer, and the attorneys Charles Howard and Charles C. Harper, the latter the Harvard-educated son of the anti–free black polemicist Robert Goodloe Harper, decided to hire an agent to promote colonization throughout the state. Within days they had obtained the services of Robert S. Finley, the son of the Reverend Robert Finley, progenitor of the national colonization movement, for the handsome annual salary of five hundred dollars and traveling expenses.[1]

Setting out in May from Baltimore, Finley, armed with colonization literature, traveled first to the Eastern Shore, where he organized numerous public meetings, made arrangements for the participation of local leaders, clergy, and influential citizens, and urged local black residents to attend. During his five-week canvass the agent found white residents of the Eastern Shore overwhelmingly supportive of the idea of colonization, and he was especially pleased to report to the managers that the Eastern Shore's black folk appeared receptive as well.[2]

Returning to the Western Shore, Finley found whites there as enthusiastic in assisting him in his efforts as those on the Eastern Shore had been, but he was dismayed by the attitude of black residents in the region. "I had the mortification to discover," Finley wrote in August to John H. B. Latrobe, son of the famed architect Benjamin H. Latrobe and principal organizer and corresponding secretary of the Maryland State Colonization Society, "that the coloured population had imbibed very enormous views and entertained very hostile feelings toward the Colonizing scheme." "There is strong reason to believe," Finley cautioned, "that their hostile feelings are very much fostered and confirmed by means to falsehood circulated through the instrumentality of emissaries from Baltimore."[3]

Finley's suspicions arose from his recent attempt, in his words, "to get up a meeting of the coloured people of Baltimore with a view of addressing them on the subject of colonization," which was "met with a prompt and universal resistance from the coloured people themselves." Within a year this "unmitigated opposition" displayed by Baltimore's people of color had grown so pronounced and organized that Finley grew frustrated and left the Colonization Society's employ. His successor, the Virginia native William McKenney, inherited Finley's malaise. When he attempted to attract potential emigrants in distant Somerset County, at the southern tail of the Eastern Shore, McKenney concluded that even "in this place some of the Blacks are catching the refractory spirit of the Baltimore *gentry.* . . . One of them has called me a *conjurer,* & was overheard earnestly stating that if any black man should permit me only to *blow my breath* upon him, he was gone."[4]

Ironically, the Eastern Shore blacks' charge of "conjurer" was a sophisticated turning of the tables; whites regularly branded black people who held to African concepts and traditions with the same derisive epithet. Now McKenney's efforts to send black folk back to Africa were being judged as silly, and he found himself labeled a "conjurer." Frustrated, the new agent lamented to manager Charles Howard that he would be forced to hasten to Baltimore "to have a large meeting of both colors on Sunday" to promote favorable reports from recent emigrants to Africa "as an offsett to the *black news* from the blacks of Baltimore." Similarly, the Colonization Society's agent James Hall found that "in the country the great thing to contend with is the *incredulity* of the coloured people—but in the city *obstinacy,* or a determination to act adverse to the wishes of the whites."[5]

The obviously organized opposition of Baltimore's people of color to the state's colonization effort, which agents Finley and McKenney discovered was slowly influencing the attitudes of Maryland's rural black populace, reveals much about the developing corporate mentality and statewide stature of the city's black community. By the 1830s Baltimore's black residents had woven a fabric of life whose texture was both uniquely urban and largely their own. Though white impositions and the state's maintenance of slavery had significantly influenced the development the city's black community, Baltimore's people of color, including slaves, had found considerable room and strength to temper such conformity. In an economic and social environment not even remotely dependent on slavery, if ever it had been, black Baltimoreans still found buffers with which to conform, but only so much as necessary to ensure their continued liberty.

The urban liberties that allowed Baltimore's free blacks to achieve a level of wealth well above that of rural free Negroes, to develop a rich and unique culture, and to forge strong organizational bonds also offered the mechanism by which to erect staunch defenses against the rising tide of racial proscriptions against them. While the organizations developed partly as avenues to advancement according to white societal norms, their associational activities offered black Baltimoreans more than economic, social, and psychological security by forestalling potential white hostility to any black groups that might threaten the social order—the kind of hostility first witnessed in the white evangelical churches. Fostering group solidarity and identity that transcended their membership, institutional mutualities offered the black residents of Baltimore, both in and outside the organizations, a means of resisting white encroachments on hard-won black liberties. Coincident with white Marylanders' insistence on free blacks' conformity to standards imposed as the safeguard of racial control and tolerance and as the mode of ultimate advancement, Baltimore's African Americans increasingly relied on the institutional ligaments of their community to bolster their autonomous existence. Partly in pursuit of progress and partly as a response to this negative shift in race relations, Baltimore's black populace matured as a community in the last decades of the antebellum period. Though divided somewhat by various social and economic crosscurrents, this community became unified and strong enough to act as a body rather than as mere individuals.[6]

Over the final three antebellum decades, black Baltimoreans found increasing need to summon such cohesion. Community divisions notwithstanding, black opposition to the colonization scheme, the domestic slave trade, and especially slavery and the reenslavement efforts in the late 1850s unified Baltimore's African American people. No issue at once divided and galvanized Baltimore's black community more than colonization. Beginning as early as 1817, it ushered in an organized black opposition to free black relocation and the maturation of community protest movements in general.

As the agents Robert Finley and William McKenney each found in turn, sentiment in favor of colonization did exist among a significant portion of

Maryland's black residents. Yet Finley was incorrect in his conclusion that such interest lay only in the rural counties. Even in Baltimore blacks found various reasons to support the emigration of free Negroes. The colonization scheme drew strength from a broad spectrum of the city's free black religious society, without regard for standing or congregation. Despite Daniel Coker's importance among the city's black people, in 1820 he left Maryland with one of the first groups of emigrants to be relocated to Liberia by the American Colonization Society. Upon his arrival, Coker wrote to his wife, who did not accompany him, "My soul cleaves to Africa in such a manner as to reconcile me to the idea of being separate from my dear friends and comforts of a Christian land. . . . Africa is a good land; tell the people to come here and they will be happy if they will be industrious."[7] As late as 1855 Charles Hooper, a black laborer, applied to the American Missionary Association for assignment in Africa, asking the agent George Whipple not to "think hard of this riting" by "a Poor ignorant unworthy A man as myself," because he "belive my father who art in Heaven Intends for me to Spand A part of My time in africa, I have often Prayed for god to send his word to the Poor heathens, I think if god has Ever spoken to any human being in The spirit he has Commanded me to Go and heal. . . ."[8]

As early as 1826 black Baltimoreans debated colonization in open forum. In December separate meetings held at the Sharp Street and Bethel churches witnessed heated controversy over the issue. One observer, who corresponded with the black New York newspaper *Freedom's Journal*, reported that in his estimation nearly two-thirds of the audience at one of the meetings was decidedly opposed to the colonization scheme. One individual pointed out that if the Colonization Society were really acting in the truest interests of black people, it would put its efforts into providing education for the state's free African Americans.[9] Despite such vocal opposition, in December 1826 several of the most prominent leaders of both Bethel and Sharp Street churches, likely assisted by the white colonizationists Charles Harper and John H. B. Latrobe, published "a memorial of the free people of color" in colonizationist publications. The memorial claimed to speak for "every quarter of the city, and every denomination," in its support for emigration to Africa. "We would remind you," the memorialists wrote, "of the time when you were in a situation similar to ours, and when your forefathers were driven by religious persecution to a distant and inhospitable shore. . . . We, too, leave our homes. . . . As long as we remain among you, we must and shall be content to be a distinct caste."[10]

Though white colonizationists authored the memorial, some of Baltimore's black residents were attracted to the tone of the appeal. They even appear to have assisted in preparing the document. Shortly after the publication of the memorial, Charles Harper, in a private letter to Ralph R. Gurley, secretary of the American Colonization Society, intimated that several of the city's "leading blacks" had offered "alterations not affecting the sense at all, but removing (and very properly) some expressions in which they might seem to speak too harshly of themselves."[11] The arguments for African colonization did induce a small number of Baltimoreans to relocate; between 1820 and 1835 Baltimore's Bethel church lost thirteen members to Liberian emigration. George R. McGill, a lay minister at the Sharp Street church and a teacher, was enticed by the offer of being a schoolmaster in Liberia, and he left Baltimore with a small group aboard the ship *Doris* in the fall of 1827. McGill returned to Baltimore two years later to extol the virtues of the African continent, encouraging immediate emigration of those who felt demeaned by white Americans because of their skin color, for "colored men from the United States, being thought by the natives to be men of information, are received and treated as white men, and denominated by the same epithet."[12]

While the hardening of racial relations reflected by Maryland's 1831 free Negro legislation and the ensuing authorization of the state's colonization society stirred the colonization debate in Baltimore, events outside the city during the 1830s piqued black interest in the movement. As the national colonization movement broadened and posed potential sites for resettlement that included not only Africa but also such less distant places as Haiti and even such domestic points as Missouri, the former British plantation colonies in the Western Hemisphere, especially British Guiana and Trinidad, proved especially attractive to African Americans. With the de jure end of British slavery in 1833 and its de facto death in 1840 following a four- to six-year period of apprenticeship, the prospect of wage employment in places advertising for laborers was particularly alluring to many of Baltimore's black workers suffering through the deep depression and widespread unemployment of the Panic of 1837.[13]

As workers throughout the northern seaboard cities searched for employment in other cities, on the evening of 25 November 1839 black Baltimoreans with renewed interest in emigration gathered at the schoolroom of the Bethel A.M.E. Church to select delegates "to visit the province of British Guiana and the Island of Trinidad, to ascertain the character of the climate, soil, natural production, and the political and social condition of the coloured inhabitants of the province and island . . . and especially whether it possesses such advantages as can justify the free coloured population of this City and State to migrate thither." Designating Thomas Green as chair, they selected by ballot two men, Nathaniel Peck, a wall colorer and Bethel lay minister who had actively promoted colonization for several years, and Thomas S. Price, a whitewasher, to journey to the British colonies, where panicky sugar planters advertised widely for laborers, agricultural and otherwise, fearing that their erstwhile "apprentices" would no longer serve them in their former capacity.[14]

Traveling with a letter of introduction signed by the city's mayor and three prominent judges (including Nicholas Brice, chief judge of the city court, whose concern with the growth of the free Negro population had apparently not subsided in the dozen years since his public letter to the governor about term manumissions), Peck and Price proceeded by train to Boston, where they embarked on a ship bound for Georgetown, British Guiana, at the mouth of the Demerara River. Arriving on 21 January 1840, they immediately met with the board of directors of the Voluntary Subscription Emigration Society in Georgetown, which agreed to underwrite the cost of the emissaries' passage and expenses, since their visit was "a subject of great importance to the Agricultural Interests" of the colony. The society also publicly advertised for solicitations on behalf of the visitors and offered to reimburse all individuals who incurred travel expenses by transporting the Baltimoreans around the province.[15]

For seven weeks the pair traveled extensively in coastal Guiana, meticulously noting all aspects of the colony—environmental, political, and social. The emissaries found the colony's tropical climate congenial and the attendant economic opportunities inviting, though somewhat limited to agricultural pursuits since the colony's economy was dominated by the sugar industry. Peck and Price posited that "many advantages are offered to industrious and enterprising capitalists, who would embark in the cultivation of vegetables [especially those common in America, which sold for much higher prices in Guiana], and rearing feathered as well as other stock for market, which would make, at present, a handsome return to the undertaker." No doubt persuaded by the generosity of their hosts and the earnestness with which the landed white Guianans regarded a prospective black exodus from Baltimore (including the offer of free passage for all who emigrated from Baltimore, paid for by the Emigration Society), the pair found the colony's social economy especially attractive, reporting that the "only distinction in society is education, character and wealth, for the higher walks—then gradations down, according to condition, &c." The writers were careful to note that black Guianans served regularly alongside whites as court assessors, clerks in public offices, and bank tellers.[16]

Realizing that any emigration from urban and mechanical Baltimore to rural and agricultural Guiana would require that black Baltimoreans have immediate access to land, Peck and Price asked the directors of the Emigration Society a number of pointed questions that explored the possibility of "cultivating cane-fields on shares": "What portion of the produce should the undertakers [emigrants] receive as reward? . . . If undertaking new fields, what quota should be received? Should the undertaker want advances in money, on what terms could he procure it?"[17] In an ironic rehearsal for Reconstruction, the emissaries pursued an avenue of economic gain already prevalent on the American agricultural landscape: sharecropping. The Emigration Society answered Peck's and Price's queries as favorably as they could, but in the end the terms they negotiated, no matter how enticing, proved to be the same labor system that would, a quarter of a century later under the guise of self-determination, again drag thousands of former American slaves into perpetual dependency when plantation agriculture in the American South was decentralized in the aftermath of the Civil War.[18] Lacking such prescience yet knowing the innate autonomy of their Baltimore constituency, Peck and Price naively saw the scheme as a viable option. After traveling to Trinidad, which the emissaries found to be "a fine and beautiful island" but less commendable for emigration than Guiana because of its "want of but few, if any mechanics," the pair returned to the United States. Arriving in Philadelphia on 11 April 1840 they hastened on to Baltimore.[19]

Immediately upon the emissaries' return, the two published a pamphlet that described their trip in detail and unqualifiedly "declare[d] their preference for Guiana." On Monday, 13 April, Peck and Price met with members of the community. Unbeknownst to them, during their absence more than a hundred had already decided their destination would be Trinidad and had signed up for passage. Present at the meeting were also three former residents—one a minister—who had emigrated to Trinidad the previous fall. They portrayed the island exceptionally favorably, telling the throng about their satisfactory employment on a sugar plantation, the generous $1.50 per day wages earned by completing three tasks (usually done by mid-afternoon), as well as decent rations that supplemented their incomes. They told of the ample employment opportunities for women and children, who could do washing or "earn as much as men picking coffee or cocoa; this is very light work and done in the shade." The trio stated confidently that "all emigrants gone out as agriculturalists and laborers are doing well, and perfectly satisfied, but that a few barbers and waiters not accustomed to work on plantations, are the only persons dissatisfied." One Reverend Jones held emphatically "that he would have given $500, although a poor man, if he had taken his family with him in the first instance."[20] Barraged with such convincing firsthand testimony, the congregation gave overwhelming support for emigration to Trinidad, despite their emissaries' recommendations for British Guiana. Within days of the meeting, 166 Baltimoreans left the city for Port of Spain, Trinidad, aboard the brigs *Northerner, Stevens*, and *Belvidera*, followed by another 87 during May and June. All told, 256 individuals emigrated from Baltimore to Trinidad in 1840, while just 5 relocated to Guiana.[21]

An analysis of the emigrants to Trinidad (which Baltimore's free Negroes preferred so resoundingly over Guiana, perhaps as a rejection of the emissaries' overzealous pursuit of sharecropping)[22] reveals that they left Baltimore as families, indicating they intended to relocate permanently. Of the 257 emigrants to Trinidad, 175, or slightly more than two-thirds, traveled as families. Of those forty-three family units, twenty-four were male-headed, ten were female-headed, and the rest were siblings traveling together. Just fifty-five single males emigrated (twelve of whom were brothers traveling together), while half as many single women emigrated. Interestingly, of those five who emigrated to British Guiana by themselves, all were either single males or males traveling without their families. Such disparity suggests that for Baltimore black families, Trinidad offered family stability while Guiana, despite its sharecropping opportunities, presented too great a risk for family relocation. The occupations of those emigrant male household heads bears out this hypothesis; of those thirty-two males identifiable in the 1837 city directory, a full one-half held skilled or semiskilled occupations or were in the service trades.[23]

As with travel to British Guiana, free black emigrants to Trinidad received free passage. All but one of the 262 emigrants to either Trinidad or British Guiana left in 1840, and of those, all but four traveled between April and June. Only one other left the city for Trinidad, in 1842. This short period of migration suggests that the economic downturn following the Panic of 1837 provided the greatest impetus to renewed interest in colonization. By mid-1840 and 1841 the city's economic fortunes had improved, and such interest waned, though the *Baltimore Sun* continued to carry advertisements for ships leaving for Trinidad.[24]

Obviously, this was no purely economic move; these émigrés were a mixed lot of skilled and semiskilled tradespeople, service workers, and unskilled laborers—lower middle-class as well as lower-class free black Baltimoreans—who saw Trinidadian emigration as the best future—if not occupationally, then culturally and socially—for themselves and, just as important, for their families. Despite the reports of their emissaries, who painted a dismal picture of the wages offered and the limited availability of employment other than in agriculture, they embarked on a risky yet irreversible odyssey, which entailed selling their household furniture to do so (or to avoid shipping costs and a 15 percent duty on it) and immediately facing possible unemployment and uncertain housing. Most interesting is the number of children and wives of Baltimore workingmen who traveled without their fathers and husbands, such as William and Frances Brown, who sent their two-year-old daughter, Sarah Ann, in April 1840, presumably in the care of others; Francis followed the following month; and William joined the family in June. Most surprising is how frequently children traveled without their parents. Nine families emigrated in this way, such as the family of Christopher Askins, a laborer living on Honey Alley who sent his nine children, all between the ages of two and sixteen, to Trinidad in April, but he did not emigrate at that time. Askins was not listed in the city directory for 1840; presumably he worked another month or two to accumulate capital or to tend to final details, and then he too joined his family.[25]

Parents who did not emigrate with their families might well have had more compelling reasons than economics to send their children ahead of them, and, more important, to make their relocation permanent. Some found that their absence, no matter how short, would jeopardize their loved ones' very freedom. Benjamin Copper bears witness to this ever-present danger. In November 1840, in preparation for emigration to Trinidad, Copper, a Baltimore free black, purchased the freedom of his slave wife, Caroline, from Samuel House, also of Baltimore, for fifty dollars. Leaving behind his now-free wife and two slave sons, Absalom and Alexander, "in the friendly care and charge" of Thomas Winston, another free black (presumably a friend of the family), along with his wife's bill of sale, Copper departed for Trinidad a year after his wife's purchase, "with the intention of returning to his residence in Baltimore City."[26]

Shortly after Copper's departure, Winston hired out Copper's two sons to Patrick Gallagher, who owned a lime kiln, and the small wage ("the hire of the youngest being only fifty cents a week over & above his cloathes & victuals") was paid to the boys' mother. Some time later Caroline Copper died. Unscrupulously, Gallagher seized the opportunity to acquire a long-term source of cheap labor at the expense of the family's misfortune. Claiming that "the father of the boys . . . has been absent from the state of Maryland for eight or nine years and still remains absent and is presumed to be dead" and that the boys' mother "a short time previous to her death requested the respondent to take charge of her children and provide for them until they should become of age," Gallagher applied to the Orphans' Court for indentures of apprenticeship for the two boys, which it granted. In 1846 the once-guardian Winston petitioned the court that the indentures were "wholly illegal & void in law," producing the bill of sale entrusted to him and asking that they be "revoked & annulled."[27] No record of the court's disposition remains, but the incident suggests the motivations behind a permanent family, rather than a temporary individual, emigration to Trinidad. Moreover, these emigrants' implacable confidence in their destination and the hardships they underwent to emigrate there suggest the depths to which racial hostility and inequities had already plunged in Baltimore by 1840.

A year after the Baltimore exodus, in 1841, a convention of free blacks from throughout Maryland met again in the city to consider a broader-based emigration effort. Numbering more than a hundred delegates (most of whom were from Baltimore), the convention met at the Light Street Methodist Church and adopted resolutions supporting colonization and the formation of auxiliaries to the Maryland State Colonization Society in all areas of the state. Between 1832 and 1841 the Colonization Society reported 627 emigrants had been sent to Africa and another 29 to Haiti. The delegates determined to redouble their efforts to increase such participation in Baltimore and elsewhere.[28] Black interest in colonization in Baltimore resurfaced after the Irish influx. John H. B. Latrobe noted an incident in 1850 in which a black drayman indicated "*his* reason for going [to Africa], that the Irish and Germans were getting into his business: that the old feeling among the whites, which had induced them to employ colored men by preference, no longer existed." The man concluded somberly "that every year made matters worse; and that seeing this, he determined to emigrate, while he was still young enough to do something in his new home."[29]

While these incidents might suggest a decided shift in black Baltimoreans' views of emigration, their support for colonization was largely spasmodic. The overwhelming majority of free Negroes in Maryland, especially those in Baltimore, remained stridently opposed to relocation efforts. Like the supporters of the movement in the city, anticolonizationists emerged from all sectors of Baltimore's black society. Opponents saw nothing of the missionary goal of emancipation; to them, colonization was no more than deportation, and, in the words of one agent, they "left no stone unturned to put obstacles in the way of our expedition."[30] Though injustices existed, Baltimore's free Negroes, like those elsewhere, believed the liberties they enjoyed and the economic advancement they had achieved in their city were worth enduring the inequities.

Though by no means the only black anticolonization voice in Baltimore, William Watkins, a teacher, was regarded by both black and white residents of the city as the leading black spokesperson of the period and proved the most indefatigable opponent of colonization. His singular stance not only helped persuade many black residents not to leave the city but also influenced the thinking of whites on the subject. At the same time, Watkins ushered in a more militant opposition to white prejudices and injustices that reverberated throughout the community and influenced far more than just the colonization controversy. Watkins had long been a frequent speaker for leading black organizations in the city, and his message of self-empowerment that routinely echoed those of his mentor, Daniel Coker, strongly encouraged autonomy and solidarity for Baltimore's black community. At a celebration of Haitian independence in 1825 (which one historian argues was the first such observance in the South), Watkins praised the growth of the black republic, declaring "that the descendants of Africa never were designed by their Creator to sustain an inferiority, or even a mediocrity, in the chain of being."[31]

Watkins saw no reason for these accomplishments to be reserved solely for the Caribbean, much less Africa; such social progress was transpiring in Baltimore and elsewhere in the United States. Writing regularly to Benjamin Lundy's *Genius of Universal Emancipation* under his pseudonym, "A Colored Baltimorean," he asked, "Why should we abandon our firesides and everything associated with the dear name of *home* . . . for the enjoyment of liberty divested of its usual accompaniments, surrounded with circumstances which diminish its intrinsic value, and render it indeed 'a dear earned morsel[?]'"[32] In 1831 Watkins attacked colonization in William Lloyd Garrison's *Liberator*, claiming that he and other black Baltimoreans would "rather die in Maryland under the pressure of unrighteous and cruel laws than be driven, like cattle, to the pestilential clime of Liberia, where grievous privation, inevitable disease, and premature death, await us in all their horrors." Tradition holds that Watkins's forceful stance turned William Lloyd Garrison against the colonization movement while Garrison was working with Lundy in Baltimore in 1830.[33]

Watkins also argued that free Negroes leaving the country would actually strengthen the institution of slavery and further degrade the status of American free Negroes. The wholesale removal of the positive influence and example of those who had succeeded would only add to the derogation of those black people—slaves and free Negroes alike—who remained. In response to a procolonization tract written by John B. Hepburn, a self-styled "Americo-African" (which Lundy had recently published in his *Genius of Universal Emancipation*), Watkins asked, with biting sarcasm, "How will our removal to Africa prove 'that our natural color is' not 'an obstacle to our moral and political improvement in these United States?' Again, will nothing but our removal thither prove 'that we possess those attributes which entitle men to the consideration of society?' Or will our remaining here prove that we do not possess those qualities?"[34]

Watkins had little patience for accommodationist stances among black Baltimoreans, especially influential church leaders. In October 1835, in an obvious response to the Nat Turner rebellion, a "White Citizen" of Baltimore expressed his concern in the *Niles' Weekly Register* about whether "the Baltimore colored population would continue to conduct themselves in an orderly and peaceable manner" and pointed to the city's black congregations as obvious vehicles for organized dissent and unrest. Three of Baltimore's free black ministers, John Fortie of Sharp Street, Nathaniel Peck of Bethel (who four years later would consider emigration), and William Livingston of St. James Protestant Episcopal, immediately offered a conciliatory response to "remove, if possible, any unfounded impressions as to there being any disposition among us, or our brethren generally of the city and vicinity of Baltimore, to countenance any views or movements which tend to disturb the peace, or alienate the feelings, to provoke the jealousies, or to jeopardize the safety of the citizens of the said community." The letter went on to explain the vested stake, both social and economic, that Baltimore's black residents had in maintaining good stead with the white community and pledged that the black people and congregations of the city would not "molest or destroy the peace and harmony of the community."[35] Similarly, five trustees of one black Methodist Episcopal church in east Baltimore published a letter openly censuring abolitionists' activities as a threat to "rivet the fetter still more closely on the slave," after the church's white elder advised them that this was the only means of saving the church from demolition.[36]

Watkins condemned these letters, as much for their overt accommodationism as for their authors' tacit acceptance of the need for such promises from an obviously responsible, law-abiding citizenry. "It is time enough," wrote Watkins, "to make disavowals, disclaimers, and pledges when we are charged with some other crime than that of our colour." In a letter to William Lloyd Garrison, Watkins revealed that his open criticism had won him threats of tar and feathering from the ministers who had authored the first letter. In words tinged with bitterness, Watkins condemned both colonization and the racial climate in nineteenth-century America that precipitated the scheme:

> Not, indeed, that we have made ourselves so by our crimes,—no but we are a "nuisance," because the Creator of all things . . . has thought proper, in his infinite wisdom, to tincture us with a darker hue than that of our white brethren. . . . This is our crime; and for this alone we are told that we can never be men, unless we

abandon the land of our birth, "our veritable home," . . . O that men would learn that knowledge and virtue, not colour, constitute the sum of human dignity. With these we are white, without them black.[37]

By the time of the ministers' letter, Watkins's passionate words had resonated strongly throughout Baltimore's black community. The city's free blacks made concerted efforts to defend their free status by preventing colonizationists from making inroads into the community. Jacob Greener, Lundy's close associate (though, he, like Watkins, held a contrary view of colonization), verbally challenged white colonizationist speakers in 1827, excoriating them for their misguided notions and arguing that "the first object of the colonization society should be to educate the coloured children" and that this should be followed by the elimination of white prejudice, "one of the blackest spots that ever cursed the globe [and] 'the stars and stripes,'" which colonization only exacerbated.[38] Further, the city's black leaders prepared a memorandum repudiating their earlier one, now voicing a lack of confidence in the colonization society because it was inconsistent with the desires of the free black community and decrying the "illiberal attacks" on the moral character of free Negroes in general. At a mass meeting held in 1831 Baltimore black residents reaffirmed their opposition to deportation, asserting that "we consider that land in which we were born our only 'true and appropriate home' and when we desire to remove we will apprise the public of the same, in due season."[39]

In addition to public demonstrations of unified opposition to colonization, Baltimore's free blacks organized more forceful, covert means of opposing the various colonization societies' efforts. Anticolonization emissaries, generally in groups, visited prospective emigrants, warning them of potential hardships in Africa, claiming misrepresentations by colonization agents, and frightening the would-be emigrants with stories of sale to either the South or the West Indies. One white agent lamented that once having persuaded a free black Baltimorean to emigrate, "in a day or two after, . . . someone had been after him, filling the mind of the emigrant . . . with alarming & false statements, and changing him from his purpose."[40]

If such tactics failed, urban free Negroes often became more coercive, denouncing emigrants as "traitors to their race" and censuring them "not only in private houses, but in public meetings." As early as 1831, as the Maryland State Colonization Society prepared to send its first group of emigrants, Baltimore freemen actually boarded the departing vessel to convince the black passengers to leave the ship before facing certain death in Africa. Their last-ditch efforts appear to have worked; only half of those sixty emigrants scheduled to sail as part of the first expedition actually departed on sailing day. So pronounced were the black anticolonizationists' efforts that the managers of the Maryland State Colonization Society pleaded with the city's watchmen to prevent such intimidation, because the emigrants were traveling at the state's expense.[41]

White and black colonizationists alike believed that Watkins's opposition was largely responsible for the truculence of Baltimore's black community on matters concerning colonization. In preparation for the 1841 convention James Hall, the agent for the Maryland State Colonization Society, wrote to Watkins, hoping that Watkins would convince "the more intelligent of the coloured population in behalf of the whole to memorialize said convention upon the subject, stating definitely what are their views and sentiments relative thereto." Watkins's reply reveals the depth of the community's aversion to colonizationists. "I am seriously of the opinion that colonizationists, *in general*, are so hostile to our remaining in the lands of our birth, so intent upon the prosecution of their scheme, believing that our existence in Maryland is an evil of fearful magnitude an evil which *must be removed*," Watkins wrote forcefully, "[that they] are doubtless prepared to propose and carry out so far as an overruling Providence will permit them, such measures as they think best calculated to accomplish their object . . . that the 'stating definitely' of our 'views and sentiments relative thereto' would be regarded by them of secondary importance."[42]

Despite seemingly uniform opposition to colonization, support for the scheme persisted in Baltimore and elsewhere in Maryland. Angered by the state and nation's anti–free Negro mood that had brought on increasing proscriptions, several Baltimore free black leaders met in the late spring of 1852 to discuss strategy for rekindling support for the scheme, which had waned during the city's economic resurgence of the late 1840s. James A. Handy, the Bethel minister, and John H. Walker, a local schoolmaster, emerged as the leaders of the group and issued a circular that decried the hypocrisy of the precepts of the Declaration of Independence, considering the exclusion of black Americans from "the blessings so freely enjoyed by the white citizens of this land," and called for a convention in July "to take into serious consideration our present condition and future prospects in this country, and contrast them with the inducements and prospects opened to us in Liberia, or any other country."[43]

When the forty-two delegates, eighteen from Baltimore and the rest from six other counties, crowded into a stuffy lower room of Washington Hall, spectators from the Baltimore black community outnumbered the delegation. Delegates who decried the deterioration of the status of black residents of the state received thunderous applause, especially one Baltimore member who remarked that even swine enjoyed more rights than they: "The hog law said at certain seasons they should run about, and at certain seasons be taken up; but the laws referring to the colored people allowed them to be taken up at any time."[44]

Yet when delegates expressed support for emigration to Africa, exclaiming that it was "the only place where the colored man could expect to be a freeman," they were met with deafening opposition from the audience. Anticolonizationists raucously hissed and shouted down speakers and even threatened the lives of delegates trying to speak. Both inside and outside the hall angry opponents "frequently assailed the delegates coming to the Convention and a large number . . . were ripe for any further opposition they could exhibit." Several delegates resigned and left the hall. One, James A. Jones of Kent County, claimed that "he had been informed that his head, if not his life, was in danger if he left the room." Frightened by the ominous atmosphere, members of the Dorchester County delegation offered to leave, remarking "that they did not think that their presence here could be of any benefit." Their motion was "received with applause, and cries of 'good' from the opponents of colonization." The Reverend Darius Stokes narrowly missed injury when a glass thrown at him whistled by his head. Only the arrival of the police allowed the convention to continue without further incident inside the hall, though even police protection could not prevent fracases from erupting outside the convention hall. So pronounced was the intimidation that it forced the convention to move the meeting to another location on the third day; this meeting was sparsely attended, and even the convention's president, the Reverend William Tasker of Frederick, sent a note to the remaining delegates claiming that "indisposition" would prevent him from attending the remainder of the convention. More important, such strident opposition caused the convention to adopt resolutions that did not support mass emigration, stating instead that the "transfer of an entire people from one country to another, must necessarily be the work of generations."[45]

Such effective, tightly organized defenses of Baltimore's black people appeared so impenetrable that one Maryland colonizationist lamented as early as 1832 that "the prejudices of the coloured people of Baltimore and other large Towns, against African Colonization, are so strong that distributing literature among them would be to throw it away." Such a stark conclusion appears to be justified, judging by the results of the 1852 convention. From distant Rochester, New York, the anticolonizationist Frederick Douglass hailed the fortitude of the free black dissidents in Baltimore and maintained that their intransigence augured racial tolerance in Maryland.

The pervasively hostile sentiment against colonization throughout the period and the equally persuasive demeanor of the Baltimore junto forced the Maryland Colonization Society to abandon recruitment efforts on the state's Western Shore. Of the emigrants sponsored by the Maryland State Colonization Society between 1832 and 1841, only fifty (less than 8 percent) were from Baltimore.[46]

Instead of reflecting deep community division, the often strident debate over the issue of colonization suggests the development of a mature social and racial identity that the Baltimore black community had made over the past several decades. Such organized dissent reflects an important stage in the sociological development of community identification. It reflects an advanced stage of the social process by which the groups moved from individual to collective to institutionalized behavior. As such, this conflict over colonization offered black Baltimoreans the opportunity to further the evolution of their own community as distinct and autonomous. That such progress was not as overtly delineated by class divisions as it was in other antebellum cities allowed community leaders (who had themselves experienced various forms of social and economic success) to gain status as spokespeople for the advancement of both their community and their race.

This concept of racial advancement is nowhere more obvious than at the infamous 1852 colonization convention held at the city's Washington Hall. The great dissension over the meeting denotes a division of the community over this weighty issue. Yet the fact that at least fourteen of the eighteen Baltimore delegates at a convention seeking to make decisions about leaving their homes and occupations for foreign places that only theoretically offered opportunity for further advancement—socially, economically, and politically—were respectable Baltimore tradesmen and professionals demonstrates they too were motivated by a commitment to community betterment that permeated the people as a whole. No downtrodden laborers chafing at class inequities, these leaders had social and economic stature similar to that of the anticolonization leaders, railed over impediments to black advancement, and with Puritan fortitude considered the prospect of relocating. Whether for or against colonization, Baltimore's black community unified around a principle far more compelling: racial progress. Baltimore's black society became, in the words of one historian of urban African Americans of the antebellum North, a "community of commitment."[47]

Emboldened by its successes in opposing colonization and having learned valuable activist strategies and tactics, Baltimore's black community used its newfound collective solidarity to protest racial injustices in people's daily lives. One of those efforts focused on obtaining public education. In 1826,

amid the North's foment for reform, Maryland passed a law creating publicly supported primary schools. Three years later the first three public
schools opened in Baltimore. According to the state law, however, only white
students could attend these schools, even though they were supported by a
property tax levied on all city owners, regardless of color.[48]

When whites refused to accept black children into the city's public
schools yet continued to require black residents to pay the school tax, the
black community rallied against this injustice. In 1839 black residents sent
a petition to the mayor and city council bearing fifty-five signatures, "Pray-
ing that Colored Persons May Be Exempted from the Payment of the
Public School Tax," because "coloured people are not at all interested in
the public schools directly or indirectly." Five years later another large
group of black residents asked the city government to appropriate a portion of the "nett proceeds of the School Tax" for two schools "in different
sections of the city . . . for the benefit of coloured children and adapted
more especially to the education of thos[e] whose circumstances prevent
them from paying a high rate of tuition." In 1850 ninety black citizens
petitioned for financial assistance from the city to assist them in "establishing public schools for the instruction of the free colored children of
the city, in the elementary branches of an English Education." A second
petition, submitted simultaneously and signed by more than a hundred
whites sympathetic to the need for black public schools (yet mindful of their
social status), called for "instruction of the [black] children . . . in such
elements of learning as may prepare them . . . with usefulness and respectability, [for] those humble stations in the community to which they are
confined by the necessities of their situation."[49]

The petitions induced the Baltimore City Council to consider the effi-
caciousness of racial proscriptions, and a number of vocal white supporters
of the black community attended the debate. Fearing that the state legislature would withdraw the city's portion of the general school fund, the city
council rejected the black residents' request for public funding for black
schools. The Joint Standing Committee on Education of the city council
reasoned that "the General Assembly of Maryland did not contemplate in
granting the City of Baltimore a portion of the school fund and in authorizing a levy for support of said schools, that it should be used in part for
black schools." Not until after the Civil War were black Baltimoreans allowed to attend the city's public schools, which they had been financially
supporting since 1826.[50]

Undeterred, the black community drew on its inner strength and resources to provide quality education for its children. Because black education in

Baltimore had long flourished in its churches, community leaders sought to establish uniform high standards among black Sabbath schools and teachers. In 1859 the Colored Sabbath School Union of Baltimore organized and met monthly to, in the words of the preamble to its constitution, "aid and assist in the mental, moral, and religious instruction of our people in every way and manner, which we think will contribute to our best interests both *for time and eternity.*"[51] Moreover, respectable black individuals set aside financial resources to guarantee that education be available for black children who could not otherwise afford to attend the private schools. Nelson Wells, a drayman, dictated in his will that municipal stock worth $3,500 be placed in a confidential trust until his wife's death to provide for the intellectual improvement of "the poor free colored children of Baltimore."[52]

In their pursuit of education, Baltimore's black people demonstrated more than a fervor for literacy and societal respectability. Their actions showed a willingness to challenge white authority within boundaries acceptable to a society dominated by slaveowners fearful of black solidarity. More important, this assertiveness, gained from the anticolonization effort, reflects the matured, unified community. In tandem with the effective opposition to colonization and organized support for public education, Baltimore's black community actively opposed the institution of slavery both in Maryland and in the nation. All of the dissident efforts of Baltimore's black community grew largely out of the long struggle against slavery—a struggle that took countless individual forms and ultimately became, as black Baltimoreans cohered into a community, a people's shibboleth.

Antislavery had enjoyed a long history in Baltimore. As early as 1789 a society formed in the city to promote "the abolition of slavery, and for the relief of free negroes and others unlawfully held in bondage." Many of its members were Quakers, whose annual and monthly meetings had condemned the practice since 1768. The group sent petitions to Congress calling for the prohibition of the practice and submitted freedom petitions on behalf of numerous black people in Baltimore (a practice the House of Delegates decried as a pernicious, yet legal, nuisance). Members even harbored escaped slaves in their efforts to end the institution. Though the society disbanded in 1792, the sentiments that had prompted its founding lingered in Baltimore, growing stronger as the economic need for slaves in the city waned. In the autumn of 1826, largely through the efforts of Benjamin Lundy, Baltimore hosted a biennial session of the American Convention for Promoting the Abolition of Slavery, and Improving the Condition of the African Race. The convention drew twenty-three delegates from both northern and southern states to discuss strategies to promote abolition in the nation and "to protect the rights of free persons of color."[53] Antislavery support in Baltimore became so pronounced that in 1840 the Englishman James Buckingham proclaimed that "all parties here seem to admit it [slavery] to be a great national evil; all appear anxious to see it abolished." Although this was undoubtedly an embellished observation, the center of antislavery sentiment in Maryland was unquestionably Baltimore.[54]

Though their bold efforts threatened to attract the enmity of white slaveowners, black ministers and teachers in Baltimore took advantage of white residents' relative ambivalence toward abolitionism to use their pulpits and podiums to stir opposition to slavery. Because of their status as leaders of the black community, ministers and teachers exerted a powerful political, social, and moral influence on the entire populace, regardless of class. As early as 1810 Daniel Coker had publicly denounced the enslavement of African Americans and demanded universal emancipation by sermonizing on the subject and publishing his views in a pamphlet titled *A Dialogue between a Virginian and an African Minister.* In a stirring speech delivered to a group of black leaders in 1825 to commemorate Haiti's independence and to oppose colonization, William Watkins praised the rise of the black republic as "irrefutable argument to prove . . . that the descendents of Africa never were designed by their Creator to sustain an inferiority, or even a mediocrity, in the chain of being; but that they are as capable of intellectual improvements as the Europeans, or people of any other nation upon the face of the earth."[55]

Together with Hezekiah Grice, a local butcher, Watkins worked to found the National Convention of the Free People of Color, an effort designed to bring together black Americans from throughout the nation to discuss issues concerning their race, such as colonization and emancipation, and to express a unified black voice on such issues. Though Grice and Watkins played an active role in planning these conventions, the movement itself quickly became dominated by black residents of New York, Philadelphia, and Wilmington. Conventions were held annually from 1830 to 1835, and periodically thereafter, largely in those northern cities. The conventions regularly condemned colonization and "oppressive, unjust, and unconstitutional" legislation that denied the rights of Negroes.[56] The conventions' stance was echoed in countless sermons, lectures, and conversations and contributed to a growing racial consciousness among Baltimore's black residents, who were encouraged to participate in the antislavery movement by shielding escaped slaves and organizing for more overt political actions.[57]

Despite the hardening of racial antipathy in Baltimore, antislavery sentiment in the city endured at least partly because of the proliferation of the domestic slave trade during the middle decades of the antebellum period. As the system of slavery fell into gradual decline in the upper counties of Maryland and as Baltimore grew precipitously, the city became the center of the slave trade for the state. James V. Deane, a former slave in Charles County, recalled seeing slaves tied to the rear of buggies and being taken to Baltimore for sale. Those masters who would not emancipate their unneeded slaves often traveled to Baltimore, where a number of traders operated, and acquired slaves to sell to planters in the Lower South, where rapidly expanding cotton production was producing an insatiable demand for slave laborers.[58]

Though Maryland did not engage in the slave trade as heavily as neighboring Virginia did, such Baltimore traders as Hope Slatter and Austin Woolfolk advertised heavily in the city's newspapers, maintained private "jails" (or enclosures) for their transient property,[59] and contributed to the shipment of hundreds of slaves each year from the city. From his office on Pratt Street, Woolfolk sent agents throughout the slaveholding sections of the state and had an office (and probably a pen) in Easton, in Talbot County on the Eastern Shore. Woolfolk and Slatter both shipped slaves to the Deep South (and gained their largest profits from such trade), but the laws regarding term slaves prompted them perforce to sell slaves locally as well. Woolfolk grew so wealthy at his craft that between 1838 and 1846 he owned sixteen separate pieces of property in the city, which were valued at more that $75,000. By the 1850s seventeen such traders operated in Baltimore.[60]

While the cruelty of the slave trade offended many Baltimore residents, the kidnapping and sale of many free blacks to the slave traders—rumored to be assisted by city authorities—stirred them to action. Because Baltimore was a magnet for fugitive slaves, the city jail was constantly used to hold runaways for return to their masters. In 1837 alone, 130 fugitive slaves were held there. The opportunities for corruption were rampant. In 1845 Charles Torrey, a Massachusetts minister who served time in the Baltimore jail for helping slaves escape, witnessed such corruption. The city's police hired black agents to entice slaves to escape to Baltimore and hide in their homes, only to betray them to the police, who held them without notice until the master offered (and they collected) a reward. Moreover, Torrey charged, local constables often searched churches for free blacks without passes (required by Maryland law in 1805), arresting them as suspected runaways and selling them to traders at low prices. As early as 1801 newspapers reported organized kidnappings of free Negroes in Baltimore (some of whom were adult black residents whom traders paid to kidnap young boys), which occurred frequently over the next two decades. In both 1811 and 1816 the Baltimore grand jury, called to investigate the kidnappings, noted slave traders' abuses of free blacks, who were "decoyed by stratagem or dragged by force into these prisons," either private jails or the city jail.[61]

In response to the growing crisis, black residents and sympathetic whites in Baltimore organized, though their strategies were quite different. In 1816, as a group of Baltimore Quakers petitioned the legislature unsuccessfully for stronger legislation against free black kidnappings, another group of concerned whites formed the Protection Society of Maryland, dedicated to curbing the kidnapping and reenslavement of free blacks.[62] The group petitioned both the House of Delegates and the U.S. Congress for similar legislation, while at the same time soliciting the support of the black community. Though preventative legislation proved limited, efforts to unify Baltimore's black people bore fruit. Local churches took collections, on one Sunday in 1860 amounting to as much as two hundred dollars, for the benefit of the Protection Society. That same year the congregation of the Ebenezer A.M.E. Church raised money to liberate one of its lay ministers from a slave trader's jail by holding a dinner at the minister's home and inviting the church choir to provide the music and the well-known ministers William H. Waters and Henry McNeil Turner to speak.[63] Moreover, black neighborhoods organized watch patrols, which patrolled the streets throughout the night and alerted either the city watchmen or Protection Society members of suspected kidnapping attempts. Dr. Bartholomew Fussell witnessed one such incident, prompted by several of Austin Woolfolk's hired men dragging a captured black woman through the streets toward his jail. Local residents quickly turned out to block the men's efforts, and they summoned Elisha Tyson, one of the city's most prominent residents and founder of the Protection Society. Through Tyson's efforts, the woman was freed.[64]

The ubiquitous antislavery efforts of black Baltimoreans, as well as the community consolidation and proven tactics of its opposition to colonization, provided a firm foundation for a resistance movement against the gravest threat yet posed to Maryland African Americans' rights as a free people: the Jacobs bill. The institutional framework that the Baltimore black community had forged in an effort to secure autonomy in their own affairs and to protect the community from racial hostility and prejudice now provided a solid edifice for their activism. Through memorials, petitions, public meetings, and newspaper correspondence, Baltimore's free Negro leadership exerted its political presence, which, in the absence of formal political rights (namely, the franchise), sought not only to solidify community sentiment but also to enlist the aid of prominent white allies who could provide crucial support. Yet the challenge the community now faced very nearly proved too great even for such organized avenues of opposition to overcome.[65]

The tactics Baltimore free Negroes used in 1859 were among an arsenal acquired over years of defending their place in Maryland society. As early as 1826 Baltimore's free blacks had appealed to the legislature for relief from the 1825 law forcing free Negroes to show proof of gainful employment or be banished from the state. Using language designed to play on whites' national pride in their virtuous republic, the appeal declared, "We reside among you and yet are strangers; natives, and yet not citizens; surrounded by the freest people and the most republican institutions in the world, and yet enjoying none of the imunities of freedom." "Though we are not slaves," it concluded, "we are not free."[66]

The following year, in response to the petition of Baltimore's white carters and draymen asking that Negroes be prohibited from plying the trade, William Watkins appealed to the city's antislavery supporters in a letter published in Benjamin Lundy's *Genius of Universal Emancipation*. With decorous language designed to avoid inflaming white hostility, Watkins argued against the "unjust and inhumane" petition, which was "designed to deprive of a means of livelihood not only individuals, but whole families whose only crime was their color." More important, black leaders like Watkins rallied the support of merchants who depended on their labor and by counterpetitioning succeeded in getting the bill dropped. Similar tactics in 1845 against the law prohibiting black gatherings and organizations resulted in exemptions for organizations composed of black members "of good character" (who paid at least five dollars in taxes), with the proviso that they obtain an annual written permit from the mayor and submit to police inspections.[67] In 1853 Baltimore's free blacks organized a convention similar to the one held the previous year to consider colonization. This meeting was held to oppose the disfranchisement of Negroes and to support the maintenance of civil rights for all, regardless of color.[68]

Such conventions, as well as petition drives, memorials, public meetings, publication of letters, and other forms of group and individual dissent, reveal the high level of political organization achieved by the black community of Baltimore in the 1840s and 1850s. Despite their divisions, black Baltimoreans could and did exert political might. Their ability to use organized tactics would prove crucial by the end of the decade, when free blacks faced the organized threat to their status as free men and women posed by Curtis W. Jacobs.

The crisis produced by the white crusade for reenslavement and the Jacobs bill engendered a level of unified, organized resistance from the black community of Baltimore exceeding even that which opposed colonization. The city's black residents rallied all potential sources of support among both free Negroes and sympathetic whites. White support came mostly from the city's religious leaders and churchfolk. Prompted by black ministers, Baltimore's white Methodist Episcopal ministers drafted a statement to the state legislature in response to the slaveholders' convention of 1858, declaring that they were "not prepared to acquiesce" to the convention's "spirit, if not their design, to drive from the state the people of colour, that are already free, and to prevent others from becoming free," as well as all "other oppressive and vexatious changes in existing laws."[69] Andrew B. Cross, a Baltimore clergyman, member of the city council, and long-time supporter of Negro rights, submitted and published in pamphlet form a lengthy letter to the legislature. Addressed to Jacobs, the letter denounced the free Negro bill as the work of "violent and extreme men" and pledged that "every denomination of Christians, with every minister of the Gospel, will be bound in conscience to lift up a voice of condemnation." Two hundred of the city's white women submitted their own petition, including the signatures of such important political figures as Reverdy Johnson and future mayor George W. Brown, "implor[ing] that the curse of the Creator of all men be not called down upon our beloved state by the adoption of such unrighteous bills, . . . that we be not ranked with the heathen nations by the passage of laws which trample underfoot every precept of the Gospel."[70]

Black Baltimoreans themselves proved tireless in rallying opposition to the Jacobs bill. All of the city's leading barbers solicited signatures for a petition to the state's lawmakers; ultimately more than a thousand blacks signed the document. Churches organized days of fasting and prayer and provided well-known local black ministers as speakers, including Henry McNeil Turner, Hiram Revels, Moses Clayton, and Noah Davis.[71] Black residents began to hold weekly meetings at local churches to decide a course of action. At one such meeting, held at Bethel in early February, black residents formed a protection society, designed to develop measures to oppose the bill. They named as its head George Hackett, a former sailor who had served aboard the U.S.S. *Constitution* and was now a local livery stable owner. As Nicholas Gilliard's son-in-law and Daniel Coker's brother-in-law, he had the advantage of being well connected in the black community. Hackett arranged a personal meeting with Curtis Jacobs to present the grievances of the city's black residents and defend the state's free Negroes. The icy confrontation proved at best inconclusive, though it showed remarkable courage on the part of the free Negro leadership and fortitude on the part of the black community in fighting the direst threat it ever faced. [72]

Fortunately for Maryland's free blacks, the Baltimore community's indefatigable efforts paid off. When the proposals of the Committee on Colored Population reached the public, the reaction was immediate and hostile. All the newspapers in Baltimore and most across the state condemned the Ja-

cobs bill as severe and oppressive. Despite Jacobs's vigorous defense, not even
the legislature could agree to the committee's plan. It passed two bills in its
stead, which fell far short of the original bill. The General Assembly let stand
the provision prohibiting future manumissions and added a provision that
allowed free Negroes over the age of eighteen to renounce their freedom
and return to lifelong slavery. A second bill addressed the issue of reenslavement, forcing free Negroes to produce evidence of having hired themselves
out for the coming year and subjecting those who failed to do so to public
auction for a one-year term. When placed before the state's voters in a ref-
erendum in the November election, more than 70 percent rejected even
these diluted bills. In Baltimore County voters stood against the bills nearly eight to one. Maryland's free Negroes would remain forever free.[73]

✤   ✤   ✤

The defeat of the reenslavement movement was unquestionably a victory
for Maryland's black population. More important, the efforts of Baltimore's
African Americans to combat the Jacobs bill had had a significant effect on
their community. The formation and strengthening of community institutions in direct response to the rising tide of white hostility and repression
had buttressed the community's defenses and crystallized its maturation. In
the face of strong differences of opinion, Baltimore's black people had galvanized themselves to respond to racial restrictions and in the process had
created a racial identity and solidarity that, for a time, overcame the city's
growing crosscurrents of economic hardship and class and color stratification that divided their community.

Over decades of growth and progress, a sense of community pride and
unity evolved among the black residents of Baltimore. By the second quarter of the nineteenth century they had established strong and active social
institutions that had transformed a small, disparate, and relatively inert
amalgam of transients into a multifaceted community that derived strength
from those institutions and exercised power through them. Resilient and
remarkably cohesive, Baltimore's African American community had proved
capable of flexing remarkable political muscle, considering blacks' lack of
formal rights. In exerting collective social rights, the community challenged
the very institution by which southern states like Maryland defined their
society and their future: slavery. On the eve of the Civil War, Baltimore's
African Americans—unlike the nation itself—still inhabited a remarkably
undivided house.

Conclusion

Once an island of racial tolerance in comparison with the rest of the state, by the last antebellum decade—and despite having the largest free Negro population of any city in the nation—Baltimore had lost its reputation as a place of refuge for free blacks. The decades-long white attack on the state's free blacks and the resultant incremental losses of freedom had taken their toll even on Baltimore's strong black community. The economic, ideological, and legislative assault on free Negroes caused black Marylanders during the late 1850s to question whether their brightest possible futures could be found in Baltimore.

After 1850 the combination of economic distress, occupational exclusion, and state enactments halted the growth of the city's black population—once the fastest growing in the nation. During the 1850s the number of free blacks in Baltimore, which had increased during the previous decade by more than 41 percent, increased by less than 1 percent, from 25,442 to 25,680. This figure stands in stark contrast to the free Negro population in Maryland, which grew during the same decade by more than 12 percent. This decline in the growth of the free black population was coupled with a continued drop in the number of slaves in the city, which meant that Baltimore's black population actually decreased, after having increased by at least 10 percent during each decade since 1790 (see table 18). During the same decade the city's white population increased by nearly a third, and when combined with the staggering growth experienced during the 1840s, whites in Baltimore numbered almost two-thirds more in 1860 than twenty years earlier.[1]

Among cities in the slave states, this phenomenon appears to have been almost exclusive to Baltimore. Though other southern states passed laws designed to reduce their free Negro reduce populations, only Charleston's free black population stagnated or declined.[2] Considering that Baltimore's black population had grown by more than a third during the previous de-

Table 18. Changes in the Baltimore Population by Race, 1790–1860

Decade	White Number	White Percentage	Black Number	Black Percentage
1790–1800	+8,975	+75.3	+4,036	+255.8
1801–1810	+15,307	+73.2	+4,734	+84.3
1811–1820	+11,848	+32.7	+4,734	+41.9
1821–1830	+13,655	+28.4	+4,227	+28.8
1831–1840	+19,437	+31.5	+2,256	+11.9
1841–1850	+59,519	+73.3	+7,222	+34.1
1851–1860	+43,854	+31.2	-490	-1.7

Sources: Wright, *Free Negro in Maryland*, 86–88; Fairbanks, *Statistical Analysis of the Population of Maryland*, 105; McSherry, *History of Maryland*, 403–4; Fields, *Slavery and Freedom on the Middle Ground*, 70.

cade, the city's lack of growth during the 1850s is particularly telling. Plagued by economic woes, crowded with white European immigrants who competed for the city's fewer available jobs, and charged with an increasingly hostile attitude toward its large free Negro population, during the 1850s Baltimore lost its status as a safe haven, and hope for Maryland's freedpeople hung in the balance.

One can find glimpses of the cessation of growth of Baltimore's black population during the decade before the Civil War. Though in nearly all years prior to 1850 blacks migrated to the city, after that year, when legislation virtually ended the flow of black people into Maryland, none entered Baltimore legally. Manumissions in the city were sharply curtailed after the 1830s and ended completely in the mid-1850s. During the 1830s, 398 manumissions were registered with the county court; a decade later, just 269 were registered. By the final decade, just 109 slaves were freed in Baltimore; all but 4 of those were freed before 1856 and none after that year.[3] Slaves, too, continued to shrink in numbers; between 1850 and 1860 the already small population fell again by nearly 25 percent, to just 2,218. Without the prospect for hiring their slaves out, rural owners did not send them to the city, and many urban owners were forced to sell their slaves either because of their own hard times or because they too could not hire them out. So complete was Baltimore's transformation from a place of refuge to one of repression that when codifying the status of black people in the city in 1858, the city council resurrected the term "negroes and other slaves," echoing the phrase used by the Maryland colonial assembly nearly 225 years earlier. Now, however, the true meaning of the phrase used by the state's founders became unmistakably clear.[4]

A decline in the number of Baltimore's free black men, who were most vulnerable to the city's economic woes, accounted for much of stagnation of the black population's growth. Between 1850 and 1860 free Negro men in the city declined by 4.5 percent, from 10,832 to 10,346. At the same time, free black women increased by nearly 5.0 percent, from 14,610 to 15,334. Yet the decline of free black males did not account solely for the cessation of Baltimore's free black population's growth during the 1850s. Though the number of free black women in the city increased by more than seven hundred during the 1850s, even this growth had slowed considerably compared with that of the previous decade. This increase was far less than that of the 1840s, when the number of free Negro women increased by 3,904 (36.5 percent), from 10,706 to 14,610. Though free Negro men were particularly hard hit by the problems of the 1850s, free black women were by no means impervious to them.[5]

Interestingly, the seeds of the free Negro population decline were sown in the 1840s. Before 1840 just 386 free blacks had requested temporary permits from the Baltimore city court to leave the state (state law passed in 1831 required that potential black travelers do so, filing a declaration citing the exact dates they would be out of the state and the destination of their travel). In 1840 alone 527 such permits were granted in the city, and 611 more in the following five years, before the state prohibited them. Many of these travelers never returned.[6] The membership of the Sharp Street church and other congregations in the city fell sharply after the mid-1840s. In 1843 the Sharp Street church alone boasted 4,000 members; by 1860 that congregation, even when combined with those at Asbury Station and Orchard Street, totaled just 2,225 parishioners. Strawberry Alley's membership declined similarly, dropping from 590 in 1854 to 338 in 1860. One of those members of the Sharp Street congregation who left the city never to return was William Watkins, the indefatigable champion of Negro rights. He was one of at least seventy-two members who went to Canada.[7]

By 1860, while Baltimore's race relations had changed considerably from those of a half-century earlier, the status of free blacks and slaves in the city had, in an ironic way, come full circle. At the turn into the nineteenth century, the city's booming economy and great demand for labor had created an ambivalent racial climate in which the standing of black residents—free and slave—was nearly indistinguishable, not so much because of the repression that cowed them into similar shades of degradation but because of the remarkable freedoms forged by each. This pervasive liberalism rendered their dual statuses as "quasi-slave" and "quasi-free" nearly synonymous. By the eve of the Civil War, in a soured economy with an overabundance of immigrant laborers, white residents of Baltimore still considered the city's free blacks and slaves similarly, although not in terms of the liberties afforded to them. Now, many white Baltimoreans joined in the concerted efforts of rural Maryland legislators to reduce the freedoms of free Negroes until all black people were virtually slaves. The effort to reenslave all free Negroes in Maryland, though thwarted, provides clear yet ominous evidence of this negative shift in attitude toward the state's black residents. The strident opposition of Baltimore free blacks to the state's colonization effort, Maryland's first attempt to limit its free Negro population, only intensified Maryland's hostility toward its free Negroes, particularly those free blacks living in the city.

Baltimore's black community presents a significant challenge to scholars of southern antebellum race relations. Ulrich B. Phillips, the eminent historian of the Old South, claimed that the central theme of southern history was the desire to preserve the supremacy of the white race; numerous others, such as Wilbur J. Cash, Carl Degler, and Grady McWhiney carried similar standards. Close scrutiny of Baltimore suggests a somewhat different interpretation. The contentions of such distinguished writers as Gunnar Myrdal, Thomas Sowell, and Barbara Fields that the American notion of race is an ideological construct rooted in historical circumstance[8]—especially economic relations—rather than any biological attribute becomes even more plausible after studying the history of Baltimore's black community, especially compared with those of Charleston and New Orleans. Though the three cities were all located in slave states, which were long thought to have common ideologies on matters of race, they had startlingly distinctive histories of race relations. Because of regional crosscurrents and different economic realities, the supposedly "solid" southern commitment to white supremacy was less than steadfast, which can be readily seen in the changing race relations in the dynamic city of Baltimore in the Upper South.

The emerging discrimination against free blacks and the decline in their population not only in late antebellum Baltimore and Maryland but also in all of the nation's states during the period provide a fascinating glimpse into the dual developments of black strength and white hostility. Precisely as Baltimore's African Americans matured socially and ideologically as a people, white Marylanders turned against them, arguing that their strength (both in numbers and in political activism) was potentially dangerous. Slavery's long-standing influence and the prevailing white racist mentality in Maryland as a whole caused the state's leaders not only to maintain the institution but, once the effects of widespread manumissions became apparent, to engage in a debate over its free Negroes that was perhaps more virulent than in any other state. In many ways Baltimore African Americans achieved their cohesion as a direct result of the obstacles that white people constructed to impede their progress. Black residents of Baltimore, borrowing one historian's terms, found in "the rotting fruit of discriminatory separation . . . the fertile seeds of community."[9] Rural white Marylanders came to fear the city's black community for the very reason it had flowered—the assertive self-consciousness of its free, and even slave, women and men. Only by mustering herculean, unified efforts did the black community help block the powerful white crusade to reenslave all free Negroes in the state of Maryland.

By the eve of the Civil War Baltimore's black people had built a mature community, which exhibited the most basic definition of the term in that it was made of members who lived in a specific locality, shared a common cultural and historical heritage, and utilized institutional organization to exert political influence to protect its own interests. Despite economic decline and rising white antipathy after 1820—in fact because of them—the once-disparate population of unskilled laborers and domestics achieved an astonishing level of social progress and coherence. Baltimore's black community exemplifies a cohesive community and provides an example far better than the stratified, class- and color-conscious black urban populations of Charleston, New Orleans (which completely excluded slaves from leadership positions and marginalized most free Negroes), and even Philadelphia. Self-educated, relatively unracked by class divisions, strongly religious, and boasting the establishment of such black organizations and associations as fraternal orders, literary associations, and debating societies that facilitated political activity and the development of racial consciousness, by 1860 Baltimore's African Americans had riveted together a cohesive urban community, both free and slave, which looked within for identification yet also exuded a solidarity that affected blacks throughout the Upper South.

Although other large nineteenth-century African American urban communities established social organizations, most suffered from internal class divisions that caused many of their social institutions to be founded by—and reserved for—the community elite. Baltimore's black community did not depend on wealth or its wealthy leadership for strength; its vitality derived from and depended on the concord of its entire populace—a populace that was overwhelmingly poor. In part, their very deprivation allowed Baltimore's African American residents to forge a community that not only avoided the divisions of other black urban communities but also allowed them to weather the racial tempests of the antebellum years. Lacking pronounced class divisions, black Baltimoreans found a unity supposedly reserved exclusively for whites, who only rarely, if ever, managed to achieve it. Despite the fact that

Baltimore's African American population stopped growing during those years, the overwhelming majority of black Baltimoreans did not leave the city for greener pastures; rather, most stayed on in the city they had helped build and worked actively and communally to oppose any further deterioration of their status.

Baltimore's African American community had achieved a level of organization unparalleled by other such communities in the slave states. The accomplishments of Baltimore's black community were all the more remarkable considering they were achieved in a state that still wore the yoke of slavery; possessed the legal, social, and ideological means for repressing black residents; and had the political might to pass the racial proscriptions witnessed during the three decades before the Civil War. The power of the slaveholding mentality exerted itself nowhere more than in Maryland, where a slaveholding minority reacted to its apparent loss of power not only by limiting what it considered the dangerous political influence of free labor Baltimore but also by turning its populace against those black residents who supposedly had no political power and were the most vulnerable to white racial and political attacks: free Negroes.

That the Baltimore black community was able to organize and mature as successfully as it did and fight for its fragile right to freedom (one that white Marylanders were determined to withdraw) serves as testament to the power of freedom in the antebellum black psyche as well as to the abilities of those "unfree" and "quasi-free" people to make real the abstraction of liberty. The accomplishments of Baltimore's black community bear witness to the indomitable spirit of those not only geographically closest to freedom but also ideologically furthest removed from slavery.

In the spring and summer of 1864, as the state's constitutional convention deliberated emancipation, unified black Baltimoreans held a series of meetings in the city protesting such issues as unequal pay for black soldiers in the Union army and the Union military authorities' attempt to force free black men into the local militia. Addressing President Lincoln directly, the "Loyial Colard men of Baltimore Citey" apprised him that they were well aware of their legal responsibilities, their rights, and especially their power as a group to forestall efforts to deny them such rights. Excluded from the state militia, they informed the President that the "Congress of theas uninted States has made us a part of the National force. . . . We have responded to the call by enlistment[.] We are allso subject to the draft[.] the will of the Loyial Colard people of Baltimore citey is as a part of the National force to be treated no wors then the lawes Demand Governing the National force."

Decrying the fact that "all efforts of the people to come to gather in mass meting to protest aganst it has ben defeated by threts," the spokesmen "hold that we ar subject to the same regulation of the National force" and curtly reminded the president of his responsibilities. "And," they added, "we are shore that the Dignetey of this Government is too Loftey to Demand a man onley by her Lawful Chanel."[10]

When Maryland officially abolished the institution of slavery, the first border state to do so, Baltimore's African Americans renewed their role as architects of freedom. "Kept in the dark long enough," black Baltimoreans now demanded of state leaders nothing less than full citizenship.[11] First, however, they celebrated their efforts in the past and their hope for the future. On 15 November, a Tuesday evening exactly two weeks after the people of Maryland had ratified its new constitution that legally abolished slavery in the state, hundreds of Baltimore's black residents gathered at Mount Vernon Hall on Howard Street for a "great and expected Demonstration of the Celebration of the Emancipation." Lasting long into the night, amid brass band music, flag waving, addresses by local ministers, and ice cream and other refreshments, the celebrants sang spirituals and hymns with the proud ardor of those whose own efforts had helped achieve their people's freedom. Along with such well-known freedom songs as "Freedom Shall Not Perish," the celebrants, mindful of past injustices, offered up throaty versions of local compositions written just for this occasion, such as the defiant "Freedom Song," which included the following lyrics:

Jacobs wanted to take our Churches,
Put the children in his clutches,
Enslave the colored population free,
And now we'd like to see him,
And certainly to greet him,
How are you Jacobs?
Maryland is free. . . .
Old Maryland, my native home is free.[12]

In 1864 black Baltimoreans eagerly looked forward to a postslavery America. Yet when the city's African Americans celebrated emancipation, they commemorated as a community a day of jubilee many years past. Theirs was a celebration not simply of gratitude to a government that had created de jure freedom for slaves but also of derision for those who had threatened to revoke free Negroes' liberties, which long tradition had taught were not privileges but rights. Such legal freedom was one that Baltimore's black people helped create for others in the slave states. Still more, black Baltimoreans had already achieved de facto freedom for themselves. As the new day of freedom dawned over the South, morning's glow reflected most brightly off the deep waters of Baltimore's harbor. In its home port, freedom rode at anchor.[13]

Notes

Abbreviations

AMA	American Missionary Association Papers, Amistan Research Center, New Orleans, Louisiana; microfilm edition, Main Library, University of Georgia, Athens.
BCA	Baltimore City Archives, Baltimore, Maryland
BCC	Records of the Baltimore County Court, Maryland State Archives, Hall of Records, Annapolis, Maryland
BC Commissioners	Records of the Baltimore City Commissioners, 1797–1899, Record Group 3, Baltimore City Archives, Baltimore, Maryland
BC Council	Papers of the Baltimore City Council, Record Group 16, Baltimore City Archives, Baltimore, Maryland
BCH	Baltimore City Court House, Baltimore, Maryland
BC Mayor	Mayor's Papers, 1797–1923, Record Group 9, Series 2: Correspondence, Baltimore City Archives, Baltimore, Maryland
BC Miscellaneous	Miscellaneous Administrative Records of Baltimore City, 1798–1939, Record Group 41, Baltimore City Archives, Baltimore, Maryland
BC Tax	Baltimore City Property Tax Records, 1798-present, Record Group 4, Baltimore City Archives, Baltimore, Maryland
Bethel	Baltimore [Bethel] A.M.E. Church Collection, 1825–1881, MSA SC 2562, Maryland State Archives, Hall of Records, Annapolis, Maryland
EPFL	Maryland Room, Enoch Pratt Free Library, Baltimore, Maryland
ERB	"Early Records of Baltimore, 1756–1800," Record Group 2, Baltimore City Archives, Baltimore, Maryland
Fortie	Fortie Family Papers, 1767–1859, Marshall Collection, MSA SC 1383, Maryland State Archives, Hall of Records, Annapolis, Maryland
HSP	Historical Society of Pennsylvania, Philadelphia, Pennsylvania

LCP   Library Company of Philadelphia, Philadelphia, Pennsylvania
Lovely Lane   United Methodist Historical Society, Lovely Lane Museum,
                    Baltimore, Maryland
MdHR   Maryland State Archives, Hall of Records, Annapolis, Mary-
                    land
MHS   Maryland Historical Society Library, Manuscripts Division,
                    Baltimore, Maryland
MSCS   Maryland State Colonization Society Papers, Maryland His-
                    torical Society, Baltimore, Maryland; microfilm edition, Main
                    Library, University of Georgia, Athens
NA   National Archives, Washington, D.C.

Introduction

1. Stampp, *Peculiar Institution;* Elkins, *Slavery.*

2. Blassingame, *Slave Community;* Gutman, *Black Family in Slavery and Freedom;* Genovese, *Roll, Jordan, Roll;* Wood, *Black Majority;* Litwack, *Been in the Storm So Long;* Raboteau, *Slave Religion;* E. Foner, *Reconstruction.*

3. Wade, *Slavery in the Cities;* Goldin, *Urban Slavery in the American South;* Starobin, *Industrial Slavery in the Old South.*

4. Litwack, *North of Slavery;* Pease and Pease, *They Who Would Be Free;* Berlin, *Slaves without Masters.* See also Curry, *Free Black in Urban America.*

5. Among the more notable of the dated regional studies are Brackett, *Negro in Maryland;* Russell, *Free Negro in Virginia;* J. M. Wright, *Free Negro in Maryland;* L. P. Jackson, *Free Negro Labor and Property Holding in Virginia;* Franklin, *Free Negro in North Carolina;* Flanders, "Free Negro in Antebellum Georgia"; Sydnor, "Free Negro in Mississippi before the Civil War"; Boucher, "Free Negro in Alabama prior to 1860"; England, "Free Negro in Antebellum Tennessee"; and Sweat, "Free Negro in Antebellum Georgia." Those published somewhat more recently include Sterkx, *Free Negro in Antebellum Louisiana;* and Wikramanayake, *World in Shadow.*

6. Berlin, "Time, Space, and the Evolution of Afro-American Society on British Mainland North America," 78. See also Berlin, "Structure of the Free Negro Caste," 297–318.

7. See Blassingame, *Black New Orleans;* T. L. Holt, *Black over White;* Katzman, *Before the Ghetto;* Kusmer, *Ghetto Takes Shape;* Osofsky, *Harlem;* Birmingham, *Certain People;* G. C. Wright, *Life behind a Veil;* Perdue, *Negro in Savannah;* and B. C. Thomas, "Baltimore Black Community, 1865–1910."

8. Nash, *Forging Freedom;* M. P. Johnson and Roark, *Black Masters;* S. White, *Somewhat More Independent.* Other studies of urban African American communities that include the antebellum period are Blassingame, *Black New Orleans;* Katzman, *Before the Ghetto;* Cottrol, *Afro-Yankees;* Horton and Horton, *Black Bostonians;* L. W. Brown, *Free Negroes in the District of Columbia;* Everett, "Free Persons of Color in New Orleans"; Gardner, "Free Blacks in Baltimore"; Powers, "Black Charleston";

and Whitman, "Slavery, Manumission, and Free Black Workers in Early National Baltimore." Curry's *Free Black in Urban America* provides important quantitative data for the antebellum black urban experience in both the North and South, but it fails to emphasize its regional distinctiveness, particularly southern.

9. For the general theoretical framework of forces that gave shape to black urban life, I have used Kusmer, "Black Urban Experience in American History," 91–122.

10. Horton, *Free People of Color*, 17.

Chapter 1: Slavery and the Growth of Baltimore

1. Douglass, *My Bondage and My Freedom*, 135–36; McFeely, *Frederick Douglass*, 18–28; Preston, *Young Frederick Douglass*, 41–44.

2. Coppin, *Unwritten History*, 10.

3. D. R. Clark, "Baltimore," 8–10; Coyle, ed., *First Records of Baltimore Town*, ix (quote).

4. Semmes, "Aboriginal Maryland," 196; Craven, *Soil Exhaustion*, 28–29; Brugger, *Maryland*, 7–18; Kulikoff, *Tobacco and Slaves*, 29–31; Menard, "British Migration to the Chesapeake Colonies," 1–46; quoted in Wilstach, *Tidewater Maryland*, 64–65; Fausz, "Present at the 'Creation,'" 7–20.

5. S. W. Bruchey, *Robert Oliver*, 30; Brackett, *Negro in Maryland*, 40; Main, *Tobacco Colony*, 34; Carr, "'Metropolis of Maryland,'" 139–44.

6. Menard, "Population, Economy, and Society in Seventeenth-Century Maryland," 71; Steffen, *From Gentlemen to Townsmen*, 11. For a description of how land patents were obtained in colonial Baltimore County, see Burnard, "Colonial Elite."

7. Brooks and Rockel, *History of Baltimore County*, 29–30; Carr and Menard, "Immigration and Opportunity," 234–35; F. F. Beirne, *Amiable Baltimoreans*, 17. Rolling Road, located in modern Baltimore's western suburbs, was named for this practice of rolling tobacco hogsheads to the Patapsco.

8. Kulikoff, *Tobacco and Slaves*, 79–81; Clemens, *Atlantic Economy and Colonial Maryland's Eastern Shore*, 170–71; Earle, *Evolution of a Tidewater Settlement System*, 24–28, 95–100. Beginning in the late 1750s, tobacco prices rebounded dramatically, and the terms of trade for tobacco compared with imported goods improved substantially as well. My thanks to Lorena Walsh for her insights into the effects of the Tobacco Inspection Act.

9. The median over the entire seventeenth century on Maryland's lower Western Shore was £50. Menard, Harris, and Carr, "Opportunity and Inequality," 169–84.

10. Land, "Economic Base and Social Structure," 644–45; Steffen, *From Gentlemen to Townsmen*, 92–96; Carr, "'Metropolis of Maryland,'" 139–40; Brooks and Rockel, *History of Baltimore County*, 13–14.

11. Quoted in Scharf, *History of Baltimore City and County*, 1:57–58; Steffen, *From Gentlemen to Townsmen*, 139; F. F. Beirne, *Amiable Baltimoreans*, 35.

12. Livingood, *Philadelphia-Baltimore Trade Rivalry*, 39; Van Ness, "Economic Development, Social and Cultural Changes," 171; Gould, "Economic Causes of the Rise of Baltimore," 231–38; Fields, *Slavery and Freedom on the Middle Ground*, 41–42; J. M. Wright, *Free Negro in Maryland*, 41–42; G. L. Browne, *Baltimore in the Nation*, 4–5; D. R. Clark, "Baltimore," 12–13. Earlier historians, such as Avery Craven, have argued that extended cultivation of tobacco without adequate crop rotation, fertilization, or prevention of erosion produced exhausted soil, too sterile to produce more than marginal-grade leaf. Such developments were most likely postrevolutionary, when population growth placed heavy pressure on land availability and thus less rotation, and deeper plowing created erosion and silting. Papenfuse, "Planter Behavior and Economic Opportunity in a Staple Economy," 297–311; Brush, "Geology and Paleoecology of Chesapeake Bay," 146–60; H. M. Miller, "Transforming a 'Splendid and Delightsome Land,'" 173–87.

13. McSherry, *History of Maryland*, 98–99; Land, *Colonial Maryland*, 135; Brugger, *Maryland*, 3–5; Clemens, "Economy and Society on Maryland's Eastern Shore," 155–60; Carr and Menard, "Land, Labor, and Economies of Scale in Early Maryland," 414–18; Trimble, "Middling Planters and the Strategy of Diversification in Baltimore County," 172–78; Brooks and Rockel, *History of Baltimore County*, 15; J. M. Wright, *Free Negro in Maryland*, 84–85.

14. Clemens, *Atlantic Economy and Colonial Maryland's Eastern Shore*, 170–205; Carr and Menard, "Land, Labor, and Economies of Scale in Early Maryland," 414–18; Carr and Walsh, "Economic Diversification and Labor Organization in the Chesapeake," 144–88; L. S. Walsh, "Slave Life, Slave Society, and Tobacco Production in the Tidewater Chesapeake," 179–87; Fields, *Slavery and Freedom on the Middle Ground*, 5; Main, "Maryland and the Chesapeake Economy," 134–40; L. S. Walsh, "Plantation Management in the Chesapeake," 400–406; Breen and Innes, *"Myne Owne Ground,"* 38–39. Breen and Innes have argued that such a process began on the Eastern Shore of Virginia in the late seventeenth century and that the transition from tobacco to grain and livestock was completed there by the turn of the eighteenth century. The process was repeated later on Maryland's upper Western Shore. As a result of this diversified and flexible agricultural base, the authors conclude that both black and white farmers participated profitably in the local economy, thus affecting greatly (if temporarily) the region's race relations.

15. Livingood, *Philadelphia-Baltimore Trade Rivalry*, 39; Van Ness, "Economic Development, Social and Cultural Changes," 171; Gould, "Economic Causes of the Rise of Baltimore," 231–38; Skaggs, *Roots of Maryland Democracy*, 36–37; F. F. Beirne, *Amiable Baltimoreans*, 36.

16. Fields, *Slavery and Freedom on the Middle Ground*, 41–42; J. M. Wright, *Free Negro in Maryland*, 41–42; G. L. Browne, *Baltimore in the Nation*, 4; quoted in D. R. Clark, "Baltimore," 12–13; Brooks and Rockel, *History of Baltimore County*, 30–32, 33–35; Gregory, "Education of Blacks in Maryland," 20; S. W. Bruchey, *Robert Oliver*, 31–32; R. Walsh, "Era of the Revolution," 89; F. F. Beirne, *Amiable Baltimoreans*, 36; Middleton, *Tobacco Coast*, 35–38; Eddis, *Letters from America*, 102.

17. Eddis, *Letters from America*, 97–98.

18. Gould, "Economic Causes of the Rise of Baltimore," 238–39; D. R. Clark, "Baltimore," 12–13; S. W. Bruchey, *Robert Oliver*, 31–32.

19. Sheller, "Artisans, Manufacturing, and the Rise of a Manufacturing Interest in Revolutionary Baltimore," 6; G. L. Browne, *Baltimore in the Nation*, 3–4.

20. Steffen, *Mechanics of Baltimore*, 6; quoted in Semmes, *Baltimore as Seen by Visitors*, 12–13.

21. Van Ness, "Economic Development, Social and Cultural Changes," 171; G. L. Browne, *Baltimore in the Nation*, 4–8, 28–29; R. Walsh, "Era of the Revolution," 81–89, 112; Steffen, *Mechanics of Baltimore*, 6–8; Fields, *Slavery and Freedom on the Middle Ground*, 42.

22. Gilmor, "Recollections of Baltimore," 241; Fields, *Slavery and Freedom on the Middle Ground*, 40; quoted in Semmes, *Baltimore as Seen by Visitors*, 2 and 13.

23. Larsen, *Urban South*, 10; D. R. Clark, "Baltimore," 73–74; R. Walsh, "Era of the Revolution," 112; Sheller, "Artisans, Manufacturing, and the Rise of a Manufacturing Interest in Revolutionary Baltimore," 4–5, 8.

24. Scharf, *History of Baltimore City and County*, 1:82; McSherry, *History of Maryland*, 403–4.

25. Abernethy, *South in the New Nation*, 13; Sharrer, "Flour Milling in the Growth of Baltimore," 322; Bernard, "Portrait of Baltimore in 1800," 344–45; Dowd, "State of the Maryland Economy," 241; quoted in S. W. Bruchey, *Robert Oliver*, 101–2.

26. McSherry, *History of Maryland*, 403–4; J. M. Wright, *Free Negro in Maryland*, 84–85; Brackett, *Negro in Maryland*, 175–76; quoted in Baltimore Town Account Book, 1772–1774, Ms. 1133, MHS.

27. McSherry, *History of Maryland*, 403–4; J. M. Wright, *Free Negro in Maryland*, 36; "Census of Deptford Hundred or Fell's Point," 274–75; Sheller, "Artisans, Manufactures, and the Rise of a Manufacturing Interest in Revolutionary Baltimore," 4–5; Baltimore County Commissioners of the Tax, Alphabetical List of Assessed Persons, 1804, Baltimore City, microfilm reel CR 39,605, MdHR. Between 1782 and 1790 Maryland's slave population increased from 83,362 to 103,036.

28. McSherry, *History of Maryland*, 403–4; J. M. Wright, *Free Negro in Maryland*, 86–88.

29. See Wade, *Slavery in the Cities;* and Goldin, *Urban Slavery in the American South.* Numerous works on American slavery have echoed the findings of these authors.

30. Figures on slaveowning are derived from Whitman, "Slavery, Manumission, and Free Black Workers in Early National Baltimore," 21.

31. Marks, "Skilled Blacks in Antebellum St. Mary's County," 545–52.

32. McSherry, *History of Maryland*, 403–4; J. M. Wright, *Free Negro in Maryland*, 86–88.

33. *Baltimore American and Commercial Daily Advertiser*, 27 September 1804 (first quote); *Federal Intelligencer, and Baltimore Daily Gazette*, 2 April 1800 (second quote); *Baltimore Daily Intelligencer*, 12 October 1794 (third quote); *Maryland Journal and Baltimore Advertiser*, 15 January 1790 (fourth quote).

34. Wade, *Slavery in the Cities*, 33–39; Steffen, *Mechanics of Baltimore*, 40–41. Of the 276 slaves in the 1783 tax assessment in Fells Point, 114 (41 percent) were working-age males between the ages of fourteen and forty-five. By contrast, only sixty-eight (25 percent) were females of the same ages.

35. BC Tax, Series 1: General Property Tax Books, 1798–1915, microfilm reel BCA 177 [1798], BCA; Second and Fourth U.S. Census, 1800, 1820, Population Schedule, Baltimore City, NA; Steffen, *Mechanics of Baltimore*, 40–41.

36. BC Tax, Series 1: General Property Tax Books, 1798–1915, microfilm reel BCA 177 [1798], BCA; J. Mullin, *Baltimore Directory for 1799*, 55, 71.

37. In 1783 Maryland banned the importation of slaves "by land or water." Because the legislature aimed this law at the African slave trade, it continued to allow Maryland residents to bring slaves into the state "for their own use," as long as those owners did not intend to resell the slaves. Subsequent laws facilitated moving slaves into the state from nearby Virginia and the District of Columbia. Slaveholders needed only to file a declaration in their respective county courts, identifying the slaves imported and specifying that their labor was reserved solely for the importing master or masters. Brackett, *Negro in Maryland*, 45–46.

38. In 1792 the legislature temporarily lifted the ban on "importation by water" to assist slaveholders who had fled Saint-Domingue to bring their chattel into Maryland. The legislature subsequently repealed this measure in 1797, in the face of widespread fears that the Caribbean slaves, bolstered by the success of the Haitian Revolution, might stir unrest or even foment insurrection among Maryland slaves. Kilty, ed., *Laws of Maryland*, 1792, chap. 56, and 1797, chap. 75.

39. Of the 227 remaining declarations filed between 1792 and 1830, 199 gave the petitioners' place of residence as either in Baltimore City or Baltimore County. Of those, 160 (80.4 percent) claimed to reside in Baltimore City. Of those not listing their residence, the largest number emigrated from Saint-Domingue and presumably lived in Baltimore City as well. BCC (Miscellaneous Court Papers), 1793–1830, MSA C1, MdHR.

40. *Baltimore Daily Intelligencer*, 10 October 1794; BC Tax, Series 1: General Property Tax Books, 1798–1915, microfilm reel BCA 177 [1798], BCA; D. R. Adams, "Prices and Wages in Maryland," 632.

41. BC Tax, Series 1: General Property Tax Books, 1798–1915, microfilm reel BCA 177 [1798], BCA; Second U.S. Census, 1800, Population Schedule, Baltimore City, NA.

42. Baltimore County Register of Wills (Petitions), 1809, MSA T621, MdHR (first quote); *DeBow's Review* 29 (1860): 615, quoted in Wade, *Slavery in the Cities*, 246 (second quote).

43. Whitman, "Slavery, Manumission, and Free Black Workers in Early National Baltimore," 21. In his excellent dissertation Whitman argues persuasively that industrial slavery in early Baltimore was adopted profitably in the urban setting.

44. Bills of sale for 2,111 slaves were registered in Baltimore between 1787 and 1830. Of those, 127 were listed simply as "children," without a stated age or sex.

Bills of sale and deeds of manumission for this period are among the Miscellaneous
Court Papers of the Baltimore County Court, 1789–1855, MSA C1, MdHR.

45. BCC (Miscellaneous Court Papers), 1792–1830, MSA C1, MdHR. In 1783,
as part of the legislature's prohibition of the international slave trade, Maryland law
required that slaveholders intending to bring slaves into Maryland file a declaration
with the county court. This declaration required the name and description of the
Negroes involved and a statement of the owner's intention to employ the slaves for
his or her personal use, as opposed to their sale.

46. Wade, *Slavery in the Cities*, 30–31; Steffen, *Mechanics of Baltimore*, 37–39. Of
the twelve female slaves James Price owned, five were between the ages of ten and
thirty-five, characteristic of domestic servants. BC Tax, Series 1: General Property
Tax Books, 1798–1915, microfilm reel BCA 177 [1798], BCA.

47. BC Tax, Series 1: General Property Tax Books, 1798–1915, microfilm reel
BCA 177 [1798], BCA; Fourth U.S. Census, 1820, Population Schedule, Baltimore
City, NA; Goldin, *Urban Slavery in the American South*, 65. In 1820 free black women
in Baltimore constituted nearly 58 percent of the city's free Negro population, outnumbering men 5,963 to 4,363. While the demand for domestics might well have
accounted for much of this disparity, the large number of free black men who worked
outside the city might explain much of it as well.

48. W. Thompson and Walker, *Baltimore Town and Fell's Point Directory*, 4; *Baltimore
Daily Intelligencer*, 1 February 1794, 25 April 1794 (quote).

49. *Baltimore American and Commercial Daily Advertiser*, 17 July 1804 (first quote);
Baltimore Gazette and Daily Advertiser, 20 March 1800 (second quote).

50. *Baltimore American and Commercial Daily Advertiser*, 7 July 1804 (first quote);
Baltimore Gazette and Daily Advertiser, 25 February 1800 (second quote), 20 March
1800 (third quote).

51. *Maryland Journal and Baltimore Advertiser*, 22 September 1789 (first quote);
Baltimore Daily Intelligencer, 6 November 1793 (second quote).

52. BC Tax, Series 1: General Property Tax Books, 1798–1915, microfilm reel
BCA 177 [1798], BCA.

53. BCC (Miscellaneous Court Papers), 1794, 1820, MSA C1, MdHR.

54. BC Tax, Series 1: General Property Tax Books, 1798–1915, microfilm reel
BCA 177 [1798], BCA; Fogel and Engerman, *Time on the Cross*, 52–55; BC Tax, Series 3: Field Assessor's Workbooks (Property Assessments), Baltimore City, 1837–
1898, BCA; McFeely, *Frederick Douglass*, 24–29.

55. Goldin, *Urban Slavery in the American South*, 36–37.

56. BC Tax, Series 1: General Property Tax Books, 1798–1915, microfilm reel
BCA 177 [1798], BCA; W. Thompson and Walker, *Baltimore and Fell's Point Directory*, 47, 54; Ambrose Clarke–von Kapff and Brune Shipping Papers, 1796–1805, Ms.
1754; *Baltimore Daily Intelligencer*, 26 February 1794 (first quote), 10 October 1794
(second quote), 5 December 1793 (third quote).

57. Baltimore County Register of Wills (Petitions), 1793, MSA T621, MdHR.

58. BC Tax, Series 1: General Property Tax Books, 1798–1915, microfilm reel

250   Notes to Pages 24–26

BCA 177 [1798], BCA; Seventh U.S. Census, 1850, Slave Schedule, Baltimore City, NA; Steffen, *Mechanics of Baltimore*, 36–37; Fields, *Slavery and Freedom on the Middle Ground*, 25; Douglass, *My Bondage and My Freedom*, 147–48 (quote).

59. In 1787 the Maryland General Assembly passed a law imposing a fine of £5 per month on masters who allowed their slaves to self-hire or live out, except during ten days at harvest time. Baltimore County was exempted from this restriction, but in 1794 the legislature rescinded this exemption and defeated a motion to exempt Baltimore City, despite the unanimous opposition of delegates from the city. In 1817 the legislature increased the exemption from ten to twenty days and raised the fine to $20 per month. Baltimore appears to have consistently defied such a prohibition. Brackett, *Negro in Maryland*, 104–6.

60. Quoted in Semmes, *Baltimore as Seen by Visitors*, 166.

61. Schweninger, *Black Property Owners in the South*, 39; Schweninger, "Underside of Slavery," 9; Ambrose Clarke-von Kapff and Brune Shipping Papers, 1796–1805, Ms. 1754, MHS (quote).

62. Alexander Robinson Ledger, Ms. 699, MHS; Wade, *Slavery in the Cities*, 325; Goldin, *Urban Slavery in the American South*, 86–93.

63. Starobin, *Industrial Slavery in the Old South*, 128–29; Wade, *Slavery in the Cities*, 64–75; Goldin, *Urban Slavery in the American South*, 36–40; *Baltimore Daily Intelligencer*, 10 October 1794; W. Thompson and Walker, *Baltimore Town and Fell's Point Directory*, 20; Douglass, *My Bondage and My Freedom*, 326–33; Eaton, "Slave Hiring in the Upper South," 663; Della, "Analysis of Baltimore's Population, 29–31; First, Second, Third, Fourth, and Fifth U.S. Census, 1790, 1800, 1810, 1820, 1830, Population Schedule, Baltimore City, NA; Eaton, "Slave Hiring in the Upper South," 674; Clayton, *Black Baltimore*, 4. Clayton suggests that living out gave greater flexibility to the slave existence and facilitated free black–slave marriages but that such arrangements appear to have been infrequent.

64. Goldin, *Urban Slavery in the American South*, 8–10.

65. Olson, *Baltimore*, 34.

66. Goldin, *Urban Slavery in the American South*, 19–20. Although the numbers are from later in the century, the federal census for 1860 reports that residents in half of the city's twenty wards hired out their slaves, but they constituted only 8 percent of the city's slaves. Hiring out flourished only in wards 5 and 6, located in the affluent central part of the city, where 30 percent of all slaves were hirelings, and since in those wards slave women outnumbered men ninety to twenty-nine, most obviously were hired as domestics. Moreover, according to the manufacturing census for 1860, Baltimore's manufacturing enterprises boasted 17,054 hands, yet at that time no more than a thousand male slaves resided in the city to take part in such labor. Eighth U.S. Census, 1860, Slave and Manufacturing Schedules, Baltimore City, NA.

67. For various interpretations of the profitability of industrial slavery, as well as the ultimate failure of it in the antebellum South, see Starobin, *Industrial Slavery in the Old South*; Goldin, *Urban Slavery in the American South*; Bateman and Weiss, *Deplorable Scarcity*; and Dew, *Bond of Iron*.

68. For an excellent discussion of industrial slavery at the Maryland Chemical Works, see Whitman, "Industrial Slavery at the Margin," 31–62.

69. Quoted in Brackett, *Negro in Maryland*, 106.

70. Brugger, *Maryland*, 7–10; Gregory, "Education of Blacks in Maryland," 1–6; L. W. Brown, *Free Negroes in the District of Columbia*, 21; McSherry, *History of Maryland*, 403–4; Griffith, *Annals of Baltimore*, 33–34; J. M. Wright, *Free Negro in Maryland*, 84–85; Brackett, *Negro in Maryland*, 175–76; Wade, *Slavery in the Cities*, 19–21, 324–25.

71. Starobin, *Industrial Slavery in the Old South*.

72. Fields, *Slavery and Freedom on the Middle Ground*, 41–42; Sheller, "Artisans, Manufacturing, and the Rise of a Manufacturing Interest in Revolutionary Baltimore," 4–5. Baltimore County's population in 1752 was 17,233, of which 11,345 were free whites; slaves made up 24.04 percent of the population.

73. Skaggs, *Roots of Maryland Democracy*, 37. By 1756 six ironworks operated in Baltimore County.

74. Blandi, *Maryland Business Corporations*, 240. From 1821 to 1852 Maryland granted 486 more charters of incorporation, which might well have further accelerated the decline of slavery in the state.

75. Fields, *Slavery and Freedom on the Middle Ground*, 47, 52–53.

76. Garonzik, "Urbanization and the Black Population of Baltimore," 18; U.S. Bureau of the Census, *Seventh Census of the United States*, 52, 705.

77. Wade, *Slavery in the Cities*, 325–27; G. L. Browne, *Baltimore in the Nation*, 28–29; Larsen, *Urban South*, 24, 47; Gardner, "Free Blacks in Baltimore," 6.

Chapter 2: The Roots of Quasi-Freedom

1. Nicholas Brice to Joseph Kent, 11 December 1827, reprinted in *Genius of Universal Emancipation*, 1 March 1828.

2. Ibid.

3. Ibid.

4. Though Brice's concerns had no immediate effect on restricting term slave behavior, in 1833 the legislature passed an "act relating to persons of Colour, who are to be free after the expiration of a term of years," which authorized county courts to sell out of the state slaves "notoriously vicious or turbulent," including those who had absconded. Courts were limited in their application in that the sale could be made only if "disinterested witnesses" testified that masters had "notified such servants of the existence and effect of this law and that this information had failed to correct his or her habits." Similarly, masters were limited in seeking redress through this law because the court costs were taken from the proceeds of the slave's or slaves' sale. *Laws of Maryland*, 1833, chap. 224.

5. Tise, *Proslavery*, 12–16; Morgan, "Slavery and Freedom," 5–29.

6. Fields, "Ideology and Race in American History"; Breen and Innes, *"Myne Owne Ground,"* 110–14; Berlin, "Time, Space, and the Evolution of Afro-American

Society"; Fredrickson, *Black Image in the White Mind;* Fredrickson, "Toward a Social Interpretation of the Development of American Racism," 1:274–75.

7. D. B. Smith, *Baltimore County Marriage Licenses,* 4, 31, 83, 103, 105, 122, 142, 146, 154, 170.

8. The 1715 legislation was followed two years later by an enactment that indentured miscreant whites for seven years as penalty for intermarriage, while enslaving the lawbreaking Negro. Piet and Piet, *Early Catholic Church Records in Baltimore,* 132; Brackett, *Negro in Maryland,* 32–33, 195–96.

9. Berlin, *Slaves without Masters,* 97–99. More stringent than Maryland, Virginia fashioned its law so that black heritage could extend into the third preceding generation. In North Carolina such ancestry could be traced legally as far as the fourth generation.

10. *Maryland Journal and Baltimore Advertiser,* 18 January 1785, quoted in Graham, *Baltimore,* 23–24.

11. E. A. Andrews, *Slavery and the Domestic Slave Trade,* 51. While there is some validity in Andrews's observation on the occupations of New York free Negroes, he was not completely accurate in his depiction. Some blacks could be found early on in the skilled trades and professions, and some, such as hack and coach drivers, did own their own businesses. Yet the overwhelming number of black residents of that city, as well as other northern cities, held menial or unskilled jobs, and the numbers grew as the century progressed; by the mid-1850s, as many as 87 percent of black laborers in New York City worked in unskilled occupations. Baltimore would soon follow this trend. Litwack, *North of Slavery,* 154–57; S. White, *Somewhat More Independent,* 157–66.

12. *Baltimore Daily Intelligencer,* 12 October 1794 (first quote); Franklin, *From Slavery to Freedom,* 107–8; Aptheker, ed., *Documentary History of the Negro People,* 1:23 (second quote); Thomas Jefferson to Banneker, 30 August 1791, in Peterson, ed., *Portable Thomas Jefferson,* 454–55.

13. Breen and Innes, *"Myne Owne Ground."*

14. For discussions of the organic nature of racial ideology, see Jordan, *White over Black;* Fields, "Ideology and Race in American History"; Fredrickson, *Black Image in the White Mind;* Fredrickson, "Toward a Social Interpretation of the Development of American Racism," 274–75; and Takaki, *Iron Cages,* vi–viii.

15. Franklin, "Slaves Virtually Free in Ante-Bellum North Carolina," 284–310; Schweninger, "Free-Slave Phenomenon," 293–307; Schweninger, "Underside of Slavery," 1–22.

16. Wade, *Slavery in the Cities,* 258–59. For the most complete study of Charleston's free blacks, see M. P. Johnson and Roark, *Black Masters.*

17. Berlin, *Slaves without Masters,* 23–28; Franklin, *From Slavery to Freedom,* 157–58; J. M. Wright, *Free Negro in Maryland,* 44–46.

18. Gardner, "Free Blacks in Baltimore," 25–27; Brackett, *Negro in Maryland,* 148–49, 152–53; Brugger, *Maryland,* 169; Gregory, "Education of Blacks in Maryland," 11; Berlin, *Slaves without Masters,* 32–34. In 1802 the Maryland legislature

offered further protection to slaves and soon-to-be freedpeople by passing a bill forbidding owners to send their term slaves out of state, where they could not be protected from resale and could not be assured of their release on the date of their legal freedom. Graham, *Baltimore*, 51.

19. All northern states ended slavery through legislative or judicial action, generally by the delayed emancipation of all children of slave mothers born after a fixed date. See Zilversmit, *First Emancipation*, for a description of the emancipation of slaves in New England, New York, New Jersey, and Pennsylvania between 1780 and 1804. For the most complete examination of the process in Pennsylvania, Maryland's neighbor to the north, see Nash and Soderlund, *Freedom by Degrees*. For a discussion of the First Emancipation in both northern and southern states and the subsequent efforts of southern state legislatures to restrict emancipation, see Berlin, *Slaves without Masters*, 15–50, 137–38n2.

20. Craven, *Soil Exhaustion*, 82–84; J. M. Wright, *Negro in Maryland*, 86–89. Cotton, too, was a seasonal crop and would lend itself well to slave labor in the Deep South, but cotton was not yet a major southern crop and was never grown in large amounts in Maryland. Although the switch from tobacco to grain usually reduced total labor force needs, farmers in Maryland added other crops to their mix, which added new kinds of off-season work that kept a certain number of agricultural workers employed year-round. Consequently, slave labor continued to be used by many grain producers in the Upper South. Irwin, "Exploring the Affinity of Wheat and Slavery in the Virginia Piedmont," 295–322.

21. Kulikoff, *Tobacco and Slaves*, 80; Fogel and Engerman, *Time on the Cross*, 86–88; Berlin, *Slaves without Masters*, 26–27; Van Ness, "Economic Development, Social and Cultural Changes," 161–62; Risjord, *Chesapeake Politics*, 15; Dunn, "Black Society in the Chesapeake," 62–63; L. S. Walsh, "Rural African Americans in the Constitutional Era in Maryland," 337–38; Fields, *Slavery and Freedom on the Middle Ground*, 5.

22. Berlin, "Structure of the Free Negro Caste," 303–4; Williamson, *New People*, 7.

23. BCC (Miscellaneous Court Papers), 1789–1854, MSA C1, MdHR; BCC (Chattel Records), 1763–1773, 208–9, 212–13, BA 0298, MdHR; Whitman, "Slavery, Manumission, and Free Black Workers in Early National Baltimore," 161n9. Dickson J. Preston has found 779 deeds of manumission involving over 1,000 slaves in Talbot County alone between 1790 and 1825; however, his research fails to identify the number of manumissions by will and concludes only that "many other slaves" were freed in this manner. Preston, *Young Frederick Douglass*, 18–19, 216–17n58.

24. BCC (Chattel Records), 1763–1773, 212–13, BA 0298, MdHR (first quote); Harford Land Records, quoted in J. M. Wright, *Free Negro in Maryland*, 45n3 (second quote); BCC (Miscellaneous Court Papers), 1846, MSA C1, MdHR (third quote).

25. As early as 1789 Baltimore printers, such as Warner and Hanna, offered print-

ed forms for manumission, with blank spaces for the name, age, and manumission
date of the prospective freedperson. By the early 1800s a majority of original manumission documents found among the Miscellaneous Court Papers of the Baltimore
County Court appear on these one-page forms.

26. Quoted in K. L. Carroll, "Religious Influences on the Manumission of
Slaves," 183; Calderhead, "How Strong Was Religion as a Force in Manumission
Activity," 49; Whitman, "Slavery, Manumission, and Free Black Workers in Early
National Baltimore," 166–67.

27. Henretta, ed., "Declaration of Independence," 120 (first quote); Caroline
County Deeds, quoted in J. M. Wright, *Free Negro in Maryland*, 46n1 (second quote);
Maryland Appeal Reports, quoted in J. M. Wright, *Free Negro in Maryland*, 44n2 (third
quote).

28. BCC (Chattel Records), 1763–1773, 212–13, BA 0298, MdHR; Baltimore
County Wills, 1794, quoted in J. M. Wright, *Free Negro in Maryland*, 49n3.

29. Tise, *Proslavery*, 33–36; Baltimore County Court, Certificates of Freedom,
1806–1816, BCA 230, BCA. Edmund Morgan places the paradoxical marriage of
slavery and freedom earlier in the eighteenth century. Morgan, *American Slavery,
American Freedom*, chap. 15.

30. BCC (Chattel Records), 1763–1773, 208–9, BA 0298, MdHR.

31. L. W. Brown, *Free Negroes in the District of Columbia*, 97–98, 102–3; Brackett,
Negro in Maryland, 148–49, 155–56. The 1796 law also provided that masters could
not manumit any slaves over the age of forty-five or unable to support themselves.

32. In Maryland in 1790 slaveowners held three such legal options by which they
could formally free their slaves: manumission by deed, by will (prohibited since 1752
but legalized in 1790), and by term sale.

33. Calderhead, "Experiment in Freedom," cited in Fields, *Slavery and Freedom
on the Middle Ground*, 30; BCC (Miscellaneous Court Papers), 1789–1830, MSA C1,
MdHR.

34. BCC (Register of Wills), 1791–95, 1796–97, 1810–15, vol. 4, 5 (quotes on
493–94), 9, BA 0435, MdHR; Berlin, *Slaves without Masters*, 152–53; L. W. Brown,
Free Negroes in the District of Columbia, 75–120 passim; J. M. Wright, *Free Negro in
Maryland*, 51.

35. M. P. Johnson and Roark, *Black Masters*, 31. Though recorded well after the
postrevolutionary period (and thus not an accurate assessment of the period), the
manumissions registered by the Maryland State Colonization Society from 1832 to
1860 do provide some indication of the pattern of manumissions. Of a total of 5,599
manumissions made in Maryland during the period, 2,870 (51.2 percent) were by
deed and 2,170 (38.8 percent) were by will. Manumissions and Emigrants, Manumission Books, Lists and Manumissions, Copies (1832–1860), microfilm reel 25,
MSCS.

36. BCC (Miscellaneous Court Papers), 1793, 1801, MSA C1, MdHR.

37. Of the 2,448 slaves freed by deeds of manumission filed in Baltimore City
or Baltimore County between 1789 and 1830, 1,701 slaves had their ages specified,

796 of whom were men and 905 of whom were women. Of the men, 378 (48 percent) were thirty-one or older when freed, while 566 (72 percent) were twenty-six or older. Of the women, 346 (38 percent) were thirty-one or older, while 564 (62 percent) were twenty-six or older. BCC (Miscellaneous Court Papers), 1789–1830, MSA C1, MdHR.

38. Of 370 male and 429 female slaves manumitted immediately by deed in Baltimore City and Baltimore County between 1789 and 1830 for whom an age was specified, 225 women (52 percent) and 234 men (63 percent) were thirty or older. BCC (Miscellaneous Court Papers), 1789–1830, MSA C1, MdHR.

39. *Niles' Weekly Register*, 16 January 1830. Because Maryland's laws on manumission until 1796 allowed masters to free slaves up to the age of fifty (lowered in 1796 to forty-five), masters could legally free superannuated slaves and could even simply lie about a slave's age in a deed of manumission. Evidence of such unlawful behavior exists in wills filed in Baltimore County between 1790 and 1822. These freed slaves often became public charges, and in an effort to curb such behavior the legislature banned the practice in 1817. Kilty, ed., *Laws of Maryland*, 1796, chap. 67; 1817, chap. 72.

40. "Half-freedom" actually resembled self-hire more than it did term slavery because it allowed slaves to live away from their masters and find their own employment, bound only by the return of a stipulated amount of labor and an annual tribute. Yet like term slavery, such practice provided for the development of black autonomy and weakened the system of racial bondage. Upon English conquest of the province in 1664, the new government abolished the practice in favor of a more traditional form of racial servitude. Berlin, "Time, Space, and the Evolution of Afro-American Society," 50–51; Goodfriend, "Burghers and Blacks," 125–44.

41. G. W. Brown, *Origin and Growth of Civil Liberty in Maryland*, 5.

42. L. W. Brown, *Free Negroes in the District of Columbia*, 87; Baltimore County Land Records, 1796–1797, 492–93, BA 0352, MdHR (quote).

43. BCC (Miscellaneous Court Papers), 1787–1830, MSA C1, MdHR. While the percentage of term sales as part of manumissions as a whole in Maryland prior to 1832 is difficult to assess, 10 percent of the 5,599 manumissions in the state after that date were performed by means of a bill of sale, a figure that might well approximate that of the earlier period. Manumissions and Emigrants, Manumission Books, Lists and Manumissions, Copies (1832–1860), microfilm reel 25, MSCS.

44. BCC (Chattel Records) 1813–14, BA 0298, MdHR (quote); BCC (Miscellaneous Court Papers), 1808, MSA C1, MdHR; Fry, *Fry's Baltimore Directory for 1812*, 79.

45. BCC (Miscellaneous Court Papers), 1807, MSA C1, MdHR.

46. BCC (Miscellaneous Court Papers), 1789–1830, MSA C1, MdHR.

47. BCC (Miscellaneous Court Papers), 1790–1830, MSA C1, MdHR. In her deed of manumission, Sarah Price freed six slaves, ranging in age from one to seventeen, all to be free at age forty-five. Obviously, while some masters manumitted their superannuated slaves for financial loss, others did so for financial gain.

48. *Laws of Maryland,* 1809, chap. 171.

49. BCC (Miscellaneous Court Papers), 1811, MSA C1, MdHR (quote). Noah Davis, a Virginia slave, moved to Baltimore and in 1846 purchased his freedom, as well as the freedom of his wife and nine children. Their owner, a wealthy widow from Fredricksburg, first gave him the option of purchasing his wife and two youngest children for $800. The remaining older children would remain in bondage, presumably until their labor had compensated her for the cost of their maintenance to date. Davis, *Narrative of the Life of Rev. Noah Davis.*

50. BCC (Miscellaneous Court Papers), 1802, 1804, MSA C1, MdHR.

51. Bancroft, *Slave-Trading in the Old South,* 21. According to Bancroft early traders were active in Maryland and Virginia, selling to planters in South Carolina and Georgia.

52. Tadman, "Slave Trading in the Ante-Bellum South," 219. For a comprehensive treatment of the U.S. domestic slave trade, see Tadman, *Speculators and Slaves.*

53. Quoted in Dillon, *Benjamin Lundy,* 6.

54. Preston, *Young Frederick Douglass,* 78.

55. BCC (Miscellaneous Court Papers), 1814, MSA C1, MdHR.

56. BCC (Miscellaneous Court Papers), 1811, MSA C1, MdHR (quote); Fry, *Fry's Baltimore Directory for 1812,* 67.

57. BCC (Miscellaneous Court Papers), 1823, MSA C1, MdHR.

58. A number of token purchases located in the Miscellaneous Court Papers of the BCC involve the reconveyance of property sold as debt security, legal acts generally made between white transactors. In 1820 Henry Snowden sold four slaves to George Bowersox for $1 as acknowledgment of Bowersox's repayment of a $300 debt he owed Snowden. Bowersox had previously conveyed these slaves to Snowden as security for the debt. BCC (Miscellaneous Court Papers), 1820, MSA C1, MdHR.

59. BCC (Miscellaneous Court Papers), 1807, 1824, MSA C1, MdHR. Token amounts are fairly common among surviving deeds of manumission. Of the 1,782 remaining individual deeds of manumission for Baltimore County between 1789 and 1830, 361 stipulate payment of any sort as part of the terms of freedom, and of those, 261 stipulate amounts of $10 or less. This suggests that those masters who felt moved to manumit their slaves generally required no payment at all, and if they did require payment, they did so only to cover the cost for the registering of the document or to ensure the legality of the transaction. Such stipulations appear far less often when masters decided to sell, rather than liberate, their slaves; when manumissions were included in bills of sale, however, the master's motives were likely less benevolent and may indicate slaves' initiative in obtaining freedom.

60. BCC (Miscellaneous Court Papers), 1819, MSA C1, MdHR; Baltimore County Register of Wills (Petitions), 1824, MSA T621, MdHR. In 1794 the Maryland legislature charged the orphans' courts of each county, normally responsible for settling estates, including guardianships of orphans, with the responsibility of indenturing every orphan child to tradespeople to prevent them from becoming charges of the colony. Most of the young black apprentices in early Maryland were likely

either orphans or slaves, and the courts assumed responsibility for monitoring estate-held slaves. Carr, "Development of the Maryland Orphans' Court," 41–62.

61. In 1803 Paul sold Guy along with two women and five boys (presumably including Guy's wife) to Thomas Kell, a Baltimore attorney, for a dollar. Kell probably conveyed Guy and his wife to Tomkins, who maintained her and her son (born two years later) until Guy either could pay Tomkins a separately arranged purchase price or worked for him a stipulated period of time. BCC (Miscellaneous Court Papers), 1803, 1807, MSA C1, MdHR.

62. BCC (Miscellaneous Court Papers), 1812, MSA C1, MdHR. During his lifetime (1749–1824) Tyson used his considerable wealth and stature to helped some two thousand of the city's African Americans achieve freedom by means similar to and even beyond those used to liberate Hamilton and Williams—in some cases reputedly having risked his life. J. S. Tyson, *Life of Elisha Tyson;* "Elisha Tyson," Vertical File, EPFL.

63. BCC (Miscellaneous Court Papers), 1793, 1813, MSA C1, MdHR.

64. Baltimore County Register of Wills (Petitions), 1809, MSA T621, MdHR; BCC (Miscellaneous Court Papers), 1834, MSA C1, MdHR.

65. At the time of Byas's manumission, Mackall filed multiple manumission deeds, and in a number of subsequent deeds he shortened the original terms of several slaves, on an individual base. Such action might indicate that for some or all of the slaves he manumitted Mackall filed the original deeds with terms that likely had been contracted previously, with possible alteration at a later date. Such an agreement could have served as incentive to future service and good behavior among his slaves. Deed of Manumission, Richard Mackall to Sundry Negroes, BCC (Miscellaneous Court Papers), 1808, MSA C1, MdHR; Deed of Manumission, Mackall to James Byas and Biggs Butler, 1809, ibid.; Deed of Manumission, Mackall to Isaac, 1813, ibid.

66. BCC (Miscellaneous Court Papers), 1822, MSA C1, MdHR. For other cases in which Isaac Tyson came to the aid of slaves, see Deed of Manumission, Tyson to James Davis, 1817, ibid.; and Bill of Sale, Thomas Dilahay to Tyson, 1822, ibid. In the first manumission, that of James Davis in 1817, Tyson noted that he had purchased Davis eight months earlier, in August 1816, from John Williamson of South Carolina. Williamson himself had just acquired Davis from another Baltimorean, Peter Carnes, and Tyson purchased Davis for $412 "to prevent him the said Davis from being Separated from his wife and children." Tyson was careful to note in the deed that he did so "fully believing he [Davis] will be able so to refund the money paid for him." Tyson might well have held Davis for those eight months to assure himself of the slave's ability to repay the debt. He acted similarly in 1822 when he freed the slave Jim immediately, after having held him for six months. Deed of Manumission, Tyson to Jim, 1822, ibid. Tyson's son, Isaac Jr., appears also to have carried on the family tradition. Deed of Manumission, Evan Ellicott and Tyson to Isaac Benson, 1830, ibid.

67. BCC (Miscellaneous Court Papers), 1819, MSA C1, MdHR.

68. BCC (Miscellaneous Court Papers), 1804, MSA C1, MdHR.

69. BCC (Miscellaneous Court Papers), 1819, MSA C1, MdHR. For a broader discussion of freedom brokers in Maryland, see Whitman, *Price of Freedom*.
70. BCC (Miscellaneous Court Papers), 1797, 1808, MSA C1, MdHR.
71. *Laws of Maryland*, 1817, chap. 112.
72. Most apparent was the state law prohibiting term slaves inherited from previous masters from being sold by their present owners without permission from the county orphans' court.
73. BCC (Miscellaneous Court Papers), 1825, MSA C1, MdHR.
74. BCC (Miscellaneous Court Papers), 1794, 1795, 1807, MSA C1, MdHR.
75. Baltimore County Register of Wills (Petitions), 1822 (first quote), 1824 (second quote), 1826 (third quote), MSA T621, MdHR; *Baltimore Sun*, 23 February 1838, quoted in Berlin, *Slaves without Masters*, 228 (fourth quote).
76. Baltimore County Register of Wills (Petitions), 1817, 1846, MSA T621, MdHR.
77. Baltimore County Register of Wills (Petitions), 1822, 1828, MSA T621, MdHR.
78. While from 1789 to 1814 just over half of all manumissions were performed immediately, from 1815 to 1830 two-thirds (768 out of 1,195) of Baltimore manumissions were immediate, and such manumissions were in the majority every year between 1815 and 1830.
79. See Wade, *Slavery in the Cities*; and Goldin, *Urban Slavery in the American South*.
80. These figures are based on 1,890 individual deeds of manumission registered in Baltimore City and Baltimore County from 1789 to 1830 that note the gender of individual slaves; those freed slaves listed without specific reference to gender, mostly children, were not included. BCC (Miscellaneous Court Papers), MSA C1, MdHR. Michael Tadman also argues that slave sales in the Upper South, like manumission, generally displayed little or no sex bias. Tadman, *Speculators and Slaves*, 11–30, 142–44.
81. Fourth and Eighth U.S. Census, 1820, 1860, Population Schedule, Baltimore City, NA. In 1820 free black women made up 5,963 of the city's 10,326 free colored persons. In 1860, 15,334 out of 25,680 free Negroes were female.
82. Goldin, *Urban Slavery in the American South*, 64–66. After separating those males and females manumitted before the age of sixteen (to ensure that those freed at extremely young ages would not greatly alter the result), the average age at manumission of males was 21.9, and for females, 29.9. The average ages of all those freed, including those freed before they were sixteen, were 20.4 for males and 27.1 for females.
83. Berlin, "Time, Space, and the Evolution of Afro-American Society," 50–51.

Chapter 3: The Urban Mélange

1. Douglass, *My Bondage and My Freedom*, 147.
2. Wade, *Slavery in the Cities*, 80–179; Olson, *Baltimore*, 34.

3. First and Second U.S. Census, 1790, 1800, Population Schedule, Maryland, NA; J. M. Wright, *Free Negro in Maryland*, 84–87; Dunn, "Black Society in the Chesapeake," 75–76. In both Queen Anne's and Kent counties free Negroes constituted more than 15 percent of the population; only the city of Petersburg, Virginia, had a comparable percentage in either of the two states. These two counties were most directly across the bay from Baltimore City.

4. "Census of Deptford Hundred or Fells' Point," 274–75; U.S. Bureau of the Census, *Negro Population of the United States*, 53–54; McSherry, *History of Maryland*, 403–4; First, Second, and Third U.S. Census, 1790, 1800, 1810, Population Schedule, Baltimore City, NA. The number of black households in Baltimore grew by 1,322.9 percent between 1790 and 1810.

5. Anderson, "Eighteenth-Century Suffrage," 143–44, 147, 150–51. From 1670 to 1776 Maryland law required ownership of fifty acres or an estate of £40 sterling to vote. The new state constitution of 1776 retained the requisite acreage but reduced the personal estate to £18 sterling. Evidence that some free blacks did vote is in legislation enacted in 1783 barring persons of color manumitted after that date from voting or holding office.

6. J. M. Wright, *Free Negro in Maryland*, 82–83.

7. W. H. Browne, ed., *Archives of Maryland*, 13:546–47 (first quote); Olson, *Baltimore*, 15 (second quote).

8. J. M. Wright, *Free Negro in Maryland*, 86–87.

9. Gutman, *Black Family in Slavery and Freedom*, 137–43. In his indispensable study of freedpeople during Reconstruction, Leon Litwack has found similar behavior among freed blacks in the Deep South in the years immediately following emancipation. In the wake of the most dramatic social event in the lives of all slaves, the legal end of slavery, most of the freed exerted their independence by leaving their home plantation but traveled only a few miles from home to seek work in the neighboring towns or (as in the case of Baltimore County ex-slaves) a nearby city. Often they never left their home counties. Litwack, *Been in the Storm So Long*, 311.

10. BCC (Certificates of Freedom), 1806–1816, BA 0290, MdHR; J. M. Wright, *Free Negro in Maryland*, 86–88. Of the four counties that declined in overall black population between 1790 and 1800, three were in southern Maryland: Calvert, Charles, and St. Mary's. Each lost primarily slave populations.

11. BCC (Certificates of Freedom), 1806–1816, BA 0290, MdHR; Fields, *Slavery and Freedom on the Middle Ground*, 34–38; J. M. Wright, *Free Negro in Maryland*, 86–87; Decter, "Notes on Method and Theory in Social History," 51–52. The number of Baltimore County free blacks born in the respective counties were Baltimore County, 220 (Baltimore City, 10); Harford, 50; Anne Arundel, 46; Calvert, 22; Talbot, 20; Queen Anne's, 15; Kent, 14; Prince George's, 8; St. Mary's, 8; Cecil, 4; Montgomery, 4; Somerset, 4; Dorchester, 3; Frederick, 2; Caroline, 1; Cumberland, 1. Of the five top counties, the three that lost slave populations from 1790 to 1800 were Anne Arundel, 370; Calvert, 204; and Talbot, 2.

12. J. M. Wright, *Free Negro in Maryland*, 86–88; Fairbanks, *Statistical Analysis of*

the Population of Maryland, 105; McSherry, *History of Maryland*, 403–4. Baltimore County's free Negro population grew from 927 in 1790 to 4,307 in 1800, while Baltimore City's population grew from 323 to 2,771. From 1800 to 1810, while Baltimore County's free black population increased to 7,208, Baltimore City's grew to 5,671. Both increases total approximately 2,900, indicating that virtually all of the county's free black growth came from the increase in Baltimore City's numbers.

13. Reuter, *Mulatto in the United States*, 112–13, 121.

14. BCC (Certificates of Freedom), 1806–1816, BA 0290, MdHR; Eighth U.S. Census, 1860, Population Schedule, Baltimore City, NA.

15. M. P. Johnson and Roark, *Black Masters*, 32–33, 203; Berlin, *Slaves without Masters*, 49–50, 109; Blassingame, *Black New Orleans*, 21–22; Jordan, "American Chiaroscuro," 183–220; Williamson, *New People*, 14–15.

16. BCC (Certificates of Freedom), 1806–1816, BA 0290, MdHR; Graham, "Manumitted Free Blacks in Baltimore," 8–18. Of the 352 entries for whom skin color was listed, 235 (66.8 percent) were either "dark," "dark brown," "black," or "very black"; 117 (33.2 percent) were listed as "very light," "light," "mulatto," "bright yellow," "yellow," or "light-dark." Among 135 women, 85 (63 percent) were listed as dark-skinned, while 50 (37 percent) were light-skinned. For a discussion of the subjectivity of color distinctions in census-taking, see Hershberg and Williams, "Mulattoes and Blacks," 396–98.

17. Of the 358 freed blacks in Baltimore from 1806–16, 84 (23.5 percent) were mulattoes. James Wright's contention that 80.2 percent of Maryland free persons of color were of mixed parentage in 1817 is wholly inaccurate, judging by more recent sources. Baltimore County Court, Certificates of Freedom, 1806–1816, BCA 230, BCA; J. M. Wright, *Free Negro in Maryland*, 26.

18. Baltimore County Court, Certificates of Freedom, 1806–1816, BCA 230, BCA; Steckel, "Slave Height Profiles from Coastwise Manifests," 363–80; Margo and Steckel, "Heights of American Slaves," 516–38; Fogel et al., "Secular Changes in American and British Stature and Nutrition," 445–81. The historian Robert Hall found similar heights for runaway slaves in Baltimore City and County from 1747 to 1790. R. L. Hall, "Slave Resistance in Baltimore City and County," 309.

19. Baltimore County Court, Certificates of Freedom, 1806–1816, BCA 230, BCA.

20. J. M. Wright, *Free Negro in Maryland*, 43; *Niles' Weekly Register*, 16 January 1830, quoted in Berlin, *Slaves without Masters*, 152–53.

21. BCC (Miscellaneous Court Papers), 1789–1830, MSA C1, MdHR.

22. BCC (Chattel Records), 1763–1773, 208, BA 0298, MdHR; BCC (Miscellaneous Court Papers), 1822, MSA C1, MdHR; Schweninger, *Black Property Owners in the South*, 15, 54–55. Quasi-free status for slaves appears to have been prevalent throughout the Upper South. See L. W. Brown, *Free Negroes in the District of Columbia*, 96; Franklin, "Slaves Virtually Free in Ante-Bellum North Carolina"; and Schweninger, "Free-Slave Phenomenon," 293.

23. Brackett, *Negro in Maryland*, 163–64, 240–41; Berlin, *Slaves without Masters*,

93; *Laws of Maryland,* 1805, 3:chap. 66. Original certificates of freedom for Anne Arundel County indicate that when freed Negroes applied for such certificates in the county where they were legally manumitted, they first brought a white witness before a justice of the peace of that county to verify their identity. One copy of the certificate, written and endorsed by the local magistrate, usually contained the required physical features and was deposited in the county clerk's office. A second copy, written by the county clerk, was given to the freedperson to carry. Anne Arundel County Court, Register of Wills, 1806–1851, folders 44 and 144, AA 0046, MdHR.

24. *Baltimore Gazette and Daily Advertiser,* 13 September 1810, cited in Graham, *Baltimore,* 68–69; D. R. Clark, "Baltimore," 51. Scott's ruling stemmed from his reasoning that jailing blacks without adequate grounds could result either in selling free Negroes into slavery to pay their jail upkeep or in unscrupulous whites' fraudulently claiming that jailed free blacks were their slaves and, upon retrieving them, selling them into perpetual slavery, probably to slave dealers who would remove them from the state. Scott's concern was not unwarranted; such incidents appear to have occurred regularly at the Baltimore jail.

25. M. P. Johnson and Roark, *Black Masters,* 174–76; Stavinsky, "Negro Artisan in the South Atlantic States," 84–150 and passim.

26. Nash, *Forging Freedom,* 72–73; L. S. Walsh, "Rural African Americans in the Constitutional Era in Maryland," 336–37; Marks, "Skilled Blacks in Antebellum St. Mary's County," 555–59; Fields, *Slavery and Freedom on the Middle Ground,* 70–71.

27. Eaton, "Slave Hiring in the Upper South," 668–69; D. R. Adams, "Prices and Wages in Maryland," 632.

28. Whitman, "Slavery, Manumission, and Free Black Workers in Early National Baltimore," 219.

29. Wade, *Slavery in the Cities,* 214–18; Quarles, "'Freedom Fettered,'" 301–2; R. L. Hall, "Slave Resistance in Baltimore City and County," 305–18; G. W. Mullin, *Flight and Rebellion,* 124–30; Goldin, *Urban Slavery in the American South,* 48.

30. *Baltimore Daily Intelligencer,* 25 June 1794, 9 July 1794 (first quote); *Baltimore American and Commercial Daily Advertiser,* 7 May 1805 (second quote).

31. *Baltimore American and Commercial Daily Advertiser,* 7 May 1805 (first quote), 25 September 1804 (second quote); *Maryland Journal and Baltimore Advertiser,* 16 February 1790 (third quote).

32. Rawick, ed., *American Slave,* 16:19–20.

33. *Baltimore American and Commercial Daily Advertiser,* 18 January 1805 (first quote), 4 February 1805 (second quote), 30 November 1804 (third quote).

34. *Maryland Journal and Baltimore Advertiser,* 28 June 1793, 5 July 1793.

35. *Baltimore Daily Intelligencer,* 25 April 1794, 9 June 1794.

36. *Maryland Journal and Baltimore Advertiser,* 21 June 1793.

37. Williamson, *New People,* 48; Renzulli, *Maryland,* 170–71, 218.

38. *Baltimore Daily Intelligencer,* 9 June 1790 (first quote), 25 April 1794 (second quote).

39. Quarles, "'Freedom Fettered,'" 301–2; Wade, *Slavery in the Cities,* 218 (quote).

40. R. L. Hall, "Slave Resistance in Baltimore City and County," 305–18.

41. The newspapers used were the *Maryland Journal and Baltimore Advertiser,* 17 September 1789–30 April 1790; the *Baltimore Daily Intelligencer,* 29 October 1793–24 October 1794; the *Baltimore Gazette and Daily Advertiser,* 25 May 1793–24 December 1793, 16 January 1800–2 April 1800; and the *Baltimore American and Commercial Daily Advertiser,* 7 July 1804–14 May 1805.

42. R. L. Hall, "Slave Resistance in Baltimore City and County," 306–7; *Baltimore Daily Intelligencer,* 24 June 1794 (first quote); *Maryland Journal and Baltimore Advertiser,* 26 March 1790 (second quote).

43. *Maryland Journal and Baltimore Advertiser,* 25 June 1793.

44. Wade, *Slavery in the Cities,* 143–44; *Baltimore American and Commercial Daily Advertiser,* 25 September 1804 (first quote), 4 February 1805 (second quote).

45. Wade, *Slavery in the Cities,* posits that urban residents' inability to control slave behavior corroded the system in southern cities after 1820, thus leading to its demise there. More persuasive is Claudia Dale Goldin's argument that urban employers' ability to substitute free workers for slaves in an economic climate that required great elasticity of labor demands contributed most significantly to slavery's decline in the cities. Goldin, *Urban Slavery in the American South.*

46. Ott, *Haitian Revolution,* 3–15, 47–72; Hartridge, "Refugees from the Island of St. Domingo in Maryland," 103–7; Scharf, *History of Baltimore City and County,* 1:82–83. See also Stoddard, *French Revolution in San Domingo;* C. L. R. James, *Black Jacobins;* Hunt, *Haiti's Influence on Antebellum America;* and BCC (Miscellaneous Court Papers), 1793–1805, MSA C1, MdHR.

47. *Baltimore Gazette and Daily Advertiser,* 13 September 1810, quoted in Graham, *Baltimore,* 68.

48. BC Tax, Series 1: General Property Tax Books, 1798–1915, microfilm reel BCA 177 [1798], BCA.

49. *Baltimore Daily Intelligencer,* 1 November 1793, 4 December 1793; Steffen, *Mechanics of Baltimore,* 40–41; Fry, *Baltimore Directory for 1810,* 43.

50. C. L. R. James, *Black Jacobins,* 6–22; *Baltimore Daily Intelligencer,* 29 October 1793–24 October 1794.

51. BC Tax, Series 1: General Property Tax Books, 1798–1915, microfilm reel BCA 177 [1798], BCA; Second U.S. Census, 1800, Population Schedule, Baltimore City, NA.

52. Olson, *Baltimore,* 30–31; BC Tax, Series 1: General Property Tax Books, 1798–1915, microfilm reel BCA 177 [1798], BCA; quoted in Hartridge, "Refugees from the Island of St. Domingo in Maryland," 103–5; *Baltimore Gazette and Daily Advertiser,* 11 July 1793.

53. Easter Duty List for Saint Mary's Parish, 1810, Sulpician Archives, Baltimore, cited in E. D. Smith, *Climbing Jacob's Ladder,* 99. The list does not designate racial characteristics for the men of color.

54. Wade, *Slavery in the Cities,* 4–16; Berlin, *Slaves without Masters,* 218–20; Fields, *Slavery and Freedom on the Middle Ground,* 70–71.

55. BCC (Certificates of Freedom), 1806–1816, BA 0290, MdHR. Out of 468, 358 (76.5 percent) had been manumitted, while 110 (23.5 percent) had been born free.

56. Ibid. Birthplaces of Baltimore County free blacks who were manumitted, outside Maryland, in numerical order, were Virginia, 10; Saint-Domingue, 5; West Indies, 3; Jamaica, 3; New York, 1; Pennsylvania, 1; Surinam, 1; and Africa, 1. Birthplaces of free blacks born free were Virginia, 3; Massachusetts, 2; Rhode Island, 1; Connecticut, 1; Pennsylvania, 1; North Carolina, 1; New Orleans, 1; and Saint-Domingue, 1.

57. *DeBow's Review* 8 (1850), 363.

58. *Baltimore Daily Intelligencer*, 5 December 1793, 21 January 1794.

59. Olson, *Baltimore*, 19; Goldin, *Urban Slavery in the American South*, 36–37.

60. S. W. Bruchey, *Robert Oliver*, 38; *Baltimore Daily Intelligencer*, 5 December 1793; Third U.S. Census, 1810, Population Schedule, Baltimore City, NA.

61. BC Tax, Series 1: General Property Tax Books, 1798–1915, microfilm reel BCA 177 [1798], BCA; Third U.S. Census, 1810, Population Schedule, Baltimore City, NA; Fry, *Baltimore Directory for 1810*, passim.

62. Pairpont, *Uncle Sam and His Country*, 219, quoted in Semmes, *Baltimore as Seen by Visitors*, 165–66.

63. Clayton, *Black Baltimore*, 3. In 1810, 204 of the city's 819 slaveholding households (24.9 percent) employed free blacks.

64. "Petition of Sundry Citizens to Prohibit Persons of Colour to Obtain Licenses to Drive Hacks, Carts, and Drays &c.," 23 January 1828, BC Council, Series 1: Administrative Files, 1797–1923, box 36, item 425, BCA, also quoted in Gardner, "Free Blacks in Baltimore," 145–46; Nagle Papers, Ms. 2052, MHS.

65. Douglass, *My Bondage and My Freedom*, 167; Ambrose Clarke-von Kapff and Brune Shipping Papers, 1796–1805, Ms. 1754, MHS.

66. Time Sheets for Laborers Working on Howard's Hill, 29 September 1795–9 January 1796, ERB, vol. 2:85–99, BCA; Time Sheets for Laborers on South Street, 29 June–13 August 1796, ERB, vol. 2:100–101, BCA; Time Sheets for Laborers for Cleaning Ditch on Howard Street, 14–29 August 1796, ERB, vol. 2:102, BCA.

67. Coyle, ed., *Records of the City of Baltimore (Special Commissioners)*, 136, 138; W. Thompson and Walker, *Baltimore Town and Fell's Point Directory*, 21, 40; Weekly Account of James Hicks to City Commissioners for Paving the Streets, 27 May 1797, ERB, vol. 2:86, BCA.

68. Coyle, ed., *Records of the City of Baltimore (Special Commissioners)*, 124–25; Della, "Analysis of Baltimore's Population," 25.

69. J. Kennedy, *Baltimore Directory for 1817–18*, 212–22; W. Thompson and Walker, *Baltimore Town and Fell's Point Directory*, 41; Graham, *Baltimore*, 274.

70. *Baltimore Sun*, 18 November 1839 (first quote), 1 August 1840 (second quote).

71. Wade, *Slavery in the Cities*, 84–87 (first quote); Steffen, *Mechanics of Baltimore*, 263–65; Clayton, *Black Baltimore*, 4; *Baltimore Sun*, 4 September 1839 (second quote).

72. Coyle, ed., *Records of the City of Baltimore (Special Commissioners)*, 288 (first quote), 296 (second quote), 330 (third quote), 316 (fourth quote).

73. J. Kennedy, *Baltimore Directory for 1817–18*, 212–22; W. Thompson and Walker, *Baltimore Town and Fell's Point Directory*, 41; Graham, *Baltimore*, 25. According to Katharine Scarborough, thirteen canvases exist, in the hands of private owners, that are attributed to Johnston, none of which is dated or signed. The subjects of the portraits are nearly always members of wealthy, aristocratic slaveholding families of Baltimore. J. Hall Pleasants, an authority on early Maryland artists, finds a "French primitive flavor" in Johnston's portraits, in which all subjects "are drawn in the same stiff manner, with a peculiar rigidity of arms and hands. With few exceptions the face is shown about three-quarters full. The eyes are always directed forward and the upper lids painted in the same manner. The mouths are all drawn in rather tightly." Though his work was not comparable to the Peales, the famous family of portrait painters of the eighteenth and nineteenth centuries, Pleasants contends that Johnston "had genuine ability." Scarborough, "Early Negro Professional Portrait Artist," uncited and undated newspaper article, "Joshua Johnston" File, Vertical File, EPFL.

74. Petition for Dancing Academy, 16 September 1805, BC Council, Series 1: Administrative Files, 1797–1923, box 5, item 206, BCA.

75. Steffen, *Mechanics of Baltimore*, 41; Della, "Problems of Negro Labor," 15.

76. Despeaux Account Book, 1810–1815, Ms. 260, Joseph Despeaux Papers, MHS; Steffen, *Mechanics of Baltimore*, 41; Berlin and Gutman, "Natives and Immigrants, Free Men and Slaves," 1182, 1185.

77. The 1817 directory listed 28 black maritime workers; in 1827 there were 68. These numbers do not include laborers, carters, draymen, and others who also worked at the harbor. J. Kennedy, *Baltimore Directory for 1817–18*, 212–22; Matchett, *Baltimore Directory for 1827*, passim; Seventh U.S. Census, 1850, Population Schedule, Ward 2, Baltimore City, in Clayton, *Black Baltimore*, 5.

78. Wade, *Slavery in the Cities*, 29–30; Semmes, *Baltimore as Seen by Visitors*, 165–66 (quotes); Hodgson, *Letters from North America*, 2:86–88.

79. Port of Baltimore, Crew Lists, Record Group 36, Bureau of Customs, boxes 1 (January–April 1806), 7 (June 1817, November 1835, 1837, January 1839, February–May 1843), NA.

80. Ibid.; *Baltimore American and Commercial Daily Advertiser,* 14 July 1804 (first quote); *Maryland Journal and Baltimore Advertiser,* 25 June 1793 (second quote); *Baltimore Daily Intelligencer,* 24 October 1794 (third quote); Robinson, *Baltimore Directory for 1804*, 36; Marks, "Skilled Blacks in Antebellum St. Mary's County," 543.

81. J. Kennedy, *Baltimore Directory for 1817–18*, 212–22; Matchett, *Baltimore Directory for 1827*, passim.

82. Nash, *Forging Freedom*, 134.

83. Douglass, *My Bondage and My Freedom*, 235, 135; J. Kennedy, *Baltimore Directory for 1817–18*, 214.

Chapter 4: The Contours of Quasi-Freedom

1. *Baltimore Daily Repository*, 26 September 1792, quoted also in Quarles, "American Revolution as a Black Declaration of Independence," 300, and Graham, *Balti-*

more, 25. For more information on Brown, see First U.S. Census, 1790, Population Schedule, Baltimore City, NA; and W. Thompson and Walker, *Baltimore Town and Fell's Point Directory*, 89.

2. Brackett, *Negro in Maryland*, 186–87n1. The initial exclusion date was 1802.

3. Jones, *Labor of Love, Labor of Sorrow*, chap. 1; D. G. White, *Ar'n't I a Woman?* chap. 1–2.

4. Franklin, *From Slavery to Freedom*, 163; BCC (Certificates of Freedom), 1806–1816, BA 0290, MdHR. Between 1806 and 1814, 15 (13.8 percent) of the 109 free blacks who had been born free were listed as physically disfigured, a much smaller number and percentage than that of former slaves and spanning a longer period of time. Seven (13.0 percent) of the males carried scars, while eight (14.5 percent) of the females were disfigured.

5. Genovese, *Roll, Jordan, Roll*, 446–50; Gutman, *Black Family in Slavery and Freedom*, 185–256 and passim; Fortes quoted in Price and Price, "Saramaka Onomastics," 342.

6. Inscoe, "Carolina Slave Names," 527–54. A number of historians have written on slave naming practices, most notably Eugene D. Genovese, Peter H. Wood, and Herbert G. Gutman. However, each concentrated on plantation slavery in the Lower South, where naming practices were somewhat different from those of the Upper South and thus reflect a different cultural experience. Genovese, *Roll, Jordan, Roll*, 51–52; Wood, *Black Majority*, 181–85; Gutman, *Black Family in Slavery and Freedom*, 185–256. Nash, *Forging Freedom*, 77–79, has provided the most recent study of slave naming practices in the North prior to emancipation.

7. Berlin, *Slaves without Masters*, 51–52; Nash, *Forging Freedom*, 80.

8. Darold D. Wax has found that between 1750 and 1769 Maryland and Virginia together imported 18,895 African slaves (compared with 36,669 in South Carolina during the same period), of which only about one third came to Maryland. Wax, "Black Immigrants," 35, 43. For more complete discussions of African slave names, see Cody, "There Was No 'Absalom' on the Ball Plantations," 563–96; and Inscoe, "Carolina Slave Names," 527–54. Cody found that between 1780 and 1799 over 14 percent of slave children born on the Ball plantation were given classical names. For a discussion of white southerners' comparisons of the societies of classical Greece and Rome with their own, see Oakes, *Slavery and Freedom*, chap. 1; and W. R. Taylor, *Cavalier and Yankee*, 35.

9. BC Tax, Series 1: General Property Tax Books, 1798–1915, microfilm reel BCA 177 [1798], BCA.

10. Ibid.; Nash, *Forging Freedom*, 81.

11. Genovese, *Roll, Jordan, Roll*, 447; First, Second, and Third U.S. Census, 1790, 1800, 1810, Population Schedule, Baltimore City, NA; BCC (Certificates of Freedom), 1806–1816, BA 0290, MdHR. Miller sees the act of naming as "the symbol of the *social* personality." Miller, "Some Aspects of the Name in Culture-History," 588.

12. First, Second, Third, and Fourth U.S. Census, 1790, 1800, 1810, 1820, Population Schedule, Baltimore City, NA; J. Kennedy, *Baltimore Directory for 1817–18*,

212; BCC (Certificates of Freedom), 1806–1816, BA 0290, MdHR. Of the 573 free black heads of households with Anglo-American names listed in the censuses from 1790 to 1810, 462 (80.7 percent) used full given names. Of 201 female heads of households with Anglo-American names, 64 (31.8 percent) used diminutive or shortened names.

13. BC Tax, Series 1: General Property Tax Books, 1798–1915, microfilm reel BCA 177 (1798], BCA; BCC (Miscellaneous Court Papers), 1789–1805, MSA C1, MdHR.

14. Genovese, *Roll, Jordan, Roll,* 445–47; *Maryland Journal and Baltimore Advertiser,* 1 January 1790 (first quote), 7 January 1790 (second quote).

15. First, Second, and Third U.S. Census, 1790, 1800, 1810, Population Schedule, Baltimore City, NA; BC Tax, Series 1: General Property Tax Books, 1798–1915, microfilm reel BCA 177 [1798], BCA; J. Kennedy, *Baltimore Directory for 1817–18,* passim Matchett, *Baltimore Directory for 1827,* passim; Matchett, *Baltimore Directory for 1849–50,* passim. For a discussion of slaves keeping the names of their first owners, see Gutman, *Slave Family in Slavery and Freedom,* 235.

16. First, Second, and Third, U.S. Census, 1790, 1800, 1810, Population Schedule, Baltimore City, NA; J. Kennedy, *Baltimore Directory for 1817–18,* 213–21; Matchett, *Baltimore Directory for 1827,* 265.

17. First, Second, Third, Fourth, and Fifth U.S. Census, 1790, 1800, 1810, 1820, 1830, Population Schedule, Baltimore City, NA; Hershberg, "Free Blacks in Antebellum Philadelphia," 193–94. Such writers as Stanley Elkins, E. Franklin Frazier, and Daniel P. Moynihan have rooted what they see as a deterioration of the black family in the institution of slavery, which they argue emasculated black males and prevented the formation of traditional father-centered families. Elkins, *Slavery;* Frazier, *Negro Family in the United States;* [Moynihan], *Negro Family.*

18. Blassingame, *Slave Community,* 172–73.

19. Seventh U.S. Census, 1850, Population Schedule, Wards 1–3, 4, Baltimore City, NA; Hershberg, "Free Blacks in Antebellum Philadelphia," 188; Hershberg and Williams, "Mulattoes and Blacks," 404.

20. Gutman, *Black Family in Slavery and Freedom,* 154–55; Hershberg, "Free Blacks in Antebellum Philadelphia," 194.

21. In 1810 Maryland, with its 111,502 slaves, ranked fourth in the country, behind only Virginia, South Carolina, and North Carolina. With the rapid growth of the new slave states of the southwest and the concomitant decline of slavery in Maryland, the state's slave population and its ranking among other slave states fell off sharply thereafter. By 1860, with 87,189 slaves, Maryland ranked thirteenth among slave states, ahead of only Delaware and Florida. Berlin, *Slaves without Masters,* 396–97.

22. Rawick, ed., *American Slave,* 12:19–20.

23. Baltimore City Archives Collection (Miscellaneous Court Papers, Index), 1831–1892, BC 0220, MdHR; Matchett, *Baltimore Directory for 1833, Corrected up to May 1833,* 169.

24. Manumissions and Emigrants, Manumission Books, Lists and Manumissions, Copies (1832–1860), microfilm reel 25, MSCS.

25. Ibid.; Clayton, *Black Baltimore*, 4; Schweninger, *Black Property Owners in the South*, 137.

26. Berlin, "Structure of the Free Negro Caste," 301; Schweninger, *Black Property Owners in the South*, 23; M. P. Johnson and Roark, *Black Masters*, 203–5.

27. Baltimore County Commissioners of the Tax, 1813 Assessment, Baltimore City, MSA C226, MdHR; Fifth U.S. Census, 1830, Population Schedule, Baltimore City, NA.

28. First, Second, Third, Fourth, and Fifth U.S. Census, 1790, 1800, 1810, 1820, 1830, Population Schedule, Baltimore City, NA; Schwartz, "Emancipators, Protectors, and Anomalies," 317–22; Curry, *Free Black in Urban America*, 44–47; Clayton, *Black Baltimore*, 11. Unquestionably, innumerable fugitive slaves lived in free black households, yet for obvious reasons were not reported to census takers.

29. Coyle, ed., *Records of the City of Baltimore (Special Commissioners)*, 136, 138; W. Thompson and Walker, *Baltimore Town and Fell's Point Directory*, 21, 40; *Federal Intelligencer, and Baltimore Daily Gazette*, 25 April 1795, cited in Schweninger, *Black Property Owners in the South*, 24. Whether Chapman was an apprentice in Gilliard's blacksmith shop or a slave is unclear.

30. Woodson, *Free Negro Owners of Slaves*, 7; BC Tax, Series 1: General Property Tax Books, 1798–1915, microfilm reel BCA 177 [1798], BCA; Manumissions and Emigrants, Manumission Books, Lists and Manumissions, Copies (1832–1860), microfilm reel 25, MSCS; Schweninger, *Black Property Owners in the South*, 24.

31. BCC (Miscellaneous Court Papers), 1805, 1808, 1809, MSA C1, MdHR.

32. BCC (Miscellaneous Court Papers), 1808, MSA C1, MdHR; BCC (Certificates of Freedom), 1806–1816, BA 0290, MdHR; *Federal Intelligencer, and Baltimore Daily Gazette*, 11 April 1805; Schweninger, *Black Property Owners in the South*, 23–24 (first quote); Graham, *Baltimore*, 261–62 (second quote). Forced to consider the possibility of paying a sum he did not have, Gilliard advertised in the same issue the sale of "AN elegant two-story frame House, and five Lots of Ground." The house appears to have been located in the Gallows Hill area, amid the residences of other tradespeople.

33. Woodson, *Free Negro Owners of Slaves*, 7; B. C. Thomas, "Baltimore Black Community," 2; M. P. Johnson and Roark, *Black Masters*, 203–18; Schweninger, *Black Property Owners in the South*, 123–24; BC Tax, Series 1: General Property Tax Books, 1798–1915, microfilm reels BCA 165–71 [1856], BCA; Curry, *Free Black in Urban America*, 45 (quote), 270–71.

34. First, Second, and Third U.S. Census, 1790, 1800, 1810, Population Schedule, Baltimore City, NA; Nash, *Forging Freedom*, 161; BC Tax, Series 3: Field Assessor's Workbooks (Property Assessments), Baltimore City, 1846, BCA; Matchett, *Baltimore Directory for 1847–48*, 36. Hackett went on to establish a successful cartering business, with a number of wagons, as well as operating a livery stable that employed whites. He ultimately operated a coal yard. Graham, *Baltimore*, 149, 158.

35. BC Tax, Series 1: General Property Tax Books, 1798–1915, microfilm reels BCA 177 [1798], BCA 165–71 [1856], BCA.

36. Second and Third U.S. Census, 1800, 1810, Population Schedule, Baltimore City, NA.

37. L. P. Jackson, *Free Negro Labor and Property Holding in Virginia*, 115–16.

38. BC Tax, Series 1: General Property Tax Books, 1798–1915, microfilm reel BCA 177 [1798], BCA.

39. BC Tax, Series 1: General Property Tax Books, 1798–1915, microfilm reel BCA 177 [1798] [1832], BCA; Baltimore Assessment Record Book, 1815, Ms. 55, MHS. During the same period the average white property holding declined by nearly a half, to slightly more than $800.

40. Schweninger, *Black Property Owners in the South*, 18–20, 78; BC Tax, Series 1: General Property Tax Books, 1798–1915, microfilm reel BCA 177 [1832], BCA; Baltimore Assessment Record Book, 1815, Ms. 55, MHS; Baltimore County Board of County Commissioners, 1828–1855, MSA C266, MdHR.

41. Nash, *Forging Freedom*, 248; Baltimore Assessment Record Book, 1815, Ms. 55, MHS; Curry, *Free Black in Urban America*, 268.

42. Nash, *Forging Freedom*, 248; Curry, *Free Black in Urban America*, 267; Du Bois, *Philadelphia Negro*, 36–37; BC Tax, Series 1: General Property Tax Books, 1798–1915, microfilm reels BCA 165–71 [1856], BCA.

43. Gardner, "Free Blacks in Baltimore," 133, 138, 301–17; Curry, *Free Black in Urban America*, 267; Matchett, *Baltimore Directory for 1851*, 316.

44. Gardner, "Free Blacks in Baltimore," 301–17. Gardner has found a total of 362 holders of at least $500 worth of real property in Baltimore in 1850 and 1860, representing 1.4 percent of the 25,442 free blacks in Baltimore in 1850, the lower population of the two years surveyed.

45. Curry, *Free Black in Urban America*, 37–48, 267–71; Schweninger, *Black Property Owners in the South*, 76. Both Curry and Schweninger found that in 1850 free black women constituted slightly less than 10 percent of free black property owners in Baltimore.

46. Schweninger, *Black Property Owners in the South*, 111–12. Schweninger found a general disparity between black property holdings in the Upper and Lower South. Consistently, the average value of property ownership in Baltimore was well below that of Charleston and Philadelphia.

47. G. L. Browne, *Baltimore in the Nation*, 190.

48. Gutman, *Black Family in Slavery and Freedom*, 102; *Maryland Journal and Baltimore Advertiser*, 25 June 1793.

49. Fourth U.S. Census, 1820, Population Schedule, Baltimore City, NA. Because the population schedules prior to 1850 did not list the names of those household residents other than heads of households, indicating merely sex, approximate ages, and free black or slave status, specific conclusions about interracial living arrangements are difficult.

50. First, Second, Third, and Fourth U.S. Census, 1790, 1800, 1810, 1820, Pop-

ulation Schedule, Baltimore City, NA; *New Baltimore Directory, and Annual Register, for 1800 and 1801*, 15; Stafford, *Baltimore Directory for 1802*, 25; Matchett, *Baltimore Directory for 1827*, 30.

51. Curry, *Free Black in Urban America*, 11–13, 256; Jordan, *White Man's Burden*, 179–89. Curry has found similar conclusions for black populations in most of the fifteen cities he studied during the antebellum period.

52. BC Tax, Series 3: Field Assessor's Workbooks (Property Assessments), Baltimore City, 1837–98, BCA; Craig, *Business Directory and Baltimore Almanac for 1842*, 422; Third U.S. Census, 1810, Population Schedule, Baltimore City, NA.

53. Fourth U.S. Census, 1820, Population Schedule, Baltimore City, NA; Clayton, *Black Baltimore*, 4.

54. George Litting Account Book, 1796–1878, Ms. 1657, MHS.

55. Wade, *Slavery in the Cities*, 30–31; Nash, *Forging Freedom*, 163–65; Steffen, *Mechanics of Baltimore*, 177; Third U.S. Census, 1810, Population Schedule, Baltimore City, NA; Fry, *Baltimore Directory for 1810*, 52, 77, 102, 121, 195.

56. BC Tax, Series 1: General Property Tax Books, 1798–1915, microfilm reel BCA 177 [1798], BCA; Third U.S. Census, 1810, Population Schedule, Baltimore City, NA; W. W. Smith, "Politics and Democracy in Maryland," 257–59. In 1822 the Maryland legislature passed a bill granting full equality for all religious groups, which took effect in 1826. That year Etting and Jacob Cohen, also Jewish, won seats on the Baltimore City Council.

57. Nash, *Forging Freedom*, 163–65; Garonzik, "Racial and Ethnic Make-up of Baltimore Neighborhoods," 397–98; Third U.S. Census, 1810, Population Schedule, Baltimore City, NA; Fry, *Baltimore Directory for 1810*; Baltimore Assessment Record Book, 1815, Ms. 55, MHS.

58. Fifth U.S. Census, 1830, Population Schedule, Baltimore City, NA; McSherry, *History of Maryland*, 403–4. In 1830, 1,427 of 14,790 free blacks (9.6 percent) lived in what had become wards 5–7, roughly constituting the area formerly encompassed by wards 2–6.

59. Fourth and Fifth U.S. Census, 1820, 1830, Population Schedule, Baltimore City, NA; Steffen, *Mechanics of Baltimore*, 19–20.

60. Condemnation Extract, Exchange Alley, ERB, vol. 1:111, BCA; Curry, *Free Black in Urban America*, 50; Third, Fourth, and Fifth U.S. Census, 1810, 1820, 1830, Population Schedule, Baltimore City, NA; S. Jackson, *Baltimore Directory*; Keenan, *Baltimore Directory for 1822 and '23*; Nash, *Forging Freedom*, 169.

61. Nash, *Forging Freedom*, 169–71; M. P. Johnson and Roark, *Black Masters*, 203–27; Borchert, *Alley Life in Washington*, chap. 1.

62. The following is taken from a compilation of the Eighth U.S. Census, 1850, Population Schedule, Baltimore City, NA; Matchett, *Baltimore Directory for 1849–50*; and Matchett, *Baltimore Directory for 1851*.

63. Morris, "Labor Controls in Maryland," 387; Lyell, *Travels in North America*, 1:102.

64. S. Jackson, *Baltimore Directory*, passim; Matchett, *Baltimore Directory for 1827*, passim.

65. S. Jackson, *Baltimore Directory*, passim; Matchett, *Baltimore Directory for 1827*, passim.

66. Fourth U.S. Census, 1820, Population Schedule, Baltimore City, NA.

67. Third U.S. Census, 1810, Population Schedule, Baltimore City, NA; Fields, *Slavery and Freedom on the Middle Ground*, 2–4; Steffen, *Mechanics of Baltimore*, 19. Steffen used the city directories for the years 1796 and 1814 to arrive at his conclusions. Since these directories did not include black residents prior to 1816, Steffen's totals were white totals. During the period, the number of white mechanics increased from 1,124 to 1,944, of a total work force of 2,479 in 1796 and 4,000 in 1814. During the same period, the number of laborers decreased from 457 to 412. Although city directories did not include all city workers, the totals are probably representative.

68. Berlin, "Structure of the Free Negro Caste," 306–7 (quote); Berlin, *Slaves without Masters*, 311.

69. M. P. Johnson and Roark, *Black Masters*, 185; Berlin, "Structure of the Free Negro Caste," 301; Wikramanayake, *World in Shadow*, 100–106; Blassingame, *Black New Orleans*, 10; Reinders, "Free Negro in the New Orleans Economy," 274.

70. Hoyt, ed., "Civilian Defense in Baltimore," 200–201, 221 (quote); Franklin, *From Slavery to Freedom*, 162; Jordan, *White over Black*, 411–12; *Baltimore Daily Intelligencer*, 13 December 1793 (quote), 28 May 1794, cited in Steffen, *Mechanics of Baltimore*, 146–49.

71. Bayly E. Marks has found that only 18 percent of black women in rural St. Mary's County, Maryland, listed skills outside agriculture. Of that 18 percent, 13 percent were free black women. Marks, "Skilled Blacks in Antebellum St. Mary's County," 541, 544.

72. Schweninger, *Black Property Owners in the South*, 84–86; J. Kennedy, *Baltimore Directory for 1817–18*, 212–22; S. Jackson, *Baltimore Directory*, passim; Matchett, *Baltimore Directory for 1827*, passim. Of 118 laundresses listed in the 1819 city directory, 38 (32.2 percent) resided at Fells Point.

73. Berlin, *Slaves without Masters*, 262.

74. G. L. Browne, *Baltimore in the Nation*, 51–52; J. Kennedy, *Baltimore Directory for 1817–18*, 212–22; Fry, *Baltimore Directory for 1810*, passim; Matchett, *Baltimore Directory for 1827*, passim.

75. G. L. Browne, *Baltimore in the Nation*, 51–65.

76. S. Jackson, *Baltimore Directory*, passim; Matchett, *Baltimore Directory for 1827*, passim; Matchett, *Baltimore Director[y], Corrected up to 1835, for 1835–36*, passim.

77. Sellers, *Market Revolution*, 135–70, 354–61, and passim; G. L. Browne, *Baltimore in the Nation*, 74–77, 127–43.

Chapter 5: Climbing Jacob's Ladder

1. *Maryland Journal and Baltimore Advertiser*, 25 June 1793.

2. For a brilliant discussion of the Africanization of white religion, see Stuckey, *Slave Culture*, 27–43 (quote on 33).

3. *North Star*, 16 February 1849, quoted in Gravely, "Rise of the African Churches in America," 73.

4. *Weekly Anglo-African*, 7 October 1859.

5. Berlin, *Slaves without Masters*, 69–70; Steffen, *Mechanics of Baltimore*, 255–56; Jordan, *White over Black*, 418–19.

6. Lincoln and Mamiya, *Black Church in the African American Experience*, 22–24. The first known black congregation in America is generally acknowledged to have been the Bluestone African Baptist Church, established in 1758 on the William Byrd plantation near Mecklenberg, Virginia.

7. Brugger, *Maryland*, 117.

8. Raboteau, *Slave Religion*, 188; Berlin, *Slaves without Masters*, 71; Gardner, "Free Blacks in Baltimore," 49–50; Lincoln and Mamiya, *Black Church in the African American Experience*, 50; Gregory, "Education of Blacks in Maryland," 21; Steffen, *Mechanics of Baltimore*, 254, 255–56. "Black Harry" Hosier, described by Bishop Thomas Coke as "one of the best preachers in the world" and by Benjamin Rush as "the greatest orator in America," became so prominent among early Methodists that he attended the 1784 General Conference at which the Methodist Episcopal Church of America was established. He and Richard Allen were the only black men in attendance. Quoted in Wesley, *Richard Allen*, 30–31.

9. Isaac, *Transformation of Virginia*.

10. Nash, *Forging Freedom*, 109–10, 193; Payne, *History of the African Methodist Episcopal Church*, 9–10.

11. Mathews, *Slavery and Methodism*, 3–10; Burtner and Chiles, *Compend of Wesley's Theology*, 7–10, 248–49; Lincoln and Mamiya, *Black Church in the African American Experience*, 50–51.

12. Mathews, *Slavery and Methodism*, 20–24, 295–99; R. Walsh, "Era of the Revolution", 119–20; Gregory, "Education of Blacks in Maryland," 21–23; Simpson, ed., *American Methodist Pioneer*, 3–10; Bangs, *Life of Freeborn Garrettson*, 59, quoted in Berlin, *Slaves without Masters*, 25 (first quote); K. L. Carroll, "Religious Influences of the Manumission of Slaves," 192 (second quote); J. M. Wright, *Free Negro in Maryland*, 47–48n6; E. T. Clark, Potts, and Payton, eds., *Journals and Letters of Francis Asbury*, 2:726 (third quote); Gardner, "Free Blacks in Baltimore," 40–41; Curry, *Free Black in Urban America*, 180–81. The issue of slavery eventually grew so divisive that at the 1844 General Conference the Methodist Episcopal church divided into two wings, one southern in support of slavery, and one northern in opposition. Mathews, *Slavery and Methodism*, chap. 6–9.

13. Brugger, *Maryland*, 170.

14. Steffen, *Mechanics of Baltimore*, 253–63; *Doctrines and Discipline of the Methodist Episcopal Church*, passim; Weems, *God's Revenge against Gambling Exemplified*, 10–22. In 1815 nearly half of white male Methodists in Baltimore were mechanics. Large-scale merchants and common workers constituted distinct minorities.

15. Baltimore City Station Records: Marriages, Baptisms, 1799–1838, 438, Lovely Lane (quotes); H. V. Richardson and Wright, "Afro-American Religion," 494–95.

16. Baltimore City Station Records, 1799–1838, 169, 173, Lovely Lane.

17. W. W. Brown, *My Southern Home*, 46.

18. Baltimore City Station Class Records, 1799–1838, 334–443, Lovely Lane (quotes); Steffen, *Mechanics of Baltimore*, 255–57. Baltimore Methodists were neither the first nor the only predominantly white denomination to perform marriage ceremonies for black parishioners. The records of St. Peter's Catholic Church from as early as 1782 are replete with examples of slave and free black marriages (as well as baptisms and burials) performed by priests for a variety of slave, free black, and mixed couples. Piet and Piet, *Early Catholic Church Records in Baltimore*.

19. Litwack, *North of Slavery*, 190; E. P. Thompson, *Making of the English Working Class*, chap. 11 and passim.

20. Curry, *Free Black in Urban America*, 195; Baltimore City Station Class Records, 1799–1838, 10–14, 196–312, 318–33, Lovely Lane; Second U.S. Census, 1800, Population Schedule, Baltimore County, NA. Each of the figures represents over 10 percent of the city's free black population as calculated in 1800 and just over 5 percent of the city's total black population.

21. Steffen, *Mechanics of Baltimore*, 257; E. D. Smith, *Climbing Jacob's Ladder*, 35; Litwack, *North of Slavery*, 197–98; Berlin, *Slaves without Masters*, 301; Trollope, *Domestic Manners of the Americans*, 2:298–99 (first quote); Wade, *Slavery in the Cities*, 160–67 (Olmsted quote on 163).

22. Baltimore City Station Class Records, 1799–1838, 391, Lovely Lane (first quote); Maryland Society for Promoting the Abolition of Slavery, "Report to the American Convention," 1796, Papers of the Pennsylvania Society for the Abolition of Slavery, HSP (second quote); Curry, *Free Black in Urban America*, 195; Steffen, *Mechanics of Baltimore*, 257; Litwack, *North of Slavery*, 197–98; Berlin, *Slaves without Masters*, 301.

23. *Maryland Journal and Baltimore Advertiser*, 7 January 1790 (first quote), 16 February 1790 (second quote).

24. Raboteau, *Slave Religion*, 180–81.

25. Litwack, *North of Slavery*, 196–98; Berlin, *Slaves without Masters*, 69–70; Wade, *Slavery in the Cities*, 271–72; Jordan, *White over Black*, 418–19; George, "Widening the Circle," 92; Nash, *Forging Freedom*, 44–45; Wesley, *Richard Allen*, 129–30; Quarles, *Negro in the Making of America*, 99.

26. Nash, *Forging Freedom*, 44–45; Graham, *Baltimore*, 40; B. C. Thomas, "Baltimore Black Community," 20; Baltimore City Station Class Records, 1799–1838, 10–14, Lovely Lane; Baltimore City Station Admissions, Removals, Deaths, 1809–1811, 153–54, Lovely Lane; Steffen, *Mechanics of Baltimore*, 256–57. Jordan, *White over Black*, contends that segregated seating occurred on a regular basis only in the Lower South, but this appears unfounded in the light of more recent studies of black churches in the Upper South.

27. J. B. Wilson, *Very Quiet Baltimoreans*, 82–87.

28. Raboteau, *Slave Religion*, 246–47; E. T. Clark, Potts, and Payton, eds., *Journals and Letters of Francis Asbury*, 3:218 (quote).

29. Sobel, *Trabelin' On*, 169–70; Genovese, *Roll, Jordan, Roll*, 280–84; Blassingame, *Slave Community*, 130–37; Nash, *Forging Freedom*, 44–45; Wade, *Slavery in the Cities*, 163 (quote).

30. Nash, *Forging Freedom*, 21, 44–45; Levine, *Black Culture and Black Consciousness*, 29; Gravely, "Rise of the African Churches in America," 62–64; Raboteau, "Richard Allen and the African Church Movement," 1–2.

31. Franklin, *From Slavery to Freedom*, 111–12; Nash, *Forging Freedom*, 98–99; Lincoln and Mamiya, *Black Church in the African American Experience*, 50–52; Raboteau, "Richard Allen and the African Church Movement," 5–7.

32. Nash, *Forging Freedom*, 191–92; Baltimore City Station Admissions, Removals, Deaths, 1809–1811, passim, Lovely Lane. As late as 1811, 149 of the 479 new members of the city's mixed churches were black.

33. Wesley, *Richard Allen*, 128–29; Gardner, "Free Blacks in Baltimore," 51–52; B. C. Thomas, "Baltimore Black Community," 21–22; Curry, *Free Black in Urban America*, 178; Berlin, *Slaves without Masters*, 71–72.

34. Gardner, "Free Blacks in Baltimore," 51–52; B. C. Thomas, "Baltimore Black Community," 21–22; E. T. Clark, Potts, and Payton, eds., *Journals and Letters of Francis Asbury*, 2:51 (first quote), 2:128–29 (second quote), 3:160 (third quote); Berlin, *Slaves without Masters*, 72. Though Philadelphia's Free African Society was nondenominational, Baltimore's Colored Methodist Society obviously was not. Others in the group included Henry Harden, Thomas Clare, Munday Janey, George Douglass, David Brister, Stephen Hill, and Caleb Suilly. Wesley, *Richard Allen*, 129–30.

35. Wesley, *Richard Allen*, 129–30; B. C. Thomas, "Baltimore Black Community," 22–24; Gardner, "Free Blacks in Baltimore," 52 (quote). This group appears to have been the only organized effort at black religious freedom in Baltimore prior to 1816.

36. Gardner, "Free Blacks in Baltimore," 52–53; *Baltimore Gazette and Daily Advertiser*, 5 July 1797.

37. Baltimore City Land Records, liber WG 69, 102 (4 April 1801), liber WG 71, 124 (16 December 1801), BCH.

38. Baltimore City Land Records, liber WG 70, 520–21 [15 March 1802], BCH (first quote); *Baltimore American and Commercial Daily Advertiser*, 6 June 1805; Gregory, "Education of Blacks in Maryland," 64–65 (second quote). Those involved in the purchase were Gilliard, Russell, William Moore, Richard Wallace, John Sunderland, Joseph Sellers, John Mingo Jr., Nero Graves, and Paraway Bradford. In 1811 these same men, referring to themselves as "Trustees of the African Church in the City of Baltimore," negotiated the purchase of another parcel of land, adjacent to this same building. Baltimore City Land Records, liber WG 115, 625–26 [30 May 1811], BCH.

39. Baltimore City Station Admissions, Removals, Deaths, 1809–1811, passim, Lovely Lane; E. T. Clark, Potts, and Payton, eds., *Journals and Letters of Francis Asbury*, 2:332; Coker, *Dialogue between a Virginian and an African Minister*, 41.

40. E. T. Clark, Potts, and Payton, eds., *Journals and Letters of Francis Asbury*, 2:466, 497, 630; Simpson, ed., *American Methodist Pioneer*, 327.

41. Litwack, *North of Slavery*, 188; quoted in Strickland, *Life of Jacob Gruber*, 323.

42. Strickland, *Life of Jacob Gruber*, 323–24 (first quote); E. T. Clark, Potts, and Payton, eds., *Journals and Letters of Francis Asbury*, 3:464 (second quote); Coker, "Sermon Delivered Extempore in the African Bethel Church," 68; Coker, *Dialogue between a Virginian and an African Minister*, 40–41. Those known black preachers were Hannibal Moore, Thomas Dublin, Richard Williams, James Coal, Thomas Hall, John Wigh, and Abner Coker.

43. A Maryland law, passed in 1692 and amended in 1715, decreed that mulatto children of free white mothers, whether the black father was free or slave, were slaves until the age of thirty-one. Kilty, ed., *Laws of Maryland*, 1715, chap. 44; Brackett, *Negro in Maryland*, 32–34; J. M. Wright, *Free Negro in Maryland*, 28–29.

44. Graham, *Baltimore*, 63; Nash, *Forging Freedom*, 231–32; Wesley, *Richard Allen*, 130–31; Gardner, "Free Blacks in Baltimore," 64–65.

45. Graham, *Baltimore*, 67; Coker, *Dialogue between a Virginian and an African Minister*, 1 (quote). Coker taught in his school for a little over ten years.

46. Coker, *Dialogue between a Virginian and an African Minister*, 39–41; Gravely, "Rise of the African Churches in America," 68; Baltimore City Station Class Records, 1799–1838, 10–14, Lovely Lane; Coker, "Sermon Delivered Extempore in the African Bethel Church," 68 (quote).

47. *Baltimore Gazette and Daily Advertiser*, 3 January 1810, quoted in Graham, *Baltimore*, 64.

48. Quoted in Graham, *Baltimore*, 67. For the fullest discussion of justifications for enslavement of blacks, see Fredrickson, *Black Image in the White Mind*, chap. 1–5; Jordan, *Black over White*, 422–24. The quote on the wall of St. Thomas's church was "The People That Walked in Darkness Have Seen a Great Light."

49. Graham, *Baltimore*, 71–73, 147–48; Raboteau, "Richard Allen and the African Church Movement," 8–9; Gardner, "Free Blacks in Baltimore," 64–65; Nash, *Forging Freedom*, 230.

50. Coker, "Sermon Delivered Extempore in the African Bethel Church," 68; Gregory, "Education of Blacks in Maryland," 64–65.

51. Graham, *Baltimore*, 72–73; Raboteau, "Richard Allen and the African Church Movement," 9–10; Coker, "Sermon Delivered Extempore in the African Bethel Church," 68–69 (quote).

52. Franklin, *From Slavery to Freedom*, 111–12; quoted in *Baltimore American and Commercial Daily Advertiser*, 6 June 1805; Nash, *Forging Freedom*, 112–15.

53. Quoted in Payne, *History of the African Methodist Episcopal Church*, 14; Raboteau, "Richard Allen and the African Church Movement," 9–11; Graham, *Baltimore*, 73; Gardner, "Free Blacks in Baltimore," 65–66, 78–79; Payne, *Recollections of Seventy-Years*, 70.

54. Membership Roll, 1825–1853, microfilm reel M1383, Bethel, MdHR; Probationer's Book, 1845–1881, microfilm reel M1383, Bethel, MdHR; quoted in Jacob Fortie Journal, Fortie Family Papers, MdHR; Nash, *Forging Freedom*, 263–65. Women enrolled in the Bethel church between 1825 and 1853 outnumbered men

873 to 407. From 1850 to 1854 alone Bethel enrolled 492 women as members, while taking just 149 men. During those twenty-eight years, 36 men achieved the rank of class leader.

55. Raboteau, *Slave Religion*, 204; Probationer's Book, 1845–1881, microfilm reel M1383, Bethel, MdHR; Baltimore City Charter Records, liber WG 20, 83 [1816], BCH; quoted in Gardner, "Free Blacks in Baltimore," 66–67.

56. *Baltimore American and Commercial Daily Advertiser*, 6 June 1805; *Baltimore Gazette and Daily Advertiser*, 25 July 1815 (quote), 16 August 1816, 4 September 1817; Graham, *Baltimore*, 74.

57. Simpson, ed., *American Methodist Pioneer*, 318–20; *Federal Intelligencer, and Baltimore Daily Gazette*, 12 August 1816, quoted in Gardner, "Free Blacks in Baltimore," 67–68 (first quote); quoted in Gravely, "Rise of the African Churches in America," 65 (second quote).

58. Graham, *Baltimore*, 74; *Baltimore Sun*, 6 August 1840, 15 September 1840 (quote).

59. *Baltimore Gazette and Daily Advertiser*, 4 September 1817; quoted in Graham, *Baltimore*, 74–76.

60. Minutes of the Society for the Relief of the Poor, 1814–17, vol. 2, Ms. 488, box 13, Fielder Israel Papers, MHS; Recommendations for Deacon's Orders, Baltimore City Station Records, 1800–1865, Lovely Lane (first quote); Minutes of the Methodist Episcopal Quarterly Conferences, Baltimore Station, 1814–19, vol. 2, Ms. 488, Fielder Israel Papers, MHS (second, third, and fourth quotes); J. Kennedy, *Baltimore Directory for 1817–18*, 109; S. Jackson, *Baltimore Directory*, 103. Mingo received this recommendation on 6 January 1818, the first black to receive such an honor in Baltimore. It is not known whether he actually was ordained.

61. Gardner, "Free Blacks in Baltimore," 65, 77–79; Curry, *Free Black in Urban America*, 191–92; Insurance Policy of African Bethel Society, 1817, Policy 4825, Baltimore Equitable Society Papers, Series 1: Policy Ledger Books, Record Group 12, microfilm reel BCA 4634, BCA; Berlin, *Slaves without Masters*, 286–88; quoted in Payne, *History of the African Methodist Episcopal Church*, 14. The Bethel congregation bought the property on Fish (then Saratoga) Street in 1827.

62. Payne, *History of the African Methodist Episcopal Church*, 14 (first quote), 15 (second quote); Gardner, "Free Blacks in Baltimore," 69–70.

63. Baltimore City and County Commissioners of Insolvent Debtors, Insolvency Docket, 1818, BC 0339, MdHR; Gardner, "Free Blacks in Baltimore," 56, 70–71; Coker, *Journal of Daniel Coker*, 42–43 (quote); E. D. Smith, *Climbing Jacob's Ladder*, 59–61, 78; Graham, *Baltimore*, 75–76. In Liberia Coker founded an A.M.E. congregation. His wife later joined him, and they eventually moved to Sierra Leone, where Coker died in about 1846.

64. Quoted in Simpson, ed., *American Methodist Pioneer*, 327; File of Appointments, Sharp Street, Strawberry Alley, and Asbury Station, 1831–1860, Lovely Lane.

65. Record of Members and Classes, 1825–1828, 1830–1832, 1840–41, Sharp Street Methodist Episcopal Church Records, 1826, Lovely Lane; Plan of Appoint-

ments, Baltimore City Station Methodist Episcopal Church, 1831, Lovely Lane; Matchett, *Baltimore Directory, Corrected up to June, 1829*, 228; Gardner, "Free Blacks in Baltimore," 55–56; Graham, *Baltimore*, 95; Rawick, ed., *American Slave*, 16:14–15. Most black physicians were informally trained, such as Eliza Foote, called "the doctor woman," who worked for a physician named Ensor in Baltimore County and used her practical experience and knowledge of medicine to treat and midwife for "the poor whites and the slaves and free Negroes of which there were a number in Baltimore." Wells was educated at the city's Washington Medical College to serve the American Colonization Society in Liberia. He never emigrated to Africa and died while fighting the severe cholera epidemic in Baltimore in 1832.

66. Membership Roll, 1825–1853, microfilm reel M1383, Bethel, MdHR; Probationer's Book, 1845–1881, microfilm reel M1383, Bethel, MdHR. Such measures of respectability that blacks expected of their leaders were even more obvious during Reconstruction.

67. *Baltimore Sun*, 19 February 1839.

68. Membership Roll, 1825–1853, microfilm reel M1383, Bethel, MdHR.

69. Payne, *Recollections*, 92–94; Lincoln and Mamiya, *Black Church in the African American Experience*, 53.

70. Payne, *Recollections*, 253–56; Stuckey, *Slave Culture*, 93–95.

71. Gardner, "Free Blacks in Baltimore," 55–64, 84–89, 94–98; E. A. Andrews, *Slavery and the Domestic Slave Trade*, 88–89; Woods, *Woods' Baltimore City Directory*; Seventh U.S. Census, 1850, Social Statistics by Ward, Baltimore City, NA; Paul, "Shadow of Equality," 31; Brackett, *Negro in Maryland*, 206; E. D. Smith, *Climbing Jacob's Ladder*, 79–80; Curry, *Free Black in Urban America*, 181–90; Berlin, *Slaves without Masters*, 297.

72. "President of Sharp Street to Wm Steuart, Mayor," 30 August 1831, BC Mayor, box 7, item 475, BCA.

73. Lovejoy, *Memoir of Rev. Charles T. Torrey*, 167.

74. Gravely, "Rise of the African Churches in America," 65; Nash, *Forging Freedom*, 193–94; Faux, *Memorable Days in America*, 108–9 (quote).

75. E. A. Andrews, *Slavery and the Domestic Slave Trade*, 89, 93.

76. *Baltimore Clipper*, 17 June 1840, quoted in Graham, *Baltimore*, 148.

77. Quoted in Strickland, *Life of Jacob Gruber*, 324.

78. Blassingame, *Slave Community*, 130–33; E. A. Andrews, *Slavery and the Domestic Slave Trade*, 88–89 (quotes).

79. Strickland, *Life of Jacob Gruber*, 323; Litwack, *North of Slavery*, 187–88; Gravely, "Rise of the African Churches in America," 65; Berlin, *Slaves without Masters*, 302–3; Anderson, "Eighteenth-Century Suffrage," 144–45; Brackett, *Negro in Maryland*, 186–87; Curry, *Free Black in Urban America*, 92, 193, 195; Clayton, *Black Baltimore*, 41–42; Nash, *Forging Freedom*, 13.

80. Litwack, *North of Slavery*, 187–88; Record of Members and Classes, 1825–1828, 1830–1832, 1840–1841, Sharp Street Methodist Episcopal Church, cited in Garner, "Free Blacks in Baltimore, 56; Plan of Appointments, Baltimore City Sta-

tion Methodist Episcopal Church, 1833, Lovely Lane; Matchett, *Baltimore Directory, Corrected up to June, 1829;* Gravely, "Rise of the African Churches in America," 65 (quote).

81. Strickland, *Life of Jacob Gruber,* 323; Litwack, *North of Slavery,* 187–88; George, "Widening the Circle," 80; Berlin, *Slaves without Masters,* 297; *Baltimore Sun,* 18 December 1838, 26 May 1840, 28 May 1840 (quote), 15 June 1840.

Chapter 6: The Maturation of a Black Community

1. J. W. Wilson, *Sketches of the Higher Classes of Colored Society in Philadelphia,* 36–37. In his book *The Philadelphia Negro,* W. E. B. Du Bois identified the writer as Joseph W. Willson. More recently, Julie Winch in her book *Philadelphia's Black Elite* identifies him as Joseph W. Wilson.

2. Baltimore City Superior Court (Certificates of Freedom), 1848–1864, BC 0165, MdHR; BCC (Certificates of Freedom), 1806–1816, BA 0290, MdHR.

3. Baltimore City Superior Court (Certificates of Freedom), 1848–1864, BC 0165, MdHR. Maryland did not keep separate birth records for African Americans in Baltimore prior to 1875.

4. Douglass, *My Bondage and My Freedom,* 141.

5. A. Mackay, *Western World,* 1:132–33, quoted in Litwack, *North of Slavery,* 182.

6. Coppin, *Unwritten History,* 17–18.

7. For a discussion of the importance of personal appearance among social classes in early America, see Prude, "To Look upon the 'Lower Sort,'" 124–59.

8. Genovese, *Roll, Jordan, Roll,* 550–61.

9. *Maryland Journal and Baltimore Advertiser,* 21 June 1793 (first quote); Larkin, *Reshaping of Everyday Life,* 182–91 (second quote).

10. Wade, *Slavery in the Cities,* 127; Douglass, *My Bondage and My Freedom,* 134, 144 (first quote); McFeely, *Frederick Douglass,* 27; *Baltimore Daily Intelligencer,* 24 October 1794 (second quote); Gardner, "Free Blacks in Baltimore," 197–98 (third quote).

11. Trollope, *Domestic Manners of the Americans,* 1:291.

12. S. White and White, "Slave Hair and African American Culture," 73–75 and passim.

13. Quoted in Semmes, *Baltimore as Seen by Visitors,* 157.

14. Quoted in Strickland, *Life of Jacob Gruber,* 323–24.

15. Trollope, *Domestic Manners of the Americans,* 1:298–99.

16. Nash, *Forging Freedom,* 217–23.

17. Wade, *Slavery in the Cities,* 73; Pairpont, *Uncle Sam and His Country,* quoted in Semmes, *Baltimore as Seen by Visitors,* 166–67.

18. Pairpont, *Uncle Sam and His Country,* quoted in Semmes, *Baltimore as Seen by Visitors,* 167.

19. Semmes, *Baltimore as Seen by Visitors,* 157 (first quote); Matchett, *Baltimore Directory for 1824,* 304, 347; Complaint against Hucksters, 20 April 1824, BC Mayor, box 4, item 831, BCA (second quote).

278 Notes to Pages 151–55

20. Wade, *Slavery in the Cities*, 73; Trollope, *Domestic Manners of the Americans*, 1:291 (quote).

21. "A Female" to Mr. Richardson, 12 March 1845, BC Council, Series 1: Administrative Files, 1797–1923, box 74A, item 474, BCA.

22. *Ordinances of the Corporation of the City of Baltimore*, 152, 335 (quotes).

23. BC Miscellaneous, Series 5: Court Records, 1815–1921, box 1, BCA.

24. Gardner, "Free Blacks in Baltimore," 146.

25. Baltimore City Court of Oyer and Terminer (Docket and Minutes), 1790, MdHR (quote); *Baltimore Gazette and Daily Advertiser*, 11 April 1805, cited in Graham, *Baltimore*, 261; Baltimore City and County Commissioners of Insolvent Debtors, Insolvency Docket, 1818, BC 0339, MdHR; *Baltimore Sun*, 10 December 1838.

26. Gregory, "Education of Blacks in Maryland," 31–34; George, "Widening the Circle," 83–86.

27. Gardner, "Free Blacks in Baltimore," 161–62; Curry, *Free Black in Urban America*, 267; J. M. Wright, *Free Negro in Maryland*, 184; Wade, *Slavery in the Cities*, 325; Schweninger, *Black Property Owners in the South*, 73–77. In 1818 the average amount of property held by Baltimore free blacks was valued at $132.93. The figures include both real and personal property.

28. Seventh and Eighth U.S. Census, 1850, 1860, Population Schedule, Baltimore City, NA; Schweninger, *Black Property Holders in the South*, 74–77; J. M. Wright, *Free Negro in Maryland*, 185–86.

29. Gardner, "Free Blacks in Baltimore," 161–63; Schweninger, *Black Property Owners in the South*, 122; Free Negro Petitions to Leave the State, BCC (Miscellaneous Court Papers), 1841, MSA C1, MdHR; Estate and Last Will and Testament of Thomas Green, BCC (Chancery Papers), MdHR 40200-5988-½, MdHR.

30. Curry, *Free Black in Urban America*, 267; J. M. Wright, *Free Negro in Maryland*, 184–86; Gardner, "Free Blacks in Baltimore," 133, 138, 301–17; Seventh U.S. Census, 1850, Population Schedule, Baltimore City, NA; BC Tax, Series 1: General Property Tax Books, 1798–1915, microfilm reels BCA 165–71 [1856], BCA.

31. J. M. Wright, *Free Negro in Maryland*, 174–75, 178–81; Copy of Will of William Matthews, 27 June 1829, BC Miscellaneous, Series 5: Court Records, 1815–1921, box 1, BCA; Franklin, *From Slavery to Freedom*, 144.

32. Curry, *Free Black in Urban America*, 40.

33. Gardner, "Free Blacks in Baltimore," 161–64; Paul, "Shadow of Equality," 21; G. L. Browne, *Baltimore in the New Nation*, 288–89; Larsen, *Urban South*, 39.

34. Seventh and Eighth U.S. Census, 1850, 1860, Population Schedule, Baltimore City, NA; Schweninger, *Black Property Holders in the South*, 74–77; BC Tax, Series 1, microfilm reels BCA 165–71 [1856], BCA; J. M. Wright, *Free Negro in Maryland*, 185–86.

35. Seventh and Eighth U.S. Census, 1850, 1860, Population Schedule, Baltimore City, NA, cited in Schweninger, *Black Property Holders in the South*, 77; Wade, *Slavery in the Cities*, 326; J. M. Wright, *Free Negro in Maryland*, 184; Curry, *Free Black in Urban America*, 40–42, 267–68. In 1860 free blacks in Baltimore owned property

(real and personal) valued at $449,138, while whites owned property worth $127 million.

36. Curry, *Free Black in Urban America*, 40–41, 267–68; J. M. Wright, *Free Negro in Maryland*, 185; Gardner, "Free Blacks in Baltimore," 163–66, 197; Matchett, *Baltimore Directory for 1824*, 137. While the per capita average, derived by dividing the total worth of property among Baltimore whites and blacks by the respective populations, is inaccurate as an estimation of average property holdings, it provides a valuable comparative figure for the size of property holdings for the two groups.

37. Nash, *Forging Freedom*, 248; Curry, *Free Black in Urban America*, 267–68; Du Bois, *Philadelphia Negro*, 36–37; BC Tax, Series 1: General Property Tax Books, 1798–1915, microfilm reels BCA 165–71 [1856], BCA. The actual 1856 figure for Baltimore was $254,697.

38. Gardner, "Free Blacks in Baltimore," 301–17. Gardner has found a cumulative total of 362 holders of at least $500 worth of real property in Baltimore in 1850 and 1860, representing 1.4 percent of the 25,442 free blacks in Baltimore in 1850, the lower population of the two years surveyed.

39. Curry, *Free Black in Urban America*, 37–48, 267–71; Schweninger, *Black Property Owners in the South*, 76. Both Curry and Schweninger found that in 1850 free black women constituted slightly less than 10 percent of free black property owners in Baltimore.

40. First, Second, Third, Fourth, and Fifth U.S. Census, 1790, 1800, 1810, 1820, 1830, Population Schedule, Baltimore City, NA; Curry, *Free Black in Urban America*, 44–47; BC Tax, Series 1: General Property Tax Books, 1798–1915, BCA 177 [1798], BCA; Baltimore Assessment Record Book, 1815, Ms. 55, MHS; *Baltimore Directory and Citizen's Register, for 1808*, 108, 144; Gardner, "Free Blacks in Baltimore," 18–20.

41. Williamson, *New People*, 32; M. P. Johnson and Roark, *Black Masters*, passim; Graham, *Baltimore*, 73; Berlin, *Slaves without Masters*, 281–82 and n49 (quotes).

42. Quoted in Semmes, *Baltimore as Seen by Visitors*, 146–47.

43. *African Repository*, January 1834, 322, quoted in Berlin, *Slaves without Masters*, 279.

44. *Baltimore Sun*, 27–29 July 1852; Gardner, "Free Blacks in Baltimore," 229–30; Nash, *Forging Freedom*, 247; Hershberg and Williams, "Mulattoes and Blacks," 395–96. Others in elite standing were teamsters, stewards, carters, and barbers.

45. Eighth U.S. Census, 1860, Population Schedule, Ward 1 and 23, Baltimore City, NA.

46. D. R. Clark, "Baltimore," 126–27; Gregory, "Education of Blacks in Maryland," 114–16.

47. BCC, Register of Wills (Indentures), 1794–1799, 328–29, 1823–1826, 359–60, BA 0337, MdHR.

48. Brackett, *Negro in Maryland*, 198. The educational clause was stricken from the state's records in 1818, though subsequent indentures continued to carry it, probably out of custom.

49. Gardner, "Antebellum Black Education in Baltimore," 361; Matchett, *Baltimore Directory for 1824*, 317; Eighth U.S. Census, 1860, Population Schedule, Ward 1 and 23, Baltimore City, NA; BCC (Chattel Records), 1823–26, 359–60, BA 0298, MdHR (quotes). Herbert Gutman has maintained that one of the most pronounced differences between apprenticeships for whites and blacks was that black apprentices were not provided a formal education as part of their indenture. It would appear that at least in Baltimore this conclusion did not hold so completely. Gutman, *Black Family in Slavery and Freedom*, 402.

50. John W. Locks was a brother of Fernandis's wife and was a lifelong friend of Frederick Douglass. The Fernandis family remained one of Baltimore's most socially elite black families well into the twentieth century. Graham, *Baltimore*, 201–3; BC Tax, Series 1: General Property Tax Books, 1798–1915, microfilm reels BCA 165–71 [1856], BCA.

51. Litwack, *North of Slavery*, 181–82. Litwack finds that in the northern states, economic success was an especially important determinant of acceptance into the upper- and middle-class black community.

52. George, "Widening the Circle," 83–84; Jacob Fortie Journal, Fortie Family Papers, MdHR; Membership Roll, 1825–1853, microfilm reel M1383, Bethel, MdHR; Davis, *Narrative of the Life of Rev. Noah Davis*, 32–36. Davis wrote his book to "raise sufficient means to free his last two children from slavery," having already purchased his wife and five eldest children from their master in Virginia.

53. Jacob Fortie Journal, Fortie Family Papers, MdHR; Plan of Appointments, Baltimore City Station Methodist Episcopal Church, 1831–59, Lovely Lane; Baltimore City Charter Records, liber AI, no. 148, folio 346, BCH; Membership Roll, 1825–1853, microfilm reel M1383, Bethel, MdHR; Matchett, *Baltimore Directory for 1837–38*; Matchett, *Baltimore Directory, or Register of Householders, for 1842*; Matchett, *Baltimore Directory for 1853–54*; George, "Widening the Circle," 83.

54. Graham, *Baltimore*, 93–94, 149; Baltimore County Commissioners of the Tax, 1813 Assessment, Baltimore City, MSA C226, MdHR.

55. Mary Anne Dickerson Album/Scrapbook, LCP; Matchett, *Baltimore Directory, or Register of Householders, for 1842*, 448; [Murphy], *Baltimore Directory, for 1845*, 138; Matchett, *Baltimore Directory for 1847–48*, 391; Matchett, *Baltimore Directory for 1851*, 324; Winch, *Philadelphia's Black Elite*, 86–87, 140, 157–60, 192n61, 63.

56. Graham, *Baltimore*, 24–25, 93–94, 127–32, 263–64; Baltimore City Charter Records, liber AI, no. 48, folio 349, BCH; Gardner, "William Watkins," 623. Watkins's son, William J. Watkins, went on to become a prolific antislavery writer and lecturer in the North and assisted Frederick Douglass in publishing his newspaper, *North Star*. Watkins's niece, Frances Ellen Watkins also went on to become an accomplished antislavery speaker and writer, as well as one of the most renowned black American poets of the era. Quarles, *Negro in the Making of America*, 105.

57. Graham, *Baltimore*, 263–64; Clipping, Jacob Fortie Journal, Fortie Family Papers, MdHR.

58. Seventh U.S. Census, 1850, Population Schedule, Ward 1, 2, 3, 4, and 10, Baltimore City, NA.

59. The Baltimore figures approximate similar patterns in postbellum Philadelphia, where in 1880, 84.9 percent of mulatto males had mulatto wives, and 93.0 percent of black males had black wives. Hershberg and Williams, "Mulattoes and Blacks," 404–6. For a study of intraracial social stratification among postbellum African Americans, see Meier, *Negro Thought in America, 1880–1915,* 150–56.

60. *Baltimore Sun,* 24 February 1841.

61. Eighth U.S. Census, 1860, Population Schedule, Ward 17, Baltimore City, NA.

62. Davis, *Narrative of the Life of Rev. Noah Davis,* 35.

63. Graham, *Baltimore,* 62–63; Gregory, "Education of Blacks in Maryland," 74–75; Gardner, "Antebellum Black Education in Baltimore," 362–63; Baltimore City Station Class Records, 1799–1838, 10–14, Lovely Lane. When Coker became minister of the Bethel church, he also conducted classes there.

64. *Baltimore Gazette and Daily Advertiser,* 3 January 1810, quoted in Graham, *Baltimore,* 65 (first and second quotes), 77 (third quote); Gregory, "Education of Blacks in Maryland," 74–75; Perdue, *Black Laborers and Black Professionals in Early America,* 121; Woodson, *Education of the Negro prior to 1861,* 140; Gardner, "Antebellum Black Education in Baltimore," 363. George Collins left Baltimore for New York in 1822, where he assisted in founding of the African Methodist Episcopal Zion church.

65. Minutes of the Asbury Sunday School Society, 1816–1824, Lovely Lane; J. M. Wright, *Free Negro in Maryland,* 202; Gardner, "Free Blacks in Baltimore," 109–11; Gregory, "Education of Blacks in Maryland," 68–69.

66. *Baltimore American and Commercial Daily Advertiser,* 6 June 1805, quoted in Berlin, *Slaves without Masters,* 75 (first quote); Douglass, *My Bondage and My Freedom,* 145–46 (second quote); *Baltimore Sun,* 24 October 1839 (third quote); D. R. Clark, "Baltimore," 126–27.

67. Graham, *Baltimore,* 149–50; M. P. Johnson and Roark, *Black Masters,* 50, 223–24.

68. Payne, *Recollections of Seventy Years,* 78–79 (first quote); "Statisticks on Destitution in Baltimore," 278–79, quoted in Berlin, *Slaves without Masters,* 303 (second quote).

69. Davis, *Narrative of the Life of Rev. Noah Davis,* 84; G. L. Browne, *Baltimore in the Nation,* 194; Gardner, "Antebellum Black Education in Baltimore," 363; Gardner, "Free Blacks in Baltimore," 126; Berlin, *Slaves without Masters,* 304–5; Curry, *Free Black in Urban America,* 155–56.

70. Gardner, "Antebellum Black Education in Baltimore," 365; Graham, *Baltimore,* 93–95; *Genius of Universal Emancipation,* 8 October 1825 (first quote), 4 March 1826 (second quote). William Lively had formal training in medicine as well as classical literature prior to opening his school. He left the city for New York in the 1830s.

71. Gregory, "Education of Blacks in Maryland," 75–76; "Condition of the Colored Population of Baltimore," 169–71. Hiram Revels, later the first black man to serve in the U.S. Senate, also ran a day school in Baltimore in the 1850s.

72. Minutes of the Asbury Sunday School Society, 20 November 1820, Lovely Lane, cited in Gardner, "Free Blacks in Baltimore," 109–10.

73. E. A. Andrews, *Slavery and the Domestic Slave Trade*, 85–86, 92–93.

74. Ibid., 87 (first quote); Douglass, *My Bondage and My Freedom*, 155, 319 (second quote).

75. Coppin, *Unwritten History*, 17–18 (first quote); Rawick, ed., *American Slave*, 16:1–2 (second quote).

76. Frazier, *Free Negro Family*, 14; Eighth U.S. Census, 1860, Population Schedule, Baltimore City, NA.

77. Seventh U.S. Census, 1850, Population Schedule, Ward 1, 2, and 10, Baltimore City, NA; Eighth U.S. Census, 1860, Population Schedule, Ward 1, 2, and 17, Baltimore City, NA.

78. Free Negro Petitions to Leave the State of Maryland, BCC (Miscellaneous Court Papers), 1832–1845, MSA C1, MdHR. The court records do not include petitions for the year 1839; presumably these are lost. A total of 1,509 free Negroes of all ages filed petitions between 1832 and 1845, of whom 1,430 were aged ten or older.

79. Seventh U.S. Census, 1850, Population Schedule, Ward 1, 2, and 10, Baltimore City, NA; Eighth U.S. Census, 1860, Population Schedule, Ward 1, 2, and 17, Baltimore City, NA; Fields, *Slavery and Freedom on the Middle Ground*, 39; Watkins, *Address Delivered before the Moral Reform Society in Philadelphia*, 14, quoted in Gardner, "Antebellum Black Education in Baltimore," 360.

80. J. M. Wright, *Free Negro in Maryland*, 200n1; Baltimore City Charter Records, liber AI, no. 148, folio 346, BCH; Gregory, "Education of Blacks in Maryland," 70. Similarly, John Fernandis and his son Jonathan Fernandis were both recognized as prominent leaders of their communities; John was illiterate, yet his son was not.

81. Litwack, *North of Slavery*, 183–84; Seventh U.S. Census, 1850, Population Schedule, Baltimore City, cited in Schweninger, *Black Property Owners in the South*, 76.

82. Petition of Persons of Color Asking Aid for the Establishment of Colored Public Schools, 7 February 1850, BC Council, Series 1: Administrative Files, 1797–1923, box 87, item 456 (missing), BCA, cited in Gardner, "Free Blacks in Baltimore," 106–9; Matchett, *Baltimore Directory for 1840–41*; Matchett, *Baltimore Directory for 1845*; Matchett, *Baltimore Directory for 1849–50*; BC Tax, Series 1: General Property Tax Books, 1798–1915, microfilm reels BCA 165–71 [1856], BCA.

83. L. J. Williams, *Black Freemasonry and Middle-Class Realities*, 103–27; Muraskin, *Middle-Class Blacks in a White Society*, 25–27.

84. *Niles' Weekly Register*, 1835, quoted in Paul, "Shadow of Equality," 38.

85. E. Tyson, *Farewell Address of Elisha Tyson*, 4–5.

86. Curry, *Free Black in Urban America*, 196–99, 204; *Liberator*, 4 June 1831, cited in Graham, *Baltimore*, 114; J. M. Wright, *Free Negro in Maryland*, 250–51; *Niles' Weekly Register* 3 October 1835; Gardner, "Free Blacks in Baltimore," 169–72, 325–26; Perdue, *Black Laborers and Black Professionals in Early America*, 132; Franklin, *From Slavery to Freedom*, 167.

87. "Condition of the Colored Population of Baltimore," 174; "The Constitution and By Laws of the Free African Civilization Society of Baltimore," cited in Gardner, "Free Blacks in Baltimore," 169–70 (quote).

88. "Condition of the Colored Population of Baltimore," 174; "Our Baltimore Letter," *Weekly Anglo-African*, 20 August 1859, 7 January 1860; Graham, *Baltimore*, 259–60; Curry, *Free Black in Urban America*, 199–201.

89. Harriet Bacon's Certificate of Membership No. 2582, People's Union Association, 4 November 1852, Fortie Family Papers, MdHR.

90. "Condition of the Colored Population of Baltimore," 174–75; B. C. Thomas, "Baltimore Black Community," 253.

91. Graham, *Baltimore*, 132–33, 255–56; Gardner, "Free Blacks in Baltimore," 174–77; Curry, *Free Black in Urban America*, 203–6; Quarles, *Negro in the Making of America*, 98–99; Gregory, "Education of Blacks in Maryland," 30, 133–36.

92. Graham, *Baltimore*, 255–56; *Weekly Anglo-African*, 20 August 1859, 12 September 1859, 2 June 1860; Curry, *Free Black in Urban America*, 203–6; Gardner, "Free Blacks in Baltimore," 172–77; Gregory, "Education of Blacks in Maryland," 30, 133–36.

93. F. Cooper, "Elevating the Race," 619–25.

94. Graham, *Baltimore*, 278–80; J. M. Wright, *Free Negro in Maryland*, 250–52; Muraskin, *Middle-Class Blacks in a White Society*, 31–35; L. J. Williams, *Black Freemasonry and Middle-Class Realities*, 38–46. In 1775 in Boston, Prince Hall, a free West Indian mulatto and minister of the Methodist church, along with fifteen other free Negroes, founded the first black lodge, which grew from Hall's desire to raise the status of black men in America, both free and slave. Accepting as members only those known to have the highest moral character, Hall envisioned that by insisting on black self-improvement (including reliability, temperance, and moral rectitude), he and his members would provide impetus for both racial equality and black social leadership. The Prince Hall Masonic Fraternity had no national agency with authority to establish chapters; local lodges were affiliated with state-level grand lodges. The Philadelphia chapter boasted such members as Absalom Jones, Richard Allen, and James Forten.

95. G. L. Browne, *Baltimore in the New Nation*, 102; Berlin, *Slaves without Masters*, 247–48, 308–15; "Condition of the Colored Population of Baltimore," 174–75; quoted in Clayton, *Black Baltimore*, 41–42; Curry, *Free Black in Urban America*, 92, 209–12.

96. *Weekly Anglo-African*, 8 August 1859; Baltimore Sun, 1 January, 10 March 1854, 11–12 May 1859; Graham, *Baltimore*, 254–55; Franklin, *From Slavery to Freedom*, 167; Wade, *Slavery in the Cities*, 143–48; Paul, "Shadow of Equality," 38.

97. *Anglo-African Magazine*, 20 August 1859, 2–39, quoted in Graham, *Baltimore*, 254–55.

98. Berlin, *Slaves without Masters*, 314–15; Curry, *Free Black in Urban America*, 212–13; *Genius of Universal Emancipation*, August 1825, 170 (quote). Gary Nash has found that black Philadelphians found other days to celebrate as well, in part from hostile white exclusion of blacks from Fourth of July festivities. Nash, *Forging Freedom*, 177, 189.

99. Curry, *Free Black in Urban America*, 208–12; Franklin, *From Slavery to Freedom*, 167; Graham, *Baltimore*, 276–77.

100. "The Constitution and By Laws of the Free African Civilization Society of Baltimore," quoted in Gardner, "Free Blacks in Baltimore," 169–70.

101. *Weekly Anglo-African*, 7 October 1859, 18 February 1860; Woods, *Woods' Baltimore City Directory*; Graham, *Baltimore*, 279.

102. Du Bois, *Souls of Black Folk*, 17.

Chapter 7: "Cursed with Freedom"

1. Fields, *Slavery and Freedom on the Middle Ground*, 7 (quote), 22.

2. Quoted in M. P. Johnson and Roark, *Black Masters*, 225.

3. G. L. Browne, *Baltimore in the Nation*, 82–86, 107–10.

4. Ibid., 117–36; Fields, *Slavery and Freedom on the Middle Ground*, 42–44; Paul, "Shadow of Equality," 11; Sixth and Eighth U.S. Census, 1840, 1860, Manufacturing Schedule, Baltimore City, NA.

5. G. L. Browne, *Baltimore in the Nation*, 107–10, 132–33.

6. "Disbursement of Poor Relief, 1st District," 1810, BC Miscellaneous, Series 1: Reports and Returns, 1798–1925, box 4, BCA; Minutes of the Board of Trustees for the Poor of Baltimore City and County, 1833–1841, Record Group 19, Series 1: HRS Records, 1798–1882, box 8, item 237, box 14, item 264, box 19, items 261–62, 267, BCA; D. G. Carroll and Coll, "Baltimore Almshouse," 139–40; "Reports on the Almshouse," BC Commissioners, Series 1: Administrative Files, 1827–28, item 287, BCA.

7. *Baltimore Sun*, 22 February 1838, quoted in Berlin, *Slaves without Masters*, 232–33 (first quote); *Baltimore Sun*, 16 September 1839, 16 October 1839, 1 June 1840 (second quote); J. M. Wright, *Free Negro in Maryland*, 248–49; D. G. Carroll and Coll, "Baltimore Almshouse," 141; Scharf, *History of Baltimore City and County*, 1:204.

8. Between 1840 and 1860 the percentage of black inmates at the Baltimore almshouse remained consistently higher than the percentage of blacks in the general population. From 1850 to 1860 black inmates constituted less than 10 percent of those held there, primarily because they were increasingly placed in the city jail and state penitentiary or sold as term slaves. Morris, "Labor Controls in Maryland," 385–400; Morris, "Measure of Bondage in the Slave States," 231–39.

9. Baltimore City and County Commissioners of Insolvency Debtors, Insolvency Docket, 1817, 1818, 1849–1850, BC 0339, MdHR; Curry, *Free Black in Urban America*, 117. The 1849 statistics are for those insolvencies between 25 May and 25 November.

10. Curry, *Free Black in Urban America*, 136–37; Berlin, *Slaves without Masters*, 259; E. A. Andrews, *Slavery and the Domestic Slave Trade*, 43 (first quote), 45 (second quote).

11. Curry, *Free Black in Urban America*, 136–37.

12. Ibid., 139; Paul, "Shadow of Equality," 19; "Report of the Board of Health," in *Ordinances and Resolutions of the City Council of Baltimore*, appendix, xxiii.

13. Buckler, *History of Epidemic Cholera*, 8–11, 16–17.

14. Gardner, "Free Blacks in Baltimore," 188–97; Wade, *Slavery in the Cities*, 134, 141; Buckler, *History of Epidemic Cholera*, 13–14, 30–32 (first quote); Howard, *Public Health Administration and the Natural History of Disease in Baltimore*, 508–9 (second quote).

15. Report of the Trustees for the Poor of Baltimore City and County, 1844, BC Miscellaneous, Series 6: Miscellaneous Administrative Papers, 1807–1927, box 1, BCA; Baltimore Eastern Dispensary Records, 1818–1894, vol. 1, Ms. 1894, MHS; J. M. Wright, *Free Negro in Maryland*, 249. During the 1840s the average percentage of blacks admitted annually to the city's Eastern Dispensary was 39.5 percent. In the 1850s that average percentage fell to 19.8.

16. Paul, "Shadow of Equality," 16. I have used Paul's tables on deaths in Baltimore from 1824 to 1860 for these figures.

17. *Niles' Weekly Register*, 16 April 1825 (first quote), 8 September 1832 (second quote), cited in J. M. Wright, *Free Negro in Maryland*, 247; *Niles' Weekly Register*, 15 September 1832 (third quote), quoted in Berlin, *Slaves without Masters*, 259. Niles, a Quaker, moved to Baltimore from Wilmington, Delaware (where he was an officer in the state's abolition society), in 1806. After editing the *Evening Post*, a Federalist newspaper, in 1811 he left it to found the *Niles' Weekly Register*. Malone, ed., *Dictionary of American Biography*, 13:521–22.

18. "Report of the Consulting Physician," *Ordinances and Resolutions of the City Council of Baltimore*, 1829, xxiii, quoted in Gardner, "Free Blacks in Baltimore," 191.

19. Brugger, *Maryland*, 210–15; Berlin, *Slaves without Masters*, 208–12.

20. Reenslavement of free blacks often occurred as a consequence of their being jailed as suspected runaways. Freedpersons unable to document their status might be held for as much as ninety days and then could be sold back into slavery for a stipulated term of service to pay the jail fees. That abuses of this law resulted in permanent reenslavement of free blacks caused a concerned legislature to amend Maryland's slave code in 1817 and 1818. *Laws of Maryland*, 1817, chap. 72, and 1818, chap. 197. For a full discussion of the slave laws of Maryland, see Brackett, *Negro in Maryland*, 26–174.

21. Berlin, "Structure of the Free Negro Caste," 307; Franklin, *From Slavery to Freedom*, 162–63; Brackett, *Negro in Maryland*, 77, 183–217; Gardner, "Free Blacks in Baltimore," 34; J. M. Wright, *Free Negro in Maryland*, 343; D. R. Clark, "Baltimore," 234–35; I. D. Reid, *Negro Community of Baltimore*, 7–8; Fields, *Slavery and Freedom on the Middle Ground*, 35; Van Ness, "Economic Development, Social and Cultural Changes," 231–33; Brugger, *Maryland*, 212. Free blacks were forbidden by law from pursuing only two trades: traveling peddlars and captains of vessels larger than scows and shallow water crafts, although in Baltimore blacks found exemptions to this legislation. The 1818 enactment that allowed free Negro lawbreakers to be sold into term servitude rather than be sentenced to jail was overturned by an 1826 enactment, when such bondpeople were being sold out of state into slavery.

22. Berlin, *Slaves without Masters*, 136; Wade, *Slavery in the Cities*, 250–51.

23. Franklin, *From Slavery to Freedom*, 157; Van Ness, "Economic Development, Social and Cultural Changes," 159–60; Fields, *Slavery and Freedom on the Middle Ground*, 24–25, 69–71, 84.

24. Fields, *Slavery and Freedom on the Middle Ground*, 24–25, 69–71, 84.

25. *Niles' Weekly Register*, 17 September 1831. Niles's opposition to free Negroes stemmed from his estimation that white masters had far too quickly thrust freedom on these former bondpeople, who had not had the opportunity to acquire life skills necessary in a free society (especially the management of property). "Blacks should be invested with correct ideas of the social duties or moral virtues," he wrote, "that they can have tolerable notions about *property.*" Moreover, Niles believed that free blacks were still largely slaves in habit, and because masters had not provided their soon-to-be-freed bondpeople with those vital bourgeois qualities of honesty, frugality, and industry, they would not be able to abandon the intemperate behaviors intrinsic in the denial of personal liberty—a tendency only reinforced by the constant interaction of free people of color and slaves in Baltimore's laissez-faire environment. "The benighted mind of a negro," reasoned the editor, "cannot shake them off, though emancipated, but by the exertion of virtues that would exalt a white man to a high rank in society." Though Niles opposed African colonization (he actually proposed a scheme of "internal colonization," by which twelve thousand young slave women would be sent annually to the North, where they would serve in households for a term of years and then be freed, thus allowing the inculcation of those virtues—and extirpation of vices—through "*moral force,*" which would "amalgamate" the races socially, and the exceedingly gradual elimination of slavery by the reduction of both the general slave population and its means of natural increase), the idea found especially great support in Maryland. That Niles called for more gradual manumission practices is ironic given the predilection Baltimore masters had long shown for such lengthy terms of service as part of bestowing freedom. *Niles' Weekly Register*, 2 December 1815, 22 May 1819.

26. *Ordinances and Resolutions of the City Council of Baltimore*, 1846, 156, quoted in Wade, *Slavery in the Cities*, 250.

27. Harper, *Letter from General Harper*, 6–7, 8–10.

28. *African Repository*, 1825, quoted in Litwack, *North of Slavery*, 20–23; Staudenraus, *African Colonization Movement*, 12–22; *Baltimore American and Commercial Daily Advertiser*, 23 January 1821 (quotes), 30 January 1821.

29. *Niles' Weekly Register*, 22 May 1819.

30. Prior to the incorporation of the Maryland State Colonization Society (MSCS) in 1831, several short-lived emigration societies were formed in Baltimore. The Maryland Haytien Company formed in 1819 in Baltimore as an alternative to the African movement. Several more groups emerged following the formation of the MSCS, including those promoting emigration to Trinidad and British Guiana. Graham, *Baltimore*, 77–78; Campbell, *Maryland in Africa*, 10–11, passim.

31. Quoted in Semmes, *John H. B. Latrobe and His Times*, 168.

32. Alford, *Prince among Slaves*, 130–31; Dillon, *Benjamin Lundy*, 87–103; *Genius*

of Universal Emancipation, June 1825, 142 (quote). Ibrahima ultimately sailed for Liberia from Baltimore.

33. Staudenraus, *African Colonization Movement,* 232–33; Campbell, *Maryland in Africa,* 34–37.

34. La Rochefoucald-Liancourt, *Travels through the United States,* 2:281 (quote); Brackett, *Negro in Maryland,* 233.

35. Brackett, *Negro in Maryland,* 233; *Genius of Universal Emancipation,* 5 March 1830 (quote).

36. Berlin, *Slaves without Masters,* 90 (quote), 364–72.

37. Eighth U.S. Census, 1860, Population Schedule, Baltimore City, NA; Swisher, *Roger B. Taney,* 92–98, 152–54; Litwack, *North of Slavery,* 52–53 (first quote); Fredrickson, *Black Image in the White Mind,* 50–51 (second quote). Ironically, despite Taney's famous ruling on black citizenship, he supported state legislation and other attempts to protect free Negroes from societal abuses and served as counselor of a rural branch of Baltimore's Free Negro Protection Society. Moreover, he demonstrated an interest in the welfare of colored people not only by manumitting his own slaves but also by purchasing other slaves to enable them to work out their freedom, lending a free Negro the purchase price of his slave wife, and supporting elderly slaves unable to earn their own livings.

38. G. Wright, *Political Economy of the Cotton South,* 125.

39. Susanna Warfield Diaries, 8 March 1849, Ms. 760, MHS; Graham, *Baltimore,* 11.

40. Lundy published his newspaper, the *Genius of Universal Emancipation,* in Baltimore from 1826 until 1839. In 1829 Lundy convinced Garrison to move from Bennington, Vermont, to Baltimore to serve as coeditor of the newspaper. Both men were persecuted for their outspoken antislavery beliefs in the growing racial antipathy of Baltimore. In 1828 Lundy was nearly killed in a confrontation with Austin Woolfolk for his written attacks on the slave trader, while Garrison spent three months in jail in 1830 after being convicted for libel for his condemnation of a ship captain from his hometown of Newburyport, Massachusetts, for transporting slaves. Filler, *Crusade against Slavery,* 25–27, 57–59; Dillon, *Abolitionists,* 30; G. L. Browne, *Baltimore in the Nation,* 100–101.

41. *Genius of Universal Emancipation,* August–September 1825; G. L. Browne, *Baltimore in the Nation,* 100–101.

42. Brackett, *Negro in Maryland,* 246; Wesley, *Negro Labor in the United States,* 15; *Planters' Advocate,* 15 June 1859, quoted in Fields, *Slavery and Freedom on the Middle Ground,* 88. In 1794, prior to the new state constitution of 1810, Baltimore white mechanics had actually blocked a provision in the city's charter disfranchising blacks, as it ran "contrary to reason and good policy, to the spirit of equal liberty and our free constitution." Steffen, *Mechanics of Baltimore,* 131.

43. Steuart, *Letter to John L. Carey,* 5–6.

44. Larsen, *Urban South,* 44–45; Fields, *Slavery and Freedom on the Middle Ground,* 47, 57; Wade, *Slavery in the Cities,* 325; Arfwedson, *United States and Canada,* 1:308–9 (first quote); Susanna Warfield Diaries, 7 April 1849, MHS (second quote).

45. Brackett, *Negro in Maryland*, 246–47; Gardner, "Free Blacks in Baltimore," 8–10; Fields, *Slavery and Freedom on the Middle Ground*, xi–xii; John P. Kennedy to Edward Johnson, 11 December 1822, BC Mayor, box 3, item 492, BCA (quote).

46. "Report of the Committee on Colored Population," *Maryland Legislative Documents*, doc. M, 47.

47. Brackett, *Negro in Maryland*, 176–77.

48. G. L. Browne, *Baltimore in the Nation*, 100; Brackett, *Negro in Maryland*, 218–19; Curry, *Free Black in Urban America*, 84–87.

49. Baltimore City Archives Collection (Miscellaneous Court Papers, Index), 1831–1892, BC 0220, MdHR.

50. J. M. Wright, *Free Negro in Maryland*, 306–7; Berlin, *Slaves without Masters*, 185–86.

51. Brackett, *Negro in Maryland*, 236–37; Ezekial Butler to Ben Thomas, 21 September 1831, box 7, item 463, BCA (first quote); "To the Editors of the Comm[ercial] Chronicle & D[aily] Marylander," 26 September 1831, BC Mayor, box 7, item 464, BCA (second quote).

52. James Christian to Jacob Small, 18 November 1831, BC Mayor, box 7, item 462, BCA.

53. *Laws of Maryland*, 1831, chap. 281, 323.

54. Brackett, *Negro in Maryland*, 236–37.

55. *Laws of Maryland*, 1831, chap. 281, 323; Brackett, *Negro in Maryland*, 236–37; I. D. Reid, *Negro Community of Baltimore*, 8–9; Gardner, "Free Blacks in Baltimore," 24; J. M. Wright, *Free Negro in Maryland*, 268–70; *Liberator*, 18 August 1832, cited in Graham, *Baltimore*, 101–2. Gardiner was acquitted of the offense on the grounds that he had been ill during his stay, which had prevented him from leaving.

56. Brackett, *Negro in Maryland*, 201–2, 209–10, 229 (first quote), 240–41 (second quote); P. S. Foner and Lewis, eds., *Black Worker*, 1:89 (third quote).

57. D. R. Clark, "Baltimore," 235. By the 1850s more than 50 percent of all inmates in the Maryland penitentiary were free Negroes, a figure that contrasted sharply with percentages in the Deep South. Ayers, *Vengeance and Justice*, 61, 295n57.

58. Quoted in Strickland, *Life of Jacob Gruber*, 323.

59. Petitions of Blacks for Permits for Gatherings, 1838, BC Mayor, box 19, items 1221–33, BCA; Petitions of Blacks for Passes, 1838, BC Mayor, box 19, items 1282–86, BCA; *Baltimore Sun*, 1 January 1841 (quote). In 1858 the curfew ordinance was amended to include potential fines of five to ten dollars per person for violation. Brackett, *Negro in Maryland*, 202, 205.

60. G. L. Browne, *Baltimore in the Nation*, 90–91, 145; Foreign Passenger Bonds, 1834, Record Group 55: Foreign Passengers, BCA.

61. G. L. Browne, *Baltimore in the Nation*, 190–92; Van Ness, "Economic Development, Social and Cultural Changes," 180, 212–13.

62. G. L. Browne, *Baltimore in the Nation*, 190–92; Van Ness, "Economic Development, Social and Cultural Changes," 180, 213; Campbell, *Maryland in Africa*, 15–16; Fields, *Slavery and Freedom on the Middle Ground*, 44.

63. G. Wright, *Political Economy of the Cotton South*, 121–25; Starobin, *Industrial Slavery in the Old South*, 119; Litwack, *North of Slavery*, 163–64; Fields, *Slavery and Freedom on the Middle Ground*, 55.

64. Fields, *Slavery and Freedom on the Middle Ground*, 3–4, 70–71, 86–87; Quarles, *Negro in the Making of America*, 89; MacLeod, "Toward Caste," 220; Curry, *Free Black in Urban America*, 33–34; Fifth, Sixth, Seventh, and Eighth U.S. Census, 1830, 1840, 1850, 1860, Population Schedule, Baltimore City, NA.

65. E. A. Andrews, *Slavery and the Domestic Slave Trade*, 73.

66. J. C. G. Kennedy, *Abstract of the Statistics of Manufactures*, 143; *Manufactures of the United States in 1860*, 228; G. L. Browne, *Baltimore in the Nation*, 182–84.

67. Berlin, *Slaves without Masters*, 231–32; Litwack, *North of Slavery*, 162–66; Curry, *Free Black in Urban America*, 83; Wesley, *Negro Labor in the United States*, 75–77; Petition by Workers of the City, 1845, BC Miscellaneous, Series 6: Miscellaneous Papers, 1807–1927, box 1, BCA; C. Mackay, *Life and Liberty in America*, cited in Semmes, *Baltimore as Seen by Visitors*, 115, 170 (quote).

68. Steuart, *Letter to John L. Carey*, 6.

69. John H. B. Latrobe to Thomas Suffern, *Maryland Colonization Journal*, October 1851, 71.

70. Della, "Analysis of Baltimore's Population," 21, 34–35; Perdue, *Black Laborers and Black Professionals in Early America*, 51; Steffen, *Mechanics of Baltimore*, 27, 47; Gardner, "Free Blacks in Baltimore," 279 (first quote); Johnston, *Notes on North America*, 2:315 (second quote).

71. Quoted in Steffen, *Mechanics of Baltimore*, 131. The Maryland Abolition Society, organized in 1797, was composed almost exclusively of artisans. Berlin, *Slaves without Masters*, 28n19.

72. Berlin, *Slaves without Masters*, 28, 60, 81, 192–93, 227–30, 234–37, 349–54; Wade, *Slavery in the Cities*, 274–75; J. M. Wright, *Free Negro in Maryland*, 161–65, 264; Wesley, *Negro Labor in the United States*, 78; Litwack, *North of Slavery*, 154–59; L. Greene and Woodson, *Negro Wage Earner*, 15–16; Della, "Analysis of Baltimore's Population," 22–23, 34–35; Della, "Problems of Negro Labor," 19–20; Fields, *Slavery and Freedom on the Middle Ground*, 205; G. L. Browne, *Baltimore in the Nation*, 100. Gary Nash and Shane White have each found similar developments in Philadelphia and New York, respectively. Nash, *Forging Freedom*; S. White, "'We Dwell in Safety.'"

73. Petition of Sundry Citizens to Prohibit Persons of Colour to Obtain Licenses to Drive Hacks, Carts, and Drays &c., 23 January 1828, BC Council, Series 1: Administrative Files, 1797–1923, box 36, item 425, BCA (quotes); Seventh U.S. Census, 1850, Population Schedule, Baltimore City, NA; Curry, *Free Black in Urban America*, 18–19; Gardner, "Free Blacks in Baltimore," 145–46; Berlin, *Slaves without Masters*, 231.

74. *Regulations of the Baltimore Cemetery*, 3 (first quote); Report of the Joint Standing Committee on Markets on the Petition of Franklin Brown and Others, 19 May 1858, BC Council, Series 1: Administrative Files, 1797–1923, box 110, item 500, BCA (second quote); Brackett, *Negro in Maryland*, 210.

75. Fields, *Slavery and Freedom on the Middle Ground,* 46–47; Curry, *Free Black in Urban America,* 98, 108–11, 303n3; *Baltimore American and Commercial Daily Advertiser,* 28 October 1822, quoted in Alexander, "Stendhal and Violence on the Baltimore Stage," 71.

76. Jordan, *White over Black,* 425; Wade, *Slavery in the Cities,* 173–74, 271–72; *Baltimore Sun,* 27 November 1837 (first quote), 6 August 1840 (second quote).

77. *Baltimore Sun,* 28 August 1838 (quote), 30 August 1838, 11 September 1838; Petition of Doctor Bond and Others, 30 August 1838, BC Mayor, box 17, item 402, BCA. The *Sun* condemned the riot, and, prompted by petitions from outraged white citizens, including a committee of the Methodist Episcopal Church's City Station, Mayor Samuel Smith offered a hundred dollar reward for apprehension of those involved.

78. *Maryland Journal and Baltimore Advertiser,* 25 June 1793, quoted in Berlin, *Slaves without Masters,* 42 (first quote); Douglass, *Life and Times,* 546; Douglass, *My Bondage and My Freedom,* 169–70 (second quote).

79. Douglass, *My Bondage and My Freedom,* 311 (first quote), 314 (second and third quotes).

80. Berlin, *Slaves without Masters,* 346–47 (first quote); Douglass, *My Bondage and My Freedom,* 315 (second quote).

81. Della, "Problems of Negro Labor," 26; Boyd, *Baltimore City Directory,* 391; Woods, *Woods' Baltimore City Directory,* 106; Gardner, "Free Blacks in Baltimore," 152; *Baltimore Sun,* 18 May 1858 (first quote), 19 May 1858 (second quote).

82. *Baltimore American and Commercial Daily Advertiser,* 5 July 1858 (first quote), 8 July 1858, 28 June 1859; Berlin, *Slaves without Masters,* 349–50; Della, "Problems of Negro Labor," 26–27; Boyd, *Baltimore City Directory,* 298; *Baltimore Sun,* 8 July 1858 (second quote).

83. *Baltimore American and Commercial Daily Advertiser,* 28 June 1859; *Baltimore Sun,* 3 June 1859, 29 June 1859; Della, "Problems of Negro Labor," 27; Gardner, "Free Blacks in Baltimore," 154–55.

84. Morris, "Labor Controls in Maryland," 386.

85. Della, "Problems of Negro Labor," 27–28; Douglass quoted in Litwack, *North of Slavery,* 166. Della has estimated that Negro labor declined as much as 38.8 percent, basing his figure on the city directories from 1849 and 1860.

86. BC Tax, Series 1: General Property Tax Books, 1798–1915, microfilm reels BCA 165–71 [1856], BCA; Della, "Problems of Negro Labor," 28; Seventh U.S. Census, 1850, Population Schedule, Baltimore City, NA.

87. Morris, "Labor Controls in Maryland," 392–93.

88. Brackett, *Negro in Maryland,* 171.

89. Ibid., 230–34.

90. Clayton, *Black Baltimore,* 7; Morris, "Labor Controls in Maryland," 398n51.

91. M. P. Johnson and Roark, *Black Masters,* 160–65.

92. Berlin, *Slaves without Masters,* 374–75; Jacobs, *Speech of Col. Curtis [W.] Jacobs,* 2; Brackett, *Negro in Maryland,* 242–46, 252–56; J. M. Wright, *Free Negro in Maryland,* 307–14; Gardner, "Free Blacks in Baltimore," 274–76; Fields, *Slavery and*

Freedom on the Middle Ground, 74–76; *Baltimore American and Commercial Daily Advertiser*, 9 June 1859 (first quote), 10 June 1859; *Baltimore Sun*, 9 June 1859 (second quote).

93. *New York Tribune*, 11 June 1859, 14 June 1859, quoted in Wesley, *Negro Labor in the United States*, 32–33.

94. *Baltimore American and Commercial Daily Advertiser*, 9 June 1859, 10 June 1859; *Baltimore Sun*, 9 June 1859, 10 June 1859 (quote); Berlin, *Slaves without Masters*, 374–75; Brackett, *Negro in Maryland*, 242–46, 252–56; J. M. Wright, *Free Negro in Maryland*, 307–14; Gardner, "Free Blacks in Baltimore," 274–76; Fields, *Slavery and Freedom on the Middle Ground*, 74–76. The 1842 convention submitted a bill designed "for the better security of negro slaves in this state, and for promoting industry and honesty amongst the free people of color." The bill passed the House, 40-31, but that March it was rejected by the Senate, 15-6.

95. *Baltimore Sun*, 10 June 1859 (first quote); J. M. Wright, *Free Negro in Maryland*, 305–6; Fields, *Slavery and Freedom on the Middle Ground*, 77; Jacobs, *Speech on the Free Colored Population*, 13 (second quote).

96. Jacobs, *Free Negro Question in Maryland*, 20.

97. Ibid., 19–20 (quote); *Baltimore American and Commercial Daily Advertiser*, 10 June 1859; Gardner, "Free Blacks in Baltimore," 276–79.

98. *Planters' Advocate*, 19 October 1859, 26 October 1859, cited in Fields, *Slavery and Freedom on the Middle Ground*, 77; *Baltimore Sun*, 14 December 1859, quoted in Berlin, *Slaves without Masters*, 374–75. In the wake of the incident at the caulkers' ball, in 1860 Baltimore strengthened its 1858 ordinance forcing free Negroes to obtain the mayor's written permission for gatherings by requiring that all such gatherings also have white supervision. Della, "Analysis of Baltimore's Population," 28.

99. Fields, *Slavery and Freedom on the Middle Ground*, 76–77. Five of the seven committee members were from the Eastern Shore.

100. Fields, *Slavery and Freedom on the Middle Ground*, 83; "Report of the Committee on Colored Population to the Legislature of Maryland," 1 February 1860, *Maryland House Documents*, 1860, doc. O, quoted in Brackett, *Negro in Maryland*, 258.

101. M. P. Johnson and Roark, *Black Masters*, 160–68; Wikramanayake, *World in Shadow*, 160–70. During the winter of 1859 and 1860 nearly every southern legislature debated free Negro enslavement; only Arkansas actually passed such a bill. Arkansas had the smallest free black population in the slave states, which made such action feasible.

102. Fields, *Slavery and Freedom on the Middle Ground*, 78–79; Brackett, *Negro in Maryland*, 258–60; J. M. Wright, *Free Negro in Maryland*, 314–15; *Weekly Anglo-African*, 18 February 1860, quoted in Gardner, "Free Blacks in Baltimore," 279–81.

103. Quoted in Fields, *Slavery and Freedom on the Middle Ground*, 78–79.

104. Jacobs, *Speech of Col. Curtis [W.] Jacobs*, 8, 12–13.

105. J. Hall, *Address to the Free People of Color of the State of Maryland*, 1–3.

Chapter 8: "Freedom Shall Not Perish"

1. Campbell, *Maryland in Africa*, 11–12, 20, 38–41; Staudenraus, *African Colonization Movement*, 17–30; Matchett, *Baltimore Directory, Corrected up to May 1833*, 85.

2. R. S. Finley to J. H. B. Latrobe, 8 August 1832, Correspondence Received, Letter Books, microfilm reel 1, MSCS.

3. R. S. Finley to J. H. B. Latrobe, 8 August 1832, Correspondence Received, Letter Books, microfilm reel 1, MSCS. For background information, see Campbell, *Maryland in Africa*, 39–42.

4. R. S. Finley to J. H. B. Latrobe, 8 August 1832, Correspondence Received, Letter Books, microfilm reel 1, MSCS (first quote); William McKenney to Charles Howard, 4 May 1833, Correspondence Received, Letter Books, microfilm reel 1, MSCS (second quote).

5. William McKenney to Charles Howard, 4 May 1833, Correspondence Received, Letter Books, microfilm reel 1, MSCS (first quote); James Hall to George Winthrop, 7 July 1842, Correspondence Sent, Agents' Books, microfilm reel 17, MSCS (second quote).

6. Berlin, *Slaves without Masters*, 66–67; Gregory, "Education of Blacks in Maryland, 35; Curry, *Free Black in Urban America*, 196–97.

7. Coker, *Journal of Daniel Coker*, 44. The American Colonization Society published Coker's letters and journal both in the newspapers and in pamphlet form, as important elements in its efforts to relocate blacks to Africa.

8. Charles B. Hooper to Rev. George Whipple, 14 December 1855, microfilm reel 79, Maryland roll 1, letter 49732, AMA.

9. *Genius of Universal Emancipation* 16 September 1826, 23 September 1826, 4 November 1826, 11 November 1826; *Freedom's Journal*, 18 May 1827; Graham, *Baltimore*, 97–99. Graham infers that the anonymous respondent quite likely was William Watkins.

10. *African Repository*, December 1826, 296–97. My thanks to John Saillant for providing me with this memorial.

11. Charles C. Harper to R. R. Gurley, 3 January 1827, American Colonization Society Papers, quoted in Graham, *Baltimore*, 99.

12. *Methodist*, 2 January 1919, 16; *Genius of Universal Emancipation*, 27 November 1829; quoted in Graham, *Baltimore*, 103–4.

13. For more complete discussions of the end of British slavery, see Mathieson, *British Slave Emancipation;* and Craton, *Sinews of Empire*.

14. Mathieson, *British Slave Emancipation*, 89–101; Peck and Price, *Report of Messrs. Peck and Price*, 3–4 (quotes); Matchett, *Baltimore Directory for 1840–41*, 281, 290.

15. Peck and Price, *Report of Messrs. Peck and Price*, 5–6.

16. Ibid., 14 (first quote), 15 (second quote).

17. Ibid., 17 (quotes).

18. E. Foner, *Reconstruction*, 173–75; J. D. Reid, "Antebellum Southern Rental Contracts," 32; Bode and Ginter, *Farm Tenancy and the Census for Antebellum Georgia*.

19. Peck and Price, *Report of Messrs. Peck and Price*, 22–24, 25 (quote).

20. *Baltimore Sun*, 4 April 1840, 13 April 1840.

21. Free Negro Petitions to Leave the State, BCC (Miscellaneous Court Papers), 1840–1841, MSA C1, MdHR; *Baltimore Sun*, 13 April 1840, 16 April 1840.

22. Peck and Price, though critical of the lack of opportunity for mechanics in Trinidad, did interview several black expatriates from New York who were employed as carpenters and "who said they were satisfied, and were doing well." Peck and Price, *Report of Messrs. Peck and Price*, 22–25 (quote on 23).

23. Free Negro Petitions to Leave the State, BCC (Miscellaneous Court Papers), 1840–1841, MSA C1, MdHR; Matchett, *Baltimore Directory for 1837–38*, passim. Sixteen of thirty-two were listed as laborers, while the remaining sixteen held such occupations as carter, drayman, porter, waiter, barber, caulker, and boot black.

24. Free Negro Petitions to Leave the State, BCC (Miscellaneous Court Papers), 1840–1841, MSA C1, MdHR; *Baltimore Sun*, 28 December 1840, 16 January 1841.

25. Matchett, *Baltimore Directory for 1837–38*, 50; Matchett, *Baltimore Directory for 1840–41*, passim.

26. Petition of Thomas Winston, 4 August 1846, Baltimore County Register of Wills (Petitions), MSA T621, MdHR.

27. Ibid.

28. Campbell, *Maryland in Africa*, 175–77; Brackett, *Negro in Maryland*, 241–42; Manumissions and Emigrants, Manumission Books, Lists and Manumissions, Copies (1832–1860), microfilm reel 25, MSCS.

29. Latrobe, *Colonization*, 25.

30. Quoted in Stopak, "Maryland State Colonization Society," 278.

31. *Genius of Universal Emancipation*, August 1825, quoted in Berlin, *Slaves without Masters*, 314–15.

32. *Genius of Universal Emancipation*, 27 November 1829, quoted in Berlin, *Slaves without Masters*, 204.

33. *Liberator*, 4 June 1831 (quote); Garrison, *Thoughts on African Colonization*, 55–56.

34. *Genius of Universal Emancipation*, 13 November 1829 (quote), 27 November 1829.

35. *Niles' Weekly Register*, 3 October 1835 (quotes).

36. Quoted in Brackett, *Negro in Maryland*, 204n1.

37. William Watkins to William L. Garrison, 31 September 1835, William L. Garrison Papers, Manuscripts Division, Boston Public Library, quoted in Graham, *Baltimore*, 119 (first quote); Gardner, "'Opposition to Emigration,'" 157 (second quote).

38. *Freedom's Journal*, 18 May 1827; Garrison, *Thoughts on African Colonization*, 21–22; Curry, *Free Black in Urban America*, 234; Graham, *Baltimore*, 97–99; Dillon, *Benjamin Lundy*, 89, 145; quoted in Berlin, *Slaves without Masters*, 204–5.

39. J. M. Wright, *Free Negro in Maryland*, 289; Graham, *Baltimore*, 98–99; quoted in Garrison, *Thoughts on African Colonization*, 21–22.

40. Quoted in Berlin, *Slaves without Masters*, 207.

41. Quoted in Campbell, *Maryland in Africa*, 27–28.

42. James Hall to William Watkins, 18 May 1841, Correspondence Sent, Agents' Books, microfilm reel 17, MSCS; Watkins to Hall, 24 May 1841, Correspondence Sent, Agents' Books, microfilm reel 17, MSCS.

43. "Typical Colonization Convention," 321–22.

44. *Baltimore Sun*, 27–29 July 1852; "Typical Colonization Convention," 338 (quote). The Baltimore hog law provided that swine could roam at will in the city streets to eat garbage during the summer months but were to be confined during the winter months.

45. *Baltimore Sun*, 27–29 July 1852; Berlin, *Slaves without Masters*, 357–59; Brackett, *Negro in Maryland*, 251–52; Gardner, "Free Blacks in Baltimore," 229–36; "Typical Colonization Convention," 318–38 (quotes).

46. Charles C. Harper to Robert R. Gurley, 1 August 1832, State Manager's Letterbook, microfilm reel 1, MSCS (quote); *Frederick Douglass's Paper*, 6 August 1852, cited in Bell, *Survey of the Negro Convention Movement*, 147; Sweet, *Black Images of America*, 36n3; Manumissions and Emigrants, Manumission Books, Lists and Manumissions, Copies (1832–1860), microfilm reel 25, MSCS.

47. Horton, *Free People of Color*, 21. See the discussion of delegates to the 1852 colonizationist convention in chapter 6 of this book.

48. Gregory, "Education of Blacks in Maryland," 110–16; Van Ness, "Economic Development, Social and Cultural Changes," 203–4.

49. Berlin, *Slaves without Masters*, 305–6, 346–47; Woodson, *Education of the Negro prior to 1861*, 307; Gardner, "Antebellum Black Education in Baltimore," 361–62; Wade, *Slavery in the Cities*, 272–73; Paul, "Shadow of Equality," 24–28; Gregory, "Education of Blacks in Maryland," 31, 116–17; Petition of James Corner and Others, 28 January 1839, BC Council, Series 1: Administrative Files, 1797–1923, box 61, item 706, BCA (first quote); Petition of Daniel Kobourn and Others Relative to Coloured Schools, 30 January 1844, BC Council, Series 1: Administrative Files, 1797–1923, box 72, item 448, BCA (second quote); Petition of Persons of Color Asking Aid for the Establishment of Colored Public Schools, 7 February 1850, BC Council, Series 1: Administrative Files, 1797–1923, box 87, item 456 (missing), BCA, quoted in Gardner, "Free Blacks in Baltimore," 106–7 (third quote); Memorial of James Wilson and Others in Favor of Establishment of Public Schools by the Colored Population, 7 February 1850, BC Council, Series 1: Administrative Files, 1797–1923, box 87, item 457, BCA (fourth quote).

50. An Ordinance to Exempt the Property of Persons of Colour from the Payment of the Public School Tax, 6–9 April 1838, BC Council, Series 1: Administrative Files, 1797–1923, box 60, item 1194, BCA; Bill to Exempt Coloured People from School Tax, 29 January 1844, BC Council, Series 1: Administrative Files, 1797–1923, box 74, item 1071, BCA; Report of the Joint Committee on Education on the Memorial of Elias Williams and Others for the Public Schools for Colored Children, 14 February 1850, BC Council, Series 1: Administrative Files, 1797–1923, box 88, item 822, BCA (quote).

51. *Weekly Anglo-African*, 3 September 1859, quoted in Graham, *Baltimore*, 256.

52. Gardner, "Antebellum Black Education in Baltimore," 365–66.

53. Gregory, "Education of Blacks in Maryland," 20–21 (first quote), 73–74; Brackett, *Negro in Maryland*, 152–53; Fishel and Quarles, eds., *Black American*, 68; *Baltimore Gazette and Daily Advertiser*, 4 February 1796, 2 January 1801; *Genius of Universal Emancipation*, 29 July 1826 (second quote), 4 November 1826, 16 December 1826. The Maryland Abolition Society deeded its building to the city's "religious people of color" in 1795, which ultimately became the Sharp Street church and academy.

54. Quoted in Semmes, *Baltimore as Seen by Visitors*, 142.

55. Gregory, "Education of Blacks in Maryland," 27; Berlin, *Slaves without Masters*, 64–65, 314–15; *Genius of Universal Emancipation*, August 1825, 170.

56. Graham, *Baltimore*, 109; Aptheker, ed., *Documentary History of the Negro People*, 1:98–105; Bell, *Survey of the Negro Convention Movement*, 13–16; quoted in Litwack, *North of Slavery*, 235–36.

57. George, "Widening the Circle," 79–90; Litwack, *North of Slavery*, 187–90.

58. Rawick, ed., *American Slave*, 16:9.

59. Henry Stockbridge, a Maryland judge, recalled in 1846 that "Slatter's Jail" was a brick-paved enclosure and two-story building with barred windows at the rear of his Pratt Street office. Semmes, *Baltimore as Seen by Visitors*, 171–72.

60. Calderhead, "How Extensive Was the Border State Slave Trade?" 43–54; Bancroft, *Slave-Trading in the Old South*, 45–66; Stampp, *Peculiar Institution*, 238; Semmes, *Baltimore as Seen by Visitors*, 142; BC Tax, Series 3: Field Assessor's Workbooks (Property Assessments), Baltimore City, 1837–45, BCA. The bills of sale for slaves in Baltimore City involving Woolfolk, the largest dealer in the state, suggest the economic precariousness of engaging in the slave trade. After having made just three sales involving five slaves in 1831, Woolfolk made twenty-one sales involving at least thirty-three slaves in 1832 and eighteen sales involving at least fifty-four slaves in 1833 (no doubt capitalizing on the combination of the Nat Turner rebellion and the anti–free Negro legislation, both of which occurred in 1831). During the next three years Woolfolk made no more than ten sales involving thirty-four slaves, and after 1836 he appears to have given up the business (reportedly as a result of poor health), manumitting, rather than selling, what appears to have been his final two slaves in 1837. Bills of Sale and Manumissions, Baltimore City, BCC (Miscellaneous Court Papers), 1831–1860, MSA C1, MdHR. See also Calderhead, "Role of the Professional Slave Trader in a Slave Economy," 195–211; and Preston, *Young Frederick Douglass*, 76–80.

61. Morris, "Labor Controls in Maryland," 388–93, 397; Lovejoy, *Memoir of Rev. Charles T. Torrey*, 167–68; Graham, *Baltimore*, 49–58, 60, 69–70, 151–52; *Baltimore American and Commercial Daily Advertiser*, 29 October 1816, quoted in D. R. Clark, "Baltimore," 235–36. Torrey died while serving his sentence in the Baltimore jail.

62. In 1827 the Protection Society was reformed as the Baltimore Society for the Protection of Free People of Color. P. S. Foner and Lewis, ed., *Black Worker*, 1:109–13.

63. *Weekly Anglo-African*, 24 March 1860, 31 March 1860; Graham, *Baltimore*, 58–59, 84–85. Born free in South Carolina in 1834, Turner had preached for the Methodist Episcopal church in Mississippi, Arkansas, and Missouri, before becoming disillusioned with the church's exclusionary practices. After joining the A.M.E. church, he was assigned to a pastorate in Baltimore in 1858 and was currently serving as minister while also studying at Baltimore's Trinity College, a black divinity school affiliated with the A.M.E. denomination, run by George T. Watkins, son of William Watkins. At Trinity College, Turner received his first formal education, studying the classics and oratory. Graham, *Baltimore*, 133–34; Coleman and Gurr, eds., *Dictionary of Georgia Biography*, 2:1008–9; "Black Georgians in History, Part 2: Henry McNeil Turner," *Atlanta Journal and Constitution*, 5 February 1974, vertical file, Hargrett Rare Books and Archives, Main Library, University of Georgia, Athens.

64. Fishel and Quarles, eds., *Black Americans*, 132–33; *Weekly Anglo-African*, 24 March 1860, 31 March 1860; Graham, *Baltimore*, 58–59, 84–85, 260. In 1826 Woolfolk gained wide notoriety for assaulting and nearly killing Benjamin Lundy, the editor of the *Genius of Universal Emancipation*, because of his editorials against him. Woolfolk was fined a dollar.

65. Winch, *Philadelphia's Black Elite*, 4–5.

66. *African Repository*, December 1826, 15.

67. *Genius of Universal Emancipation*, 12 January 1828, (first quote); Berlin, *Slaves without Masters*, 231; Gardner, "Free Blacks in Baltimore," 146–47 (second quote); Brackett, *Negro in Maryland*, 203–4.

68. Gregory, "Education of Blacks in Maryland, 36–37."

69. "Memorial of Methodist Episcopal Ministers against the Slaveholders' Convention," n.d. [1859], Ms. 488, box 13, Fielder Israel Papers, MHS.

70. Quoted in *Weekly Anglo-African*, 3 March 1860.

71. Turner and Revels both served as A.M.E. pastors in the city during the 1850s, before going on to other states, where they achieved more national recognition during Reconstruction. Turner was the first black chaplain in the U.S. Army, a politician and civil rights activist in Reconstruction Georgia, and a bishop of the A.M.E. church; Revels was the first black man to sit in the U.S. Senate, voted there from the state of Mississippi.

72. *Weekly Anglo-African*, 18 February 1860, 3 March 1860; Graham, *Baltimore*, 154–59; Fields, *Slavery and Freedom on the Middle Ground*, 80–81; Gardner, "Free Blacks in Baltimore," 25.

73. Fields, *Slavery and Freedom on the Middle Ground*, 81–82; Brackett, *Negro in Maryland*, 262n1.

Conclusion

1. Sixth, Seventh, and Eighth U.S. Census, 1840, 1850, 1860, Population Schedule, Baltimore City, NA; Fairbanks, *Statistical Analysis of the Population of Maryland*, 106.

2. Wade, *Slavery in the Cities*, 325–27.

3. Baltimore City Archives Collection (Miscellaneous Court Papers, Index), 1831–1892, BC 0220, MdHR.

4. Fairbanks, *Statistical Analysis of the Population of Maryland*, 105; *Ordinances of the Mayor and the City Council of Baltimore*, 1858, 369, quoted in Della, "Analysis of Baltimore's Population," 31 (quote).

5. *Ordinances of the Mayor and the City Council of Baltimore*, 1858, 369, cited in Della, "Analysis of Baltimore's Population," 31.

6. Baltimore City Archives Collection (Miscellaneous Court Papers, Index), 1831–1892, BC 0220, MdHR.

7. File of Appointments, Sharp Street, Asbury Station, and Strawberry Alley Congregations, 1831–1860, Lovely Lane; *Methodist*, 2 January 1919, 16; Graham, *Baltimore*, 126.

8. Myrdal, *American Dilemma;* Sowell, *Economics and Politics of Race;* Fields, "Ideology and Race in American History."

9. Horton, *Free People of Color,* 74.

10. "Loyial Colard men of Baltimore Citey to His Exelencey The pesident of theas uninted States of america," 20 August 1864, in Berlin et al., eds., *Freedom*, 507–9. African Americans were enrolled temporarily during Jubal Early's invasion of Maryland in the summer of 1864.

11. Ibid.

12. "Freedom, Jubilee: Liberty," Broadside, 15 November 1864, LCP.

13. Fields, *Slavery and Freedom on the Middle Ground*, 129–30.

Bibliography

Primary Sources

Archival Material

Baltimore City Archives, Baltimore, Maryland
    Baltimore City Property Tax Records, 1798–1915. Record Group 4.
        Series 1: General Property Tax Books, 1798, 1856, 1860. Microfilm reels
            BCA 145–47, 165–71, 177.
        Series 3: Field Assessor's Workbooks (Property Assessments), Baltimore
            City, 1837–1898.
    Baltimore County Court. Certificates of Freedom, 1806–1816. Microfilm reel
        BCA 230.
    Baltimore Equitable Society Papers. Record Group 12, Series 1: Policy Led-
        ger Books. Microfilm reel BCA 4634.
    "Early Records of Baltimore, 1756–1800." 2 vols. Record Group 2.
    Foreign Passengers. Record Group 55.
    Mayor's Papers, 1797–1923. Record Group 9, Series 2: Correspondence.
    Minutes of the Board of Trustees for the Poor of Baltimore City and County,
        1833–1841. Record Group 19, Series 1: HRS Records, 1798–1882.
    Miscellaneous Administrative Records, 1798–1939. Record Group 41.
        Series 1: Reports and Returns, 1798–1925.
        Series 5: Court Records, 1815–1921.
        Series 6: Miscellaneous Administrative Papers, 1807–1927.
    Papers of the Baltimore City Commissioners, 1797–1899. Record Group 3,
        Series 1: Administrative Files, 1827–1828.
    Papers of the City Council. Record Group 16, Series 1: Administrative Files,
        1797–1923.
Baltimore City Court House, Baltimore, Maryland
    Baltimore City Charter Records.
    Baltimore City Land Records.
Historical Society of Pennsylvania, Philadelphia, Pennsylvania
    Pennsylvania Society for Promoting the Abolition of Slavery Papers.
        Maryland Abolition Society, Membership List.
        Maryland Society for Promoting the Abolition of Slavery, "Report to the
            American Convention," 1796.

Library Company of Philadelphia, Philadelphia, Pennsylvania
    "Freedom, Jubilee: Liberty," Broadside, 15 November 1864.
    Mary Anne Dickerson Album/Scrapbook
Maryland Historical Society Library, Manuscripts Division, Baltimore, Maryland
    Alexander Robinson Ledger. Ms. 699.
    Ambrose Clarke-von Kapff and Brune Shipping Papers, 1796–1805. Ms. 1754.
    Baltimore Assessment Record Book, 1815. Ms. 55.
    Baltimore Eastern Dispensary Records, 1818–1894. 2 vols. Ms. 1894.
    Baltimore Town Account Book, 1772–1774. Ms. 1133.
    Fielder Israel Papers. Ms. 488.
    George Litting Account Book, 1796–1878. Ms. 1657.
    Joseph Despeaux Papers. Ms. 260.
    Maryland State Colonization Society Papers. 36 microfilm reels.
    Nagle Papers. Ms. 2052.
    Susanna Warfield Diaries. Ms. 760.
Maryland State Archives, Hall of Records, Annapolis, Maryland
    Anne Arundel County Court. Register of Wills, 1806–1851. Record Group
        AA 0046.
    Baltimore City and County Commissioners of Insolvent Debtors. Record
        Group BC 0339.
    Baltimore City Archives Collection. Miscellaneous Court Papers. Index, 1831–
        1892. Record Group BC 0220.
    Baltimore City Court of Oyer and Terminer. Docket and Minutes, 1790.
        Record Group C183.
    Baltimore City Superior Court. Certificates of Freedom, 1848–1864. Record
        Group BC 0165.
    Baltimore County Board of County Commissioners, 1828–1855. Record
        Group MSA C266.
    Baltimore County Commissioners of the Tax. Alphabetical List of Assessed
        Persons, 1804, 1813, Baltimore City. Record Group C266.
    Baltimore County Court.
        Certificates of Freedom, 1806–1816. Record Group BA 0290.
        Chancery Papers. Record Group MdHr 40200.
        Chattel Records, 1763–1773, 1813–1814, 1823–1826. Record Group BA
            0298.
        Miscellaneous Court Papers, 1785–1855. Record Group MSA C1.
        Register of Wills, 1791–1797, 1810–1815. Record Group BA 0435.
        Register of Wills. Indentures, 1794–1799, 1823–1826. Record Group BA
            0337.
    Baltimore County Land Records, 1796–1797. Record Group BA 0352.
    Baltimore County Land Records. General Index, 1659–1800. Record Group
        BA 0352.
    Baltimore County Register of Wills (Petitions), 1789–1860. Record Group
        MSA T621.

Bethel [Baltimore] A.M.E. Church Collection, 1825–1881. Record Group MSA SC 2562. 12 microfilm reels.

Fortie Family Papers, 1767–1869. Marshall Collection. Record Group MSA SC 1383.

Somerset County Court. Certificates of Freedom, 1832–1839. Record Group MSA 50238-1.

Morgan State University Library, Baltimore, Maryland

Bliss Forbush Collection. "Memorial Concerning the African race," undated, Appeals to the Legislature, 1787–1818.

National Archives, Washington, D. C.

Bureau of Customs. Record Group 36, Port of Baltimore, Crew Lists, 1806–1843.

U.S. Census Office.

First Census of the United States, 1790. Population Schedule. Baltimore City, Maryland.

Second Census of the United States, 1800. Population Schedule. Baltimore City, Maryland.

Third Census of the United States, 1810. Population Schedule. Baltimore City, Maryland.

Fourth Census of the United States, 1820. Population Schedule. Baltimore City, Maryland.

Fifth Census of the United States, 1830. Population Schedule. Baltimore City, Maryland.

Sixth Census of the United States, 1840. Population and Manufacturing Schedule. Baltimore City, Maryland.

Seventh Census of the United States, 1850. Population, Slave, and Manufacturing Schedules. Baltimore City, Maryland.

Seventh Census of the United States, 1850. Social Statistics by Ward. Baltimore City, Maryland.

Eighth Census of the United States, 1860. Population, Slave, and Manufacturing Schedules. Baltimore City, Maryland.

Sharp Street Methodist Episcopal Church, Baltimore, Maryland

Records of Members and Classes, 1825–1828, 1830–1832, 1840–1841.

Sulpician Archives, Baltimore, Maryland

Records of Saint Mary's Parish. Easter Duty List, 1810.

United Methodist Historical Society, Lovely Lane Methodist Museum, Baltimore, Maryland

Baltimore City Station Admissions, Removals, Deaths, 1809–1811.

Baltimore City Station Class Records, 1799–1838.

Baltimore City Station Records: Marriage, Baptisms, 1799–1838.

Minutes of the Asbury Sunday School Society, 1816–1824.

Plan of Appointments for Sharp Street, Strawberry Alley, and Asbury Station, 1831–1860.

Sharp Street Methodist Episcopal Church Records, 1826.

University of Georgia Main Library, Athens, Georgia
  American Missionary Association Papers. 132 microfilm reels.
  Maryland State Colonization Society Papers. 31 microfilm reels.

Books, Essays, Articles, and Reports

Adams, George E. *Life and Character of William Crane.* Baltimore: n.p., 1868.
"An Account of the Colony of the Lord Baron of Baltamore, 1633." In *Narratives of Early Maryland,* edited by Clayton Colman Hall. New York: Barnes and Noble, 1910).
Andrews, Ethan Allen. *Slavery and the Domestic Slave Trade in the United States.* Boston: Light and Stearns, 1836. Reprint. Freeport, N.Y.: Books for Libraries, 1971.
Aptheker, Herbert, ed. *A Documentary History of the Negro People in the United States.* 3 vols. Secaucus, N.J.: Citadel, 1951–73.
Arfwedson, C. W. *The United States and Canada in 1832, 1833, and 1834.* 2 vols. London: Richard Bentley, 1834.
At a Meeting of "the Maryland Society for Promoting the Abolition of Slavery, and the Relief of Free Negroes, and Others, Unlawfully Held in Bondage," Held at Baltimore, the 4th of February, 1792. Baltimore: William Goddard and James Angell, 1792.
"Autobiography of John Davis, 1770–1864." *Maryland Historical Magazine* 30 (March 1935): 11–39.
Baltimore Equitable Society for the Insuring of Houses from Loss by Fire. Baltimore: n.p., 1804.
Bangs, Nathan. *The Life of the Rev. Freeborn Garrettson.* 2d ed. New York: J. Emory and R. Waugh, 1830.
Brown, George W. *The Origin and Growth of Civil Liberty in Maryland.* Baltimore: J. D. Toy, 1850.
Brown, William Wells. *My Southern Home.* Boston: A. G. Brown, 1880.
Buckler, Thomas H. *A History of Epidemic Cholera as It Appeared at Baltimore City and County Almhouses in the Summer of 1849, with Some Remarks on the Medical Topography and Diseases of This Region.* Baltimore: J. Lucas, 1851.
Burn, James D. *Three Years among the Working Classes in the United States during the War.* London: Smith, Elder, 1865.
Byllesby, Langton. *Observations on the Sources and Effects of Unequal Wealth.* New York: L. J. Nichols, 1826.
Carey, John L. *Slavery in Maryland, Briefly Considered.* Baltimore: J. Murphy, 1845.
Chase, Samuel. *To the Citizens of Baltimore-Town, May 4, 1794.* Baltimore: n.p., 1794.
Chickering, Jesse. *Immigration into the United States.* Boston: C. C. Little and J. Brown, 1848.
Clark, Elmer T., J. Manning Potts, and Jacob S. Payton, eds. *The Journals and Letters of Francis Asbury.* London: n.p., 1958.
Coker, Daniel. *A Dialogue between a Virginian and an African Minister.* In *Negro Protest Pamphlets,* edited by Dorothy Porter. New York: Arno, 1969.
———. *Journal of Daniel Coker.* Baltimore: John D. Toy, 1820.

———. "A Sermon Delivered Extempore in the African Bethel Church in Baltimore, Jan. 21, 1816." In *A Documentary History of the Negro People in the United States*, edited by Herbert Aptheker. New York: Citadel, 1951.

"The Condition of the Colored Population of Baltimore." *Baltimore Literary and Religious Magazine* 4 (April 1838): 169–74.

Constitution of the Carpenters' Society of Baltimore. Baltimore: n.p., 1791.

Constitution of the Maryland Society, for Promoting the Abolition of Slavery, &c., September 8, 1789. Baltimore: William Goddard and James Angell, 1789.

Coppin, Levi J. *Unwritten History.* N.p.: by the author, 1919. Reprint. New York: Negro Universities Press, 1968.

Coyle, Wilbur F., ed. *First Records of Baltimore Town and Jones' Town, 1729–1797.* Baltimore: City Library, 1905.

Custis, George Washington Parke. *An Address Occasioned by the Death of General Lingan, Who Was Murdered by the Mob at Baltimore, Delivered at Georgetown, September 1, 1812.* Boston: Bradford and Read, 1812.

Davis, Noah. *A Narrative of the Life of Rev. Noah Davis, a Colored Man, Written by Himself, at the Age of Fifty-Four.* Baltimore: John F. Weishampel Jr., 1859.

Dixon, James. *Personal Narrative of a Tour through a Part of the United States and Canada.* New York: Lane and Scott, 1849.

The Doctrines and Discipline of the Methodist Episcopal Church in America. Philadelphia: n.p., 1801.

Douglass, Frederick. *Life and Times of Frederick Douglass.* Rev. ed. New York: Crowell-Collier, 1962.

———. *My Bondage and My Freedom.* New York: Miller, Orton and Mulligan, 1855. Reprint. New York: Dover Publications, 1969.

Eddis, William. *Letters from America, Historical and Descriptive; Comprising Occurrences from 1769, to 1777, Inclusive.* London: by the author, 1792.

Election Laws of the State of Maryland, Now in Force: With Such Portions of the Constitution as Relate to the Elective Franchise. Baltimore: n.p., 1856.

Facts and Documents Relative to the Late Attack on Liberty of the Press in Baltimore. Philadelphia: n.p., 1812.

Faux, William. *Memorable Days in America.* London: W. Simpkin and R. Marshall, 1823.

Fearon, Henry B. *Sketches of America.* London: n.p., 1818.

Foner, Philip S., and Ronald L. Lewis, eds. *The Black Worker: A Documentary History from Colonial Times to the Present.* 7 vols. Philadelphia: Temple University Press, 1978–83.

Garrettson, Freeborn. *The Experiences and Travels of Mr. Freeborn Garrettson, Minister of the Methodist Episcopal Church in North America.* Philadelphia: Joseph Crukshank, 1791.

Garrison, William L. *The Maryland Scheme of Expatriation Examined.* Boston: Garrison and Knapp, 1834.

———. *Thoughts on African Colonization; or an Impartial Exhibition of the Doctrines,*

Principles and Purposes of the American Colonization Society, Together with the Resolutions, Addresses and Remonstrances of the Free People of Color. Boston: Garrison and Knapp, 1832.

Gilmor, Robert. "Recollections of Baltimore, Read before the Maryland Historical Society, 9 May 1844." *Maryland Historical Magazine* 7 (September 1912): 236–44.

Goddard, William. *The Prowess of the Whig Club, and the Manoeuvers of the Legion.* Baltimore: n.p., 1777.

Griffith, Thomas W. *Annals of Baltimore.* Baltimore: W. Wooddy, 1833.

Hall, James. *An Address to the Free People of Color of the State of Maryland.* Baltimore: n.p., 1859.

Harper, Robert G. *A Letter from General Harper to Elias Caldwell.* Baltimore: R. J. Matchett, 1818.

Hersey, John. *Advice to Christian Parents.* Baltimore: n.p., n.d.

Hewitt, John H. *Shadows on the Wall; or, Glimpses of the Past.* Baltimore: Turnbull Brothers, 1877.

Hodgson, Adam. *Letters from North America.* 2 vols. London: Hurst, Robinson, 1824.

Hurd, John C. *The Law of Freedom and Bondage in the United States.* Boston: Little, Brown, 1861.

Interesting Papers Relative to the Recent Riots at Baltimore. Philadelphia: n.p., 1812.

Jacobs, Curtis W. *The Free Negro Question in Maryland.* Baltimore: John W. Woods, 1859.

———. *Speech of Col. Curtis [W.] Jacobs, on the Free Colored Population of Maryland.* Annapolis, Md.: Elihu S. Riley, 1860.

Johnston, James F. W. *Notes on North America, Agricultural, Economical, and Social.* 2 vols. Edinburgh and London: W. Blackwood and Sons, 1851.

La Rochefoucald-Liancourt, François A. *Travels through the United States of North America.* 2 vols. London: R. Phillips, 1799.

Latrobe, John H. B. *Colonization: A Notice of Victor Hugo's Views of Slavery in the United States, in a Letter from John H. B. Latrobe, of Baltimore, to Thomas Suffern, of New York.* Baltimore: John D. Toy, 1851.

———. *Memoir of Benjamin Banneker.* Baltimore: John D. Toy, 1845.

Learned, Joseph D. *A View of Policy of Permitting Slaves in the States West of the Mississippi, Being a Letter to a Member of Congress, by Joseph D. Learned, Esq.* Baltimore: J. Robinson, 1820.

"Letter from a Colored Man in Baltimore." *African Repository* 29 (April 1853): 98–99.

Lovejoy, J. C. *Memoir of Rev. Charles T. Torrey, Who Died in the Penitentiary of Maryland, Where He Was Confined for Showing Mercy to the Poor.* Boston: J. P. Jewett, 1847.

Lyell, Charles. *Travels in North America, in the Year 1841–2.* 2 vols. New York: Wiley and Putnam, 1845.

Mackay, Alexander. *The Western World; or, Travels in the United States in 1846–47.* 3 vols. London: R. Bentley, 1849.

Mackay, Charles. *Life and Liberty in America.* 2 vols. London: Smith, Elder, 1859.

Maryland Colonization Society. *Annual Reports*. Baltimore: Maryland Colonization Society, 1850.

McCreary, George W. *The Ancient and Honorable Mechanical Company of Baltimore*. Baltimore: Kohn and Pollock, 1901.

McJilton, John N. *Report of the Delegate to the Educational Conventions of Buffalo and Boston: To the Commissioners of Public Schools of Baltimore, and Address on the Teacher's Calling, Nationally Considered, Delivered at Buffalo*. Baltimore: Bull and Tuttle, 1860.

McKay, Charles F. *The Mortality of Baltimore, with Reference to the Principles of Life Insurance*. New York: n.p., 1850.

McSherry, James. *History of Maryland, 1634 to 1848*. Baltimore: John Murphy, 1849.

Merrill, Walter M., ed. *The Letters of William Lloyd Garrison*. 2 vols. Cambridge, Mass.: Belknap, 1971.

Methodist. 2 January 1919.

Minutes of the Annual Conference of the Methodist Episcopal Church for the Years 1773–1828. New York: n.p., 1840.

Minutes of the General Assembly of the Presbyterian Church, 1821–1835, 1836–1841, 1842–1847, 1848–1849. Philadelphia: n.p., n.d.

Minutes of the General Assembly of the Presbyterian Church in the United States of America from Its Organization in A.D. 1798 to A.D. 1820. Philadelphia: n.p., 1847.

Minutes of the General Assembly of the Presbyterian Church in the United States of America New School, 1838–1851. New York, n.p., n.d.

Minutes of the Proceedings of a Convention of Delegates from the Abolition Societies Established in Different Parts of the United States at Philadelphia, on May 3, 1797. Philadelphia: n.p., 1797.

Minutes Taken at the Several Annual Conferences of the Methodist Episcopal Church, 1810–1820, 1821–1829. Philadelphia: n.p., n.d.

Minutes Taken at the Several Conferences of the Methodist Episcopal Church, in America, for the Year 1800. Philadelphia: n.p., 1800.

Minutes Taken at the Several Conferences of the Methodist Episcopal Church, in America, for the Year 1815. Philadelphia: n.p., 1815.

Naff, John H. "Recollections of Baltimore, Thrown Together as They Were Collected, at Different Times, from Conversations with the Elders of the City." *Maryland Historical Magazine* 5 (June 1910): 104–23.

Olmsted, Frederick Law. *A Journey in the Seaboard Slave States, with Remarks on Their Economy*. New York: Dix and Edwards, 1856.

Pairpont, Alfred J. *Uncle Sam and His Country*. London: Simpkin, Marshall, 1857.

Payne, Daniel A. *A History of the African Methodist Episcopal Church*. Nashville, Tenn.: Publishing House of the A.M.E. Sunday-School Union, 1891.

———. *Recollections of Seventy-Years*. Nashville, Tenn.: Publishing House of the A.M.E. Sunday School Union, 1888. Reprint. New York: Arno, 1968.

Peck, Nathaniel, and Thomas Price. *Report of Messrs. Peck and Price, Delegates to Visit British Guiana and the Island of Trinidad for the Purpose of Ascertaining the Advan-*

tages to Be Derived by Colored People Migrating to Those Places. Baltimore: Woods and Crane, 1840.

Pierce, William L. *The Year: A Poem in Three Cantoes.* New York: David Longworth, 1813.

A Plan of the Female Humane Association Charity School. Baltimore: Warner and Hannah, 1800.

Porter, Dorothy, ed. *Negro Protest Pamphlets.* New York: Arno, 1969.

A Portrait of the Evils of Democracy: Submitted to the Consideration of the People of Maryland. Baltimore: n.p., 1816.

Rawick, George P., ed. *The American Slave: A Composite Autobiography.* 19 vols. Westport, Conn.: Greenwood, 1972.

———. *The American Slave: A Composite Autobiography, Supplement.* 12 vols. Westport, Conn.: Greenwood, 1977.

Raymond, Daniel. *Elements of Political Economy.* 2 vols. Baltimore: F. Lucas Jr. and E. J. Coale, 1823.

———. *The Missouri Question.* Baltimore: Schaeffer and Maund, 1819.

Regulations of the Baltimore Cemetery with Suggestions to Lot-Holders, and the Act of Incorporation, 1850. Baltimore: John Murphy, 1850.

Report of a Meeting of the Maryland Society for Promoting the Abolition of Slavery and the Relief of Free Negroes, and Others Unlawfully Held in Bondage, Joseph Townsend, Secretary. Baltimore: William Goddard and James Angell, 1792.

Report of Cases Argued and Adjudged in the Court of Appeals of Maryland and in the High Court of Chancery of Maryland (1826–1829). Baltimore: Curlander, 1884.

Report of the Committee of Grievances and Courts of Justice of the House of Delegates of Maryland, on the Subject of the Recent Mobs and Riots in the City of Baltimore. Annapolis, Md.: Jonas Green, 1813.

Rules of Order for the Government of the Board of Trustees and the By-Laws Defining the Duties of the Officers of the Baltimore City Almshouse, Bayview Asylum. Baltimore: n.p., 1866.

Rules to Be Observed by the Hands Employed in the Brick-Making Business. Baltimore: n.p., 1802.

Semmes, John E. *John H. B. Latrobe and His Times.* Baltimore: Norman, Remington, 1917.

A Series of Letters and Other Documents Relating to the Late Epidemic [of] Yellow Fever. Baltimore: William Warner, 1820.

Smith, Henry. *Recollections and Reflections of an Old Itinerant: A Series of Letters.* New York: Lane and Tippett, 1848.

"Statisticks of Destitution in Baltimore." *Baltimore Literary and Religious Magazine* 3 (June 1837): 278–79.

Steuart, R[ichard] S. *Letter to John L. Carey on the Subject of Slavery.* Baltimore: J. Murphy, 1845.

Stirling, James. *Letters from the Slave States.* London: J. W. Parker and Son, 1857.

Stockbridge, Henry, Sr. "Baltimore in 1846, Read before the Maryland Historical

Society, 10 December 1875." *Maryland Historical Magazine* 6 (March 1911): 20–34.

Strickland, W. P. *The Life of Jacob Gruber.* New York: Carlton and Porter, 1860.

Trollope, Frances. *Domestic Manners of the Americans.* 2 vols. New York: Dodd, Mead, 1832.

Tyson, Elisha. *The Farewell Address of Elisha Tyson, of the City of Baltimore, to the People of Colour, in the United States of America.* Baltimore: William Wooddy, 1824.

Tyson, John Shoemaker. *Life of Elisha Tyson, the Philanthropist.* Baltimore: Benjamin Lundy, 1825.

Tyson, Martha Ellicott. *A Sketch of the Life of Benjamin Banneker, from Notes Taken in 1836.* Baltimore: Maryland Historical Society, 1854.

Varle, Charles. *A Complete View of Baltimore.* Baltimore: Samuel Young, 1833.

Watkins, William. *Address Delivered before the Moral Reform Society in Philadelphia, August 8, 1836.* Baltimore: Merrihew and Gunn, 1836.

Weems, M. L. *God's Revenge against Gambling Exemplified in the Miserable Lives and Untimely Deaths of a Number of Persons of Both Sexes.* 4th ed. Philadelphia: n.p., 1822.

Whiteman, Maxwell, ed. *Minutes and Proceedings of the First Annual Meeting of the American Moral Reform Society.* Philadelphia: n.p., 1837.

Wilson, Joseph W. *Sketches of the Higher Classes of Colored Society in Philadelphia.* Philadelphia: Merrihew and Thompson, 1841.

Government Documents

Baltimore City Health Department. *The First Thirty-Five Annual Reports, 1815–1849.* Baltimore: n.p., 1953.

Browne, William Hand, ed. *Archives of Maryland.* 72 vols. Baltimore: Maryland Historical Society, 1883–1972.

Coyle, Wilbur F., ed. *Records of the City of Baltimore (Special Commissioners), 1782–1797.* Baltimore: Wilbur F. Coyle, 1909.

Fairbanks, W. L. *A Statistical Analysis of the Population of Maryland.* Baltimore: Maryland Development Bureau of the Baltimore Association of Commerce, 1931.

Howard, William T. *Public Health Administration and the Natural History of Disease in Baltimore, Maryland, 1797–1920.* Washington, D.C.: Carnegie Institution, 1924.

Kennedy, Joseph C. G. *Abstract of the Statistics of Manufactures, according to the Returns of the Seventh Census.* Senate Documents, 35th Cong., 2d Sess., vol. 10, 1859–60.

Kilty, William, ed. *Laws of Maryland, 1799–1818.* 8 vols. Annapolis, Md.: n.p., 1806–20.

Laws of Maryland. Annapolis, Md.: n.p., 1805, 1809, 1817, 1818, 1831, 1833.

Manufactures of the United States in 1860; Compiled from the Original Returns of the Eighth Census. Washington, D.C.: Government Printing Office, 1865.

Maryland House Documents. Annapolis, Md.: n.p., 1860.

Maryland House of Delegates, Committee of Grievances and Courts of Justice. *Report of the Committee of Grievances and Courts of Justice of the House of Delegates in Mary-*

land, on the Subject of the Recent Mobs and Riots in the City of Baltimore, Together with the Depositions Taken before the Committee. Annapolis, Md.: n.p., 1813.

Maryland Legislative Documents. Annapolis, Md.: n.p., 1843.

Ordinances of the Corporation of the City of Baltimore. Baltimore: John Cox, 1876.

The Ordinances of the Mayor and the City Council of Baltimore. Baltimore: n.p., 1858.

Ordinances and Resolutions of the City Council of Baltimore. Baltimore: n.p., 1829, 1846, 1850, 1851.

U.S. Bureau of the Census. Negro Population of the United States, 1790–1915. Washington D.C.: Government Printing Office, 1918.

———. Population of the United States in 1860. Washington D.C.: Government Printing Office, 1864.

———. The Seventh Census of the United States: 1850. Washington, D.C.: Government Printing Office, 1850.

City Directories

Baltimore Directory and Citizen's Register, for 1808. Baltimore: n.p., 1808.

Boyd, William H. The Baltimore City Directory. Baltimore: Richard Edwards and William Boyd, 1858.

Craig, Daniel H. Craig's Business Directory and Baltimore Almanac for 1842. Baltimore: Daniel H. Craig, 1842.

Fry, William. The Baltimore Directory for 1810. Baltimore: G. Dobbin and Murphy, 1810.

———. Fry's Baltimore Directory for 1812. Baltimore: B. W. Sower, 1812.

Jackson, Samuel. The Baltimore Directory, Corrected up to June, 1819. Baltimore: Richard J. Matchett, 1819.

Keenan, C. The Baltimore Directory, for 1822 and '23. Baltimore: Richard J. Matchett, 1822.

Kennedy, James. The Baltimore Directory for 1817–18. Baltimore: James Kennedy, 1817.

Matchett, Richard J. Baltimore Directory for 1824. Baltimore: Richard J. Matchett, 1824.

———. Matchett's Baltimore Directory for 1827. Baltimore: Richard J. Matchett, 1827.

———. Matchett's Baltimore Directory, Corrected up to June, 1829. Baltimore: [R. J. Matchett], 1829.

———. Matchett's Baltimore Directory, Corrected up to May 1833. Baltimore: Richard J. Matchett, 1833.

———. Matchett's Baltimore Director[y], Corrected up to 1835, for 1835–36. Baltimore: R. J. Matchett, 1835.

———. Matchett's Baltimore Directory for 1837–38. Baltimore: Richard J. Matchett, 1837.

———. Matchett's Baltimore Directory for 1840–41. Baltimore: R. J. Matchett, 1840.

———. Matchett's Baltimore Directory, or Register of Householders, for 1842. Baltimore: Richard J. Matchett, 1842.

————. *Matchett's Baltimore Directory for 1847–48.* Baltimore: R. J. Matchett, 1847.
————. *Matchett's Baltimore Directory for 1849–50.* Baltimore: Richard J. Matchett, 1849.
————. *Matchett's Baltimore Directory for 1851.* Baltimore: Richard J. Matchett, 1851.
————. *Baltimore Directory for 1853–54.* Baltimore: Richard J. Matchett, 1853.
Mullin, John. *The Baltimore Directory, for 1799.* Baltimore: Warner and Hanna, 1799.
[Murphy, John]. *The Baltimore Directory, for 1845.* Baltimore: John Murphy, 1845.
The New Baltimore Directory, and Annual Register, for 1800 and 1801. Baltimore: Warner and Hanna, 1800.
Robinson, James. *The Baltimore Directory for 1804.* Baltimore: Warner and Hanna, 1804.
Stafford, Cornelius W. *The Baltimore Directory for 1802.* Baltimore: John W. Butler, 1802.
Thompson, William, and James L. Walker. *The Baltimore Town and Fell's Point Directory.* Baltimore: Pechin, 1796.
Woods, John J. *Woods' Baltimore City Directory.* Baltimore: John J. Woods, 1860.

Newspapers and Periodicals

Anglo-African Magazine. New York, New York.
African Repository. Washington, D.C.
Baltimore American and Commercial Daily Advertiser. Baltimore, Maryland.
Baltimore Clipper. Baltimore, Maryland.
Baltimore Daily Intelligencer. Baltimore, Maryland.
Baltimore Daily Repository. Baltimore, Maryland.
Baltimore Gazette and Daily Advertiser. Baltimore, Maryland.
Baltimore Sun. Baltimore, Maryland.
DeBow's Review (or *Commercial Review of the South and West*). New Orleans, Louisiana.
Federal Intelligencer, and Baltimore Daily Gazette. Baltimore, Maryland.
Frederick Douglass's Paper. Rochester, New York.
Freedom's Journal. New York, New York.
Genius of Universal Emancipation. Baltimore, Maryland.
Liberator. Boston, Massachusetts.
Maryland Colonization Journal. Baltimore, Maryland.
Maryland Journal and Baltimore Advertiser. Annapolis, Maryland.
New York Tribune. New York, New York.
Niles' Weekly Register. Baltimore, Maryland.
Planters' Advocate. Annapolis, Maryland.
Weekly Anglo-African. New York, New York.

Secondary Sources

Dissertations and Manuscripts

Boucher, Morris R. "The Free Negro in Alabama prior to 1860." Ph.D. diss., University of Iowa, 1950.

Burnard, Trevor G. "A Colonial Elite: Wealthy Marylanders, 1691–1776." Ph.D. diss., Johns Hopkins University, 1988.

Clark, Dennis R. "Baltimore, 1729–1829: The Genesis of a Community." Ph.D. diss., Catholic University of America, 1976.

Davidson, Thomas E. "Free Blacks and the County Courts of Colonial Maryland— Law versus Custom." Unpublished manuscript, Maryland Historical Society.

Deal, Joseph D., III. "Race and Class in Colonial Virginia: Indians, Englishmen, and Africans on the Eastern Shore during the Seventeenth Century." Ph.D. diss., University of Rochester, 1981.

England, James M. "The Free Negro in Antebellum Tennessee." Ph.D. diss., Vanderbilt University, 1941.

Everett, Donald E. "The Free Persons of Color in New Orleans, 1830–1865." Ph.D. diss., Tulane University, 1952.

Franch, Michael S. "Congregation and Community in Baltimore, 1840–1860." Ph.D. diss., University of Maryland at College Park, 1984.

Gardner, Bettye Jane. "Free Blacks in Baltimore, 1800–1860." Ph.D. diss., George Washington University, 1974.

Garonzik, Joseph. "Urbanization and the Black Population of Baltimore, 1850–1870." Ph.D. diss., State University of New York at Stony Brook, 1974.

Gregory, Clarence K. "The Education of Blacks in Maryland: An Historical Survey." Ed.D. diss., Columbia University Teachers College, 1976.

Lawrence-McIntyre, Charsee. "Free Blacks: A Troublesome and Dangerous Population in Antebellum America." Ph.D. diss., State University of New York at Stony Brook, 1984.

Paul, William G. "The Shadow of Equality: The Negro in Baltimore, 1864–1911." Ph.D. diss., University of Wisconsin, 1972.

Powers, Bernard Edward, Jr. "Black Charleston: A Social History, 1822–1885." Ph.D. diss., Northwestern University, 1982.

Stavinsky, Leonard P. "The Negro Artisan in the South Atlantic States, 1800–1860: A Study of Status and Economic Opportunity with Special Reference to Charleston." Ph.D. diss., Columbia University, 1958.

Sweat, Edward F. "The Free Negro in Antebellum Georgia." Ph.D. diss., University of Indiana, 1957.

Thomas, Betty C. "The Baltimore Black Community, 1865–1900." Ph.D. diss., George Washington University, 1974.

Walker, Paul Kent. "The Baltimore Community and the American Revolution: A Study in Urban Development, 1763–1783." Ph.D. diss., University of North Carolina at Chapel Hill, 1973.

Whitman, T. Stephen. "Slavery, Manumission, and Free Black Workers in Early National Baltimore." Ph.D. diss., Johns Hopkins University, 1993.

Books and Articles

Abernethy, Thomas P. *The South in the New Nation, 1789–1819*. Baton Rouge: Louisiana State University Press, 1961.

Adams, Donald R., Jr. "Prices and Wages in Maryland, 1750–1850." *Journal of Economic History* 46 (September 1986): 625–45.

Adams, William F. *Ireland and the Irish Emigration to the New World from 1815 to the Famine*. New Haven, Conn.: Yale University Press, 1932.

Alden, John R. *The First South*. Baton Rouge: Louisiana State University Press, 1961.

Alexander, Douglas. "Stendhal and Violence on the Baltimore Stage." *Maryland Historical Magazine* 66 (Spring 1971): 68–71.

Alford, Terry. *Prince among Slaves: The True Story of an African Prince Sold into Slavery in the American South*. New York: Harcourt Brace Jovanovich, 1977.

Anderson, Thornton. "Eighteenth-Century Suffrage: The Case of Maryland." *Maryland Historical Magazine* 76 (June 1981): 141–58.

Andrews, Matthew Page. *History of Maryland: Province and State*. Garden City, N.Y.: Doubleday, 1929.

———. *The Negro in the American Revolution*. New York: International Publishers, 1940.

———. "The Quakers and Negro Slavery." *Journal of Negro History* 25 (July 1940): 331–62.

Ayers, Edward L. *Vengeance and Justice: Crime and Punishment in the Nineteenth-Century American South*. New York: Oxford University Press, 1984.

Baker, Gordon Pratt, ed. *Those Incredible Methodists: A History of the Baltimore Conference of the United Methodist Church*. Baltimore: Commission on Archives and History, 1972.

Baker, Howard F. "National Stocks in the Population of the United States as Indicated by Surnames in the Census of 1790." *American Historical Association Annual Reports* 1 (1932): 246–67.

Baker, Jean H. *The Politics of Continuity: Maryland Political Parties from 1858 to 1870*. Baltimore: Johns Hopkins University Press, 1973.

Baldwin, Brooke. "The Cakewalk: A Study in Stereotype and Reality." *Journal of Social History* 15 (Winter 1982): 205–18.

Bancroft, Frederic. *Slave-Trading in the Old South*. Baltimore: J. H. Furst, 1931. Reprint. New York: Frederick Ungar, 1959.

Bateman, Fred, and Thomas Weiss. *A Deplorable Scarcity: The Failure of Industrialization in the Slave Economy*. Chapel Hill: University of North Carolina Press, 1981.

Beirne, D. Randall. "The Impact of Black Labor on European Immigration into Baltimore's Oldtown, 1790–1810." *Maryland Historical Magazine* 83 (Winter 1988): 331–45.

Beirne, Francis F. *The Amiable Baltimoreans*. Baltimore: Johns Hopkins University Press, 1951.

———. *Baltimore: A Picture History, 1858–1958.* New York: Hastings House, 1957.

Bell, Howard. *A Survey of the Negro Convention Movement, 1830–1861.* New York: Arno, 1969.

Bender, Thomas. *Community and Social Change in America.* Baltimore: Johns Hopkins University Press, 1978.

Berlin, Ira. *Slaves without Masters: The Free Negro in the Antebellum South.* New York: Oxford University Press, 1974.

———. "The Structure of the Free Negro Caste in the Antebellum United States." *Journal of Social History* 9 (Spring 1976): 297–318.

———. "Time, Space, and the Evolution of Afro-American Society on British Mainland North America." *American Historical Review* 85 (February 1980): 44–78.

Berlin, Ira, and Herbert G. Gutman. "Natives and Immigrants, Free Men and Slaves: Urban Workingmen in the Antebellum American South." *American Historical Review* 88 (December 1983): 1175–1200.

Berlin, Ira, and Ronald Hoffman, eds., *Slavery and Freedom in the Age of the American Revolution.* Charlottesville: University Press of Virginia, 1983. Reprint. Urbana: University of Illinois Press, 1986.

Berlin, Ira, Steven F. Miller, Joseph P. Reidy, and Leslie S. Rowland, eds. *Freedom: A Documentary History of Emancipation, 1861–1867.* Series 1, vol. 2, *The Wartime Genesis of Free Labor: The Upper South.* New York: Cambridge University Press, 1993.

Berlin, Ira, and Philip D. Morgan, eds. *Cultivation and Culture: Labor and the Shaping of Slave Life in the Americas.* Charlottesville: University Press of Virginia, 1993.

Bernard, Richard M. "A Portrait of Baltimore in 1800: Economic and Occupational Patterns in an Early American City." *Maryland Historical Magazine* 69 (Winter 1974): 341–60.

Berthoff, Rowland. "Conventional Mentality: Free Blacks, Women, and Business Corporations as Unequal Persons, 1820–1870." *Journal of American History* 76 (Winter 1989): 753–84.

Bilhartz, Terry D. *Urban Religion and the Second Great Awakening: Church and Society in Early National Baltimore.* Rutherford, N.J.: Farleigh Dickinson University Press, 1986.

Birmingham, Stephen. *Certain People: America's Black Elite.* Boston: Little, Brown, 1977.

"Black Georgians in History, Part 2: Henry McNeil Turner." *Atlanta Journal and Constitution,* 5 February 1974.

Blackmar, Elizabeth. *Manhattan for Rent, 1785–1850.* Ithaca, N.Y.: Cornell University Press, 1989.

Blandi, Joseph. *Maryland Business Corporations, 1783–1852.* Baltimore: Johns Hopkins University Press, 1934.

Blassingame, John W. "Before the Ghetto: The Making of the Black Community in Savannah, Georgia, 1865–1880." *Journal of Social History* 6 (Summer 1973): 463–88.

———. *Black New Orleans, 1860–1880*. Chicago: University of Chicago Press, 1973.
———. "The Recruitment of Negro Troops in Maryland." *Maryland Historical Magazine* 58 (March 1963): 20–29.
———. *The Slave Community: Plantation Life in the Antebellum South*. New York: Oxford University Press, 1972.
Bode, Frederick E., and Donald Ginter. *Farm Tenancy and the Census for Antebellum Georgia*. Athens: University of Georgia Press, 1986.
Bogen, David S. "Annapolis Poll Books of 1800 and 1804: African American Voting in the Early Republic." *Maryland Historical Magazine* 86 (Spring 1991): 57–65.
Boles, John B., ed. *Maryland Heritage: Five Baltimore Institutions Celebrate the American Bicentennial*. Baltimore: Maryland Historical Society, 1976.
———. "Tension in a Slave Society: The Trial of the Reverend Jacob Gruber." *Southern Studies* 18 (Summer 1979): 179–97.
Bolster, W. Jeffrey. "'To Feel like a Man': Black Seamen in the Northern States, 1800–1860." *Journal of American History* 76 (Winter 1989): 1173–99.
Borchert, James. *Alley Life in Washington: Family, Community, Religion, and Folklife in the City, 1850–1970*. Urbana: University of Illinois Press, 1980.
Brackett, Jeffry R. *The Negro in Maryland: A Study of the Institution of Slavery*. Baltimore: Johns Hopkins University, 1889.
Bragg, George F. *History of the Afro-American Group of the Episcopal Church*. Baltimore: Church Advocate Press, 1922.
———. *Men of Maryland*. Alexandria, Va.: Chadwyck-Healy, 1914. Reprint. Baltimore: Church Advocate Press, 1925.
Brawley, Benjamin. *A Social History of the American Negro*. New York: Macmillan, 1913. Reprint. New York: Macmillan, 1970.
Breen, T. H., and Stephen Innes. *"Myne Owne Ground": Race and Freedom on Virginia's Eastern Shore, 1640–1676*. New York: Oxford University Press, 1980.
Bridenbaugh, Carl. *The Colonial Craftsman*. Chicago: University of Chicago Press, 1961.
Bridges, William E. "Family Patterns and Social Values in America, 1825–1875." *American Quarterly* 17 (Spring 1965): 3–11.
Bridner, Elwood. "The Fugitive Slaves in Maryland." *Maryland Historical Magazine* 66 (Spring 1971): 33–50.
Brooks, Neal A., and Eric G. Rockel. *A History of Baltimore County*. Towson, Md.: Friends of the Towson Library, 1979.
Brown, Letitia Woods. *Free Negroes in the District of Columbia, 1790–1846*. New York: Oxford University Press, 1972.
Brown, Richard D. *Modernization: The Transformation of American Life, 1600–1865*. New York: Hill and Wang, 1976.
Browne, Gary L. *Baltimore in the Nation, 1789–1861*. Chapel Hill: University of North Carolina Press, 1980.
Bruchey, Eleanor S. "The Development of Baltimore Business, 1800–1914." *Maryland Historical Magazine* 64 (Spring 1969): 18–42.

———. "The Industrialization of Maryland, 1860–1914." In *Maryland: A History, 1632–1974*, edited by Richard Walsh and William L. Fox. Baltimore: Maryland Historical Society, 1974.

Bruchey, Stuart Weems. *Robert Oliver, Merchant of Baltimore, 1783–1819*. Baltimore: Johns Hopkins Press, 1956.

Brugger, Robert J. *Maryland: A Middle Temperament, 1634–1980*. Baltimore: Johns Hopkins University Press, 1988.

Bruns, Roger, and William Fraley. "'Old Gunny': Abolitionist in a Slave City." *Maryland Historical Magazine* 68 (Winter 1973): 369–82.

Brush, Grace S. "Geology and Paleoecology of Chesapeake Bay: A Long-term Monitoring Tool for Management." *Journal of the Washington Academy of Science* 76 (1986): 146–60.

Burtner, Robert W., and Robert E. Chiles. *A Compend of Wesley's Theology*. New York: Abingdon, 1954.

Calderhead, William. "How Extensive Was the Border State Slave Trade?" *Civil War History* 18 (March 1972): 42–55.

———. "How Strong Was Religion as a Force in Manumission Activity: Anne Arundel County, a Case Study." In *Hall of Records' Conference on Maryland History, in Honor of Morris L. Radoff*. Annapolis, Md.: Hall of Records Commission, 1974.

———. "The Role of the Professional Slave Trader in a Slave Economy: Austin Woolfolk, a Case Study." *Civil War History* 23 (September 1977): 195–211.

Campbell, Penelope. *Maryland in Africa: The Maryland State Colonization Society, 1831–1857*. Urbana: University of Illinois Press, 1971.

Carr, Lois Green. "The Development of the Maryland Orphans' Court, 1654–1715." In *Law, Society, and Politics in Early Maryland: Proceedings of the First Conference on Maryland History, June 14–15, 1974*, edited by Aubrey C. Land, Lois Green Carr, and Edward C. Papenfuse. Baltimore: Johns Hopkins University Press, 1977.

———. "'The Metropolis of Maryland': A Comment on Town Development along the Tobacco Coast." *Maryland Historical Magazine* 69 (Summer 1974): 124–45.

Carr, Lois Green, and Russell R. Menard. "Immigration and Opportunity: The Freedman in Early Colonial Maryland." In *The Chesapeake in the Seventeenth Century: Essays on Anglo-American Society*, edited by Thad W. Tate and David L. Ammerman. Chapel Hill: University of North Carolina Press, 1979.

———. "Land, Labor, and Economies of Scale in Early Maryland: Some Limits to Growth in the Chesapeake System of Husbandry." *Journal of Economic History* 49 (June 1989): 407–18.

Carr, Lois Green, Philip D. Morgan, and Jean B. Russo, eds. *Colonial Chesapeake Society*. Chapel Hill: University of North Carolina Press, 1988.

Carr, Lois Green, and Lorena S. Walsh. "Economic Diversification and Labor Organization in the Chesapeake, 1650–1820." In *Work and Labor in Early America*, edited by Stephen Innes. Chapel Hill: University of North Carolina Press, 1988.

Carroll, Douglas G., Jr., and Blanche D. Coll. "The Baltimore Almshouse: An Early History." *Maryland Historical Magazine* 66 (Summer 1971): 135–52.

Carroll, Kenneth L. "An Eighteenth-Century Episcopalian Attack on Quaker and Methodist Manumission of Slaves." *Maryland Historical Magazine* 80 (Summer 1985): 139–50.

———. "Maryland Quakers and Slavery." *Maryland Historical Magazine* 45 (September 1950): 215–25.

———. "Nicholites and Slavery in Eighteenth-Century Maryland." *Maryland Historical Magazine* 79 (Summer 1984): 126–33.

———. *Quakerism on the Eastern Shore.* Baltimore: Maryland Historical Society, 1970.

———. "Religious Influences on the Manumission of Slaves in Caroline, Dorchester, and Kent Counties." *Maryland Historical Magazine* 56 (Fall 1961): 176–97.

———. "Voices of Protest: Eastern Shore Abolition Societies, 1790–1820." *Maryland Historical Magazine* 58 (Summer 1963): 350–59.

Cash, Wilbur J. *The Mind of the South.* New York: Alfred A. Knopf, 1941.

Cassell, Frank A. "The Great Baltimore Riot of 1812." *Maryland Historical Magazine* 70 (Fall 1975): 241–59.

———. *Merchant Congressman in the Young Republic: Samuel Smith of Maryland, 1752–1839.* Madison: University of Wisconsin Press, 1971.

———. "The Structure of Baltimore's Politics in the Age of Jefferson, 1795–1812." In *Law, Society, and Politics in Early Maryland: Proceedings of the First Conference on Maryland History, June 14–15, 1974,* edited by Aubrey C. Land, Lois Green Carr, and Edward C. Papenfuse. Baltimore: Johns Hopkins University Press, 1977.

Cassity, Michael. *Defending a Way of Life: An American Community in the Nineteenth Century.* Albany: State University of New York Press, 1989.

Catterall, Helen T., ed. *Judicial Cases concerning American Slavery and the Negro.* 5 vols. Washington, D.C.: Carnegie Institution, 1926. Reprint. New York: Negro Universities Press, 1968.

"Census of Deptford Hundred or Fell's Point, 1776." *Maryland Historical Magazine* 25 (September 1930): 271–75.

Clark, Raymond B. *Index to Baltimore County, Maryland, Wills, 1660–1777.* Arlington, Va.: by the author, 1982.

Clayton, Ralph. *Black Baltimore—1820–1870.* Bowie, Md.: Heritage Books, 1987.

———. *Slavery, Slaveholding, and the Free Black Population of Antebellum Baltimore.* Bowie, Md.: Heritage Books, 1993.

Clemens, Paul G. E. *The Atlantic Economy and Colonial Maryland's Eastern Shore: From Tobacco to Grain.* Ithaca, N.Y.: Cornell University Press, 1980.

———. "Economy and Society on Maryland's Eastern Shore, 1689–1733." In *Law, Society, and Politics in Early Maryland: Proceedings of the First Conference on Maryland History, June 14–15, 1974,* edited by Aubrey C. Land, Lois Green Carr, and Edward C. Papenfuse. Baltimore: Johns Hopkins University Press, 1977.

Cody, Cheryll A. "There Was No 'Absalom' on the Ball Plantations: Slave Naming Practices in the South Carolina Low Country, 1720–1865." *American Historical Review* 92 (May 1987): 563–96.

Coleman, Kenneth, and Charles Stephen Gurr, eds. *Dictionary of Georgia Biography.* 2 vols. Athens: University of Georgia Press, 1983.

Conkin, Paul. *Prophets of Prosperity: America's First Political Economists.* Bloomington: Indiana University Press, 1980.

Cooper, Frederick. "Elevating the Race: The Social Thought of Black Leaders, 1827–50." *American Quarterly* 24 (December 1972): 604–25.

Cooper, William J. *Liberty and Slavery: Southern Politics to 1860.* New York: Alfred A. Knopf, 1983.

Cottrol, Robert. *The Afro-Yankees: Providence's Black Community in the Antebellum Era.* Westport, Conn.: Greenwood, 1982.

Craton, Michael. *Sinews of Empire: A Short History of British Slavery.* Garden City, N.Y.: Anchor Press/Doubleday, 1974.

Craven, Avery O. *Soil Exhaustion as a Factor in the Agricultural History of Virginia and Maryland, 1606–1860.* Urbana: University of Illinois Press, 1926.

Curry, Leonard P. *The Free Black in Urban America, 1800–1850: The Shadow of the Dream.* Chicago: University of Chicago Press, 1981.

———. "Urbanization and Urbanism in the Old South: A Comparative View." *Journal of Southern History* 40 (February 1974): 43–60.

Davidson, Thomas E. "Free Blacks in Old Somerset County, 1745–1755." *Maryland Historical Magazine* 80 (Summer 1985): 151–56.

Deal, Douglas. "A Constricted World: Free Blacks on Virginia's Eastern Shore, 1680–1750." In *Colonial Chesapeake Society*, edited by Lois Green Carr, Philip D. Morgan, and Jean B. Russo. Chapel Hill: University of North Carolina Press, 1988.

Decter, Avi Y. "Notes on Method and Theory in Social History: Free Blacks in St. Mary's County, Maryland, 1850–1860." In *Hall of Records' Conference on Maryland History, in Honor of Morris L. Radoff.* Annapolis, Md.: Hall of Records Commission, 1974.

Degler, Carl N. *Neither Black nor White: Slavery and Race Relations in Brazil and the United States.* New York: Macmillan, 1971.

Della, M. Ray, Jr. "An Analysis of Baltimore's Population in the 1850's." *Maryland Historical Magazine* 68 (Spring 1973): 20–35.

———. "The Problems of Negro Labor in the 1850's." *Maryland Historical Magazine* 66 (Spring 1971): 14–32.

DePauw, Linda Grant. "Land of the Unfree: Legal Limitations on Liberty in Pre-revolutionary America." *Maryland Historical Magazine* 68 (Winter 1973): 355–67.

Dew, Charles B. *Bond of Iron: Master and Slave at Buffalo Forge.* New York: W. W. Norton, 1994.

———. "Slavery and Technology in the Antebellum Southern Iron Industry: The Case of Buffalo Forge." In *Science and Medicine in the Old South*, edited by Ronald L. Numbers and Todd L. Savitt. Baton Rouge: Louisiana State University Press, 1989.

DiLisio, James E. *Maryland: A Geography.* Boulder, Colo.: Westview, 1983.

Dillon, Merton L. *The Abolitionists: The Growth of a Dissenting Minority.* DeKalb:

Northern Illinois University Press, 1974. Reprint. New York: W. W. Norton, 1979.

———. *Benjamin Lundy and the Struggle for Negro Freedom*. Urbana: University of Illinois Press, 1966.

Doherty, Robert W. "Social Basis of the Presbyterian Schism, 1837–1838: The Philadelphia Case." *Journal of Social History* 2 (Fall 1968): 69–79.

Dowd, Mary Jane. "The State of the Maryland Economy, 1776–1807." *Maryland Historical Magazine* 57 (June 1962): 90–132; 57 (September 1862): 229–58.

Drake, Thomas E. *Quakers and Slavery in America*. New Haven, Conn.: Yale University Press, 1950.

Du Bois, W. E. B. *The Negro Artisan*. Atlanta, Ga.: [Atlanta University Press], 1902.

———. *The Philadelphia Negro: A Social Study*. Philadelphia: University of Pennsylvania, 1899. Reprint. New York: Benjamin Blom, 1967.

———. *The Souls of Black Folk*. Chicago: A. C. McClurg, 1903.

Dumenil, Lynn. *Freemasonry and American Culture, 1880–1930*. Princeton, N.J.: Princeton University Press, 1984.

Dunaway, Wayland Fuller. "Pennsylvania as an Early Distributing Center of Population." *Pennsylvania Magazine of History and Biography* 55 (April 1931): 134–69.

Duncan, Richard R. "The Era of the Civil War." In *Maryland: A History, 1632–1974*, edited by Richard Walsh and William L. Fox. Baltimore: Maryland Historical Society, 1974.

Dunn, Richard S. "Black Society in the Chesapeake, 1776–1810." In *Slavery and Freedom in the Age of the American Revolution*, edited by Ira Berlin and Ronald Hoffman. Charlottesville: University Press of Virginia, 1983. Reprint. Urbana: University of Illinois Press, 1986.

Dvorak, Katharine L. *An African-American Exodus: The Segregation of the Southern Churches*. Brooklyn, N.Y.: Carlson, 1991.

Earle, Carville V. *The Evolution of a Tidewater Settlement System: All Hallow's Parish, Maryland, 1650–1783*. Chicago: University of Chicago Press, 1975.

Earle, Carville V., and Ronald Hoffman. "Staple Crops and Urban Development in the Eighteenth-Century South." *Perspectives in American History* 10 (Winter 1976): 7–78.

Eaton, Clement. "Slave Hiring in the Upper South: A Step towards Freedom." *Mississippi Valley Historical Review* 46 (March 1960): 663–78.

Eblen, Jack E. "Growth of the Black Population in Antebellum America, 1820–1860." *Population Studies* 26 (October 1972): 273–89.

Elkins, Stanley. *Slavery: A Problem in American Institutional and Intellectual Life*. Chicago: University of Chicago Press, 1959.

Ellefson, C. Ashley. "Free Jupiter and the Rest of the World: The Problems of a Free Negro in Colonial Maryland." *Maryland Historical Magazine* 66 (Spring 1971): 1–13.

Evitts, William J. *A Matter of Allegiances: Maryland from 1850 to 1861*. Baltimore: Johns Hopkins University Press, 1974.

Farley, Reynolds. "The Urbanization of Negroes in the United States." *Journal of Social History* 1 (Spring 1968): 241–58.

Fausz, J. Frederick. "Present at the 'Creation': The Chesapeake World That Greeted the Maryland Colonists." *Maryland Historical Magazine* 79 (Spring 1984): 7–20.

Feldberg, Michael. *The Turbulent Era: Riot and Disorder in Jacksonian America.* New York: Oxford University Press, 1980.

Ferguson, Charles W. *Organizing to Beat the Devil: Methodists and the Making of America.* Garden City, N.J.: Doubleday, 1971.

Fields, Barbara J[eanne]. "Ideology and Race in American History." In *Race, Region, and Reconstruction: Essays in Honor of C. Vann Woodward,* edited by J. Morgan Kousser and James McPherson. New York: Oxford University Press, 1982.

———. *Slavery and Freedom on the Middle Ground: Maryland during the Nineteenth Century.* New Haven, Conn.: Yale University Press, 1985.

Filler, Louis. *The Crusade against Slavery, 1830–1860.* New York: Harper and Brothers, 1960.

Finnie, Gordon. "The Anti-Slavery Movement in the Upper South before 1840." *Journal of Southern History* 35 (May 1969): 319–42.

Fishel, Leslie H., Jr., and Benjamin Quarles, eds. *The Black American: A Documentary History.* New York: William Morrow, 1970.

Fitchett, E. Horace. "The Origin and Growth of the Free Negro Population of Charleston, South Carolina." *Journal of Negro History* 26 (October 1941): 421–37.

———. "The Status of the Free Negro in Charleston, South Carolina." *Journal of Negro History* 32 (October 1947): 430–51.

Flanders, Ralph B. "The Free Negro in Antebellum Georgia." *North Carolina Historical Review* 9 (July 1932): 250–72.

Fogel, Robert W., and Stanley L. Engerman. *Time on the Cross: The Economics of American Negro Slavery.* Boston: Little, Brown, 1974.

Fogel, Robert W., Stanley L. Engerman, Roderick Floud, Gerald Friedman, Robert A. Margo, Kenneth Sokoloff, Richard H. Steckel, T. James Trussell, Georgia Villaflor, and Kenneth W. Wachter. "Secular Changes in American and British Stature and Nutrition." *Journal of Interdisciplinary History* 14 (Autumn 1983): 445–81.

Foner, Eric. *Reconstruction—America's Unfinished Revolution.* New York: Harper and Row, 1988.

Foner, Laura. "The Free People of Color in Louisiana and St. Domingue: A Comparative Portrait of Two Three-Caste Slave Societies." *Journal of Social History* 3 (June 1970): 406–29.

Foner, Philip S. *Blacks in the American Revolution.* Westport, Conn.: Greenwood, 1976.

———. "The First Negro Meeting in Maryland." *Maryland Historical Magazine* 66 (Spring 1971): 60–67.

———. *History of Black Americans: From the Compromise of 1850 to the End of the Civil War.* Westport, Conn.: Greenwood, 1983.

Franklin, John Hope. *The Free Negro in North Carolina, 1790–1860.* Chapel Hill: University of North Carolina Press, 1943.

———. *From Slavery to Freedom: A History of Negro Americans.* 7th ed. New York: McGraw-Hill, 1993.

———. "Slaves Virtually Free in Ante-Bellum North Carolina." *Journal of Negro History* 28 (July 1943): 284–310.

Frazier, E. Franklin. *The Free Negro Family: A Study of Family Origins before the Civil War.* Nashville, Tenn.: Fisk University, 1932.

———. *The Negro Church in America.* New York: Schocken Books, 1963.

———. *The Negro Family in the United States.* Chicago: University of Chicago Press, 1939.

Fredrickson, George M. *The Black Image in the White Mind: The Debate on Afro-American Character and Destiny, 1817–1914.* New York: Harper and Row, 1971.

———. "Toward a Social Interpretation of the Development of American Racism." In *Key Issues in the Afro-American Experience,* vol. 1, edited by Nathan I. Huggins, Martin Kilson, and Daniel M. Fox. New York: Harcourt Brace Jovanovich, 1971.

Fuke, Richard Paul. "The Baltimore Association for the Moral and Educational Improvement of the Colored People, 1864–1870." *Maryland Historical Magazine* 66 (Winter 1971): 369–404.

———. "A Reform Mentality: Federal Policy toward Black Marylanders, 1864–1868." *Civil War History* 22 (September 1976): 214–35.

Furstenberg, Frank, Jr., Theodore Hershberg, and John Modell. "The Origins of the Female-Headed Black Family: The Impact of the Urban Environment." In *Philadelphia: Work, Space, Family and Group Experience in the Nineteenth Century,* edited by Theodore Hershberg. New York: Oxford University Press, 1981.

Gardner, Bettye J. "Antebellum Black Education in Baltimore." *Maryland Historical Magazine* 71 (Fall 1976): 360–66.

———. "'Opposition to Emigration: A Selected Letter of William Watkins (The Colored Baltimorean).'" *Journal of Negro History* 67 (Summer 1982): 155–58.

———. "William Watkins: Antebellum Black Teacher and Anti-slavery Writer." *Negro History Bulletin* 39 (September-October 1976): 623–25.

Garitee, Jerome R. *The Republic's Private Navy: The American Privateering Business as Practiced by Baltimore during the War of 1812.* Middletown, Conn.: Wesleyan University Press, 1977.

Garonzik, Joseph. "The Racial and Ethnic Make-up of Baltimore Neighborhoods, 1850–70." *Maryland Historical Magazine* 71 (Fall 1976): 392–402.

Garrett, Jane N. "Philadelphia and Baltimore, 1790–1840: A Study of Intra-regional Unity." *Maryland Historical Magazine* 55 (March 1960): 1–13.

Gatewood, Willard B. "Aristocrats of Color: South and North—The Black Elite, 1880–1920." *Journal of Southern History* 54 (February 1988): 3–20.

Genovese, Eugene D. *Roll, Jordan, Roll: The World the Slaves Made.* New York: Pantheon Books, 1974.

George, Carol V. R. "Widening the Circle: The Black Church and the Abolitionist

Crusade, 1830–1860." In *Antislavery Reconsidered: New Perspectives on the Abolitionists*, edited by Lewis Perry and Michael Fellman. Baton Rouge: Louisiana State University Press, 1979.

Gilchrist, David T., ed. *The Growth of the Seaport Cities, 1790–1825: Proceedings of a Conference Sponsored by the Eleutherian Mills–Hagley Foundation, March 17–19, 1966.* Charlottesville: University Press of Virginia, 1967.

Gilje, Paul A. "The Baltimore Riots of 1812 and the Breakdown of the Anglo-American Mob Tradition." *Journal of Social History* 13 (Summer 1980): 547–64.

Gilliard, John T. *The Catholic Church and the American Negro.* Baltimore: St. Joseph's Society Press, 1930.

Glenn, Norvil D. "Negro Prestige Criteria: A Case Study in the Bases of Prestige." *American Journal of Sociology* 68 (May 1963): 645–57.

Goldin, Claudia Dale. *Urban Slavery in the American South, 1820–1860: A Quantitative History.* Chicago: University of Chicago Press, 1976.

Goodfriend, Joyce D. "Burghers and Blacks: The Evolution of a Slave Society at New Amsterdam." *New York History* 59 (1978): 125–44.

Gould, Clarence P. "The Economic Causes of the Rise of Baltimore." In *Essays in Colonial History Presented to Charles McLean Andrews by His Students.* New Haven, Conn.: Yale University Press, 1931.

Graham, Leroy. *Baltimore, the Nineteenth-Century Black Capital.* Lanham, Md.: University Press of America, 1982.

———. "Manumitted Free Blacks in Baltimore, 1806–1816." *Maryland Magazine of Genealogy* 5 (Spring 1982): 7–22.

Gravely, Will B. "Rise of the African Churches in America (1786–1822)." *Journal of Religious Thought* 14 (Fall 1984): 315–32.

Gray, Lewis C. *History of Agriculture in the Southern United States to 1860.* 2 vols. Washington, D.C.: Carnegie Institution, 1933.

Green, Constance M. *The Secret City: A History of Race Relations in the Nation's Capital.* Princeton, N.J.: Princeton University Press, 1967.

Greene, Lorenzo, and Carter G. Woodson. *The Negro Wage Earner.* Washington, D.C.: Association for the Study of Negro Life and History, 1930.

Greenwald, William I. "The Ante-Bellum Population, 1830–1860." *Mid-America* 36 (July 1954): 176–89.

Griffin, Clifford S. "Religious Benevolence as Social Control, 1815–1860." *Mississippi Valley Historical Review* 44 (December 1957): 423–44.

Griffin, Richard W. "An Origin of the Industrial Revolution in Maryland: The Textile Industry, 1789–1826." *Maryland Historical Magazine* 61 (March 1966): 24–36.

Grimes, Michael A. "More Baltimore Cabinetmakers and Allied Tradesmen, 1800–1845." *Maryland Historical Magazine* 83 (Fall 1988): 244–46.

Grimshaw, William H. *Official History of Freemasonry among the Colored People in North America.* New York: Broadway, 1903. Reprint. Salem, N.H.: Ayer, 1984.

Guertler, John T., ed. *The Records of Baltimore's Private Organizations: A Guide to Archival Resources.* New York: Garland, 1981.

Gutman, Herbert G. *The Black Family in Slavery and Freedom, 1750–1925*. New York: Random House, 1976.

———. *Work, Culture, and Society in Industrializing America: Essays in American Working-Class and Social History*. New York: Vintage Books, 1977.

Guy, Anita Aidt. "The Maryland Abolition Society and the Promotion of the Ideals of the New Nation." *Maryland Historical Magazine* 84 (Winter 1989): 342–49.

Hall, Clayton Colman, ed. *Baltimore: Its History and People*. New York: Barnes and Noble, 1912.

———, ed. *Narratives of Early Maryland*. New York: Barnes and Noble, 1910.

Hall, Robert L. "Slave Resistance in Baltimore City and County, 1747–1790." *Maryland Historical Magazine* 84 (Winter 1989): 305–18.

Hall of Records' Conference on Maryland History, in Honor of Morris L. Radoff. Annapolis, Md.: Hall of Records Commission, 1974.

Hancock, Harold B. "Not Quite Men: The Free Negroes in Delaware in the 1830's." *Civil War History* 17 (December 1971): 320–31.

Handlin, Oscar, and Mary Handlin. "Origins of the Southern Labor System." *William and Mary Quarterly*, 3d ser., 7 (April 1950): 199–222.

Handy, James. *Scraps of African Methodist Episcopal History*. Philadelphia: A.M.E. Book Concern, 1902.

Harding, Vincent. "Religion and Resistance among Antebellum Negroes, 1800–1860." In *The Making of Black America*, edited by August Meier and Elliott Rudwick. 2 vols. New York: Atheneum, 1969.

Hartridge, Walter C. "The Refugees from the Island of St. Domingo in Maryland." *Maryland Historical Magazine* 38 (June 1943): 103–22.

Harvey, Katharine A. "Practicing Medicine at the Baltimore Almshouse, 1828–1850." *Maryland Historical Magazine* 74 (September 1979): 223–37.

Henretta, James, ed. "The Declaration of Independence, July 4, 1776." In *The Course of United States History: An Anthology*, edited by David Nasaw. 2 vols. Chicago: Dorsey, 1987.

Hershberg, Theodore. "Free Blacks in Antebellum Philadelphia: A Study of Ex-Slaves, Freeborn and Socio-economic Decline." *Journal of Social History* 5 (Spring 1972): 183–209.

———, ed. *Philadelphia: Work, Space, Family and Group Experience in the Nineteenth Century*. New York: Oxford University Press, 1981.

Hershberg, Theodore, and Henry Williams. "Mulattoes and Blacks: Intra-group Color Differences and Social Stratification in Nineteenth-Century Philadelphia." In *Philadelphia: Work, Space, Family and Group Experience in the Nineteenth Century*, edited by Theodore Hershberg. New York: Oxford University Press, 1981.

Herskovits, Melville J. *The Myth of the Negro Past*. New York, Harper and Brothers, 1941. Reprint. Boston: Beacon, 1958.

Hoffman, Ronald. *A Spirit of Dissension: Economics, Politics, and the Revolution in Maryland*. Baltimore: Johns Hopkins University Press, 1973.

Hoffman, Ronald, Thad W. Tate, and Peter J. Albert, eds. *An Uncivil War: The South-*

ern Backcountry during the American Revolution. Charlottesville: University Press of Virginia, 1985.

Holt, Michael F. "The Politics of Impatience: The Origins of the Know-Nothingism." *Journal of American History* 60 (September 1973): 309–32.

Holt, Thomas L. *Black over White: Negro Political Leadership in South Carolina during the Reconstruction.* Urbana: University of Illinois Press, 1977.

Horton, James Oliver. "Blacks in Antebellum Boston: The Migrant and the Community, an Analysis of Adaptation." *Southern Studies* 21 (Fall 1982): 277–93.

———. *Free People of Color: Inside the African American Community.* Washington, D.C.: Smithsonian Institution Press, 1993.

Horton, James Oliver, and Lois E. Horton. *Black Bostonians: Family Life and Community Struggle in an Antebellum City.* New York: Holmes and Meier, 1979.

Howard, William T. *Public Health Administration and the Natural History of Disease in Baltimore, Maryland, 1797–1920.* Washington, D.C.: Carnegie Institution of Washington, 1924.

Hoyt, William D., Jr., ed. "Civilian Defense in Baltimore, 1814–1815." *Maryland Historical Magazine* 39 (September 1944): 199–224; 39 (December 1944): 293–309; 40 (March 1945): 7–23; 40 (June 1945): 137–53.

Huggins, Nathan I., Martin Kilson, and Daniel M. Fox, eds. *Key Issues in the Afro-American Experience.* 2 vols. New York: Harcourt Brace Jovanovich, 1971.

Hunt, Alfred N. *Haiti's Influence on Antebellum America: Slumbering Volcano in the Caribbean.* Baton Rouge: Louisiana State University Press, 1988.

Innes, Stephen, ed. *Work and Labor in Early America.* Chapel Hill: University of North Carolina Press, 1988.

Inscoe, John C. "Carolina Slave Names: An Index to Acculturation." *Journal of Southern History* 49 (November 1983): 527–54.

Irwin, James R. "Exploring the Affinity of Wheat and Slavery in the Virginia Piedmont." *Explorations in Economic History* 25 (March 1988): 295–322.

Isaac, Rhys. *The Transformation of Virginia, 1740–1790.* Chapel Hill: University of North Carolina Press, 1982.

Jackson, Luther P. *Free Negro Labor and Property Holding in Virginia, 1830–1860.* New York: D. Appleton, 1942. Reprint. New York: Russell and Russell, 1971.

———. "Manumission in Certain Virginia Cities." *Journal of Negro History* 15 (July 1930): 278–314.

Jacob, Kathryn A. "The Woman's Lot in Baltimore Town, 1729–97." *Maryland Historical Magazine* 71 (Fall 1976): 283–95.

James, C. L. R. *The Black Jacobins: Toussaint L'Ouverture and the San Domingo Revolution.* New York: Vintage Books, 1963.

James, Sydney V. *A People among People: Quaker Benevolence in Eighteenth-Century America.* Cambridge, Mass.: Harvard University Press, 1963.

Jenkins, William Sumner. *Pro-slavery Thought in the Old South.* Chapel Hill: University of North Carolina Press, 1935.

Johnson, Franklin. *The Development of State Legislation concerning the Free Negro.* New York: n.p., 1918.

Johnson, Michael P., and James L. Roark. *Black Masters: A Free Family of Color in the Old South.* New York: W. W. Norton, 1984.

Johnson, Paul E. *A Shopkeeper's Millennium: Society and Revivals in Rochester, New York, 1815–1837.* New York: Hill and Wang, 1978.

Johnson, Whittington B. "Free Blacks in Antebellum Savannah: An Economic Profile." *Georgia Historical Quarterly* 64 (Winter 1980): 418–31.

———. "The Origin and Nature of African Slavery in Seventeenth Century Maryland." *Maryland Historical Magazine* 73 (September 1978): 236–45.

Jones, Jacqueline. *Labor of Love, Labor of Sorrow: Black Women, Work, and the Family, from Slavery to the Present.* New York: Basic Books, 1985.

Jordan, Winthrop. "American Chiaroscuro: The Status and Definition of Mulattoes in the British Colonies." *William and Mary Quarterly,* 3d ser., 19 (April 1962): 183–220.

———. *The White Man's Burden: Historical Origins of Racism in the United States.* New York: Oxford University Press, 1974.

———. *White over Black: American Attitudes toward the Negro, 1550–1872.* Chapel Hill: University of North Carolina Press, 1968.

Karinen, Arthur E. "Maryland Population: 1631–1730." *Maryland Historical Magazine* 54 (December 1959): 365–407.

Kasson, John. *Civilizing the Machine: Technology and Republican Values in the United States, 1776–1900.* New York: Grossman, 1976. Reprint. New York: Penguin, 1977.

Katzman, David M. *Before the Ghetto: Black Detroit in the Nineteenth Century.* Urbana: University of Illinois Press, 1973.

Kellow, Margaret M. R. "Indentured Servitude in Eighteenth-Century Maryland." *Histoire sociale* 17 (November 1984): 229–55.

Kimmel, Ross M. "Free Blacks in Seventeenth-Century Maryland." *Maryland Historical Magazine* 71 (Spring 1976): 19–25.

Klein, Herbert S. *African Slavery in Latin American and the Caribbean.* New York: Oxford University Press, 1986.

Klein, Rachel N. "Frontier Planters and the American Revolution: The South Carolina Backcountry." In *An Uncivil War: The Southern Backcountry during the American Revolution,* edited by Ronald Hoffman, Thad W. Tate, and Peter J. Albert. Charlottesville: University Press of Virginia, 1985.

Knights, Peter R. *The Plain People of Boston, 1830–1860: A Study in City Growth.* New York: Oxford University Press, 1971.

Koger, Azzie Briscoe. *Negro Baptists in Maryland.* Baltimore: Clarke, 1946.

Kornweibel, Theodore, Jr. *In Search of the Promised Land: Essays in Black Urban History.* Port Washington, N.Y.: Kennikat, 1981.

Kotlikoff, Laurence J., and Anton J. Rupert. "Manumission of Slaves in New Orleans, 1827–1846." *Southern Studies* 19 (Summer 1980): 172–81.

Kousser, J. Morgan, and James McPherson, eds. *Race, Region, and Reconstruction: Essays in Honor of C. Vann Woodward.* New York: Oxford University Press, 1982.

Krech, Shepard, III. "Black Family Organization in the Nineteenth Century: An

Ethnological Perspective." *Journal of Interdisciplinary History* 12 (Winter 1982): 429–52.

———. *Praise the Bridge That Carries You Over: The Life of Joseph L. Sutton.* Boston: G. K. Hall, 1981.

Kulikoff, Allan. "The Beginnings of the Afro-American Family in Maryland." In *Law, Society, and Politics in Early Maryland: Proceedings of the First Conference on Maryland History, June 14–15, 1974*, edited by Aubrey C. Land, Lois Green Carr, and Edward C. Papenfuse. Baltimore: Johns Hopkins University Press, 1977.

———. "The Economic Growth of the Eighteenth-Century Chesapeake Colonies." *Journal of Economic History* 39 (March 1979): 275–88.

———. *Tobacco and Slaves: The Development of Southern Cultures in the Chesapeake, 1680–1800.* Chapel Hill: University of North Carolina Press, 1986.

———. "Uprooted Peoples: Black Migrants in the Age of the American Revolution, 1790–1820." In *Slavery and Freedom in the Age of Revolution*, edited by Ira Berlin and Ronald Hoffman. Charlottesville: University Press of Virginia, 1983. Reprint. Urbana: University of Illinois Press, 1986.

Kusmer, Kenneth L. "The Black Urban Experience in American History." In *The State of Afro-American History: Past, Present, and Future*, edited by Darlene Clark Hine. Baton Rouge: Louisiana State University Press, 1986.

———. *A Ghetto Takes Shape: Black Cleveland, 1870–1930.* Urbana: University of Illinois Press, 1976.

Land, Aubrey C. *Colonial Maryland: A History.* Millwood, N.Y.: KTO, 1981.

———. "Economic Base and Social Structure: The Northern Chesapeake in the Eighteenth Century." *Journal of Economic History* 25 (December 1965): 639–54.

———. "The Planters of Colonial Maryland." *Maryland Historical Magazine* 67 (Spring 1972): 109–28.

———. "Provincial Maryland." In *Maryland: A History, 1632–1974*, edited by Richard Walsh and William L. Fox. Baltimore: Maryland Historical Society, 1974.

Land, Aubrey C., Lois Green Carr, and Edward C. Papenfuse, eds. *Law, Society, and Politics in Early Maryland: Proceedings of the First Conference on Maryland History, June 14–15, 1974.* Baltimore: Johns Hopkins University Press, 1977.

Larkin, Jack. *The Reshaping of Everyday Life, 1790–1840.* New York: Harper and Row, 1988.

Larsen, Lawrence H. *The Urban South: A History.* Lexington: University Press of Kentucky, 1990.

Laurie, Bruce. "Fire Companies and Gangs in Southwark: The 1840s." In *The Peoples of Philadelphia: A History of Ethnic Groups and Lower-Class Life, 1790–1940*, edited by Allen F. Davis and Mark Haller. Philadelphia: Temple University Press, 1973.

———. *Working People of Philadelphia, 1800–1850.* Philadelphia: Temple University Press, 1980.

Leakin, George Armistead. "The Migrations of Baltimore Town." *Maryland Historical Magazine* 1 (March 1906): 45–56.

LeFurgy, William G. *Baltimore's Wards, 1797–1978*. Baltimore: [Baltimore] City Archives and Records Management Office, 1980.

———. *The Records of a City: A Guide to the Baltimore City Archives*. Baltimore: [Baltimore] City Archives and Records Management Office, 1984.

Lemon, James T. *The Best Poor Man's Country: A Geographical Study of Early Southeastern Pennsylvania*. Baltimore: Johns Hopkins University Press, 1972. Reprint. New York: W. W. Norton, 1980.

Levine, Lawrence W. *Black Culture and Black Consciousness: Afro-American Folk Thought from Slavery to Freedom*. New York: Oxford University Press, 1977.

Lincoln, C. Eric, and Lawrence H. Mamiya. *The Black Church in the African American Experience*. Durham, N.C.: Duke University Press, 1990.

Litwack, Leon F. *Been in the Storm So Long: The Aftermath of Slavery*. New York: Alfred A. Knopf, 1979.

———. *North of Slavery: The Negro in the Free States, 1790–1860*. Chicago: University of Chicago Press, 1961.

Livingood, James W. *The Philadelphia-Baltimore Trade Rivalry, 1780–1860*. Harrisburg: Pennsylvania Historical and Museum Commission, 1947.

Macdonough, Oliver. "The Irish Famine Emigration to the United States." *Perspectives in American History* 10 (Winter 1976): 357–448.

MacLeod, Duncan J. "Toward Caste." In *Slavery and Freedom in the Age of the American Revolution*, edited by Ira Berlin and Ronald Hoffman. Charlottesville: University Press of Virginia, 1983. Reprint. Urbana: University of Illinois Press, 1986.

Main, Gloria L. "Maryland and the Chesapeake Economy, 1670–1720." In *Law, Society, and Politics in Early Maryland: Proceedings of the First Conference on Maryland History, June 14–15, 1974*, edited by Aubrey C. Land, Lois Green Carr, and Edward C. Papenfuse. Baltimore: Johns Hopkins University Press, 1977.

———. *Tobacco Colony: Life in Early Maryland*. Princeton, N.J.: Princeton University Press, 1982.

Malone, Dumas, ed. *Dictionary of American Biography*. 20 vols. New York: Charles Scribner's Sons, 1934.

Mandel, Bernard. *Labor, Slave and Free: Workingmen and the Anti-slavery Movement in the United States*. New York: Associated Authors, 1955.

Margo, R. A., and Richard H. Steckel. "The Heights of American Slaves: New Evidence on Slave Nutrition and Health." *Social Science History* 6 (December 1982): 516–38.

Marks, Bayly E. "Clifton Factory, 1810–1860—An Experiment in Rural Industrialization." *Maryland Historical Magazine* 80 (Spring 1985): 45–65.

———. "Skilled Blacks in Antebellum St. Mary's County, Maryland." *Journal of Southern History* 53 (November 1987): 537–64.

Mathews, Donald G. *Religion in the Old South*. Chicago: University of Chicago Press, 1978.

———. "The Second Great Awakening as an Organizing Process, 1780–1830: An Hypothesis." *American Quarterly* 21 (Spring 1969): 23–43.

———. *Slavery and Methodism: A Chapter in American Morality, 1780–1845.* Princeton, N.J.: Princeton University Press, 1965.

Mathieson, William Law. *British Slave Emancipation, 1838–1849.* London: Longmans, Green, 1932. Reprint. New York: Octagon Books, 1967.

Matison, Sumner E. "Manumission by Purchase." *Journal of Negro History* 33 (October 1948): 146–67.

McCusker, John J., and Russell R. Menard. *The Economy of British America, 1607–1789.* Chapel Hill: University of North Carolina Press, 1985.

McDougall, Harold A. *Black Baltimore: A New Theory of Community.* Philadelphia: Temple University Press, 1993.

McFeely, William S. *Frederick Douglass.* New York: W. W. Norton, 1991.

Mehlinger, Louis R. "The Attitude of the Free Negro toward African Colonization." *Journal of Negro History* 1 (July 1916): 140–54.

Meier, August. *Negro Thought in America, 1880–1915: Racial Ideologies in the Age of Booker T. Washington.* Ann Arbor: University of Michigan Press, 1963.

Menard, Russell R. "British Migration to the Chesapeake Colonies in the Seventeenth Century." In *Colonial Chesapeake Society,* edited by Lois Green Carr, Philip D. Morgan, and Jean B. Russo. Chapel Hill: University of North Carolina Press, 1988.

———. *Economy and Society in Early Colonial Maryland.* New York: Garland, 1985.

———. "Farm Prices of Maryland Tobacco, 1659–1710." *Maryland Historical Magazine* 68 (Spring 1973): 80–85.

———. "Five Maryland Censuses, 1700 to 1712: A Note on the Quality of the Quantities." *William and Mary Quarterly,* 3d ser., 37 (Fall 1980): 616–26.

———. "From Servants to Slaves: The Transformation of the Chesapeake Labor System." *Southern Studies* 16 (Winter 1977): 355–90.

———. "Population, Economy, and Society in Seventeenth-Century Maryland." *Maryland Historical Magazine* 79 (Spring 1984): 71–92.

Menard, Russell R., P. M. G. Harris, and Lois Green Carr. "Opportunity and Inequality: The Distribution of Wealth on the Lower Western Shore of Maryland, 1638–1705." *Maryland Historical Magazine* 69 (Summer 1974): 169–84.

Meyer, Eugene L. *Maryland Lost and Found: People and Places from Chesapeake to Appalachia.* Baltimore: Johns Hopkins University Press, 1986.

Middlekauff, Robert. *The Glorious Cause: The American Revolution, 1763–1789.* New York: Oxford University Press, 1982.

Middleton, Arthur P. *Tobacco Coast: A Maritime History of Chesapeake Bay in the Colonial Era.* Newport News, Va.: Mariners' Museum, 1953.

Miller, Floyd J. *The Search for a Black Nationality: Black Emigration and Colonization, 1787–1863.* Urbana: University of Illinois Press, 1975.

Miller, Henry M. "Transforming a 'Splendid and Delightsome Land': Colonists and Ecological Change in the Chesapeake, 1607–1820." *Journal of the Washington Academy of Science* 76 (March 1986): 173–87.

Miller, M. Sammy. "Patty Cannon: Murderer and Kidnapper of Free Blacks." *Maryland Historical Magazine* 72 (Fall 1977): 419–23.

Miller, Nathan. "Some Aspects of the Name in Culture-History." *American Journal of Sociology* 32 (January 1927): 588–611.

Montgomery, David. "The Working Classes of the Pre-industrial American City, 1780–1830." *Labor History* 9 (Winter 1968): 3–22.

Morgan, Edmund S. *American Slavery, American Freedom: The Ordeal of Colonial Virginia.* New York: W. W. Norton, 1975.

———. "Slavery and Freedom: The American Paradox." *Journal of American History* 59 (June 1972): 5–29.

Morris, Richard B. "Labor Controls in Maryland in the Nineteenth Century." *Journal of Southern History* 14 (August 1948): 385–400.

———. "The Measure of Bondage in the Slave States." *Mississippi Valley Historical Review* 41 (September 1954): 231–39.

Morriss, Margaret S. *Colonial Trade of Maryland, 1689–1715.* Philadelphia: Porcupine, 1976.

[Moynihan, Daniel Patrick]. *The Negro Family: The Case for National Action.* Washington, D.C.: Government Printing Office, 1965.

Mullin, Gerald W. *Flight and Rebellion: Slave Resistance in Eighteenth-Century Virginia.* New York: Oxford University Press, 1972.

Munroe, John A. "The Negro in Delaware." *South Atlantic Quarterly* 56 (Winter 1957): 428–44.

Muraskin, William A. *Middle-Class Blacks in a White Society: Prince Hall Freemasonry in America.* Berkeley: University of California Press, 1975.

Myrdal, Gunnar. *An American Dilemma.* New York: Harper and Brothers, 1944.

Nash, Gary B. *Forging Freedom: The Formation of Philadelphia's Black Community, 1720–1840.* Cambridge, Mass.: Harvard University Press, 1988.

———. "Maryland's Economic War with Pennsylvania." *Maryland Historical Magazine* 60 (September 1965): 231–44.

Nash, Gary B., and Jean R. Soderlund. *Freedom by Degrees: Emancipation in Pennsylvania and Its Aftermath.* New York: Oxford University Press, 1991.

Nelson, Lee H. "Brickmaking in Baltimore, 1798." *Journal of the Society of Architectural Historians* 18 (March 1959): 18–25.

Nicholls, Michael L. "Passing through This Troublesome World: Free Blacks in the Early Southside." *Virginia Magazine of History and Biography* 92 (January 1984): 50–70.

North, Douglass C. *The Economic Growth of the United States, 1790–1860.* New York: W. W. Norton, 1966.

Numbers, Ronald L., and Todd L. Savitt, eds. *Science and Medicine in the Old South.* Baton Rouge: Louisiana State University Press, 1989.

Nurnberger, Ralph D. "The Great Baltimore Deluge of 1817." *Maryland Historical Magazine* 69 (Winter 1974): 405–8.

Oakes, James. *Slavery and Freedom: An Interpretation of the Old South.* New York: Alfred A. Knopf, 1990.

Olson, Sherry H. *Baltimore: The Building of an American City.* Baltimore: Johns Hopkins University Press, 1980.

Osofsky, Gilbert. "Abolitionists, Irish Immigrants, and the Dilemmas of Romantic Nationalism." *American Historical Review* 80 (October 1975): 889–912.

———. *Harlem: The Making of a Ghetto, 1900–1920.* New York: Harper and Row, 1966.

Ott, Thomas O. *The Haitian Revolution, 1789–1804.* Knoxville: University of Tennessee Press, 1973.

Owens, Hamilton. *Baltimore on the Chesapeake.* Garden City, N.Y.: Doubleday, 1941.

Owsley, Frank L. *Plain Folk of the Old South.* Baton Rouge: Louisiana State University Press, 1949.

Papenfuse, Edward C. *In Pursuit of Profit: The Annapolis Merchants in the Era of the American Revolution, 1763–1805.* Baltimore: Johns Hopkins University Press, 1975.

———. "Planter Behavior and Economic Opportunity in a Staple Economy." *Agricultural History* 46 (Fall 1972): 297–311.

Parish, Peter. "The Edges of Slavery in the Old South: Or, Do Exceptions Prove Rules?" *Slavery and Abolition* 4 (April 1983): 106–25.

Patterson, Orlando. *Slavery and Social Death: A Comparative Study.* Cambridge, Mass.: Harvard University Press, 1982.

Pease, William H., and Jane H. Pease. "The Negro Convention Movement." In *Key Issues in the Afro-American Experience,* edited by Nathan I. Huggins, Martin Kilson, and Daniel M. Fox. New York: Harcourt Brace and Jovanovich, 1971.

Perdue, Robert E. *Black Laborers and Black Professionals in Early America, 1750–1830.* New York: Negro Universities Press, 1975.

———. *The Negro in Savannah, 1865–1900.* New York: Exposition, 1973.

Perry, Lewis, and Michael Fellman, eds. *Antislavery Reconsidered: New Perspectives on the Abolitionists.* Baton Rouge: Louisiana State University Press, 1979.

Pessen, Edward. *Riches, Class, and Power before the Civil War.* Lexington, Mass.: D. C. Heath, 1973.

Peterson, Merrill D., ed. *The Portable Thomas Jefferson.* New York: Viking, 1975.

Petrella, Frank. "Daniel Raymond, Adam Smith, and Classical Growth Theory: An Inquiry into the Nature and Causes of the Wealth of America." *History of Political Economy* 19 (July 1987): 239–59.

Phillips, Christopher. "The Dear Name of Home: Resistance to Colonization in Antebellum Baltimore." *Maryland Historical Magazine* 91 (Summer 1996): 181–202.

———. "The Roots of Quasi-Freedom: Manumission and Term Slavery in Early National Baltimore." *Southern Studies* 4 (Spring 1993): 39–66.

Phillips, Glenn O. "Maryland and the Caribbean, 1634–1984: Some Highlights." *Maryland Historical Magazine* 83 (Fall 1988): 199–214.

Piet, Mary A., and Stanley G. Piet. *Early Catholic Church Records in Baltimore, Maryland, 1782 through 1800.* Westminster, Md.: Family Line Publications, 1989.

———. "The Organized Educational Activities of Negro Literary Societies, 1828–1846." *Journal of Negro Education* 5 (Winter 1936): 556–66.

Pred, Allan R. *Urban Growth and the Circulation of Information: The United States System of Cities, 1790–1840*. Cambridge, Mass.: Harvard University Press, 1973.

Preston, Dickson J. *Young Frederick Douglass: The Maryland Years*. Baltimore: Johns Hopkins University Press, 1980.

Price, Jacob M. "Economic Function and the Growth of American Port Towns in the Eighteenth Century." *Perspectives in American History* 8 (April 1974): 123–86.

Price, Richard, and Sally Price. "Saramaka Onomastics: An Afro-American Naming System." *Ethnology* 11 (Fall 1972): 341–67.

Prude, Jonathan. "To Look upon the 'Lower Sort': Runaway Ads and the Appearance of Unfree Laborers in America, 1750–1800." *Journal of American History* 78 (June 1991): 124–59.

Purviance, Robert. *Narrative of Events Which Occurred in Baltimore Town during the Revolutionary War*. Baltimore: n.p., 1849.

Quarles, Benjamin. "The American Revolution as a Black Declaration of Independence." In *Slavery and Freedom in the Age of the American Revolution*, edited by Ira Berlin and Ronald Hoffman. Charlottesville: University Press of Virginia, 1983. Reprint. Urbana: University of Illinois Press, 1986.

———. *Black Abolitionists*. New York: Oxford University Press, 1969.

———. "'Freedom Fettered': Blacks in the Constitutional Era in Maryland, 1776–1810—An Introduction." *Maryland Historical Magazine* 84 (Winter 1989): 299–304.

———. *The Negro in the American Revolution*. Chapel Hill: University of North Carolina Press, 1961.

———. *The Negro in the Making of America*. New York: Macmillan, 1964.

Raboteau, Albert J. "Richard Allen and the African Church Movement." In *Black Leaders of the Nineteenth Century*, edited by Leon Litwack and August Meier. Urbana: University of Illinois Press, 1988.

———. *Slave Religion: The "Invisible Institution" in the Antebellum South*. New York: Oxford University Press, 1978.

Rachleff, Peter J. *Black Labor in the South: Richmond, Virginia, 1865–1890*. Philadelphia: Temple University Press, 1984.

Ransom, Roger, and Richard Sutch. *One Kind of Freedom: The Economic Consequences of Emancipation*. New York: Oxford University Press, 1977.

Read, Allen Walker. "The Speech of Negroes in Colonial America." *Journal of Negro History* 24 (July 1939): 247–58.

Reid, Ira D. *The Negro Community of Baltimore*. Baltimore: National Urban League, 1934.

Reid, Joseph D., Jr. "Antebellum Southern Rental Contracts." *Explorations in Economic History* 13 (January 1976): 69–83.

Reinders, Robert C. "The Free Negro in the New Orleans Economy, 1850–1860." *Louisiana History* 6 (Summer 1965): 273–85.

Renzulli, L. Marx. *Maryland: The Federalist Years*. Rutherford, N.J.: Fairleigh Dickinson University Press, 1972.

Reuter, Edward B. *The Mulatto in the United States.* Boston: Gorham, 1918. Reprint. New York: New American Library, 1969.

[Reynolds, William M.]. *A Brief History of the First Presbyterian Church of Baltimore.* Baltimore: Williams and Wilkins, 1913.

Rich, Linda G. *Neighborhood, a State of Mind.* Baltimore: Johns Hopkins University Press, 1981.

Richards, Leonard L. *"Gentlemen of Property and Standing": Anti-abolitionist Mobs in Jacksonian America.* New York: Oxford University Press, 1970.

Richardson, Clement, ed. *The National Cyclopedia of the Colored Race.* Montgomery, Ala.: National Publishing, 1919.

Richardson, Harry V., and Nathan Wright, Jr. "Afro-American Religion." In *The Black American Reference Book,* edited by Mabel M. Smythe. Englewood Cliffs, N.J.: Prentice-Hall, 1976.

Ridgway, Whitman H. *Community Leadership in Maryland, 1790–1840: A Comparative Analysis of Power in Society.* Chapel Hill: University of North Carolina Press, 1979.

Risjord, Norman K. *Chesapeake Politics, 1781–1800.* New York: Columbia University Press, 1978.

Robinson, Henry S. "Some Aspects of the Free Negro Population of Washington, D.C., 1800–1862." *Maryland Historical Magazine* 64 (Spring 1969): 43–64.

Rollo, Vera F. *The Black Experience in Maryland.* Lanham, Md.: Maryland Historical Press, 1980.

Rosenberg, Charles E. *The Cholera Years: The United States in 1832, 1849, and 1866.* Chicago: University of Chicago Press, 1962. Reprint. Chicago: University of Chicago Press, 1987.

Rouse, Michael F. *The Study of the Development of Negro Education under Catholic Auspices in Maryland and the District of Columbia.* Baltimore: Johns Hopkins University Press, 1935.

Rukert, Norman G. *The Port, Pride of Baltimore.* Baltimore: Bodine and Associates, 1982.

Runcie, John. "'Hunting the Nigs' in Philadelphia: The Race Riot of August 1834." *Pennsylvania History* 39 (April 1972): 187–218.

Rury, John L. "Philanthropy, Self-Help, and Social Control: The New York Manumission Society and Free Blacks, 1785–1810." *Phylon* 46 (September 1985): 231–41.

Russell, John H. *The Free Negro in Virginia, 1619–1865.* Baltimore: Johns Hopkins University Press, 1913. Reprint. New York: Dover Publications, 1969.

Rutter, Frank Roy. *South American Trade of Baltimore.* Baltimore: Johns Hopkins University Press, 1897.

Scharf, J. Thomas. *The Chronicles of Baltimore; Being a Complete History of "Baltimore Town" and Baltimore City from the Earliest Period to the Present Time.* Baltimore: Turnbull Brothers, 1874.

———. *History of Baltimore City and County.* 2 vols. Baltimore: Louis H. Everts, 1881. Reprint. Baltimore: Regional Publishing, 1971.

———. *History of Maryland from the Earliest Period to the Present Day.* 3 vols. Baltimore: J. B. Piet, 1879. Reprint. Hatsboro, Pa.: Tradition, 1967.

Schlesinger, Arthur M., Jr. *The Age of Jackson.* Boston: Little, Brown, 1945.

Schultz, Edward T. *History of Freemasonry in Maryland.* Baltimore: J. H. Medairy, 1885.

Schwartz, Philip J. "Emancipators, Protectors, and Anomalies: Free Black Slaveowners in Virginia." *Virginia Magazine of History and Biography* 95 (July 1987): 317–38.

Schweninger, Loren. *Black Property Owners in the South, 1790–1815.* Urbana: University of Illinois Press, 1990.

———. "The Free-Slave Phenomenon: James P. Thomas and the Black Community in Ante-bellum Nashville." *Civil War History* 22 (December 1976): 293–307.

———. "A Negro Sojourner in Antebellum New Orleans." *Louisiana History* 20 (Fall 1979): 305–14.

———. "The Underside of Slavery: The Internal Economy, Self-Hire, and Quasi-Freedom in Virginia, 1780–1865." *Slavery and Abolition* 12 (September 1991): 1–22.

Sellers, Charles G. *The Market Revolution: Jacksonian America, 1815–1846.* New York: Oxford University Press, 1991.

Semmes, Raphael. "Aboriginal Maryland, 1608–1689. In Two Parts. Part Two: The Western Shore." *Maryland Historical Magazine* 24 (June 1929): 157–72.

———. *Baltimore as Seen by Visitors, 1783–1860.* Baltimore: Maryland Historical Society, 1953.

———. *Crime and Punishment in Early Maryland.* Baltimore: Johns Hopkins University Press, 1938.

Senese, Donald J. "The Free Negro and the South Carolina Courts, 1790–1860." *South Carolina Historical Magazine* 68 (Spring 1967): 140–53.

Sharrer, G. Terry. "Flour Milling in the Growth of Baltimore, 1750–1830." *Maryland Historical Magazine* 71 (Fall 1976): 322–33.

Sheller, Tina H. "Artisans, Manufacturing, and the Rise of a Manufacturing Interest in Revolutionary Baltimore Town." *Maryland Historical Magazine* 83 (Spring 1988): 3–17.

———. "The Origins of Public Education in Baltimore, 1825–1829." *History of Education Quarterly* 22 (Spring 1982): 23–43.

Simpson, Robert Drew, ed. *American Methodist Pioneer: The Life and Journals of the Rev. Freeborn Garrettson, 1752–1827.* Madison, N.J.: Academy Books for Drew University Library, 1984.

Skaggs, David Curtis. *Roots of Maryland Democracy, 1753–1776.* Westport, Conn.: Greenwood, 1973.

Smith, Dawn Butler. *Baltimore County Marriage Licenses, 1777–1798.* Westminster, Md.: Family Line Publications, 1989.

Smith, Edward D. *Climbing Jacob's Ladder: The Rise of Black Churches in Eastern American Cities, 1740–1877.* Washington, D.C.: Smithsonian Institution Press, 1988.

Smith, W. Wayne. "A Marylander in Africa: Letters of Henry Hannon." *Maryland Historical Magazine* 69 (Winter 1974): 398–404.

———. "Politics and Democracy in Maryland, 1800–1854." In *Maryland: A History, 1632–1974*, edited by Richard Walsh and William L. Fox. Baltimore: Maryland Historical Society, 1974.

Smythe, Mabel M., ed. *The Black American Reference Book.* Englewood Cliffs, N.J.: Prentice-Hall, 1976.

Sobel, Mechal. *Trabelin' On: The Slave Journey to an Afro-Baptist Faith.* Princeton, N.J.: Princeton University Press, 1979.

Soderlund, Jean R. *Quakers and Slavery: A Divided Spirit.* Princeton, N.J.: Princeton University Press, 1985.

Sowell, Thomas. *The Economics and Politics of Race: An International Perspective.* New York: William Morrow, 1983.

Stampp, Kenneth M. *The Peculiar Institution: Slavery in the Ante-bellum South.* New York: Vintage Books, 1956.

Starke, Barbara M. "A Mini View of the Microenvironment of Slaves and Freed Blacks Living in the Virginia and Maryland Areas from the Seventeenth through the Nineteenth Centuries." *Negro History Bulletin* 41 (September-October 1978): 878–80.

Starobin, Robert S. *Industrial Slavery in the Old South.* New York: Oxford University Press, 1970.

Staudenraus, P. J. *The African Colonization Movement, 1816–1865.* New York: Columbia University Press, 1961.

Steckel, Richard H. "Slave Height Profiles from Coastwise Manifests." *Explorations in Economic History* 16 (September 1979): 363–80.

Steffen, Charles G. "Changes in the Organization of Artisan Production in Baltimore, 1790 to 1820." *William and Mary Quarterly*, 3d ser., 36 (January 1979), 101–17.

———. *From Gentlemen to Townsmen: The Gentry of Baltimore County, Maryland, 1660–1776.* Lexington: University Press of Kentucky, 1993.

———. *The Mechanics of Baltimore: Workers and Politics in the Age of Revolution, 1763–1812.* Urbana: University of Illinois Press, 1984.

———. "The Pre-industrial Iron Worker: Northhampton Iron Works, 1780–1820." *Labor History* 20 (Winter 1979): 89–110.

Stegmaier, Mark J. "Maryland's Fear of Insurrection at the Time of Braddock's Defeat." *Maryland Historical Magazine* 71 (Winter 1976): 467–83.

Sterkx, Herbert E. *The Free Negro in Antebellum Louisiana.* Rutherford, N.J.: Farleigh Dickinson University Press, 1972.

Stickle, Douglas F. "Death and Class in Baltimore: The Yellow Fever Epidemic of 1800." *Maryland Historical Magazine* 74 (September 1979): 282–99.

Stoddard, T. Lothrop. *The French Revolution in San Domingo.* Boston and New York: Houghton Mifflin, 1914.

Stopak, Aaron. "The Maryland State Colonization Society." *Maryland Historical Magazine* 63 (September 1968): 275–98.

Stuckey, Sterling. *Slave Culture: Nationalist Theory and the Foundations of Black America*. New York: Oxford University Press, 1987.

Sullivan, David K. "William Lloyd Garrison in Baltimore, 1829–1830." *Maryland Historical Magazine* 68 (Spring 1973): 64–79.

Sweet, Leonard I. *Black Images of America, 1784–1870*. New York: W. W. Norton, 1976.

Swisher, Carl B. *Roger B. Taney*. Hamden, Conn.: Archon Books, 1961.

Sydnor, Charles S. "The Free Negro in Mississippi before the Civil War." *American Historical Review* 32 (July 1927): 769–88.

Tadman, Michael. "Slave Trading in the Ante-bellum South: An Estimate of the Extent of the Inter-regional Slave Trade." *Journal of American Studies* 13 (August 1979): 195–220.

———. *Speculators and Slaves: Masters, Traders, and Slaves in the Old South*. Madison: University of Wisconsin Press, 1989.

Taeuber, Karl E., and Alma Taeuber. *Negroes in Cities: Residential Segregation and Neighborhood Change*. Chicago: Aldine, 1965.

Takaki, Ronald. *Iron Cages: Race and Culture in Nineteenth-Century America*. New York: Oxford University Press, 1979.

Tate, Thad W., and David L. Ammerman, eds. *The Chesapeake in the Seventeenth Century: Essays on Anglo-American Society*. Chapel Hill: University of North Carolina Press, 1979.

Taylor, George R. *The Transportation Revolution, 1815–1860*. Armonk, N.Y.: M. E. Sharpe, 1951. Reprint. New York: Holt, Rinehart, and Winston, 1964.

Taylor, Henry L. "On Slavery's Fringe: City-Building and Black Community Development in Cincinnati, 1800–1850." *Ohio History* 95 (Winter-Spring 1986): 5–33.

Taylor, William R. *Cavalier and Yankee: The Old South and American National Character*. Garden City, N.Y.: Anchor Books, 1963.

Thernstrom, Stephen. *Poverty and Progress: Social Mobility in a Nineteenth Century City*. Cambridge, Mass.: Harvard University Press, 1964.

———. "Urbanization, Migration, and Social Mobility in Late Nineteenth-Century America." In *Towards a New Past: Dissenting Essays in American History*, edited by Barton J. Bernstein. New York: Vintage Books, 1968.

Thomas, Thaddeus. *The City Government of Baltimore*. Baltimore: Johns Hopkins Press, 1896.

Thompson, E. P. *The Making of the English Working Class*. New York: Pantheon Books, 1963.

———. "Time, Work-Discipline, and Industrial Capitalism." *Past and Present* 38 (December 1967): 56–97.

Tise, Larry E. *Proslavery: A History of the Defense of Slavery in America, 1701–1840*. Athens: University of Georgia Press, 1987.

Trimble, Logan C. "Middling Planters and the Strategy of Diversification in Baltimore County, Maryland, 1750–1776." *Maryland Historical Magazine* 85 (Summer 1990): 171–78.

"A Typical Colonization Convention." *Journal of Negro History* 1 (July 1916): 318–38.

Van Ness, James S. "Economic Development, Social and Cultural Changes, 1800–1850." In *Maryland: A History, 1632–1974*, edited by Richard Walsh and William L. Fox. Baltimore: Maryland Historical Society, 1974.

Vexler, Robert I. *Baltimore: A Chronological and Documentary History, 1632–1970*. Dobbs Ferry, N.Y.: Oceana Publications, 1975.

Wade, Richard C. *Slavery in the Cities: The South, 1820–1860*. New York: Oxford University Press, 1964.

Wagandt, Charles L. *The Mighty Revolution: Emancipation in Maryland, 1862–1864*. Baltimore: Johns Hopkins University Press, 1964.

Walker, Mack. *Germany and the Emigration, 1816–1885*. Cambridge, Mass.: Harvard University Press, 1964.

Walsh, Lorena S. "Community Networks in the Early Chesapeake." In *Colonial Chesapeake Society*, edited by Lois Green Carr, Philip D. Morgan, and Jean B. Russo. Chapel Hill: University of North Carolina Press, 1988.

———. "Plantation Management in the Chesapeake, 1620–1820." *Journal of Economic History* 49 (June 1989): 393–406.

———. "Rural African Americans in the Constitutional Era in Maryland, 1776–1810." *Maryland Historical Magazine* 84 (Winter 1989): 327–41.

———. "Slave Life, Slave Society, and Tobacco Production in the Tidewater Chesapeake, 1620–1820." In *Cultivation and Culture: Labor and the Shaping of Slave Life in the Americas*, edited by Ira Berlin and Philip D. Morgan. Charlottesville: University Press of Virginia, 1993.

Walsh, Richard. "The Era of the Revolution." In *Maryland: A History, 1632–1974*, edited by Richard Walsh and William L. Fox. Baltimore: Maryland Historical Society, 1974.

Walsh, Richard, and William L. Fox, eds. *Maryland: A History, 1632–1974*. Baltimore: Maryland Historical Society, 1974.

Ward, David. *Cities and Immigrants: A Geography of Change in Nineteenth-Century America*. New York: Oxford University Press, 1971.

Warner, Sam Bass, Jr. "If All the World Were Philadelphia: A Scaffolding for Urban History, 1774–1930." *American Historical Review* 74 (October 1968): 26–43.

———. *The Private City: Philadelphia in Three Periods of Its Growth*. Philadelphia: University of Pennsylvania Press, 1968.

Warren, Marion E. *Baltimore—When She Was What She Used to Be, 1850–1930*. Baltimore: Johns Hopkins University Press, 1983.

Wax, Darold D. "Black Immigrants: The Slave Trade in Colonial Maryland." *Maryland Historical Magazine* 73 (Winter 1978): 30–45.

———. "The Image of the Negro in the *Maryland Gazette*, 1745–75." *Journalism Quarterly* 46 (Spring 1969): 73–80.

Weber, Adna. *The Growth of Cities in the Nineteenth Century: A Study in Statistics*. New York: Macmillan, 1899.

Weishampel, J. F. *History of Baptist Churches in Maryland*. Baltimore: by the author, 1885.

Werner, John M. *Reaping the Bloody Harvest: Race Riots in the United States during the Age of Jackson, 1824–1849*. New York: Garland, 1986.

Wesley, Charles H. *Negro Labor in the United States, 1850–1925*. New York: Vanguard, 1927.

———. *Richard Allen, Apostle of Freedom*. Washington, D.C.: Associated Publishers, 1935.

Wheeler, William Bruce. "The Baltimore Jeffersonians, 1788–1800: A Profile of Intra-factional Conflict." *Maryland Historical Magazine* 66 (Summer 1971): 153–68.

White, Deborah Gray. *Ar'n't I a Woman? Female Slaves in the Plantation South*. New York: W. W. Norton, 1985.

White, Shane. "Impious Prayers: Elite and Popular Attitudes toward Blacks and Slavery in the Middle-Atlantic States, 1783–1810." *New York History* 67 (July 1986): 261–83.

———. *Somewhat More Independent: The End of Slavery in New York City, 1770–1810*. Athens: University of Georgia Press, 1991.

———. "'We Dwell in Safety and Pursue Our Honest Callings': Free Blacks in New York City, 1783–1810." *Journal of American History* 75 (September 1988): 445–70.

White, Shane, and Graham White. "Slave Hair and African American Culture in the Eighteenth and Nineteenth Centuries." *Journal of Southern History* 61 (February 1995): 45–76.

Whitman, T. Stephen. "Industrial Slavery at the Margin: The Maryland Chemical Works." *Journal of Southern History* 59 (February 1993): 31–62.

———. *The Price of Freedom: Slavery and Manumission in Baltimore and Early National Maryland*. Lexington: University Press of Kentucky, 1997.

Wikramanayake, Marina. *A World in Shadow: The Free Black in Antebellum South Carolina*. Columbia: University of South Carolina Press, 1973.

Williams, Loretta J. *Black Freemasonry and Middle-Class Realities*. Columbia: University of Missouri Press, 1980.

Williams, William Appleman. *The Contours of American History*. Cleveland, Ohio: World Publishing, 1961. Reprint. New York: W. W. Norton, 1988.

Williamson, Joel. *New People: Miscegenation and Mulattoes in the United States*. New York: Free Press, 1980.

Wilson, Carol. *Freedom at Risk: The Kidnapping of Free Blacks in America, 1780–1865*. Lexington: University Press of Kentucky, 1994.

Wilson, Edward. *Historical Facts about Sharp Street Memorial Church*. Baltimore: Wells, 1963.

Wilson, Jane B. *The Very Quiet Baltimoreans: A Guide to the Historic Cemeteries and Burial Sites of Baltimore*. Shippensburg, Pa.: White Mane Publishing, 1991.

Wilstach, Paul. *Potomac Landings*. New York: Tudor Publishing, 1920.

———. *Tidewater Maryland*. New York: Tudor Publishing, 1931.

Winch, Julie. *Philadelphia's Black Elite: Activism, Accommodation, and the Struggle for Autonomy, 1787–1848*. Philadelphia: Temple University Press, 1988.

Wood, Peter H. *Black Majority: Negroes in Colonial South Carolina from 1670 through the Stono Rebellion*. New York: Alfred A. Knopf, 1974.

Woodson, Carter G. *The Education of the Negro prior to 1861*. New York: G. P. Putnam, 1915.

———. *Free Negro Heads of Families in the United States in 1830*. Washington, D.C.: Association for the Study of Negro Life and History, 1925.

———. *Free Negro Owners of Slaves in the United States in 1830*. Washington D.C.: Association for the Study of Negro Life and History, 1924.

———. *The History of the Negro Church*. Washington, D.C.: Associated Publishers, 1921.

———, ed. *The Mind of the Negro as Reflected in Letters Written during the Crisis, 1800–1860*. Washington, D.C.: Association for the Study of Negro Life and History, 1926.

Wright, Gavin. *The Political Economy of the Cotton South: Households, Markets, and Wealth in the Nineteenth Century*. New York: W. W. Norton, 1978.

Wright, George C. *Life behind a Veil: Blacks in Louisville, Kentucky, 1865–1930*. Baton Rouge: Louisiana State University, 1985.

Wright, James M. *The Free Negro in Maryland, 1634–1860*. New York: Columbia University, 1921.

Yacovone, Donald. "The Transformation of the Black Temperance Movement, 1827–1854: An Interpretation." *Journal of the Early Republic* 8 (Fall 1988): 281–97.

Zilversmit, Arthur. *The First Emancipation: The Abolition of Slavery in the North*. Chicago: University of Chicago Press, 1967.

Index

Mingo, James, 158
Mingo, John, 137, 273n38, 275n60
Mississippi, 175, 186, 296nn63, 71
Missouri, 296n63; and colonization/emi-
gration, 186, 215
Moale, Richard, 22
Moale, William E., 49
Moffitt, Joseph, 48
Monticello, Va., 68
Moore, George, 51
Moore, Hannibal, 274n42
Moore, Matilda, 51
Moore, William, 273n38
Moral Reform Society (Philadelphia),
169
Mount Vernon Hall (Baltimore), 241
Moynihan, Daniel P., 266n17
Mulattoes: in Baltimore, 21, 62–63, 68,
71–73, 105–7, 156–57, 161–63,
260nn16, 17; French Caribbean, 71,
72–73; in Lower South, 62–63, 105–6,
156; in Maryland, 37, 62–63, 105–6,
274n43; in Upper South, 63
Muller, Caspar O., 49
Myers, Daniel, 169
Myrdal, Gunnar, 238

Nabb, Catherine, 49
Nagle, Henry, 75
Nash, Gary, 2, 37–38, 283n98, 289n72
National Convention of the Free People
of Color, 229. See also Negro conven-
tion movement
Nazarites, order of (Baltimore), 175
Negro convention movement, 228–29
Nelson, Charles, 85
Newburyport, Mass., 287n40
New Jersey, 68
New Orleans, La., 73; black occupations·
in, 109, 202; free black community in,
3, 63, 154, 155, 157, 238
New York, 18, 33, 73, 131
New York, N.Y., 13, 29, 118, 134, 143,
178, 214, 229, 281nn64, 70, 293n22;
occupations of free blacks in, 252n11,
289n72
Nicholas, Marceline, 94
Niles, Hezekiah, 42, 63, 181–82, 185,
186, 189, 285n17, 286n25
Niles' Weekly Register, 14, 42, 181, 222,
285n17
Nisbitt, William, 77–78

Norfolk, Va., 26, 69, 80
North Carolina, 18, 33, 73; race relations
in, 252n9
Northerner (brig) 218
North Star, 118
Norwood, Mary, 48
Norwood, Samuel, 96

Oberlin College, 172
Odd Fellows. See Order of Odd Fellows
O'Donnell, Deborah, 49
O'Donnell, Sarah, 49
Old Town (Baltimore), 82, 104, 106, 150
Olmsted, Frederick Law, 124
Order of Odd Fellows (Baltimore), 173,
174, 175
O'Roarke, Devezeaux, 43
Orphans' Court (Maryland), 158,
256n60; of Baltimore County, 23, 48,
49, 54, 219–20
Osborn, Joseph, 76
Osgood, William, 67
Owings, Samuel, 49

Pairpont, Alfred, 24, 75, 79, 149, 150
Panic of 1837, 178, 179
Parks, Anthony, 93
Parraway, Samuel, 96
Parrish, Daniel, 94
Patapsco River, 7, 8, 10, 11
Paul, John, 49, 257n61
Payne, Daniel, 140, 165
Pearce, James Alfred, 205
Pease, Jane H., 1
Pease, William H., 1
Peck, Rev. Francis J., 175
Peck, Rev. Nathaniel, 139, 169, 216–18,
222, 293n22
Pennsylvania, 18, 71, 73, 119, 191; as
outlet for escaped slaves, 47, 53, 68;
Quakers in, 61; slavery in, 34; Supreme
Court, 133–34; and trade with Balti-
more, 11
People's Union Association (Baltimore),
171–72
Peters, Eliza, 139
Petersburg, Va., 259n3
Philadelphia, Pa., 11, 13, 29, 61, 71, 103,
143, 165, 178, 193, 194, 217; anti-
slavery activity in, 124; free black com-
munity in, 2, 92, 98–99, 146, 155, 157,
160–61, 162, 173, 229, 283nn94, 95,

CHRISTOPHER PHILLIPS is an assistant professor of history at Emporia State University. He received a B.A. from Illinois Wesleyan University and a Ph.D. from the University of Georgia. He is the author of *Damned Yankee: The Life of General Nathaniel Lyon.*

Kenneth and John B. Rayner and the Limits of Southern Dissent   *Gregg Cantrell*

Lynching in the New South: Georgia and Virginia, 1880–1930
W. Fitzhugh Brundage

Local People: The Struggle for Civil Rights in Mississippi   *John Dittmer*

Indians at Hampton Institute, 1877–1923   *Donal F. Lindsey*

A Voice of Thunder: The Civil War Letters of George E. Stephens
Edited by Donald Yacovone

Freedom's Port: The African American Community of Baltimore, 1790–1860
Christopher Phillips

REPRINT EDITIONS

King: A Biography (Second Edition)   *David Levering Lewis*

The Death and Life of Malcolm X (Second Edition)   *Peter Goldman*

Race Relations in the Urban South, 1865–1890
Howard N. Rabinowitz; foreword by C. Vann Woodward

Race Riot at East St. Louis, July 2, 1917   *Elliott Rudwick*

W. E. B. Du Bois: Voice of the Black Protest Movement   *Elliott Rudwick*

The Negro's Civil War: How American Negroes Felt and Acted during the War
for the Union   *James M. McPherson*

Lincoln and Black Freedom: A Study in Presidential Leadership   *LaWanda Cox*

Slavery and Freedom in the Age of the American Revolution
Edited by Ira Berlin and Ronald Hoffman

Diary of a Sit-In (Second Edition)
Merrill Proudfoot; introduction by Michael S. Mayer

They Who Would Be Free: Blacks' Search for Freedom, 1830–61
Jane H. Pease and William H. Pease

The Reshaping of Plantation Society: The Natchez District, 1860–80
Michael Wayne

Rice and Slaves: Ethnicity and the Slave Trade in Colonial South Carolina
Daniel C. Littlefield

Race Riot: Chicago in the Red Summer of 1919   *William M. Tuttle, Jr.*

UNIVERSITY OF ILLINOIS PRESS
1325 SOUTH OAK STREET
CHAMPAIGN, ILLINOIS 61820-6903
WWW.PRESS.UILLINOIS.EDU